THE BURNING OF WILDGOOSE LODGE
Ribbonism in Louth
Murder and the Gallows

The Burning of Wildgoose Lodge

Ribbonism in Louth
Murder and the Gallows

RAYMOND MURRAY

Raymond Murray

To Molly, Pat + Colette

With every Blessing

14 February 2005

CUMANN SEANCHAIS ARD MHACHA
THE ARMAGH DIOCESAN HISTORICAL SOCIETY

For my sister Teresa

© Cumann Seanchais Ard Mhacha, 2005
© Raymond Murray

All rights reserved
ISBN 0 9511490 2 4

Printed by R. & S. Printers, The Diamond, Monaghan

Preface

In the 1970s I used to accompany my friend Kevin McMahon to Dublin Castle when he was researching agrarian disturbances in South Armagh in the second half of the nineteenth century. His completed study, co-authored with Thomas McKeown, has been published in a series of articles in *Seanchas Ard Mhacha*. At that time my interest in the infamous story of the atrocity of Wildgoose Lodge, a tragedy connected with the Ribbonmen, had been awakened by my reading of T.G.F. Paterson's essay on the subject and, not to be idle in my friend's company, I set about seeking further information on it in the national archives. Soon afterwards I used some of my newly-found material in an article on Wildgoose Lodge in the *County Louth Archaeological and Historical Journal* (1986). For many years the distress and misfortune connected with it haunted me and at last I have committed my findings to paper.

The Wildgoose Lodge tragedy had at that time also spurred the literary critics Benedict Kiely and Daniel Casey to action, not surprisingly, since both writers have had a lifelong enthusiasm for the works of the Tyrone author William Carleton who made it the subject of one of his great short stories. Daniel Casey in his essays on Wildgoose Lodge has admirably dovetailed its mixture of history and lore and Benedict Kiely in his musings has deftly evoked the atmospheric horror of death and revenge.

In this book I have tried to find out the truth of what really happened, what led to the murders and what were the consequences. It involved a clash between the state and the poor, the powerful and the powerless, class division, and the 'land question'. My main resources have been government papers and newspapers and these, of course, have their own prejudicial colouring. Occasionally, however, even in these the voice of the people is heard and I have supplemented them by the inclusion of the views of some liberal critics of government policy and the analysis of a few nineteenth century historians who, being near to the period of Wildgoose Lodge, have a sympathetic attitude to the social problems in question. My method has been to let the documents speak for themselves, and so I have to a great extent published them in full, allowing the reader to sense the climate of the times. There is a great variety in the spelling of names and places in the documents and newspapers and these I have retained, but in general comment, for the main characters, I have used the spelling of Samuel Pendleton, chief magistrate of police in Louth.

For his prompt help and kindness I thank first of all Noel Ross, editor of the *County Louth Archaeological and Historical Journal*, and I am grateful also to Pádraig Ó Néill, Kevin McMahon, Fr Ignatius Fennessy, OFM, Bríd Mhic Sheáin, and Fr Seán Quinn. I am greatly indebted to the staff and custodians of the papers I consulted: the National Archives, Dublin; the National Library, Dublin; the Royal Irish Academy, Dublin; Roinn Bhéaloideas Éireann, University College, Dublin; the Public Record Office of Northern Ireland, Belfast; the Public Record Office, London; Louth County Library, Dundalk; Louth County Archives, Dundalk; the County Museum, Dundalk; the Newspaper Library, Belfast Public Library; the Library in Queen's University, Belfast; the Library, Franciscan House of Studies, Dún Mhuire, Killiney; the Linenhall Library, Belfast; the Irish and Local Studies Library, Southern Education & Library Board, Armagh; the Cardinal Tomás Ó Fiaich Memorial Library & Archive, Armagh. I thank Pádraig Ó Néill and the County Louth Archaeological and Historical Society for permission to quote from the published diary of Henry McClintock.

I thank my sister Teresa for her support during the writing of this book, which I dedicate to her. *Mo bhuíochas mór do Chumann Seanchais Ard Mhacha a thoiligh an leabhar a fhoilsiú.*

Contents

Preface

1. The History and the Lore   1
   Introduction
   Uncovering the Facts

2. Poverty and Ribbonmen   11
   Ribbonmen
   Famine and Fever

3. Rule by Despotism   56
   Law and Order
   Judge William Fletcher

4. The First Attack on Wildgoose Lodge   81
   The Lodge
   The First Attack
   Trial of Michael Tiernan, Patrick Shanley & Philip Conlon
       (Trial Judge – Judge St George Daly)

5. The Burning of Wildgoose Lodge   99
   The Burning
   Reaction of the Magistrates
   Baronies Proclaimed

6. The Disturbed State of Louth and Bordering Areas   134
   Events in 1814-15
   Events in 1816
   Events in 1817
   Events in 1818-19

7. Approvers and Arrests   162
   Arrests
   Approvers

8. Arrest, Trial & Execution of Patrick Devan   194
   Arrest of Patrick Devan
   Trial of Patrick Devan
       (Trial Judge – Judge Baron James McClelland)
   Execution of Patrick Devan

9. Trials and Executions (1)   221
       Trial of Hugh McCabe, John Kieran & James Campbell
       Trial of Terence Marron, Patrick Malone (1) & Patrick Craven
       Trial of Michael Floody, Patrick Meegan & Hugh McLarny, and Bryan Lennon
       (Trial Judge – Judge William Fletcher)
       Judge Fletcher's Criticism of the Catholic Clergy
       Execution of Hugh McCabe, John Kieran, James Campbell, Terence Marron, Patrick Malone (1), Patrick Craven, Michael Floody, Patrick Meegan, Hugh McLarny and Bryan Lennon

10. Trials and Executions (2)   264
       Trial of James Smyth, Patrick McQuillan, & Lawrence Gaynor
       Trial of Thomas McCullogh
       Trial of William Butler, Thomas Sheenan, & John Keegan
       (Trial Judge – Judge William Fletcher)
       Execution of Thomas McCullogh, Patrick McQuillan, James Smyth, Thomas Sheenan, John Keegan
       Dr James Marron, Parish Priest of Tallanstown

11. Trials and Executions (3)   297
       Trial of William Butler, Owen Gaynor & Michael Kearnan
       (Trial Judge – Judge Baron James McClelland)
       Execution of Owen Gaynor and Michael Kearnan
       Murder of Terence Cassidy

12. Rewards and Payments   311

13. The Gibbets   322

14. Conclusion   325

Notes   336

Concise Biographies   344

Bibliography   351

Index of Selected Place-names   357

1
The History and the Lore

INTRODUCTION

In the early hours of the morning of Wednesday 30 October 1816 eight people perished in a fire at Wildgoose Lodge at Reaghstown, parish of Tallanstown (Arthurstown), barony of Ardee, County Louth. The burning of the house was deliberate. Two of the victims were Edward Lynch, the tenant, and his son-in-law, Thomas Rooney. They had given information to the government authorities regarding a raid for arms at Lynch's house the previous April as a result of which three men were tried, convicted and hanged. The Ribbonmen carried out these savage murders in revenge for the prosecution of their members. Ribbonmen were a 19th century oath-bound, secret society, regional in character, principally organised in Dublin, north Leinster, north Connacht and in south and central Ulster. In the northern region comprising Louth, Meath, Monaghan, Cavan and South Armagh, in the 1815-19 period, they were mainly involved in agrarian protest and this would have been the sphere of influence as regards this particular atrocity. These Ribbonmen regarded themselves as defenders of the livelihood and interests of the rural poor at a time of economic crisis and social disaster. By an alternative system of law comprising reprisal and a ruthless use of force they tried to establish stability for the Irish peasantry, which the Irish government refused to do. It was a practice of secret societies occasionally to involve members from another district when a serious crime was to be committed, partly to strengthen their solidarity, partly to escape detection. When members were imprisoned they collected money to support them and their families and they contributed towards their legal defence fees. Subsequently after sordid trials infected with perjury and informers eighteen men were hanged for the Reaghstown murders, some of them protesting their innocence to their dying breath. Three of those hanged for the murders at Wildgoose Lodge were also indicted for the original burglary.

This incident is not referred to in general histories. Even the volume *Ireland under the Union, I. 1801-70* of *A New History of*

Ireland does not mention it. It is touched on in Norman Gash's *Mr Secretary Peel: The Life of Sir Robert Peel to 1830* (paperback with revisions, 1985) and A.P.W. Malcomson's *John Foster: The politics of the Anglo-Irish Ascendancy* (1978). Ramsay Colles in *The History of Ulster* (iv, 1920) mentions the 'spirit of turbulence' in the baronies of Dundalk, Ardee and Louth in 1815. Michael Beames includes it briefly in context in *Peasants and Power: the Whiteboy Movements and their Control in Pre-Famine Ireland* (1983) and couples it, as did William Carelton, with the multiple murder of the Sheas in Tipperary 'where the occupants were caught on pitchforks attempting to escape from a blazing house – thirteen people died in this incident, including three Kerry labourers'. A short account of the tragedy in a modern local history, *The Book of Dundalk* (1946) by Padraic Ua Dubhthaigh is quite inaccurate. Early local histories in County Louth, such as Brett's *Reminiscences of Louth* (1857), err in the few details they give. John D'Alton and J. Roderick O'Flanagan in their *History of Dundalk* (1864) have a special chapter on it but give more misinformation than fact. George Henry Basset's *Louth County Guide and Directory* (1886) picks up inaccuracies from their book. John Mathews, editor of the *Dundalk Examiner*, set about remedying this situation in a series of articles in 1881, which were printed posthumously in booklet form on 6 November 1897. It is an interesting account but Mathews pursues the very thing he attacks by resorting to traditions and folklore and he cannot resist imaginative narrative, acting more as zealot than historian. One regrets that he did not give a better guide to his sources. The atrocity, therefore, did not so much go down in history as in lore, but then, paradoxically, mythology creates its own history. Michael J. Murphy, a noted folklore collector who died 18 May 1996, gathered some traditions about it for the Irish Folklore Commission. But the person most responsible for giving it national and even international publicity and ensuring its notoriety was the celebrated writer William Carleton (1794-1869) who first published his gothic short story on Wildgoose Lodge under the title 'Confessions of a Reformed Ribbonman' in *The Dublin Literary Gazette* in 1830 and then included it under the title 'Wildgoose Lodge' in the 1835 edition of *Traits and Stories of the Irish Peasantry*, an edition translated into German and published at Leipzig in 1837. Leon de Wailly translated it into French in 1861 with two other sketches. It has been republished many times in English. Carleton's version predates local history accounts. It had a profound influence on them and seems to have even coloured local folk traditions. Carleton is a good storyteller, a gift he inherited from his father who was steeped in Irish lore. His writings give valuable insights into local social conditions and customs and also into his own personality. The pilgrimage, the patron, the wedding, the fascination of the priest evoke in him emotions of common humanity and simplicity and these are often set against a background of landlordism, rackrenting, eviction, emigration, famine, fever and death. Wrongs and injustice, gloom and horror, mingle with occasional comedy and light heartedness. Carleton abhorred violence and is passionate in portraying its evil, but he often writes for effect, even in his autobiography, and so one has to be cautious in searching for the truth behind his literary imagination. His relation of the burning of Wildgoose Lodge is powerful, frightening and bitter. The Gothic shadows touched with a tinge of blasphemy, the shared fearful atmosphere of a Gaelic fireside ghost story, and the hard chilling English realistic tradition evoke the satanic element in man before which helpless humanity and Christianity flee. This is all very well if Carleton had let his story stand as literature but since he could not dismiss the basic factuality of the tragedy he added a historical note to his powerful literary indictment of violence. Thus he gave credence to his fiction and in particular he seized on the character of the ringleader of the burning, Patrick Devan, to present him as satanic, the very embodiment of evil. Here is his note:

> This tale of terror is, unfortunately, too true. The scene of hellish murder detailed in it lies at Wildgoose Lodge, in the county of Louth, within about four miles of Carrickmacross, and nine of Dundalk. No such multitudinous murder has occurred, under similar circumstances, except the burning of the Sheas, in the county of Tipperary. The name of the family burned in Wildgoose Lodge was Lynch. One of them, shortly before this fatal night, prosecuted and convicted some of the neighbouring Ribbonmen, who visited him with severe marks of their displeasure, in consequence of his having refused to enrol himself as a member of their body. The language of the story is partly fictitious; but the facts are pretty closely such as were developed during the trial of the murderers. Both parties were Roman Catholics, and either twenty-

five or twenty-eight of those who took an active part in the burning, were hanged and gibbeted in different parts of the county of Louth. Devann, the ringleader, hung for some months in chains, within about a hundred yards of his own house, and about half a mile from Wildgoose Lodge. His mother could neither go into nor out of her cabin without seeing his body swinging from the gibbet. Her usual exclamation on looking at him was – 'God be good to the sowl of my poor marthyr!' The peasantry, too, frequently exclaimed, on seeing him, 'Poor Paddy!' A gloomy fact that speaks volumes!

The note is very inaccurate especially in listing twenty-five or twenty-eight men hanged and gibbeted. Carleton's personal antipathy to the murders at Wildgoose Lodge and his opposition to agrarian crime controlled by the tyranny of secret societies are borne out in the strong moral tones he instils into the introduction to his short stories:

Stimulated by this romantic love of adventure, I left my native place, and directed my steps to the parish of Killanny, in the county of Louth, the Catholic Clergyman of which was a nephew of our own Parish Priest, brother to him who proposed going to Munster with me, and an old school-fellow of my own, though probably twenty years my senior. This man's residence was within a quarter or half a mile's distance of the celebrated Wild-goose Lodge, in which some six months before a whole family, consisting of, I believe, eight persons, men women, and children, had been, from motives of personal vengeance, consumed to ashes. I stopped with him for a fortnight, and succeeded in procuring a tuition in the house of a wealthy farmer named Piers Murphy, near Corcreagh. ...

In my own youth, and I am now forty-four years, I do not remember a single school under the immediate superintendence of either priest or parson, and that in a parish the extent of which is, I dare say, ten miles by eight... The instruction of the children was altogether a matter in which no clergy of any creed took an interest. This was left altogether to hedge schoolmasters, a class of men who, with few exceptions, bestowed such an education upon the people as is sufficient almost, in the absence of all other causes, to account for much of the agrarian violence and erroneous principles which regulate their movements and feelings on that and similar subjects ...

With respect to the darker side of the Irish character, I feel that, consistently with that love of truth and impartiality which has guided, and I trust ever shall guide, my pen, I could not pass them over without further notice. I know that it is a very questionable defence to say that some, if not principally all, of their crimes originate in agrarian or political vengeance. Indeed, I believe that, so far from this circumstance being looked upon as a defence, it ought to be considered as an aggravation of the guilt; inasmuch as it is, beyond all doubt, at least a far more manly thing to inflict an injury upon an enemy face to face, and under the influence of immediate resentment, than to crouch like a cowardly assassin behind a hedge and coolly murder him without one moment's preparation, or any means whatsoever of defence. This is a description of crime which no man with one generous drop of blood in his veins can think of without shame and indignation. Unhappily, however, for the security of human life, every crime of the kind results more from the dark tyranny of these secret confederacies, by which the lower classes are organized, than from any natural appetite for shedding blood. Individually, the Irish loathe murder as much as any people in the world; but in the circumstances before us, it often happens that the Irishman is not a free agent, - very far from it; on the contrary, he is frequently made the instrument of a system, to which he must become either an obedient slave or victim.

Carleton returns to the theme in his autobiography. There he recounts again his visit to Fr Edward McArdle in Killany in the autumn of 1817. Killany parish, diocese of Clogher, lies chiefly in County Monaghan but part of it, seventeen townlands, is in County Louth. It seems Fr McArdle was a curate in Killany until he became parish priest there about 1820 and apparently died in 1826[1]. Carleton says in his autobiography that Fr McArdle 'lodged in a farmer's house at a distance of about three miles from the town of Carrickmacross, and about two or one and a half from the celebrated Wildgoose Lodge, the scene of the dreadful tragedy which had occurred the preceding year'[2]. While he was visiting the priest, Carleton relates, he saw the gibbeted corpse of Devan dangling from ropes of slime in a tar sack and heard the story from the sergeant of the guard of soldiers on the body. This could be true as Patrick Devan, a local leader of Ribbonmen, was hanged at Wildgoose Lodge and gibbeted nearby at Corcreagh on 24 July 1817, but it could not be true, as he claimed, that he saw at this time the gibbets of the others executed for the crime, since those executions did not take place until 1818. He says the soldier's story 'clung to me until I went to bed that night – it clung to me through my sleep wih such vivid horror that sleep was anything but a relief to me. When Mr McArdle came home that evening, he gave me in reply to my inquiry an account of the whole tragedy, and pointed out Wildgoose Lodge, which was visible from the garden of the house in which he lodged'. Carleton soon after this spent some time as a tutor in the family of Piers Murphy, Corcreagh and would have heard stories there of the atrocity at Wildgoose Lodge. Carleton's autobiography is coloured with his hatred of secret societies and impassioned pathos for the victims and, although he obviously read up some newspaper accounts, as he says he did, his account is full of errors. But let us turn now to his literary endeavour, powerfully told in the first person, and sense some of the foreboding evil in these paragraphs from his story. Demonic elements of nature provide a cloak for the conspiracy to wreak revenge.

Extracts from Carleton's Story

It was about the middle of winter. The day was gloomy and tempestuous almost beyond any other I remember; dark clouds rolled over the hills about me, and a close sleet-like rain fell in slanting drifts that chased each other rapidly towards the earth on the course of the blast. The outlying cattle sought the closest and calmest corners of the fields for shelter; the trees and young groves were tossed about, for the wind was so unusually high that it swept in hollow gusts through them, with that hoarse murmur which deepens so powerfully on the mind the sense of dreariness and desolation.

As the shades of night fell, the storm, if possible, increased. The moon was half gone, and only a few stars were visible by glimpses, as a rush of wind left a temporary opening in the sky. I had determined, if the storm should not abate, to incur any penalty rather than attend the meeting; but the appointed hour was distant, and I resolved to be decided by the future state of the night.

Ten o'clock came, but still there was no change; eleven passed, and on opening the door to observe if there were any likelihood of its clearing up, a blast of wind, mingled with rain nearly blew me off my feet. At length it was approaching to the hour of midnight; and on examining it a third time, I found it had calmed a little, and no longer rained.

I instantly got my oak stick, muffled myself in my great coat, strapped my hat about my ears, and, as the place of meeting was only a quarter of a mile distant, I presently set out.

The appearance of the heavens was lowering and angry, particularly in that point where the light of the moon fell against the clouds, from a seeming chasm in them, through which alone she was visible ...

At length I arrived at a long slated house, situated in a solitary part of the neighbourhood; a little below it ran a small stream, which was now swollen above its banks, and rushing with mimic roar over the flat meadows beside it. The appearance of the bare slated building in such a night was particularly sombre, and to those, like me, who knew the purpose to which it was usually devoted, it was or ought to have been peculiarly so. There it stood, silent and gloomy, without any appearance of human life or enjoyment about or within it. As I approached, the moon once more had broken out of the clouds, and shone dimly upon the wet, glittering slates and windows, with a death-like lustre, that gradually faded away as I left the point of observation, and entered the folding-door. It was the parish chapel.

Great evil is accentuated in the sacrilegious activities of the beastly conspirators. The rituals of Ribbonmen replace the Catholic Mass rite. The Captain is celebrant of the ceremony. Murmurs echo the tones of the Latin Low Mass. Holy Communion is veiled in the sharing of whiskey to enliven the perverted will; the oath to sacrifice the condemned family is solemnly sworn on the altar and missal. A wicked laugh mocks the stillness of God's presence. As if blown by an unseen malicious power the candle gutters out.

The scene which presented itself here was in keeping not only with the external appearance of the house, but with the darkness, the storm, and the hour, which was now a little after midnight. About forty persons were sitting in dead silence upon the circular step of the altar. They did not seem to move; and as I entered and advanced, the echo of my footsteps rang through the building with a lonely distinctness, which added to the solemnity and mystery of the circumstances about me. The windows were secured with shutters on the inside, and on the altar a candle was lighted, which burned dimly amid the surrounding darkness, and lengthened the shadow of the altar itself, and those of six or seven persons who *stood* on its upper steps, until they mingled in the obscurity which shrouded the lower end of the chapel. The faces of the men who *sat* on the altar steps were not distinctly visible, yet their prominent and more characteristic features were in sufficient relief, and I observed, that some of the most malignant and reckless spirits in the parish were assembled. In the eyes of those who stood at the altar, and whom I knew to be invested with authority over the others, I could perceive gleams of some latent and ferocious purpose, kindled, as I soon observed, into a fiercer expression of vengeance, by the additional excitement of ardent spirits, with which they had stimulated themselves to a point of determination that mocked at the apprehension of all future responsibility, either in this world or the next.

The welcome which I received on joining them was far different from the boisterous good humour that used to mark our greetings on other occasions; just a nod of the head from this or that person, on the part of those *who sat*, with a *dhud dhemur tha thu?* in a suppressed voice, even below a common whisper: but from the standing group, who were evidently the projectors of the enterprise, I received a convulsive grasp of the hand, accompanied by a fierce and determined look, that seemed to search my eye and countenance, to try if I were a person likely to shrink from whatever they had resolved to execute ... Along with the grasp, they did not forget to remind me of the common bond by which we were united, for each man gave me the secret grip of Ribbonism in a manner that made the joints of my fingers ache for some minutes afterwards.

There was one present, however – the highest in authority – whose actions and demeanour were calm and unexcited. He seemed to labour under no unusual influence whatever, but evinced a serenity so placid and philosophical, that I attributed the silence of the sitting group, and the restraint which curbed in the out-breaking passions of those who *stood*, entirely to his presence. He was a schoolmaster, who taught his daily school in *that* chapel, and acted also, on Sunday, in the capacity of clerk to the priest – an excellent and amiable old man, who knew little of his illegal connexions and atrocious conduct.

When the ceremonies of brotherly recognition and friendship were past, the Captain (by which title I shall designate the last-mentioned person) stooped, and, raising a jar of whiskey on the corner of the altar, held a wine-glass to its neck, which he filled, and with a calm nod handed it to me to drink. I shrank back, with an instinctive horror, at the profaneness of such an act, in the house, and on the altar of God, and peremptorily refused to taste the proffered draught ...

... But in the course of his meditation, I could observe, on one or two occasions, a dark shade come over his countenance, that contracted his brow into a deep furrow, and it was then, for the first time, that I saw the satanic expression of which his face, by a very slight motion of its muscles, was capable. His hands during this silence, closed and opened convulsively; his eyes shot out two or three baleful glances, first to his confederates, and afterwards vacantly into the deep gloom of the lower part of the chapel; his teeth ground against each other, like those of a man whose revenge burns to reach a distant enemy, and finally, after having wound himself up to a certain determination, his features relapsed into their original calm and undisturbed expression. At that moment a loud laugh, having something supernatural in it, rang out wildly from the darkness of the chapel ...

Carleton brings out the magnitude of the atrocity in a graphic description of the merciless killing of one of the women in the lodge:

... The hour now was about half-past two o'clock. Scarcely had the last words escaped from the Captain's lips, when one of the windows of the house was broken, and a human head, having the hair in a blaze, was descried, apparently a woman's, if one might judge by the profusion of burning tresses, and the softness of the tones, notwithstanding that it called, or rather shrieked, aloud, for help and mercy. The only reply to this was the whoop from the Captain and his gang, of 'No mercy – no mercy!' and that instant the former, and one of the latter, rushed to the spot, and ere the action could be perceived, the head was transfixed with a bayonet and a pike, both having entered it together. The word 'mercy' was divided in her mouth; a short silence ensued, the head hung down on the window, but was instantly tossed back into the flames!

It was interest in Carleton that revived curiosity in the burning of Wildgoose Lodge. Benedict Kiely in his biography of Carleton, *Poor Scholar*, commented, '... the terrible story of Wildgoose Lodge ... was nothing unique in a country where men were bitterly discontented about rent and tithes, where men really knew slavery and oppression and the black neighbourhood of perpetually threatening hunger, where men hated each other because of differing creeds'.³ This particular outrage, however, is essentially agrarian rather than religious.

UNCOVERING THE FACTS

The first tentative move to uncover the facts of the atrocity was made by T.G.F. Paterson (1888-1971), former curator of Armagh County Museum, prompted also by his study of Carleton. He wrote, 'Carleton's version was my first introduction to the tragedy of Wildgoose Lodge and as a boy I thought the story pure fiction. Later I realized from other sources that the account was based on stark reality, and finding many discrepancies in the various narratives, recently decided on some research in the files of contemporary newspapers, a study less productive of decisive results than anticipated. Two years ago, accompanied by Mr H. G. Tempest, I paid a visit to the site of Wildgoose Lodge. A sense of calamity pervades the place, a feeling intensified by its lonely and isolated position. So long as the story persists in the local folklore it is evident that no house will rise again on that particular spot'. These words are from his article entitled 'The Burning of Wildgoose Lodge' published in 1950 in the *County Louth Archaeological Journal* (xii, 2). His valuable contribution in sorting out some contemporary press accounts was a first step towards unravelling the facts. He gave a fair idea of what happened even though his study was incomplete. Benedict Kiely, also drawn to the subject through his interest in Carleton, visited Wildgoose Lodge and in seven articles in the *Irish Times*, 12 July 1972 to 21 September 1972, meandered meditatively through the horrible story of murder, revenge and state punishment. It is not surprising that ghostly articles on Wildgoose Lodge followed in *Ireland's Own* and *The Ulster Tatler* and that it became the subject of an occasional ballad.[4]

In 1974 and 1975 Daniel J. Casey, Professor of English, State University of New York, returned to the subject with two articles in the same Louth journal (xviii, 2,3) entitled 'Wildgoose Lodge: the Evidence and the Lore' in which he examined historical accounts and newspaper resources, gathered some of the more recent local traditions and then set about analysing the folk traditions. He also perused the new creative writing on the subject, which then included two plays 'Wildgoose Lodge' by Jack McQuoid and Michael Duffy (produced by Sam Hanna Bell, BBC Northern Ireland Home Service, Radio 4, 2 February 1968) and 'Reprisal' (first entitled 'Terrorism' in the unpublished script) by Éamonn Smullen (Project Arts Theatre Production, Dublin, 1971). Facts needed to be obtained because there had been doubts regarding aspects of the trials and the executions and even as to who and how many died in the fire. One major problem surrounded the number who were actually hanged for the outrage. In 1986 I published a selection of documents from the National Archives of Ireland in an article in the *County Louth Archaeological and Historical Journal* (xxi, No.2), which clarified many of the problems. For example, one particular document written by Samuel Pendleton, Chief Magistrate of Police in County Louth, lays out the names of those charged, when arrested, by whom evidence was given, nature of sentence and date of execution in the cases of those capitally convicted.

2
Poverty and Ribbonmen

RIBBONMEN

Prior to the 1798 Rising of the United Irishmen, the Defender movement, a secret political society formed to defend Catholics and resolve economic grievances, was strong in County Louth and there is a record of constant agrarian strife there from 1790 to 1798. There were incidents of Catholics raiding Protestant houses for arms in Louth, Meath and Cavan. After the interlude of Defender/United Irish co-operation in Louth, largely brought about by the mediation of James Napper Tandy and Fr James Coigly, who was a curate in Dundalk and chaplain to the prison there, 1793-96, and following the distress caused by economic decline, Ribbonism, a new movement to protect the poor, pursued once more the social policy and custom of Defenderism. Thomas Bartlett has written in *The Fall and Rise of the Irish Nation*, 'That there was a close link between Defenderism and Ribbonism was soon apparent: when a "Ribbonman's oath" was discovered in Leitrim in 1812, it contained the words "I do further swear that I am now a true Defender" and collections of Ribbon oaths and catechisms also revealed the movement's indebtedness to Defenderism, especially its anti-Protestant aspect'.[5] A new generation of agitators in the northern counties could still reach back to the Defender and Peep o'Day Boys' sectarian conflicts and the strong dissatisfactions of the Oakboys and Steelboys against injustice. Land was the only resource in Ireland and contest in sharing and controlling it inevitably led to conflict. Ribbonism no doubt was also prompted to action by the Whiteboy and Rockite activities in Munster, the midlands and south Leinster, which cast a cultural influence of agitation all over Ireland. In those regions and in parts of Connacht local secret agrarian associations abounded for periods of a few years in the first half of the nineteenth century with appelations, apart from Whiteboys, such as Threshers (Thrashers), Carders, Whitefeet, Blackfeet, Terry Alts and Levellers. Two feuding factions in the south-east of Ireland, the Caravats and

Shanavests, mixed personal and agrarian grievances with crime, cruelty and terror. All of these and their heirs tended to be classified under the 'Whiteboy' label but all subsequently subsumed under the generic term of Ribbonism (the Molly Maguires were a later off-spring group dominant in Leitrim, Longford and Roscommon in 1844-47 and under that name also formed a protest movement in North America). Constant governmental use of the term Ribbonism, even from the first quarter of the 19th century, to cover all groups engaged in agrarian agitation and crime, error as it was, inevitably influenced the newspapers and the public in general to follow suit in such use of the term, just as they had followed the authorities a previous decade ago in labelling all peasant unrest as 'defenderism'. However, it is from the 1820s that *formal* Ribbonism as distinct from agrarian societies became more organised in its formation of lodges and its neo-masonic rituals, an inheritance from the Defenders, gaining its strength among the artisans and working class in Dublin and the eastern counties and parts of Ulster, and even appearing among some Irish communities in Britain. In this 'true' Ribbonism there lurked a national political ideology derived from the Defenders and in rural areas there was a deep feeling, impractical, as it seemed, to repossess land and undo the confiscations of the past. There was no national organisation in Ribbonism and there were no national leaders but there were occasional 'provincial meetings' and some unpleasant conflicting urban-rural contacts and meetings, and, as in the case of Patrick Devan, schoolteacher, weaver and parish clerk, there were sometimes educated men or the odd more prosperous farmer who acted as local leaders. Public houses were a favourite place of meeting. Lecky in his book on Daniel O'Connell remarks that disturbances were 'not always due to distress or confined to the poorest districts'.[6] Revolt occurs more often among those who have gained some prosperity and are in danger of losing it or are ambitious for higher status. The weakest, though nursing their resentments, generally remain tranquil.[7] Ribbonism added a sectarian dimension to the agrarian disturbances and was aided by the Pastorini prophecies which heralded the destruction of Protestantism.[8] It was generally based on the poor, lower middle-class, and working class Catholics. Sectarianism was stronger in the regions where Ribbonmen contended with Orangemen and where their advance in gaining tenancies and sharing a new prosperity by individual effort in the linen industry aroused fear and jealousy among Protestant tenants. The slackening of the Penal Laws, the pride of place and independent mentality created by the Irish Volunteers and the increasing desire for Catholic emancipation added to those fears. The sectarian undertones of Defenderism still lingered in peasant culture as is clear from various Ribbon oaths of the period in County Louth and its neighbouring counties and this would have been sufficient to give Protestants the idea that there was a conspiracy of hostility towards them. Carleton in his short story 'Wildgoose Lodge' has Captain Devaun order his men in Stonetown Chapel to take two oaths, one to carry out their action and one to maintain secrecy. They may bear a resemblance to the oaths in the Ribbon culture he was familiar with:

> He then turned round, and taking the Missal between his hands placed it upon the altar. Hitherto every word was uttered in a low precautionary tone; but on grasping the book he again turned round, and looking upon his confederates with the same satanic expression which marked his countenance before, he exclaimed, in a voice of deep determination, first kissing the book!
> 'By this sacred an' holy book of God, I will perform the action which we have met this night to accomplish, be that what it may; an' this I swear upon God's book, and God's althar!'
> On concluding, he struck the book violently with his open hand, thereby occasioning a very loud report.
> At this moment the candle which burned before him went suddenly out, and the chapel was wrapped in pitchy darkness; the sound as if of rushing wings fell upon our ears, and fifty voices dwelt upon the last words of his oath with wild and supernatural tones, that seemed to echo and to mock what he had sworn ...
> He then turned round, and, placing his right hand on the missal, swore, ' In the presence of God and before his holy altar, that whatever might take place that night he would keep secret from man or mortal, except the priest, and that neither bribery, nor imprisonment, nor death, would wring it from his heart'.

The general tone of Ribbon oaths, the activities of Louth, Meath and South Armagh Ribbonmen, the methods of police and magistrates in proceeding against them and the co-operation of the courts may be illustrated by the following examples.

On 23 July 1815 at the Summer Assizes in Trim, James Reilly was tried before Mr Justice Daly upon an indictment which charged him with taking an unlawful oath, commonly called 'The Ribbonman's Oath'. The *Belfast News Letter* 4 August 1815 published the proceedings.

> Th. Battersby, Esq. examined by Mr Espinasse. Is a Magistrate of County Meath; saw the prisoner on the morning of 29th Nov. last. He had been apprehended at Oldcastle the preceding night, in consequence of directions given to the Police Officers. Upon being interrogated, he made a confession, which witness took down. Witness told him he was not to expect any thing in consequence of making such confession. Witness then produced the paper, which was signed by him, and by the prisoner.
> Mr McNally (*for the defence*) objected to this confession being read, as it had been extorted from him. The magistrate, in his cross-examination said that [the] prisoner was not sent to jail for some days, as he had intimated that he was disposed to give information against others. He was removed to a school-house, and witness *heard* that a weight was fastened to one of his legs, on account of his having attempted to escape.
> Mr McNally then examined prisoner's brother and another, who deposed that they saw the prisoner in the school-house with a 56lb weight fastened to one of his legs by a plough chain; but this was after his confession.
> The Judge permitted the confession to be read. It was as follows: 'That on the 8th of September last, at the mile-house, near Drogheda, he was sworn to the purport of the Oath, No.1 (now found on him) by a man who called himself Hugh Flinn and said he came from Carrickmacross. Says he swore Peter Fray and James Gerarty, both of Granard, weavers, about a fortnight since to the Oath No.2, which he drew out himself. Understands the purport of the Society was to have no dealings with Protestants, and to support each other in all cases of necessity. Paper No.4 he got from a man who lives near Bailieborough, County Cavan; he believes his name is Michael Smyth. Prayer-book found in his pocket belongs to himself. Knows a number of the Society in his own county. Cannot break his oath by telling how many, or their names. The Society was not to rob any person of money or arms, but to be ready when called on by the Committee or their Agents. Cannot tell when the Committee met or who presided. Expects he will get from them money to support him now, while in confinement. Cannot tell how it may be conveyed to him. No Freemason or Orangeman to be of their Society – none but pure Catholics'.
> John Manning, police constable, stated that having directions to arrest a man, who was charged with administering 'the Ribbonman's Oath', and that he would find the oath in his hat, witness, accompanied by E.

Miller, searched several public-houses, and about half-past ten in the night of 28th November, found the prisoner in the house of Peter Smyth. Witness went up to the prisoner and pulled off his hat. Prisoner snatched a parcel of papers out of his hat, and endeavoured to give them to another person, but they were secured by Miller. Prisoner made great resistance, and was with difficulty removed from the public-house.

E. Miller corroborated the former witness, and produced the papers which were taken from prisoner's hat. They had been exhibited to the prisoner when before the Magistrate, and he admitted them to be his. The papers were then read.

OATH, No.1

'In the name of the Father, Son, and Holy Ghost. Amen. What is your name? – I do come here, and make oath on the Evangelists and Catholic Church, and enter into the following resolutions, that I will keep secret of all that I will here see this day, until death and after.

That I will keep secret, and help, and aid, and assist, and support those articles until death and after, and lead to a Catholic life.

That you will not connect with any Protestant, or Freemason, or any other connection that is against you, but those that is connected with us.

That you shall not quarrel, riot, brag, or boast out of the strength of your confederacy.

That you will not rob, nor steal, nor defraud any brother to the valuation of from one sixpence to a shilling to your knowledge, or knowing, without making a restitution.

That no man shall be taken in here, on your vigor or strength, without two or more of the same Society.

That you shall not appear before Judge, Bar, or Jury, and Justice, for the injury of your said brother.

That if any thing derives between you and your said brother, that you will leave it to the decision of two or more of the said brothers.

That you shall not leave one penny with a Protestant, which you will get with a Roman Catholic as cheap.

That no man shall be received here, but a true Catholic, and that alone, unless he is duly inspected into his character, by two or more of the same Society.

That you are not to let yourself be knowing to any man, unless he is tried by word, or sign, and to not divulge your secret in drunkenness – in your sobriety, in dread, or fear, or let yourself knowing to any man, but a brother.

That you will attend at all true and lawful causes, and if not, that you shall give true and lawful account for your non-attendance.

That you are to stand for each other in all true and lawful causes, until death'.

PAPER. No.2

+ 'In the name of Father, Son, and Holy Ghost! - What is your name? I do come here and make oath on the Holy Evangelists and Catholic Church – I will enter into the following resolution, in the presence of the Almighty God, and the Blessed Virgin, that I never will turn King's evidence against any man in this society, in the honour of the Holy Cross; that I will keep secret from this day, until death'.

The PAPER. No.3 was nearly similar to No. 1 but did not contain so many articles.
The PAPER. No. 4 was a copy of verses, or song; it was not received in evidence.

The learned Judge summed up the evidence, and the Jury, without leaving the box, found the prisoner *Guilty*.

His Lordship expressed in strong terms his sense of the crime. The prisoner was an instrument in the hands of wicked men who professed the Catholic religion, in order to accomplish their desperate projects. The Catholic professes the Christian religion, to no part of which can this engagement be reconciled. The introduction of religion was a veil to mislead the ignorant, and obscure the most nefarious designs. The prisoner appeared to be an active and zealous agent of such men, and therefore too dangerous to be suffered to remain in the country. He was ordered to be transported for seven years.

A Ribbon oath dating from 1823, endorsed by John Foster, 'From W. Filgate. Oath administered to an Association of Riband Men' runs as follows:

I William Wilson do swear in the presence of our Brotherly Members, by the contents of this book, and by the Seal of Christ, that I will maintain and endeavour to support our one true religion and that I will destroy all heretics, as far as in my power agreeable to order, and will not spare person or property no one excepted. I do also swear and acknowledge that I will be ready to assist the secret members of this Society against every heretic that is perpetually loading and trampling our blest communion; and I do further swear by our Holy Father the Pope to be ready if possible, nothing but sickness to prevent my efforts, in 24 hours' warning to carry this our glorious and long wished for design into real execution against heretics of every sect who fatten on the tenth part of labour; and that neither torture or death shall make me divulge any part of the above obligation. So help me God by the Cross and true Seal of a Saviour and bind me faithful to this obligation. Amen.[9]

Urban and rural combinations of Ribbonmen, as has been observed, had little or no contact with each other and, since the land question was of prime concern for country people in the succeeding famine crises of 1817, 1822, 1831, 1835-6-7, 1842 and 1845-52, agrarian protest predominated in rural movements and was locally based. Already, as an introduction to the distress and violence of these years in County Louth there had been an outbreak of violence in north Meath and the southern Cavan border due to the failure of the potato crop in 1811 and 1812. There were other social issues besides the possession of land, such as payment of tithes, and in some places the excessive burden of priests' dues. In the 1816-17 period, when famine and fever struck, rent rates and the price of provisions were dominant grievances. The Catholic poor, silently for the most part, resented the great social status cleavage between rich and poor, between 'respectability' and the 'lower orders', a divide regarded as divinely providential by the gentry and often by churchmen. The rising Catholic middle class too was overshadowed by the ascendancy. This dual form of society prevailed in County Louth, a hierarchical system with paternalistic tones; a county dotted with fine elegant mansions looked down on damp cabins and lowly cottages. The labouring classes and cottier tenants had little or no opportunity of formal education; they were ill-fed and ill-clothed. In all walks of life the gentry dominated and regimented those under them. The rural poor also resented the contempt, power and oppression of an alien government represented in the ruthless Protestant ascendancy and their control over police, soldiers and the courts. They reviled greedy landlords, most of whom were magistrates. They threatened them with anonymous notices, but were careful for the most part not to attack them directly. The landlords wreaked their own revenge in a judicial process that was often a form of injustice, intimidation and terror. There was no redress for the grievances of the poor through the judicial system. It treated them with obscene cruelty and they sometimes showed their contempt for it by naked perjury. The executive in Dublin Castle, without any consideration of the causes of discontent, looked on the 'lower orders' of Irish people as inferior human beings, by nature prone to violence, and propounded this view in their private letters to the government at Westminster. They made little distinction between the law-abiding in 'the lower orders' and the secret societies. In the absence of universal right and justice, underground peasant movements formed their own legal system in secret assemblies, cutivated their own values and codes and dealt out their own cruel penalties. Paradoxically, with no recognition of dignity for the peasantry within the state system, the formation of secret societies, loosely federated, was a preparation for O'Connell's democracy. With Catholic Emancipation would come the birth of constitutional politics. The softer picture is a society of peasants who inherited a clan culture of close kinship and a folk memory of communal ownership. There was a tradition of great generosity and charity among well to do farmers and the poor alike, a compassion instilled into them by the Catholic Church. The Irish language was spoken in much of the rural areas of Louth and its rich culture was embedded in poetry, story and oral tradition. This cultural world had a vision of ultimate liberation and was unknown to the ascendancy. The rise of the Catholic chapels and the votes of forty-shilling freeholders were the only earthly visible sign of the first growth of independent attitudes. Otherwise the estate framework dominated the rural areas.

The activities of agrarian associations fluctuated with the rise and fall of the mainly agrarian economy and the fortunes of personal interests. The lesson learned from the mass slaughter of the United Irishmen pushed aside all ideas of insurrection. A local underground coercive protection society, which could control its members and punish informers, and engage sporadically in a type of destructive and murderous guerrilla warfare, was more attractive. In Louth and its neighbouring counties the threatening letter and poster, houghing of farm animals, destruction of crops, firing of farmhouses and ricks, the intimidation of witnesses and assassination of chosen offenders, informers in particular, were adopted from the methods of the 'Whiteboy' movements. Such activity was meant to build up an atmosphere of deterrence. Ribbonism had its own security code. Secrecy was sacrosanct. A sacred oath and vengeful punishment of betrayers, including murder, were its basic defence against infiltration and knowledge of its plans. Tom Garvin in his article 'Defenders, Ribbonmen and Others' quotes Michael Davitt's appreciation of the Ribbonmen's maintenance of secrecy in comparison with later organisations:

> Spies were sent into its ranks by Dublin Castle ... but the secrets of the society, the nature of its leaders, its methods of government and of

> action were far more successfully concealed than those of any other oath-bound combination among the Irish people. This was due, primarily, to a wise precaution against keeping books, documents, or records that would reveal information if lost or seized. In this respect these peasant conspirators were far wiser in their plans than the educated organizers and leaders of the Fenian Brotherhood [of the 1860s] ... it can be safely affirmed that the more or less uneducated Ribbonmen have shown themselves to be more skilled in the methods of secret conspiracy than the more cultured class of their countrymen who founded Fenianism, to a large extent upon the Ribbon lodges of Ireland.[10]

One might venture to say that agrarian disturbances in the early 19th century helped to develop the politicisation of the rural poor. Although it did not harness them for an organised national movement, it did prepare them for a role in the Catholic emancipation campaign and a shallow political alliance at that period with the large Catholic tenant farmers who hitherto had sometimes been the target of their attacks. The land struggle was a bitter one, varying with new structures in society, the reduction of the labouring class and especially changes from tillage to grazing. It lasted more than a century.

FAMINE AND FEVER

In his seminal article, 'The importance of agrarian classes: agrarian class structure and collective action in nineteenth-century Ireland' (1978)[11] Samuel Clark corrects the simplistic picture of a perennial common interest among the rural Catholic population in a long struggle against the landowners. That great social cleavage did exist but there were also social groups within the occupiers of land. The majority of landlords in pre-Famine Ireland were tenants with large holdings who for profitable purposes sublet portions of their land. The sub-tenants inevitably were more vulnerable in times of crisis than the direct tenants or middlemen. The rural poor were at the bottom of the social pyramid, some of them landless labourers, some of them labourer-landholders who had cabins and small potato gardens. Access to the land, the very source of livelihood, and the regulation of its terms and distribution, was a prime factor in agrarian protest. Fortunes fluctuated with social and economic change; all grades of rural society could fall victim and lose their position. Tradesmen enjoyed a reasonable standard of living, as the landlords and farmers were dependant on their skills. In County Louth in the first quarter of the nineteenth century the linen trade still supplied a home industry of spinning and weaving in the wintertime. The food of the poorer classes consisted mainly of potatoes, buttermilk and stirabout. Clark identifies five classes in rural Ireland: 'landless labourers, labourer-landholders, small independent land-holders, large independent landholders (large farmers) and landowners'. Fortunes could be haphazard and peasant farmer and labourer could interchange. Michael Beames in his explanation of the terms 'cottiers' and 'conacre' in their various distinctions defines 'cottier' in the counties Dublin, Louth, Meath, Armagh, Down and Cavan as similar to 'cottager' in England and 'merely means the occupier of a cabin, without any reference to his occupation, the size of the ground, if any, attached to his cabin or any such circumstances' and defines 'conacre' as 'a form of holding, from half a rood to two acres in size taken from the farmer or landlord to grow potatoes, and less commonly oats for one season'.[12] Rural tradesmen also sought their piece of land to supplement their meagre income. Land obviously became scarce with the rapidly growing population after 1800 and at the same time a piece of potato ground was essential for survival. The increase in population saw also an increase in the poorest type of houses, often one-roomed overcrowded thatched cottages, a major factor in a poor quality of life.

Even before the post-Napoleonic war crisis the Irish peasantry found it difficult to eke out a living. They were often subjected to oppression. Sir George Cornhall Lewis in his book *Local Disturbances in Ireland* (1836) quotes from *An Inquiry into the Causes of Popular Discontents in Ireland* by an Irish Country Gentleman (London, 1804):

> 'It has not been unusual in Ireland', he says, ' for great landed proprietors to have regular prisons in their houses for the summary punishment of the lower orders. Indictments preferred against gentlemen for similar exercise of power beyond law are always thrown out by the grand juries. To horsewhip or beat a servant or labourer is a frequent mode of correction. But the evil is not so great among the gentlemen of large property, whose manners have generally been

softened by education, travelling, and the progress of humanity and civilization. A horde of tyrants exists in Ireland in a class of men that are unknown in England; in the multitude of agents to absentees; small proprietors, who are the pure Irish squires; middle-men, who take large farms, and squeeze out a forced kind of profit, by reletting them in small parcels; lastly, the little farmers themseves, who exercise the same insolence they receive from their superiors, on those unfortunate beings, who are placed at the extremity of the scale of degradation, the Irish peasantry'.[13]

Richard Willcocks, chief magistrate in the barony of Middlethird, Tipperary, in a letter to Gregory at Dublin Castle, gives a clear picture of the situation of labourers, farmers and landowners in that barony in 1816, a picture that would probably reflect the general situation in County Louth. Both Peel and Gregory respected his opinion and judgements.

Cashel: April 17, 1816

> I have had the honour to receive your letter of the 11th instant, requesting that I would, for the information of Mr Peel, answer certain queries therein mentioned. In reply to which I beg to aquaint you for Mr Peel's information that I have collected the best authentic information in my power, which together with my own information makes me to answer the queries in the following manner:
> The Labourers in this Barony, and I believe in general throughout the country, are paid in two ways. Some hold a Cabbin and from half an acre to an acre of ground, for which they pay 2 to 4 guineas a year. The persons [sic] who pay for such Cabbin and Ground works the year round with his employer for sixpence a day. He who pays 3 guineas a year gets eightpence a day, and if the labourer pays a higher rent he gets tenpence a day the year round. In general the labourer also gets the grass of a cow from his employer, for which he pays from two to four guineas a year, which is also taken out in labour at the same rate as for the Cabbin and Land. He also gets a potato ground at a fair price. These labourers get no lease from their employers.
> The other class of labourers who hold no land, and who are the more numerous, generally get from eightpence to tenpence a day the year round, but at the time of making up the harvest, and the digging of the potatoes, the labourers who come into the country from Limerick and Kerry and those of this county who are not bound by the year, get much higher wages, such as from two and sixpence to two shillings a day. It is my opinion that the labouring classes of this county are fairly dealt with, and taking all circumstances into view, they have no reason to complain of their state or condition, they are in general well clothed, and their food plenty and wholesome.
> As to the poorest and lowest order of farmers, I take their state and

condition at present to be very pitiable, particularly those who have taken lands within the last 6 or 8 years. Farmers of this decription hold from 10 to 30 or 40 acres of land, for which they pay 40 shillings to four pounds an acre, according to the quality of the land, and from the present prices for the produce of land it is impossible that those rents can be paid. I consider the condition of poor farmers for years back to be bad. In order to pay a high rent, tithe and county charges, and to support a wife and from three to five children, he was obliged to bring evey article of produce to market, even the straw that ought to make his manure, all which did not leave him a surplus to lay out or expend on the improvement of his land, and the consequence is that the land has become quite worn out and exhausted, and don't produce half the crop it would, had it been treated as it ought.

I find that some years back, and before lands became so very valuable as they lately have been, the leases granted by the Landlords were in general three lives or 21 years, but latterly the general run of leases has been for one life or 21 years. And the rate of Tithes for some years back has been about twelve shillings an acre for wheat, bere, barley and potatoes; oats or meadow land eight shillings an acre, sixpence the ewe, and one shilling the lamb. It does not appear to me that there has been much variation in the rate of tithe latterly.

There is a difference made in the rent of lands titheable, and those which are not. I have been informed that the lands or the greater part of them in the parish of Holy Cross, part of which is in the Barony of Middlethird, are tithe free, and that those lands have hitherto set from six to eight shillings an acre higher than lands titheable of equal quality in the adjoining parish, and I believe in general this is about the difference in rent in such cases.

Upon the whole, taking into view the last 6 or 8 years, I think the petty farmer has now a right to complain, for although he got high prices for the last 5 or 6 years, it is well known that lands carried an equal rise in rent, and it is equally well known that the prices of the present day will not pay half the rent which the farmer is bound to pay by the leases granted within the last 8 or 10 years. His exertions to cultivate the land, if bound to this high rent, will cease and his inevitable ruin must follow unless the prices of the produce rise or the Landlords lower their rents. In my opinion much remains to be done on the part of the Landlord to ameliorate the condition of this class of men. It appears to me that the high rents are by far a much greater grievance than, and infinitely more oppressive than, the Tythes.

There is an immense population in this part of the Country, and land is the only manufacture in the south of Ireland, so that having no other means of employment, by which they could support their families, the tenants would give any price for land sooner than be without it, for let their ability be what it may to pay the rent by having possession of the land, they were certain of having the means of supporting their families ...

As regards honesty. I think in general there is great honesty among the lower orders from one to the other, and fidelity in their dealings.

Disposition of the people. I think in general the common people are civil and respectful to the upper classes, except when unlawful combination gets among them. They are in general lively, and fond of rural sports and amusements ...

Lodging and fuel. The habitation is a small, and I am sorry to say in general a filthy Cabbin, which very often contains a cow or a pig in the same appartment with some of the family. Their beds are in general straw, or the chaff of oats in a coarse bed-tick. Their fuel, if convenient to a bog, is plenty, but in many places scarce and dear when at a distance. The lower orders in general have not a right to cut turf, but the farmers when they take land get from the Landlord the right and privilege of cutting turf, and the poorer classes purchase from them, and either pay in work or money, but I cannot say at what price.

Middlemen. The land in Tipperary generally is not let by the Landlord to the Cottier, but most certainly through the intervention of the middlemen, and in many cases heretofore the middlemen had a greater income out of the land than the landlord. The middleman will take a piece of land from 100 to 200 acres, and will job this out to Cottiers at more than double the rent which he pays himself, but I think this grievous system of high setting practised by the middlemen is now likely to be crushed or put down, for there is now large arrears of rent due to them by the Cottiers, which I believe they are not able nor do they intend to pay. The Land therefore will fall back upon the middleman, and he must make a new setting at a fair price.[14]

Laws passed in the post peace period, between 1815 and 1818, facilitated landlords more and more in discouraging sub-letting and processing eviction. Deflation lasted to the 1830s and still the middlemen were tied to the agreements made with the landlords who were reluctant to make abatements. Undertenants were hardly able to pay heir rents in time of distress. The burden of high rents was passed down the scale from estate owners to big middlemen, to farmers, to sub-tenants. William O'Connor Morris in his book *Present Irish Questions* (1901) gives a good summary of the land problem in Ireland in the post Napoleonic war era:

Partly owing to the corn laws of the Irish Parliament, partly to the extension of the Parliamentary franchise, in 1793, to the great mass of the Catholic peasantry, but principally to the effects of the long war with France, Ireland, it may be said, was well-nigh changed from a pastoral to an agricultural country; large farms were generally replaced by small; the land in most districts was divided into little tillage holdings; the cottar system multiplied apace; the population, about three millions of souls in the day of Arthur Young (his book *Tour in Ireland* was published in 1780), increased to more than six millions at the Peace of 1815; and this population becoming every year more dense, for the most part eked existence out on a precarious root. The economc and social consequences were very great, and continued in operation during a long series of years. The competition for the possession of land became intensely keen; rents were unnaturally forced up in thousands of cases; the value of landed property enormously rose; all this encouraged extravagance among the landed gentry, and especially induced them largely to encumber their estates. At the same time the wages of labour distinctly declined; the condition of the Irish labouring peasant, when Edward Wakefield, a very industrious and able observer, wrote on the state of Ireland in 1812, was markedly worse than it had been in the time of Arthur Young. Yet these effects were not the most serious, at least, the most lasting, effects of the revolution taking place in landed relations. As the large farm system was being broken up, as the small farm system had come in its stead, and as poulation had rapidly grown, the occupiers of the soil had more and more made the permanent additions to their holdings; they had built, fenced, and reclaimed land, more and more; and in the general eagerness to obtain possession of land, considerable sums were often paid for farms on their transfer. The concurrent rights of the tenant classes in Ireland had thus become enormousy increased; they often amounted, equitably, to a real joint-ownership; yet these rights were without the support of law, and were liable to be extinguished often at the mere will of the landlord ...

The land system, nevertheless, was not much disturbed while the high prices of the war prevailed; there was a good deal indeed of disorder connected with the land, but society was not deeply affected. And it is only just to observe that the landlords, as a class, did respect the concurrent rights of their tenants in the soil; the conclusive proof is that these could not have grown up had they been generally, or even largely, set at nought. But a great and calamitous change passed over Ireland when the comparative wealth caused by the war collapsed, and when the return to cash payments made the effects worse. Rents suddenly fell greatly, and even disappeared; the wages of labour, which had usually been paid through what may be called a wretched truck system, were reduced to a remarkable degree; hundreds of thousands of the cottar peasantry sank to the lowest depths of indigence. A great social convulsion, in a word, took place; this culminated in famine in several counties; a miserable population was deprived of the means of subsistence. In these circumstances the owners of the soil acted as a class would ordinarily act; many, impoverished themselves, let things drift; many made themselves conspicuous for good works of charity; a minority had recourse to severe measures, like the English landlords of the sixteenth century, to get rid of a mass of poverty clinging in despair to the land. The old divisions of race and faith unquestionably aggravated this state of things; but the Government of the day showed little forethought, and, in fact, was infinitely the most to blame; it met the emergency, not by wise and healing measures, but by legislation, which made the eviction of the peasant from his holding easy and cheap, and by having recourse to repression unjust and severe in the extreme. In too many instances, 'clearances' of estates, an evil word, were witnessed; hundreds of families were driven from their homes and cast on the world; as the necessary result, in numberless cases, the equitable rights of the Irish tenant were ruthlesly destroyed. As a matter of course, Whiteboyism, never completely suppressed, broke out in formidable agrarian disorder; the peasantry, deprived of the protection of law, leagued themselves together to enforce a law of their own; crime multiplied to an immense extent; all the machinery of coercion could not wholly keep it under.[15]

In the growing crisis in the post-war period the impoverished crowds and rural gangs often vented their anger and grievance not only against those who controlled the land, middlemen, farmers with long leases, landlords and their agents but also against tenants who had taken land from which the previous occupant had been evicted. Conflict also arose when rural labourers were denied 'conacre', the renting of a small plot generally used to grow potatoes to feed their family. Problems arose after 1815 either by the constraint of higher rent, landlords and middlemen attempting to keep the rents at the inflated wartime levels, a tendency on the landlords' part to accept tenants only as tenants-at-will, and the movement of farmers from tillage to pasturage agriculture. In Meath in particular pasture offered high profits and small tenants were pushed out. While there was opposition and horror against the barbarity of the methods of the 'Ribbonmen', often among the rural poor themselves, their cause in defending themselves against ejectment, their sense of their property 'right', community kinship and social relationship, and the cruelty and broad injustice of the law in facilitating by an act of parliament in 1816 the law of ejectment, continued to arouse waves of sympathy.

In the Napoleonic period there was a huge demand from Britain and her allies for provisions for their armies.[16] County Louth as elsewhere in Ireland benefited. Much of these provisions were exported through the port of Dundalk. The team authors of the book *"Down the Quay": A History of Dundalk Harbour* (1988) give a succinct account of the early nineteenth development of Dundalk port: 'In 1803 the new Custom House was built and there was a military guard placed where goods were stored at the quays. Goods could not be removed from outside the Butter Crane Wall, now the site of Shorts Hire Service, without knowledge of the Revenue Officers, since it lay within 50 yards of the Custom House gate under the watchful eye of the guard posted outside the gate day and night. The trade which had been encouraged by the building of new quays, extensive stores and a new Custom House suffered a severe setback after the Napoleonic wars during the period of transition from war to peace. Exports for the year ending January 1813 (including corn, beef, pork, bacon, butter and livestock) amounted to £345,638. By January 1817 this had fallen to £70,241'.[17] Raymond D. Crotty comments in his book *Irish Agricultural Production: its volume and structure* (1966), 'The years 1815-20 marked a turning point of vast importance in the history of Irish agriculture. Within a few years of the Battle of Waterloo as government expenditure was contracted and "sound money" policies were pushed through, prices broke and the period of long term inflation which had persisted there since 1760 gave way to a period of deflation which lasted up to the 1840s'.[18] The new prosperity had led to a great increase in land values. Landlords demanded inflated rents. When the war ended the bottom fell out of the market for produce, the English market, so precious for Ireland, was flooded by foreign wheat and oats, and the tenants, faced with the general fall in prices, could no longer pay the high rents due to a fall in income. When the landlords did not prudently take into account the starker market levels, tension inevitably rose with their tenants. Kevin B. Nowlan in his essay 'Agrarian unrest in Ireland, 1800-1845' (1959) wrote, 'In the years following 1815, landlords and middlemen tried to keep rents at the inflated wartime levels as far as possible, with the result that very large numbers of tenants fell into arrears in their payment of rent. Then again, in the post-war years, cattle prices tended to resist the fall in agricultural prices better than grain. This appears to have led some landlords to reduce the number of tillage farms, a process which inevitably involved the eviction of tenants'.[19] Although landowners would have benefited by a change to pasture, they had not the capital to advance it quickly. Cattle prices did fall somewhat but that did not deter landlords from attempts to move from tillage to pastorage and thus reduce the numbers of their tenants. The steep rise in population was obviously another factor in the increase in poverty. Eviction did not happen on a wide scale in County Louth but, as happened in other parts of the country, and with the lack of industrial outlet, payment of rents, taxes, cess, tithes and church dues increased the burden of poor people. It ran deep in the nature of the peasant to maintain his holding; it was a family tragedy to default on payment of rent or fail to maintain a holding on the highest bid when a lease expired. Those threatened with eviction then naturally made a common cause of resistance with the unemployed cottiers.

Action in fighting social oppression, as has been remarked, surged when relative prosperity ended, when the climate was wet and cold and harvests failed and when the price of stock fell. Shortage of money matched the shortage of food. Joseph Lee in his 'The Ribbonmen'wrote: 'The chronology of Ribbon activities reflects the primacy of economic factors. Although outrage was endemic throughout much of the countryside in the half century before the Famine, the three major eruptions – 1814-16, 1821-23, and 1831-34 - can be traced directly to economic causes. Grain prices fell 30 per cent after the bumper harvest of 1813, having been exceptionally high during the previous four years. The winter of 1813 proved unusually severe, and grain prices fell a further 15 per cent in 1814-15. Farmers were unable to pay a rent which had been agreed when prices were higher, and labourers in turn were thrown out of work. Agitation against threatened evictions, continuing high rents and falling wages swept through several counties'.[20] The year 1817 saw no relief from bad weather; incesssant rain fell throughout the summer but the weather improved in the autumn and the harvest was better than expected.

The rise of the Ribbonmen in Louth in the 1814-16 period points, therefore, to poverty caused by the poor harvests, lack of employment for a fast-growing population dependent on the land, and the general low economy which affected everybody. The potato had become the main source of subsistence for large sections of the population and for a great number of people it was the only source. Failures in the potato crop in 1816 and 1817 created want and famine. 1813-1814 and 1815-1816 saw severe winters. In the summer and autumn of 1816 the weather was particularly wet. Potatoes rotted in the ground and the corn seeded in the fields. There was some respite at the end of September but in the beginning of October the storms recommenced with vigour.

One can follow the apprehensions, sufferings and repercussions of the disastrous harvest of 1816 and the typhus fever that followed the better harvest of 1817.[21] Deprivation, hunger and fever dominate the various reports and testimonies. They are important for the understanding of the wave of violence that ensued and form the background to the events at Wildgoose Lodge. Heavy rains at the end of September and beginning of October ruined the 1816 harvest. Outrages increased as hungry people expressed their bitterness at the export of food from the seaports, attempted plunder, or rioted against the traders who hoarded food in the hope of larger profits.

Paterson in his article on Wildgoose Lodge quotes from the *Census of Ireland* (Vol. 1, Part V), which gives a frightening picture of the severity of the climate, hunger and fever in 1816 and 1817:

> During the summer and autumn of 1816 and 1817, from whatsoever quarter the wind came it was accompanied by rain. Thus during two successive years the season of harvest was too cold and moist to bring the fruits of the earth to maturity, and turf, the chief fuel of the poor, could not be cut or saved.
> To make matters worse, fever began to spread extensively in the spring and continued until the summer of 1818. In Ulster it made greater and more rapid progress than elsewhere, though conditions were bad in Munster and Connaught, and in Leinster later in the year.
> By midsummer bread was more than twice its usual price and potatoes were above three times their average cost. In several parts of Ireland, particularly in the north, the poor were forced to gather wild esculent plants to allay the pains of hunger.
> Conditions were worsened by the transition from war to peace and the consequent lessened demand for agricultural produce, a factor resulting in great distress amongst the farming community and its dependants.[22]

The *Newry Magazine* for 1816 chronicles the weather and harvest for these years in Ireland and Britain:

> *Agricultural Report, 10 May 1816*: 'The almost unprecedented severity of last winter, has very much retarded the growth of the young wheats, and rendered them less vigorous and healthy than is usual at this season of the year. In the midland counties of England, heavy rains have greatly impeded agricultural labours, and much arable lands

have been inundated by floods, that their owners have been unable to cultivate them effectually, and they as yet remain waste. Through a large tract of Great Britain, the barley sowing has been greatly retarded by incessant rains, the lands having been absolutely saturated with water ...

A smaller proportion of ground than usual has been this year cultivated in England – many farms having been deserted by their proprietors, and many thrown out for pasturage. In Ireland, we are happy to say, the late discouraging prices of agricultural products have not prevented our farmers from ploughing and sowing their lands. There is a considerable export of that article to France. The redundant stock, lately on hands, is beginning to disappear and the Irish farmer will reap the advantage due to his industry and perseverance. An immense quantity of flaxseed has been sown. This is chiefly to be attributed to two causes, viz. 1st, to the unusual cheapness of American seed – 2d, to the early and continued frost which in the beginning of November last, had rendered it impractical to labour large tracts of potato lands, which the farmers intended for wheat. These have been sown with flaxseed, and a very great crop may be expected'.

Agricultural Report: 30 August 1816: 'The inclement and wintry summer, with which we have been visited in these islands, has manifestly impeded the ripening of our crops, and of course retarded the harvest. In England, the hawthorn blossoms had scarcely fallen from the hedges, on the 20th July; the elder trees were then but beginning to flower, and in the northern and midland counties, the grain, generally speaking, was not in full ear.

Throughout the whole of Great Britain, much of the wheat crops had been prostrated by the rain ...

In Ireland also, the harvest has been retarded by cold unnatural weather, and perpetual rains. Wheat promised to be a very luxuriant crop, but much of it had been beaten to the ground, and blight and mildew may, we fear, be expected to ensue, if change of weather shall not very soon take place. As yet, the straw is (generally speaking) clear in colour, but the ear is tardy in filling with farinaceous matter. If we shall not soon be favoured by Providence with a series of sunny weather, it is to be dreaded that grain, particularly barley and wheat, will begin to grow and malt on the foot.

Our potato crop is abundant. Oats and barley do not fill well, yet a seasonable change of weather would produce a correspondent beneficial effect on the general crops of the kingdom, and place us above all dread of want or even of scarcity. The hay-making season has, this summer, been by no means a time of hilarity and pastime ... it has been a period of labour and vexation ... Much has been flooded by the swell of rivers ... much injured in lap-cock, and much damaged on the foot. The flax crop is abundant, but it will be difficult to save it in the present season'.

Agricultural Report, 26 October 1816: 'The late advantageous change of weather, has rescued a large portion of our grain crops, which had been

prostrated by incessant rains, from total destruction. The wheat has latterly sustained more injury than any other species of grain. Mildew and blight are prevalent, and much of the lying corn had vegetated before it was completely fit for reaping.
The new oat-meal, which is at present brought to market, is vastly inferior to that of the preceding year. The worst of the damaged grain, as yet reaped, has in the first instance, been threshed off, hastily kiln-dried, and manufactured into meal.
Much of the corn in cold and backward soils is still uncut, and a large quantity has not yet been carted from the fields.
The produce of every species of grain is, by no means, proportioned, in this country, to the bulk of the straw. Potatoes are not deficient in quantity, but very materially so in quality.
It is to be dreaded, that during the ensuing winter the poor will suffer most severely from want of fuel. It was utterly impossible for the agriculturalist, or his labourers to make the usual quantity of turf, and the small proportion of that necessary article, which they have been able to save and remove from the bogs, is so extremely wet, that it will scarcely answer for culinary purposes. Those benevolent members of society, who feel for the distresses and miseries of their indigent fellow-creatures, ought now to establish funds, for the purchase of coals and cheap grates, to be distributed among poor house-keepers, at moderate prices. The good which would result from such a plan would be incalculable.
The late harvest and the wetness of the grounds will render it a difficult if not impossible task to get the seed wheat into the earth, whether fallows or potato lands, in the usual season. This will, of course, have a bad effect in keeping up the process of that valuable article, during the whole of the ensuing summer; unless the ports shall be opened, by virtue of the corn laws, for the admission of foreign grain'.

Robert Curtis in *The History of the Royal Irish Constabulary* (1869) has a childhood memory of the 1816 period:

After the termination of the French war, in 1815, thousands of the British army were disbanded, and numbers of them being Irishmen, returned as idlers – some of them with small pensions – to their native land. The following summer of 1816 was, perhaps, the wettest which can be remembered before or since. The wheat crop all over Ireland was so smutted, malted and damaged, that a sound loaf of Irish flour could not be procured in any part of the kingdom; and it was a common trick amongst school-boys, of which the author of this history was then a very small unit, to pull the soft out of the bread with which they had been served, but which they could not eat, and throw it against the wall, where it stuck like putty! The potatoes, too, which formed the poor man's principal support, were, from the constant rain, no better than balls of soap; whole acres of them in the low lands were flooded, and could not be come at, if even fit for use. After a while some relief came from England (which had not fared much better itself) and from America; but malty bread, and unwholesome substitutes, had done their work upon the poor, and produced in the following year, 1817, a fearful amount of fever and dysentery. The suffering and poverty caused by two such years, with hundreds of disbanded soldiers, ill calculated from their previous lives for anything but idleness, turned loose amongst the population, with more indigenous material, soon produced formidable disturbances; and, in 1818, most portions of the south of Ireland were in a state of turbulence and disorder, where *'carding'* and *'half roasting'* were sometimes conceded as *mercies*, instead of sudden death.[23]

In answer to Peel's anxiety to know the facts of the situation reports were returned on request from various parts of the country.[24] The Earl of Courtown wrote from Courtown to Gregory on 9 October 1816, 'The state of the harvest in this neighbourhood is very melancholy, and if it does not please God to give us some dry weather very soon, it will all be destroyed'. On the same day W. H. Trotter wrote to Peel:

> I trust you will excuse me for taking the liberty of calling your attention to the state of the crops at this period. In the barony where I preside, Lecale, admitted to be the best grain county in the north of Ireland, there is not one-twentieth part of the crop cut and not a single field drawn. The wheat, barley and oats are actually vegetating in the ear before they cut and the potatoes in the low grounds are rotting – those in other places are of a wretched bad quality – horror and dismay appear in the countenances of the landholders and the labouring poor are much worse. Great apprehensions are entertained amongst the farmers that the latter will resort to violence and robbery during the winter, and no doubt many of the idle and profligate will take advantage of the public distress for the purpose of plunder – may I take the liberty of suggesting the prudence of suspending the distillation of all grain for the malting of barley even for a month until it can be ascertained whether any grain can be saved.

B.T. Balfour of Townley Hall, County Louth, gave a full report on 9 October 1816:

> I have lately been through a part of the North and West of the land, through Monaghan, Fermanagh, Cavan and Sligo. I had the benefit of my own observation in addition to what I learn from my connections and correspondences in the corn trade. To answer first your enquiry respecting the stock of old grain on hand. There is very little wheat either in this county or in Meath in the hands of merchants and millers and none in those of farmers. This I know from those persons coming

to us for flour who never deal with us when they can get it elsewhere. There is not I believe altogether a supply left for 6 weeks of the usual consumption except with us. We have about 4000 barrels either here or in Limerick and Liverpool which will keep us in flour till January. There is a trifling quantity of oats in the hands of farmers, and very little in those of merchants but I believe there may be some oatmeal in the hands of small county dealers as the low prices last year induced those that could afford to keep it to do so, and it is more easily kept in meal than in oats. This will now be kept back as the appearance of scarcity has always that effect on that description of people.

With regard to other parts of the kingdom I shall know more in a few days, having written to Limerick, Cork, Waterford and Clonmel to endeavour to make purchases. As to the present crop it is in river. The wheat is spouting whether it is cut or uncut. The oats are beaten into the earth and either rotten or sprouted. The potatoes watery and beginning to rot. A great quantity of the potatoes and oats are actually under water and the ducks swimming among them. In addition the distilleries are at work and consuming to the utmost of their power. They will of course attract the immediate notice of Government but I need not suggest to you that in the circumstances with which we are threatened it is not mere destructive unconscious regulation that will be expected from them (the Government). More undoubtedly will be expected than may be recoverable or practicable but most surely whatever is by any means practicable will fall within the strict line of their duty to perform. It is not a mere question of humanity, though that would be sufficient, but the tranquillity if not the existence of the country may be at stake. The probable effects of combined disaffection and starvation upon millions cannot be contemplated without something more than apprehension. Terror is too strong a word. The lower classes however will not have all the misery to themselves. Those who have generally lived by rent must prepare themselves to live by their wits. This may be done by those who have no incumbrances but how interest money or connections are to be paid I know not. I hate croaking but I defy the most sombre pencil to paint the present prospect in colours darker than those of nature.

Queries and answers were received by Peel from Colonel Alexander Armstrong, B[rigade] Major, Louth, Armagh and Monaghan, dated 10 October 1816:

In what state is the corn which is cut? Either totally rotten or growing again.
In what state is that which remains to be cut and would a continuance of fine weather now enable the farmer to save it? In most places it is growing from the ear, besides it has got so very ripe the wet weather not allowing the peope to cut and that if the weather should take up ever so fine a vast quantity must be lost by seeding.
What is the state of the potato crop? Very indifferent in general and so wet

they are likely to bring dysenteries and other dreadful complaints.
Has the turf been generally cut and saved, and what are the prospects of the poor with respect to fuel for the coming winter? A vast deal of turf has been cut and very little saved – a most melancholy prospect for the poor who are going miles to pull the heath from the mountains. When that is expended I don't know what they can recourse to.
What is the price p. barrel of wheat, oats, and barley? Very little brought to market as yet – at Armagh on the 8th inst. oatmeal was £1 5. 0. per cwt; at Lurgan on the 4th £1 8. 0. p. cwt and first flour 7s. p. stone – oatmeal in Carrickmacross this day (10th Octr) £1 2. 9. p. cwt.
In addition to this the hay in the neighbourhood of Richhill and along the banks of the Blackwater and the Ban rivers has been mostly swept away by the floods and carried to Lough Neagh.

On 10 October 1816 Major General Burnet, stationed in Armagh, made his report by private letter to Peel's request for facts:

I have received from Head-Quarters a copy of your letter of the 8th inst. to L. Gen. Lord Forbes respecting the state of the harvest in this Country, and am extremely concerned that I must report it to be most deplorable.
The season in the North of Ireland has been very backward and the late rains destroyed a very large proportion of both grain and hay.
My duty has led me to travel within the last ten days through the counties of Armagh, Cavan, Fermanagh, Louth, Monaghan and Tyrone and I everywhere observed the upland hay to have been only tolerably well saved, and the grain that was cut had not been taken off the land by reason of the bad weather. With respect to to the low grounds they are in general flooded, the grain lodged and some fresh growing from the ears – most of that as well as the hay is in the water and I fear totally destroyed.
Oats have risen considerably in the different markets and in this town from thirteen pence to two shillings and two pence per stone – and bread is rising in proportion.
Although there was in general a prospect of a good crop of potatoes, they are not dry and if a speedy change of weather does not take place, and there should come an early frost, I fear this food of the people will fail.
The turf is wet and bad and much of it under water and in my late tour of more than 140 miles there was scarcely any to be seen at the cottages and in very many places cars could not get to draw it in.
Scarcely any of the crops of grain has been got in and that which is in the low grounds I fear will not be saved. The poor are suffering more from the rising prices of meal and potatoes, and want of work as no harvest work can be done in this weather.
As you required an early communication I lose no time in reporting the result of my personal observations, and will have the honor to transmit

> Major Genl Dalzell's report, who has lately been on duty in the North, as soon as I receive it.
> P.S. I ought to have stated that the price of potatoes is nearly doubled within the last three weeks.

The rapid growth of population added a further dimension to the want and distress. Rents, cess and tithes increased the suffering. Armed with his fresh facts Peel wrote from Ireland to Sidmouth, the Home Secretary, on 10 October 1816, announcing the prospect of famine following the rain and floods at harvest time which had ruined the potato, grain and hay crops.[25] He had already the previous day in a letter to the Prime Minister, Lord Liverpool, relayed his observation on the failure of the turf harvest.

> The great comfort of the Irish peasant has hitherto been the abundant supply of fuel which he could command in winter. It makes amends for the wretchedness of his hovel and the want of clothing. But this year very little turf has been saved, and it is now so thoroughly wet that it would require several days continuance of fine weather to bring it into a state in which it could be used. If there is a severe winter the want of fuel will be a greater source of misery than the want of food.
> (cf. note 21, p.2)

The *Newry Magazine* No. 11, November & December 1816, gives some other indications of relief work to help the 1816 famine victims:

> The unusual severity of the season, having put it out of the power of many of the lower orders, to procure fuel and provisions adequate to their wants, considerable exertions have been very generally made throughout the kingdom to afford them relief. The Prince Regent has ordered £5000 for the relief of the poor of Spital fields and £2000 for those of Dublin.
> In Newry, a considerable sum has been raised for procuring fuel for the poor; and it is proper particularly to mention the liberal donation of 100*l*, British, granted by Mr. J. M'Camon formerly of Newry, and latterly of Berbice and London, for the relief of the poor of that town.
> His Grace the Lord Primate, subscribed £100, towards the fund of the Armagh Committee, and Leonard Dobbin, Esq., gave two tons of oatmeal, for the relief of the poor of that place.

The same issue of the *Newry Magazine* makes some interesting side remarks on the effects of the severe weather:

The barometer was observed to stand unusually high, in the latter end of November. On the 30th of that month, it stood in Newry, at 30 inches 8 tenths, which is perhaps a greater height than has been remarked in this country, for many years.
It is singular that in the last few months, the sparrows have almost entirely disappeared in this quarter of the country. Some say that they have perished in consequence of eating the grain scattered in the fields, which had been rendered pernicious to them by the incessant rain.

As was expected the winter of 1816-17 following the bad harvest intensified the suffering of the poor. The *Newry Magazine* fills in the picture:

Agricultural Report, 4 January 1817: The continuance of wet weather in Great Britain, during the whole of October (1816), and the beginning of the succeeding month, most materially retarded the labours of the harvest, late as it was, and on the 17th of November a great proportion of the bean crop, as well as the barley and oat crop, was still in the fields.
An average quantity of wheat has been this year sown in England, and the young shoots promise well. Oats yield abundantly in straw, but the grain, both in quantity and quality, is, through the larger part of Great Britain, far below an average crop.
In Ireland, beyond all doubt, our crops are miserably deficient. Our wheat, malted in the stook, produces a species of weak and clammy flour, which will not rise in the loaf. The oats are deficient, at least one-third in bulk, and still more so with respect to the yield in shelling and meal, when compared with the quantity ground. The potato crop, more nearly approaches a fair average than any other of our agricultural proceeds, but the quantity of nutritious matter which it contains, is far less than usual.
A greater breadth of wheat lands have been sown this season than we had reason to suppose would have been practicable. Wheat is a hardy grain, and can endure a degree of moisture in the ridge at sowing time, which would totally destroy oats. Notwithstanding this, it is to be dreaded that the continual rains with which our lands have been deluged, will prove very injurious to this valuable crop.
The scarcity of fuel is now severely felt. Quick-set fences are totally disappearing in some parts of the country – and young plantations of timber are destroyed in others and used for fire wood.

One of the sources amply quoted by Paterson in his article on Wildgoose Lodge is a book *Retrospect of a Military Life* (Edinburgh, 1846) by a Scottish soldier James Anton of the 42nd Foot who came to Ireland with his regiment in May 1817 and was quartered in various towns, reaching Dundalk in June 1818.

Paterson relies too heavily on him regarding the facts of the Wildgoose Lodge atrocity. Anton seems to have got them second-hand, but he was in Dundalk before some of the executions and may have done guard duty at the gibbets. He says, 'detachments were posted at the respective gibbets to prevent any of their criminal associates from consigning the bodies to the graves'. Paterson, however, rightly appreciates Anton's shrewd comments as an outside observer on the social conditions of Ireland and of Louth in particular. Anton writes,

> In May, 1817 we received the route for Ireland. We arrived there that same month and were quartered in the towns of Armagh and Newry from both of which places the regiment sent out detachments to garrison a number of small villages, within a circle of about ten miles from those towns.
> Armagh had been the headquarters of the regiment in 1808 and it was the same on this occasion. Newry had also been the station of a regimental detachment at that time and so it was on this, and, in consequence of the general good feeling that then existed between the inhabitants and the soldiers, we were welcomed with no ordinary degree of rejoicing, that is to say, if people borne down by sickness and famine can be said to rejoice, for at that time a very distressing famine prevailed over all the province of Ulster: the potatoes, which constitute the principal food of the inhabitants are usually sold in plentiful years at two-pence or three-pence per stone but this year the same quantity was selling at eighteen-pence, and they were scarcely fit for man or beast; frosted and bitter to the taste, the one half had to be cast to the ash-pit. Yet, on this food many of the people supported themselves without complaining. Such was the dearth of provisions that the soldiers received an increase of three-pence per day of pay. The mail and stage coaches were surrounded on their arrival and departure by crowds of poor famishing females with squalid children pulling at their milkless breasts, or tugging at the wretched rags that scarcely covered their mothers' nakedness. Every countenance was marked by affliction; the voice of the mother calling for charity, and the children imploring the mother for food, of which she had none to give. So accustomed were passengers to those solicitations for alms that their hearts became callous to the voice of supplication; the exhausted hand of charity shrunk from relieving the poor, and they were left to perish in a land far famed for hospitality; but the sources were now dried up and no bold advocate pleaded for assistance or relief within the walls of the British Parliament-House.
> During this time of unprecedented distress in the Province of Ulster, I heard of no extraordinary exertions making to raise subscriptions for the relief of the famishing. Some generous landlords exerted themselves greatly to alleviate distress of their own tenantry, yet this

was but a partial relief.

Five years after this famine of 1817, I happened to be quartered in the Province of Munster, where a similar calamity was said to exist; and for the relief of the famishing a very munificent grant was voted by the government and immense sums contributed by the benevolence of the whole empire, yet to compare the dearth and famine of 1822 with that of 1817 would be like comparing the Tees to the Thames, or the Deal to the Shannon.[26]

Official relief of distress as Anton pointed out was slow and limited. In March 1817 Peel introduced a scheme to import oats to be sold cheaply for seed but it failed miserably. The oats were too dear and of a poor quality. It was not until June that a measure was taken to relieve distress by setting up a central committee of seven members who relayed funds to local voluntary relief committees. On 16 June also the poor employment act was enacted to initiate the provision of public works. Local relief committees were set up in many cities, towns and villages to gather funds to relieve distress.

Impending crisis is discernible in the concern among the 'principal' inhabitants of Drogheda who met at the Tholsel on 15 January 1817 following a public notice for the purpose of relieving the distress of the 'manufacturing and labouring classes':

> The Right Hon. The Mayor presided. Mr St George Smith shortly opened the business for which they met, and reminded them to follow the plan adopted by the city of Derry, who came forward with a loan as well as a donation. He read a statement of the disbursement of the sums described in 1812, for the same laudable [sic], which seemed highly satisfactory; and that a balance remained in the hands of the treasurer amounting to near £50. A committee was then to call on the inhabitants for aid, and to carry into effect, and direct the application of the funds so raised; the meeting then adjourned. Mr Mayor, with true feelings of providence for the distresses of the poor, subscribed the entire sum he is entitled to by virtue of his office, which amounts to 230*l*; this with the grant usually given by the Corporation for a dinner, will realise the amount to £500, which will be thrown into the general fund. (*Belfast News-Letter*, 17 January 1817).

The *Newry Magazine*, May and June 1817, reflected back on the situation of agriculture in the spring:

> During the whole of last Spring the heavy clay lands were wrought with some difficulty. The continued action of the sun and an unusually long protracted drought had condensed the ploughed surface of the earth into solid masses, and it was found impracticable to pulverise the ground for the admission of drill potatoes, without the incessant use of the mallet. Till the middle of June, our crops of oats, barley, potatoes and flax, had a most unpromising appearance. About that period, however, a favourable change of weather took place and the most beneficial results have ensued. Much heat, followed by grand and awful peals of thunder and magnificient displays of lightning, gave strong indications that the atmosphere was surcharged with electric matter. Torrents of rain succeeded, which gradually diminished into a series of less violent and more benign showers, under whose genial influence the whole face of pasture changed. Lately the surface of the ground was parched, rent and almost naked. Now it is chargd with a rich and deep verdure. Our oats, barley and potatoes have assumed a new and most pleasing aspect. The wheat looks healthy and luxuriant – much of it is shot, and the whole gives fair promise of a very ample crop.
> Our flax crop is remarkably backward, but since the late alteration in the weather, it is considerably improved.
> Early meadows are not remarkably luxuriant; but from those late ones which abound with the natural grasses of the country, a great abundance of hay may be expected. The late rains have vastly improved our clovers as well as our pasture lands.
> We never recollect a season, in which so many early potatoes had been planted, as in the present. Some new potatoes have already been sold in our markets, and we may every day expect a more abundant supply.

A report in the *Freeman's Journal*, 18 August 1817, feared for the harvest:

> We trust (says the *Cork Southern Register* of Aug. 14), the other Counties have not experienced the same visitation which has prevailed in this for some days. The rains since Sunday evening have been heavy and consistent, accompanied with storms. In this neighbourhood the cornfields present the events of both being much lodged and beat down. Nevertheless, if dry weather and heat were now to ensue the injury which has been done would be returned in a great measure, but it continues wet and boisterous.

Famine developed when the potato crop was late in coming in, not until September 1817. Buyers intercepted farmers on their way to the markets and bought up their produce to sell it at an exorbitant price when it became scarce. Labourers starved during this period of economic depression and lack of food. To add to the crisis, typhus fever spread throughout Ireland. It began late in 1816 and continued until the spring of 1819. Typhus was the travelling companion of unemployment, starvation, poor housing, insanitary conditions, wet climate and lack of fuel. Timothy P. O'Neill observes in his article 'Fever and Public Health in pre-Famine Ireland': 'The absence of fires and hot water created the optimum conditions for the breeding of the typhus carrying louse. The poor had no means of heating themselves or washing their clothes, which they usually wore day and night. Huddled together for mutual warmth in conditions of squalor they inevitably became infested with vermin'.[27] Beggars, journeymen, and community social and religious customs like wakes and patrons helped spread the fever.

William Carleton described with pathos the human suffering wrought by fever in his novel *The Black Prophet*, basing some scenes in part on the famines of 1817 and 1822. He included a long note taken from Dr J. Corrigan's pamphlet:

> It is as well to state here that the season described in this tale is the dreadful and melancholy one of 1817; and we may add, that in order to avoid the charge of having exaggerated the almost incredible sufferings of the people in that year, we have studiously kept our descriptions of them within the limits of the truth. Doctor Corrigan in his able and very seasonable pamphlet *On Fever and Famine as Cause and Effect in Ireland* ... has confirmed the accuracy of the gloomy pictures I was forced to draw. Here follows an extract or two:
> 'It is scarcely necessary to call to recollection the summer of 1816, cold and wet – corn uncut in November, or rotting in the sheaves on the ground; potatoes not ripened (and when unripe there cannot be worse food) containing more water than nutriment; straw at such an extravagant price as to render the obtaining of it for bedding almost impossible, and when procured, retaining from its half-fermented state so much moisture, that the use was, perhaps, worse than the want of it. The same agent that destroyed the harvest spoiled the turf. Seldom had such a multiplication of evils come together. In some of the former years, although food and bedding were deficient, the portion saved was of good quality, and fuel was not wanting; but in 1816 every comfort that might have compensated for partial want was absent. This description applies to the two years of 1816 and 1817. In midsummer of 1817, the blaze of fever was over the entire country. It had burst forth almost in a thousand different points. Within the short space of a month, in the summer of 1817, the epidemic sprung forth in Tramore, Youghal, Kinsale, Tralee and Clonmel, in Carrick-on-suir,

Roscrea, Ballina, Castlebar, Belfast, Armagh, Omagh, Londonderry, Monasterevin, Tullamore, and Slane. This simultaneous break-out shows that there must have been some universal cause ...
The poor were deprived of employment, and were driven fom the doors where before they had always received relief, lest they should introduce disease with them. Thus destitution and fever continued in a vicious circle, each impelling the other, while want of presence of mind aggravated the terrible infliction. Of the miseries that attend a visitation of epidemic fever, few can form a conception. The mere relation of the scenes that occurred in the country, even in one of its last visitations, makes one shudder in reading them. As Barker and Cheyne observe in their Report, a volume might be filled with instances of the distress occasioned y the visitation of fever in 1817.
'On the road leading from Cork, within a mile of the town (Kanturk), I visited a woman labouring under typhus; on her left lay a child very ill, at the foot of the bed another child just able to crawl about, and on her right the corpse of a third child who had died two days previously, which, the unhappy mother could not get removed' – *Letter from Dr O'Leary, Kanturk*. ...

The poor suffered most but all classes were affected. Newspapers, in almost every edition, carried reports on the fever from all parts of Ireland. For example the *Dublin Evening Post*, 2 September 1817, published a letter from a physician complaining that little precaution was being taken against fever in Dublin city and a letter from Ennis dated 30 August gives a picture of a worsening situation:

The weather has been rather more favourable here than in the County of Cork or Limerick. The out crops and potatoes are very fine upon the good limestone grounds; upon the cold mountainy soil, they are rather backward, but have as yet sustained no *irremedial* damage.
A fever of a very pestilential character has made its appearance at New Market-on-Fergus, to which several persons have fallen victims; among others, Mr McMahon the Catholic Bishop's nephew, a fine young man of three and twenty. The epidemic fever, which has prevailed throughout the country for the entire year, is most decidedly becoming more malignant and general in this part of the world.
Fine new potatoes in the Ennis market for four pence halfpenny.

The *Newry Magazine* (November- December, 1817) had a more heartsome agricultural report for September and October:

During the greater part of September and October, the weather continued remarkably fine, resembling in every respect, the termination of a pleasing spring and commencement of a mild summer. The harvest did not burst at once upon the farmer, but came on in a gradual and regular succession, and thus enabled him (generally speaking) to reap his grain, without any very disadvantageous competition for labourers. Indeed, so great was the disparity in point of time, with respect to the ripening of crops, that whilst large quantities of our grain have been long ago converted into meal, many fields of oats remain even yet uncut and as green, as if the current month were July. Betwixt Newry and Armagh, and in many parts of the county Monaghan, where the remarkable drought prevalent during last spring had retarded vegetation or prevented the young shoots from bursting through the bound and arid surface of the land – this unnatural state of the grain crops is very general. However distressing this untoward circumstance may be to the owners of these fields, an abundance has been already reaped, in other districts, to feed the population of this country, and allow a large quantity for exportation.

Our oats yield well in shelling and in meal. The wheat, as yet brought to market, is not in general of a prime quality; but it ought to be remembered, that the very worst grain has, in the first instance, been thrashed off to procure straw for thatching corn stacks. The late potatoes do not turn out so well as those of an early kind – Some nocturnal frosts which prevailed early in October withered the stems and prevented all further increase of bulk and weight in the bulbs. Hay is abundant, and the open weather has kept pastoral lands in high verdure.

A few welcome measures on the part of the slow-moving government, notably the setting up of a fever committee, similar to its earlier famine committee, to channel funds to local fever committees, and the charitable work of these local relief committees did not, however, solve the problem. The task of medical relief was too much for the poorly supplied and inadequately staffed dispensaries and hospitals and there were not enough of these. The typhus epidemic raged throughout Ireland from 1817 to 1819 and resulted in some 65,000 deaths. This is the moderate estimate of F. Barker and J. Cheyne in *An account of the rise, progress and decline of fever lately epidemical in Ireland, together with communications from physicians in the provinces* I (Dublin,1821). K.H. Connell has estimated that out of a probable population of 5,832,000 about 44,300 died from fever in 1817-19.[28] The newspapers sadly and continuously announced the deaths of people in their prime and published medical precautions that should be taken to avoid catching fever. Peel hesitated to take action. On 30 September 1817 he had set up a national fever committee of three people to assess applications for aid and afford relief as the government judged expedient. His policy was to aid local contributions. He wrote to Gregory, 30 January 1818, 'For heaven's sake do not let us get too much involved with fever commissioners and mendicity commissioners ... be very hard hearted for we are establishing a noxious precedent'.[29] It was not until April 1818 that £15,000 was provided for the care of fever patients. Peel wrote to Sir Edward Baker in May 1818, 'I think before the summer comes a great exertion should be made to put down the fever. If it costs £20,000 I care not; the money will be well expended when the distribution is entrusted to those who compose the Fever Committee'.[30] From the autumn of 1816 through to the summer of 1817 the government, as we have seen, had dithered in providing relief for the famine victims. Lord Lieutenant Whitworth was incompetent in the situation and Peel was anxious to have information at his disposal before he would act. The poor employment act of 1817 was a first step. In the end among all the officials it was Peel who at last acted positively to have £37,000 in money given to a central committee for distribution to voluntary committees in local areas for the administration of relief. A further sum of £18,000 was given to a select committee to further measures to combat the typhus fever.[31]

The Report of the 'Select Committee on the Contagious Fever in Ireland' was printed in *Parliamentary Papers: Session 27 January 1818- 10 June 1818 (Vol. vii)* and throws light on the causes and spread of the disease, attempted remedies and efforts to contain it. Here are some of its observations:

> The great increase of the malady may, we think, be dated pretty generally through the Island from the Spring of 1817; in some places commencing with the months of March or April, in others, not until July, and even August. The Reports of the Fever Hospitals of Cork and Waterford, clearly trace the great increase of Fever in those cities to a period much earlier; in Cork as far back as the Autumn of 1816; in Waterford to January 1817. We advert to these reports particularly, because as far as respects these large and populous cities, they furnish, in detail, the most ready means of judging accurately as to the progress and extent of the disease, from the monthy tables of admissions and deaths which are annexed to them. ...
> From the want of Dispensaries or Hospitals generally dispersed, we

have no detailed accounts of a very large part of Ireland, nor any account whatever of some entire counties, as Mayo and Donegal, except a statement that in this latter county it has prevailed very considerably; we can however have no doubt, that where no such establishments existed, great numbers of the poor must have undergone very great sufferings. One of the causes to which progress of the disease is very generally ascribed, the crowds of wretched mendicants, by whom the country has been traversed in all directions, affords a melancholy proof and illlustration of this opinion.

The mortality has been much greater among the higher ranks of society, whom the disease has attacked, than in the labouring classes; and the physicians and other medical attendants, as well as the clergy of different denominations have felt its destructive force in much more than an ordinary proportion, as the discharge of duty, uniting with the claims of humanity, exposed them peculiarly to its visitation.

The Apppendix to the Report surveys different regions and some of these are relevant to County Louth and its environs:

Monaghan: 20 April 1818. Hospital opened 16 August 1817 to 16 April 1818, admitted 700, died 37; rather above one in nineteen; 15 remain in hospital. Funds exhausted, and in debt above £200, after allowing for grand jury presentments not yet due. Total of expenses, £953. Many applying in vain for admission, from want of funds, to which Government contributed £100, and the rest was derived from grand jury presentments and subscriptions. (Mr *Lucas*)

Dundalk: Commencement 27 August, admissions 588, died 19; about one in thirty; supported by subscriptions above £800; necessary to separate sick from healthy, even compulsorily, to check disease. (Visount *Jocelyn*)

Navan: Mr Nicholls. 1 April 1818. Fever at its height end of autumn. Since then declines; occasionally however resuming its violence; now shorter and milder than it was; nine-tenths of the families have been in some degree affected, and about three-fourths in each family of the poorer classes. No fever hospital. Causes: feeding on damaged corn and wild rape, want of fuel, bad clothing and lodging, and want of employment.

Armagh: Mr Simpson. Commencement April 1817; at its greatest height in September 1818; 200 then lying ill in the town at one time, now only two or three cases in town, but still prevalent in country. Causes: want of food, cold and wet weather, want of fuel, want of cleanliness, insufficient ventilation from stopping up windows, depression of mind from want of employment. No fever hosptal; had such been early established, and sick separated from the healthy, the contagion would have been much checked; greatly extended by travelling mendicants.

Dungannon: 4th May 1818. Dr Sinclair. Fever hospital could only afford room to 211 patients, between 20 June 1817 and 3rd February 1818, when it closed. Numbers relieved at dispensary in same period, 1663, besides numbers in country round of whom no account was kept. Causes: unwholesome food in scanty portions; want of fuel; damp and comfortless habitations; and contagious influence greatly extended by travelling mendicants. First means of remedy: separation of diseased from healthy; strict cleanliness; thorough ventilation; cold bath or ablution with vinegar and water, as case required; affusion of cold water most beneficial; of 211 in hosptal but 7 died. (N.B. All the reports of Dr Barry, of Cork; Dr Bracken of Waterford, and several others, agree in the superior efficacy of the affusion of cold water, or by sponging the body, when it can be applied in the early stages of the complaint.)

Cavan: Mr Roe and Dr Murray; April 1818. Commencement of much fever in May 1817, amongst lower classes; spread in summer and autumn to middle and higher ranks; much done for relief of the diseased by Countess of Farnham and Bishop of Kilmore; has been latterly confined to lower ranks; still prevails there considerably. Causes: scanty and unwholesome food, want of employment, great consequent distress. Fever not likely soon to disappear, as this cause not likely to be removed. Swarms of mendicants spread the contagion.

Drogheda: Dr Fairclough, and others; 1st April 1818. Fever increased in August, at its height end of November; from that time declining, but still more prevalent than usual. Causes: debility from bad quality and scanty supply of food to lower classes, want of employment, despondency, and slothful and dirty habits in consequence. No fever hospital here at first; a house used in October, by private subscriptions and Government aid, for those malignant cases, as far as it could afford accommodation. Interior of houses of fever patients whitewashed, fresh straw given, and old straw removed or burned, and fumigation employed to stop contagion.

In conclusion regarding admission to the hospitals the Report says:

> The Admissions were more numerous in the winter months, at the end of the year, at which we need not be surprised; for although cold, in certain circumsatnces, has an obvious tendency to check febrile disease, and has been accordingly applied as a remedy in the treatment of Fever; yet, when combined with damp or wet, filth, and hunger (which is most severely felt in cold weather) it can be no longer regarded as a useful auxiliary, but as a pernicious enemy. The obvious effect of the combination of these evils is, to bring the poor more closely together in their filthy habitations, and to induce them to resort to the use or abuse of whiskey, substituting slow poison for wholesome food. But since the latter end of the year 1816, the food of the people has been of a bad quality, and, what is perhaps still worse, deficient in quantity. When to all these is superadded the depression of mind necessarily attending upon such circumstances, we need not wonder at the great and spreading extension of Fever in this country, whatever may be considered as its origin. Many, very many, of the poor, in most large

towns, generally live in a kind of despair; they even hold their lives cheap, when compared with those in better circumstances.

A special problem developed in regard to fever in the prisons and it illustrates vividly callousness on the part of the government. A letter dated 14 June 1817 from Dublin Castle was passed on to London:

> The general gaols in Ireland being at present extremely crowded, and a contagious disorder pervading in some of them, I am commanded by the Lord Lieutenant to desire you will signify to Lord Sidmouth His Excellency's request that His Lordship will give directions that a vessel may be engaged as soon as possible, to receive on board in the harbour of Cork 350 to 360 male convicts and to convey them to New South Wales and I am to request and I am to aquaint you that directions could be given here for providing some provisions, clothing, and medicines as will be necessary for the use of the convicts on their voyage ...[32]

As a further measure to relieve crowding in the prisons, official correspondence from Dublin to London over the summer of 1818, mentions preparations for the conveyance of some 180 to 200 female convicts to New South Wales.[33]

Brett in his *Reminiscences of Louth* (1857), writing considerably near to the period, gives us the local scene in Louth, 'A scarcity of food prevailed throughout the county to an alarming extent in the year 1817 in consequence of the failure of the previous harvest. The sufferings of the poor were deplorable. Epidemics and infectious diseases, and particularly fever, in most cases proved fatal. Hospitals were established, and charitable persons, who possessed sufficient means, exerted themselves in endeavouring to alleviate the sufferings of the poor and the afflicted. The clergy of all denominations were actively and constantly engaged in works of charity on that trying occasion. The Rev. E. Thackeray, the truly benevolent and kind-hearted Vicar of Dundalk, was untiring in his efforts to relieve the prevailing distress. The ministrations of the Catholic Clergy were required night and day; their good works were performed without intermission, and, from frequent exposure to contagion, some of them fell victims to that awful malady, typhus fever. Medical men were also unable to arrest the progress of the disease, and it caused the death of some members of the profession. The proprietors of the Dundalk Distillery had a considerable quantity of oats and barley in their stores, which they directed to be ground into meal and sold to the poor at a very low price. But the aspect of the country was changed, by the glorious weather of the following year, 1818, and the people resumed their former cheerfulness. Peace and plenty were in a great degree restored'.[34]

Dundalk in particular was severely struck by the fever. The *Dublin Evening Post* reported on 30 December 1817 on the fever in Clonmel, Ennis, Kilkenny, Newry, Armagh, and Derry and singled out Dundalk as the most affected:

> No part of Ireland has been visited with so much severity by this pestilential calamity, as Dundalk – and no place has displayed such noble efforts to relieve and assist the unhappy sufferers who have been afflicted by it. A temporary Hospital has been opened there since August last, which was constantly occupied by seventy or eighty patients. This Establishment, together with medicines, etc for the *extern* Patients, has been supported by voluntary contributions from the Inhabitants of the Town and Vicinity, amounting to upwards of seven hundred pounds, in addition to a grant of one hundred and twenty-five pounds from Government. The pecuniary concerns of this most benevolent Institution have been carefully managed by a Committee of Gentlemen, at the head of which is Lord Jocelyn, who meet every morning for the admission of Patients, & for the purpose of having such houses fumigated as have been visited by the contagion.
> For medical aid the Committee have been heretofore chiefly indebted to the indefatigable exertions of Doctor Gillican, a young Physician of the first eminence, and the most rising reputation, who devoted not only the whole of his time, but also his purse, to the objects of the Institution – his motives being too pure to accept of any other requital than what the feelings of his own heart afforded him. Under his assiduous auspices, the Committee had the happiness to witness a great amelioration of the distemper. But we lament to say, that their joy has been suddenly turned into mourning, by the death of this invaluable man, who has become the victim of his humanity; he caught the fever, and has died. Of two young Gentlemen, Apothecaries, who shared his labours, one has already shared his fate – and the life of the other is despaired of. Three servants of the Hospital have been also attacked by this dreadful pestilence. Under such desolating circumstances, an appeal is made to all those parts of the Country which have escaped the ravages of this plague. We have no doubt but that our Readers will feel gratified in bestowing a small tribute upon this mournful occasion, to assist the efforts of the benevolent Inhabitants of Dundalk; and thereby evince their gratitude to Providence for their own safety.

There follows in the report the text of Lord Jocelyn's appeal, 11 December 1817, on behalf of the committee, asking for help beyond the charity already contributed by the gentlemen residing around Dundalk and especially asking those in the habit of coming to Dundalk to contribute. Funds were exhausted; no fewer than three hundred and sixty-five persons had already been treated in the hospital and sixty-eight of those still remained there. There are poignant accounts in the same issue of the newspaper of the deaths and funerals of Dr George Gillichan, Dundalk, and Fr Mark Nowlan, O.P., Drogheda, who died of the fever. Dr Gillichan, native of Dundalk, received his diploma in Edinbugh and returned to Dundalk to practice. He had received a rich fortune from his late father but was devoted to his career. It was he who recommended the establishment of a fever hospital when typhus appeared – 'his purse was ever open to the necessities of the poor, and often, after raising them from the bed of sickness by his skill, he relieved them from misery by the extension of his bounty'. Dr Gillichan died on 24 December 1817 and was buried on 28 December.

Henry McClintock wrote in his diary:

> **Tuesday 23d December 1817, Dundalk.** Frost & rainy afterwards – I did not leave the house having taken some calomel –'we dined at home as usual.
> **Wednesday 24th** Hard frost – I am not very well – took more calomel last night & Epsom salts this day – I stayed in my room almost the entire day – poor Doctor Gillichan died at two oclock this day of the fever which is raging here violently – there have been upwards of eighty patients in the fever hospital here at once.[35]
> **Thursday 25th, Christmas Day.** Very hard frost – I kept my bed 'till three oclock feeling very weak & sickish – went downstairs to dinner – my mother dined with us – Louis & Marianne dined with us – three days ago Mr Cassorly (a young apothecary of most excellent character & ability) died of the fever also.
> **Friday 26th** Hard frost in the morng – eveng wet – I did not get up until twelve oclock but I am much better – I dined in the parlour with Bessy.

Fr Mark Nowlan of the Dominican Convent, Linenhall Street, Drogheda, caught the fever while attending a poor family, all lying in the fever. He died after a week's illness on 20 December and was buried on 22 December – 'How dearly this exemplary and much lamented Clergyman was beloved by all classes, was evinced on the occasion of his funeral, which took place on Monday. The arrangements were conducted by some of the most respectable Gentlemen in Drogheda. At an early hour in the day, the whole Town presented the most doleful appearance; not a single shop was to be seen open. At two o'clock the body was brought out; at this moment, the cries and lamentation of the multitude who waited outside, were most affecting. The Procession, which was composed of the most respectable part of the community of all persuasions, wearing scarfs and hatbands, and which, when formed, extended about three quarters of a mile in length, moved on in slow and solemn pace to the church-yard which is some distance from the Town. On arriving there, the church-yard was crowded almost to suffication. When the coffin was about to be deposited in the grave, the demonstrations of grief and affliction approached almost to insanity, and prevented the interment for nearly half an hour, in despite of the expostulations of Clergymen present. At length the scene was closed for ever on this respectable and worthy man, whose memory will be long cherished, and his loss deeply regretted by his numerous friends, who esteemed him for his many virtues, and by the People of the Town and Neighburhood, to whom he ministered the solemn and pious offices of religion with a zeal and affection which endeared him equally to all'.

Harold O'Sullivan wrote of conditions in Dundalk in 1817, 'In Dundalk a soup kitchen was established in the ground floor of the Market House aided by grain supplied by the distillery. When the typhus epidemic started in August a temporary fever hospital was established in the old charter School-house in Anne Street under the administration of a local committee aided by grants from the Grand Jury. Accommodation was provided for ninety patients and by December upwards of 400 persons had been admitted. In that month Doctor Gillichan and two apothecaries who had been assisting him contracted the disease and died. In a letter from Viscount Jocelyn (Lord Roden's son) to Robert Peel describing the situation an appeal was made for further assistance since the other physicans in the town were too busy with their practices and the doctors in the Infirmary (Louth) at Park Street were unable to do more. The epidemic continued into the new year, after which it declined and eventually petered out'.[36] Some further information on Louth is available from the Ardee Dispensary Minute Book, 1813-1851. The Dispensary community health service, established in Ardee in 1813, catered for the sick poor, was non-sectarian in character, especially in its management, but it was, however, in the control of the landed gentry and one of its rulings prevented its service being extended to tenants of non-subscribers. Harold O'Sullivan who has published a general commentary on the Ardee Dispensary and the minutes of its meetings gives some details on the famine and typhus epidemic in the crisis period 1816-18: 'The first notice of the epidemic is contained in the Visitation Book when, on the 12th August, 1817, the Visitor reported that on inspecting the books he perceived that the typhus fever was rapidly increasing in the town and neighbourhood. He deemed it expedient to request the Treasurer to order two-dozen of porter and one gallon of spirits to be sent to Doctor Runcie to be distributed amongst the patients. Later in the month lime was purchased and labourers employed "in white-washing the houses of the lower orders of Ardee, in expectation of checking the progress of the contagion, the costs to be defrayed out of the extraordinary funds of the dispensary". In September whitewashing was still in progress. Reporting to Dublin Castle in that month, a Doctor Lee of Ardee stated, "Fever was very prevalent since last month, principally amongst the poor when food has been very bad; not very fatal". Details of the epidemic are not given in the Minutes for the reason that the Annual Reports did not commence until 1819. Up to that year 5, 259 persons had been relieved, 1,166 having been attended to in the year 1818-19. It was with pleasure the Committee remarked that the county was never at any period more free from typhus fever'.[37] The Management Committee of Ardee Dispensary in June 1817 was as follows: 'Chichester Fortescue, John Taaffe, Robert Young, John Fitz' Ruxton, Patrick Ward, Revd. John Doyne, Revd. B. Loughran (who replaced Rev. P. McGuire, resigned.)'. We will meet some of these men again in the course of the unravelling of the Wildgoose Lodge story. Harold O'Sullivan noted the spread of dispensaries in Louth, 'In County Louth the first to be established was in Dundalk in 1805, attached to the County Infirmary. Another was established by John (Speaker) Foster in Collon in the same year. In 1835 there were ten in operation: Ardee, Ballymascanlon, Carlingford, Castlebellingham, Collon, Dunleer, Dundalk, Drogheda, Louth and Termonfeckin'.

Fever continued into the spring of 1818 and reached its peak in the summer and autumn of 1818. In Meath and Louth it became widespread in May and June 1817 and 'disappeared when employment became plentiful with the revival of the linen trade in 1818'.[38] A long letter from 'Medicus', 14 March 1818, published in the *Dublin Evening Post*, 17 March 1818, attributed the continuance of fever to cold and famine.

In *Tempest's Annual* (1952) T.G.F. Paterson published extracts from *Ireland exhibited to England, a Political and Moral History of the population* by A. Atkinson (Volume I published in London, 1823, but apparently written in 1817). The extracts refer to Louth and to Dundalk in particular and Paterson adds some useful notes of reference. Atkinson describes the overcrowded jail in Crowe Street (called after the governor of the jail, John Crowe) where the Wildgoose Lodge prisoners were confined. H. G. Tempest confirms this in his *Gossiping Guide to Dundalk*, 'In 1816 the Rev. Elias Thackeray reported that the gaol was very small, but well regulated, and that preparations were being made for a new one, £16,000 having been voted by the Grand Jury'. Here are some of Atkinson's remarks:

> Previous to our departure from this place we thought it might be of some service to the country to publish a few remarks upon the condition of the poor in this district (in the spring of 1817) a season of distress that will be long remembered by the poor of Ireland who have survived it. In the consequence of this persuasion we addressed the following letter to the Editor of the *Newry Telegraph:*
> *(We extract the following from the letter-Ed. T.A.)*
> The cottages, in a considerable proportion, present you with a view of men out of employment, and of women and children, from whose naked or famished appearance, humanity revolts. Nor is this portrait confined to any single portion of the country through which I have recently travelled; it is a correct delineation of the condition of the poor, in several parts of the counties of Meath and Louth (although the inhabitants of those wretched cabins which are to be found in the suburbs of several towns present you with the strongest features of their country's misery), a spectacle which extends itself, if my information be correct, to the more northern counties of our country, with equal marks of depression and distress. I do not mean to charge the gentry, and still less the little farmers, resident in those counties,

with having fostered a disposition of cruelty towards the poor - on the contrary many of the former, as individuals, are extremely charitable; and from the doors of the latter the wandering poor are never repulsed, if they have any thing to give them. But the sickly and famished mother of children, who cannot fly from home, who must embrace misery and death in the midst of her hovel, with her children around her, I speak it boldly and from knowledge, is often unnoticed and unknown; and in the towns and cantons of this country must undoubtedly so continue, until death relieve her from her load of suffering, unless persons whose hearts are impregnated with the seeds of humanity, soon present a bulwark to the tide of misery, which now overflows this country; and this, in the judgment of many humane and intelligent persons, can never be effectually done but by parochial societies, which shall not only make collections and have sermons preached for this purpose, but which shall select from their body the most humane and reflecting persons to visit the poor in their cottages, and to ascertain, by actual inspection, the necessities of each that so the charities of the public may be justly and accurately applied.

In proof of the utility of such societies it may be a necessary, though painful duty, to call upon the inhabitants of any town where no such patriotic society has yet been formed, to step out and see how the poor of their own neighbourhoods are circumstanced. Let the opulent inhabitants of Kingscourt, Ardee, and many other towns which we might name, stoop from the splendour of those seats which they have rendered worthy of their country and take a peep into those abodes of wretchedness, *which* (within a pistol-shot of the finest combinations of art and nature) present the senses of the stranger with an aggregate of all which the imagination could devise, to complete a picture of horror - a picture which might, indeed, be exceeded by Milton's genius of destruction, or Blair's horrors of the grave; but which, in the *ipso facto* scenes of human life, can only be excelled by the prospect of a dungeon in which the putrid carcasses of the inhabitants combine with clanking chains, and the fetid effluvia of a vault, to give us, alas! a lively representation of the future condition of those sons of prosperity, who instead of manifesting their gratitude to heaven for the bounty which has distinguished them, by their charity to that nature of which they partake, sedulously avoid those objects which bring to their recollection that there is such a thing as misery in the world; and that the millions which every year are basely squandered at the card-table would, in the hands of a wise and judicious charity, effectually relieve it.

To persons so base and unprincipled as to sacrifice to a passion unbottomed in nature, the dearest interests of their country, it is, of course, unnecessary to address ourselves on any subject which has country for its object. The majority of the opulent are not, however, thus deeply degraded, and therefore it is that we shall proceed to address them on the subject of our country - our poor distressed country; and finally, to suggest to the Irish government, with that respect which becomes us as subjects of the king, such means of relieving the poor in the immediate neighbourhood of Dundalk as we have heard noticed by one or two of its inhabitants, as combining with an extensive employment of the poor, some important advantages to the police and commerce of Louth, of which this town may be considered as the capital.

Before we proceed to this latter part of our subject (which, so far, as regards the formation of a harbour at Giles' quay, we presume to introduce upon the authority of others), it may not be improper to mention that shortly after our arrival at Dundalk, having heard that the necessities of the poor in several parts of the counties of Monaghan and Armagh obliged them to repair to the bolting-mills of the county for the purpose of procuring small quantities of bran to blend with potatoes for the support of life, we rode one morning to the flour-mill of Mr. Callan, a respectable trader in this town, and there had an opportunity of placing ourselves in perfect possession of the facts of this statement. We found thirty or forty poor persons who had travelled a considerable distance to procure this poor material, which they proposed to blend with potatoes, or with a little meal, if they could procure it (as the best mode of spinning out the little stock of provisions which they had left), until the ensuing harvest should arrive, to rescue them from impending famine. To these specimens of the general distress it must be acknowledged that the charity exercised by the respectable inhabitants of Dundalk towards the poor of that place has in some degree rendered this town an exception. Here no less than 300 poor persons, on an average, receive daily from a cookery maintained by subscription, one wholesome and nutritious meal. But has this rule been generally adopted? Has any such institution taken place in the towns of Kingscourt and Ardee, already noticed? In the back lanes of this latter town we heard that famine had made such rapid progress that the poor were dying of a noxious disease and that it was not safe to visit them. So far for the charity of those places. But, perhaps the necessary *medical* provisions for a starving people, together with their preparation for a better world, had so much occupied the thoughts of their good superiors, as to cause the insignificant accommodations of food and raiment to be forgotten!

We shall now proceed to point out these modes of extending relief to the inhabitants of Dundalk and its neighbourhood, which come properly under the control of the government of the country. We have heard it said that a considerable quantity of oats intended for seed was shipped by government last spring for the towns of Belfast, Newry, and some other ports on this coast; and that the price laid on this oats (32*s*. per barrel) rendering it inaccessible to farmers of the lower class, a large proportion of it, very fortunately, remains undisposed of – 800 barrels of this oats are said to be now lying in the port of Dundalk, in good order, which, if ground into meal and disposed of to the *poor only*, at prices somewhat lower than the standard prices of the market, would have the happiest effect; as by this means, the quantity of food in the market would be increased, and a check placed upon the growing prices of the *meal factor*.

In aid of this grand object, *a mitigation of the miseries of the poor*, another and still more powerful assistant than that of a reduction in the prices of provisions, presents itself –namely that of furnishing them with proper employment – and here a new field of inquiry opens itself before us. The county of Louth has, we understand, had it in contemplation to build a new bridge over the river of Dundalk, on the great northern road to Belfast, and a new jail in the town of Dundalk. The necessity of this latter public work will soon appear to any person who will take the trouble of entering one of those cells on the ground floor of the present prison, in which 12 or 14 unfortunate victims of the law were unavoidably huddled together when we visited that prison a few days previous to their trial in the spring of 1817. It is true, this prison, though totally inadequate to the necessities of the county (and presenting, when fully inhabited, a sad spectacle to the eye of humanity) is kept as clean as possible; and as well aired as the plan of an old prison completely overstocked with prisoners will admit of, yet its inadequacy to the present purposes of the law, the premature inflictions of punishment, which confinement in that prison must impose upon accused persons and the present circumstances of distress which loudly call for employment and which offer the labourer's exertions at a very reduced price, are surely motives of sufficient weight to induce the county to set about this work forthwith.

In addition to these useful sources of employment to the labouring poor it has also been suggested that material advantages would be derived to the trade navigating the Irish sea, if a pier was erected at a place called Giles's quay, on the north east side of the bay of Dundalk

...

I once more beg leave to suggest to the inhabitants of Dundalk and to every town where a similar charity has been established, that, however valuable a daily cookery may be rendered to the healthful poor, its benefits are not likely to be extended to the sick cottager, unless parochial societies, formed for this and other purposes of charity, shall appoint proper visitors to inspect and report upon the condition of the sick and infirm poor, in their respective districts.

Atkinson continues in his main text:

The lands around Dundalk are said to be of good quality and well calculated for the growth of wheat and other species of grain. The several articles of agricultural produce are chiefly disposed of in the Dundalk market, which, for the sale of corn, has been long eminent; and in former years a considerable proportion of the money which the landholder received for the produce of his farm was expended in this town in purchasing the necessary articles and comforts that his farm would not supply; the money thus returned to its former channel and the consequence was wealth and prosperity. At present, however, it is otherwise. The produce of the farmer's industry must now go to pay those exorbitant war rents and accumulating imposts, which, to a land of liberty and plenty, accomplish all the purposes of an oppressive and grinding despotism; leaving the farmer nothing for his labour, and the country merchant, who shines by the reflection of his wealth, in a state of bankruptcy and despair. The consequences of this revolution (facilitated by an expenditure of the natural revenue of the country in Italy and France, and for which our modern gentry have acquired an inextinguishable rage) may be easily conceived by the political economist. The revenue of the crown, it is said, maintains its ground; perhaps this may be the case, or perhaps not; but if the affirmative be the fact we must only say that the prosperity of the country since the bankrupt calendar, the mendicity associations, the intolerable overflow of our prisons and law courts, and the general distress, which pervade all classes of the people, proclaim to our rulers in characters that cannot be misunderstood, the distress of the nation, and the progress of that calamity which is now the lot of Europe, and from which few are exempted, save those who derive their wealth from an interest in the public taxes!

Rank and Fashion. Dundalk may be considered as the centre of the rank and fashion of that district of the Irish coast which extends from Castlebellingham and Dunleer to Jonesborough and Ravensdale, in the neighbourhood of Newry. The Northern Rangers, a celebrated hunting club, assemble in this place; and some of the gentry of the surrounding country exhibit in their manners and appearance, a degree of taste and elegance that would not disgrace a court.

We are bound also by our own experience to acknowledge that individuals, in the decent ranks of society, preserve that attention to hospitality and letters for which the country was once eminently remarkable, and which still (notwithstanding its misfortune) constitute a feature of its character in the history of Nations.

Genius and Disposition of the People. The population, as you advance northward of Dundalk, combine with a pleasing simplicity, a proper degree of the activity and intelligence of Ulster. They are, in general, peaceably disposed, and although some enormities had been committed in Louth a little previous to our passage through that county (in the spring of 1817) – [*he is referring to the burning of Wildgoose Lodge*] yet a shadow of criminality did not attach to the inhabitants of Dundalk, nor to the country towards Ulster, beyond it. The insurrection act was in operation at this time in a part of Louth, and the country felt much interest in the trial of a young clergyman at Dundalk, who, after an attentive examination of his case and that many testimonies had been borne to his loyalty by the protestant gentry of the country, was honourably acquitted ...[39]

The traveller of intelligence, who explores the County of Louth in pursuit of statistical information will find (with the exception of Collon, which is a little manufacturing colony) a very material difference between that district of the county which extends along the coast from Drogheda towards Newry, and possesses more or less of a manufacturing spirit, and those districts of the interior, which may be regarded as exclusively agricultural. These latter, as to the appearance, manners, and language of the peasantry approximate, in our view, to the character of the labouring peasantry of Meath, and those agricultural districts of Cavan, which unite with Louth in the opposite direction; while the population of the coast, that is, from Drogheda towards Newry approximate more nearly, in our judgement, to the character of Ulster. This difference in the manners and circumstances of the Louth population, has, probably, its origin in those geographical distinctions of the county which gave birth to its commercial and agriculural relations ...

Emigration provided another outlet from the poverty, fever and hunger of the 1815–17 period. While not expanding on that theme, I present a little sidelight on the emigration from the *Newry Magazine* (November and December, 1817):

> In consequence of the great distress experienced by many Irish emigrants, a meeting of Irishmen, and descendants of Irishmen was held at Harmony Hall, New York, on the 25th of November last, for the purpose of promoting a settlement for their relief. On this occasion it was resolved, that they should endeavour to procure from Congress, a tract of land, in the Illinois territory, to be settled by emigrants from Ireland; and that it be recommended to Irishmen, and descendants of Irishmen, in other cities and towns of the union, to form similar societies.

3
Rule by Despotism

LAW AND ORDER

The disorder in Ireland in 1815-17, stemming from the decline in the economy, social problems, poverty and famine, did not prompt the government into urgent remedial reforms but rather propelled them into action in re-establishing coercive laws and organising police and army to deal with violence. This followed on a tradition of coercion establised by the Whiteboy Acts and the savage use of the army.

In September 1812, Robert Peel (1788-1850), twenty-four years of age, took office in Dublin as Chief Secretary, assistant to the Lord Lieutenant. He remained in Ireland in this important post until August 1818. His power derived from the authority of the Lord Lieutenant. He was in effect prime minister, the key figure in both the executive and administrative branches of the Irish government, the Irish link to the cabinet and the House of Commons. He maintained a regular correspondence on Irish affairs with Sidmouth, the Secretary of State and was supported by the Prime Minister Lord Liverpool in the Irish policy he pursued. His attitude to governing Ireland is well summed up in one of his letters: 'I believe an honest despotic government would be by far the fittest government for Ireland'.[40] William Gregory, twenty-two years older than Peel, intelligent and experienced in Irish affairs, was Chief Under-Secretary from 1812-1830. He was appointed 5 October 1812. Lord Whitworth, former soldier and diplomat, succeeded Richmond as Lord Lieutenant in August 1813.

Both Peel and Gregory had easy good relationships with one another and with Whitworth. All three were ardent Protestants, took the 'Protestant side' in the Irish religious animosities and strongly opposed Catholic emancipation. Official religion, however, did not countenance biblical justice, the vindication of the poor and the needy, of the marginalized. Norman Gash in his book *Mr Secretary Peel* gives a good picture of the rest of the government team which continued after Viceroy Richmond, 'Of the other officials at the Castle the most important were the Lord Lieutenant's three legal advisers. Manners, the Lord Chancellor, once described as looking like the ghost of Charles I, was an English importation. Reputed a bad lawyer, he was by way of compensation a good Protestant and a devoted shooter of woodcock; in political matters he was said to be influenced by William Saurin, the Attorney General. In 1812 both were in their middle fifties but Saurin was a product of the Irish bar. The son of an Ulster Presbyterian minister and grandson of a Huguenot refugee, with his harsh foreign features and black glittering eyes under shaggy brows, Saurin brought both intelligence and fanaticism to the Protestant party at the castle. He had headed the opposition of the Irish lawyers to the Union in 1800 and later became one of the most violent opponents of Catholic emancipation. The third member of the legal triumvirate, and the only true Irishman among them, was Charles Kendal Bushe, who like Saurin was a Trinity College man. Broad-shouldered, a little corpulent by the time Peel knew him, with long intelligent face, he impressed people most by his bright blue eyes, mellow voice, and witty conversation; politically he was inclined to be more liberal than his two colleagues'.[41]

Peel regarded the Catholic Church as more an impediment than an aid to quelling disturbances despite the stern opposition of bishops against violence and the efforts of some priests, in danger to themselves, who spoke out against agrarian crime and co-operated with the civil authorities.[42] He was irritated by the refusal of most people to cooperate with the government. The 'State of the Country Papers' in the National Archives, Dublin, for the period of County Louth disturbances1813-1819, the background to the story of Wildgoose Lodge, provide examples throughout Ireland of atrocities committed by secret societies and non-political criminals, including burning of houses, murder, rape, and the intimidation and murder of witnesses who gave evidence in prosecutions. Limerick, Westmeath, Kildare, and Tipperary especially saw continual outbreaks of agrarian disturbances in the first quarter of the nineteenth century, revived after the failure of the potato crop in 1812 and the bad harvest of 1816. Following convictions of agrarian agitators at the Spring Assizes in Mullingar in1814, six men were hanged and four transported.⁴³

Peel's great quarrel, however, was with the 'country gentlemen' who were the magistrates and grand jurors in the counties. He thought many of them were incompetent, often motivated by self-interest and neglecting their duties in enforcing local law and order effectively. He wrote to Lord Desart, 24 February 1814, 'We have a right to call on country gentlemen for the performance of the ordinary duties of a magistrate, but in the event of a commotion and a general disposition to acts of outrage, we can scarcely expect from them, at least we can only find in very rare circumstances, that degree of activity and vigilance which is necessary for their suppression'.⁴⁴ The government always kept a wary eye out for any signs of radical political organisations in Ireland and from 1813 Peel was anxious to introduce legislation to deal with agrarian disturbances. The parochial or county constables, frequently called watchmen in the towns, were few in number and reduced in practice to collecting the county cess.⁴⁵ The un-uniformed baronial constabulary (the 'Barneys'), appointed by the 'country gentlemen' who made up the grand jury and under the control of the magistrates, were grossly inadequate for the task of preserving public order, even when reinforced by the military. Their main duties had been reduced to searching for stolen goods. The large military force, dissipated and scattered throughout the country, was unsuited for police work. Furthermore the military was generally under the direction of a timid local magistrate who feared intimidation and reprisals. The militia regiments were undisciplined and only added to the danger in difficult situations. The yeomen were often sectarian in character. For example, on 30 May 1814, the fair day in Shercock, County Cavan, the yeomanry fired on a Catholic crowd who were attacking two Protestant houses in the town. The next day Fitzhenry (*recte* Fitzherbert) Ruxton of Ardee wrote to Dublin Castle stating that he had visited the scene and saw the bodies of five dead Catholics and two wounded. He reported that he was told that as many as nine or ten had been killed and the same number wounded. He spoke of 'the irritation and the desire for revenge to be observed among the country people, and of the triumph publicly shown by the yeomanry at their success'.

He was fearful that unless a military force was sent to Shercock 'the mischief has only begun and many more lives will be lost'.⁴⁶

Peel's response to the disorders, and this was a priority with him, was to introduce two bills in 1814, the renewal of the Insurrection Act and the establishment of a new policing system. Gauging the difficulties he was meeting in the House of Commons he proceeded first with the Peace Preservation Act. His vision is well summed up by Galen Broeker in his book *Rural Disorder and Police Reform in Ireland 1812-36* (1970), 'At the centre was a stipendiary (chief) magistrate – a paid, full-time police official with the powers of a magistrate, appointed by and responsible to the Irish government. The stipendiary magistrate had under his exclusive control a body of special constables, also selected by the government. The Peace Preservation Force, as it came to be called, was sent to a disturbed area after a specified number of the local magistrates had requested the lord lieutenant to proclaim the area in a state of disturbance. While the force was operating, the stipendiary or chief magistrate was superior to the other magistrates of the area, who functioned under his direction. The cost of the operation was paid by the area involved, and when tranquillity was restored the Force was either withdrawn or disbanded. Thus, during periods of serious disorder, the traditional machinery of rural law enforcement was to be augmented by trained policemen in mobile units under the authority of the central government'.⁴⁷ The superintending magistrates were to be responsible immediately to the government. The Peace Preservation Act (54 Geo. III, c. 131), received its second reading without opposition on 1 July 1814 and was passed on 25 July. Broeker outlines its main provisions: 'The lord lieutenant, acting with the advice of the Irish privy council could proclaim any county, county of a city or town, barony or half-barony, or any combination of these, to be in a state of disturbance requiring a chief magistrate and an "extraordinary" establishment of police. In practice, the Castle proved reluctant to act against the wishes of the magistrates of the area involved, and bitter argument often preceded the appearance of the Force in a disturbed area. A chief magistrate of police was to be appointed for each barony or half-barony within a proclaimed area "as shall seem best", and might be removed or replaced by the government at any time. The chief magistrate was to have the powers of a justice of the peace in his district and for a seven-mile radius beyond. He had to reside in his assigned area, and could leave only in the course of duty or with permission from the lord lieutenant. All magistrates within his district were to be under his jurisdiction and were required to assist him in all ways. The lord lieutenant would appoint for the "aid and support of such chief magistrates", a clerk, a chief constable, and sub-constables up to fifty in number, all of whom were to be under the control of the chief magistrate with specific orders to obey no other magistrate unless ordered to do so'.[48] Expense for the new police force fell on the proclaimed area and so it was in the interest of local magnates to restore order in record time. Many of the recruits to the new force were ex-soldiers and were commanded by military officers. The mounted section was known as the 'Dragoon Police'. T.G.F. Paterson writes, 'They were a picturesque crowd, uniformed in blue jackets, red cuffs and collars, red and gold lace girdles, tall beaver caps with feathers, and long scarlet cloaks reaching over their horses' tails. Each horse carried two men, for behind the rider, on a small pad, sat a second trooper with a short rifle'.[49] Baronial constables continued as before. Two amendment acts followed to streamline the measures taken and these were passed on 29 November 1814 and March 1817. In 1822 the County Constabulary was established, later in 1836 forming the Irish Constabulary, a permanent body of police for the whole country.

Peel regarded violence as inherent in the disposition and nature of Irish people and, while facing practicalities in passing emergency laws and law and order bills and pursuing the implementation of them, he occasionally reveals his prejudice towards the 'the lower orders'. He wrote to Gregory, 24 June 1814, 'I said the Bill (*the Peace Preservation Act*) was not meant to meet any temporary emergency, but was rendered necessary by the past state of Ireland for the last fifty years and by the probable state of it for the next five hundred'.[50] In one letter he described Tipperary as 'by far the most troublesome county in Ireland'. Disturbance was due 'to sheer wickedness, encouraged by the apathy of one set of magistrates and the half connivance of another'. 'For the last thirty years', he wrote, 'and probably for the last three hundred, this same county of Tipperary has been conspicuous even in the Irish annals of violence and barbarity, having less excuse in the distress and suffering of its inhabitants than most parts of Ireland. But there is more than one district in the south of Ireland in which plenty and prosperity incite to crime rather than repress it'.[51]

Encouraged by the reception of his Police Bill, Peel, moved again for the renewal of the Insurrection Act, striking another blow for the restoration of 'order' in Ireland, and succeeded in having it re-enacted. It had been repealed in 1810. The bill, 54 Geo. III, c. 180, was passed on 30 July 1814. It was to be effective for three years. Broeker sums up the provisions of the act: 'The act provided that seven magistrates in special session could inform the lord lieutenant that their county was in a disturbed state. The lord lieutenant, acting on the advice of the Irish privy council, could proclaim the county or any part of it to be in a disturbed condition. All people living in the proclaimed area were required to remain in their homes from sunset to sunrise, under penalty of seven years' transportation. All who demanded arms or administered illegal oaths (without the use of violence), or who possessed weapons and refused to give them to the authorities, were liable to the seven-years' transportation penalty. When the act was finally applied, after its re-enactment in 1814, the most important provision proved to be that authorizing the suspension of trial by jury in the proclaimed area. Persons arrested under the act were tried before a court of general sessions, presided over by an assistant barrister, who was assisted by as many magistrates as could be persuaded to attend. Apparently crimes of a capital nature were reserved to the courts of criminal assize. The assistant barrister usually attempted to get as many magistrates as possible to sit with him; one assistant barrister stated that he refused to try a serious case with fewer than six magistrates present. The assistant barrister usually guided the deliberations of the magistrates, and a convicted man could apply to the court for a review, after which the court would decide whether or not to request a pardon from the lord lieutenant'.[52]

JUDGE WILLIAM FLETCHER

One of the most defiant criticisms of Peel's measures was delivered by Judge William Fletcher in his lengthy charge to the Grand Jury at County Wexford, at the Summer Assizes, 1814. It was published, with some editing, in the *Annual Register*, 1814. His remarks are important since they are an argument from within and he himself was to figure prominently in some of the trials of those accused of the Wildgoose Lodge atrocity.

F. Elrington Ball in *The Judges in Ireland, 1221-1921* marks out the career of Judge William Fletcher as follows:

> **William Fletcher:** was eldest son of George Fletcher of Dublin, physician, and Mary, eldest daughter of Stephen Meyler; was born 1750; matriculated in Dublin University 1765; appears as a scholar 1769; graduated as bachelor of arts 1770 and as bachelor of medicine 1774; entered the Middle Temple 1776; was called to the Irish bar 1778; married Sarah Whitley of Maryborough 1780; proceeded doctor of laws 1785; practised as a civilian; was elected member for Tralee 1795; became a king's counsel same year; was appointed a justice of the Common Pleas 1806; delivered a charge on current political questions, in county Wexford 1814; was subject of a petition to the house of commons 1816; resided in Dublin successively in Cumberland-street and in Merrion-square, and near Dublin at Montrose; died at Montrose 1823; left issue.[53]

In his charge at Wexford Assizes Judge Fletcher began by looking back thirty years at the county of Wexford, which to the surprise of many had exploded into revolt despite its previous tranquil state and the industrious habits of the peasantry. He welcomed the current state of tranquillity in Wexford and decried the exaggeration and misrepresentation of disturbances by media and other advertisement; indeed he cited a personal experience where an incident, in which he was involved, was presented out of all recognition. The visitor from England, interested in writing a book of travel, returned, he maintained, full of prejudice, armed with information from the squires, 'each rivalling the other in entertaining their guest, all busy in pouring falsehoods into his ears, touching the disturbed state of the country, and the vicious habits of the people'. Mischieveous presentation was also true of other parts besides Wexford and alarmists gave all local crime the colouring of political disturbance. In his circuits throughout other counties in Ireland Fletcher observed disturbances among the 'lower orders' but there were many causes for them. He said, 'never during the entire period of my judicial experiences (comprising sixteen circuits) have I discovered or observed any serious purpose, or settled scheme of assailing his Majesty's Government, or any conspiracy connected with internal rebels or foreign foes; but various deep rooted and neglected causes, producing similar effects throughout this country, have conspired to create the evils which really and truly exist'. Not mincing his words he proceeded to elaborate on these causes: avidity in acquiring and renting lands leading to high payments and high rents causing displacement of traditional residents and bringing in the unwanted stranger; the enormous paper currency leading to banks failing and ruining multitudes; the large county assessments, especially for roads to suit landlords only and the burden to provide them falling heavily on the poor; the harassment caused by the unfair church tythes – 'they are a tax upon industry, upon enterprise, and upon agricultural skill'; the abuse of the county presentment Code of Ireland for the purposes of 'fraud and peculation'; the abuse of oaths of registration for elections, bordering on perjury; the 'hasty mode of pronouncing decrees upon Civil Bills, which was common before Assistant Barristers were nominated for the several counties'; illicit distillation especially in the north-west; increasing absenteeism of landlords. He continued: 'Vexed with those exactions … can we be surprised that a peasant, of unenlightened mind, of uneducated habits, should rush upon the perpetration of crimes, followed by the punishment of the rope and the gibbet?'

He noticed a weakening in the connection of the Catholic pastor with his flock - 'the flock, goaded by their wants, and flying in the face of the pastor, with a lamentable abandonment of all religious feeling, and a dereliction of all regard to that pastoral superintendence, which is so essential to the tranquillity of the country. For, if men have no prospect here, but of a continued series of want, and labour, and privation; and if the hopes and fears of a future state are withdrawn from them, by an utter separation from their own pastor, what must be the state of society? The ties of religion and morality being thus loosened, a frightful state of things has ensued. Perjury has abounded. The sanctity of oaths has ceased to be binding, save where they administer to the passion of parties. The oaths of the Orange Associations, or of the Ribbonmen, have, indeed, continued to be obligatory. As for oaths administered in a court of justice, they have been set at naught'.

'Is there no remedy', he asked, 'but Act of Parliament after Act of Parliament, in quick succession, framed for coercing and punishing? Is there no corrective, but the rope and the gibbet? Yes, Gentlemen, the removal of those causes of disturbance, which I have mentioned to you, will operate as the remedy. ... Is it not high time for those permanent absentees to offer some assistance, originating from themselves, out of their own private purses, towards improving and ameliorating the condition of the lower orders of the peasantry upon their great domains, and rendering their lives more comfortable? ...Gentlemen, I will tell you what those absentees ought particularly to do; they ought to promote the establishment of houses of refuge, houses of industry, school houses, and set the example upon their own estates, of building decent cottages, so that the Irish peasant may have, at least, the comforts of an "English sow"; for an English farmer would refuse to eat the flesh of a hog, so lodged and fed as an Irish peasant is ... If your farms fall out of lease, set them not up to be let by public auction; encourage your tenantry to build comfortable dwellings for themselves, give them a property in their farms, and an interest in the peace of the county. These are the remedies for the discontents of the people; they will be found much better than the cord and the gibbet'.

Regarding education he said – 'It is in vain to flatter yourselves that you can improve their minds (the poor) if you neglect their bodies. Where have you ever heard of a people desirous of education, who had not clothes to cover them, or bread to eat?'

He went into some detail on the unfairness of tythes: 'Far be it from me to say, that tythes are not due to the clergy. By the law of the land, they have as good a title to their tythes as any of you have to your estates; and I am convinced, that the clergyman does not, in any instance, exact what he is strictly entitled to. But this mode of assessment has been much complained of; and it is particularly felt in this country, because the Catholic receives no spiritual comfort from his Protestant rector; he knows him only through the Tythe Proctor, and he has moreover his own pastor to pay. This is the reason why he thinks it is a grievance; and, I must admit, that although the clergyman does not receive all that he is entitled to, and although it may not be a grievance in another country, yet the tythe system is a painful system for Ireland'.

The magistracy in Ireland came in for heavy criticism from Judge Fletcher and he returned to the theme a few times. 'The country has seen a magistracy, over-active in some instances, and quite supine in others. This circumstance has materially affected the administration of the laws in Ireland. In this respect I have found that those societies, called Orange Societies, have produced most mischievous effects; and particularly in the North of Ireland. They poison the very fountains of justice; and even some magistrates, under their influence, have, in too many instances, violated their duties and their oaths. I do not hesitate to say, that all Associations of every description in this country, whether of Orangemen or Ribbonmen, whether distinguished by the colour of Orange or of Green, all combinations of persons, bound to each other (by the obligation of an Oath) in a league for a common purpose, endangering the peace of the country, I pronounce them to be contrary to law. And should it ever come before me to decide upon the question, I shall not hesitate to send up bills of indictment to a Grand Jury against the individuals, members of such an Association, wherever I can find the charge properly sustained. Of this I am certain, that, so long as those Associations are permitted to act in the lawless manner they do, there will be no tranquillity in this country; and particularly in the north of Ireland. There those disturbers of the public peace, who assume the name of Orange Yeomanry, frequent the fairs and markets, with arms in their hands, under the pretence of self-defence, or of protecting the public peace, but with the lurking view of inviting attacks from the Ribbon Men, confident that, armed as they are, they must overcome defenceless opponents, and put them down. Murders have been repeatedly perpetrated upon such occasions; and, though legal prosecutions have ensued, yet, such have been the baneful consequences of these factious Associations, that, under their influence, Petty Juries have declined (upon some occasions) to do their duty. These facts have fallen under my own view. It was sufficient to say, such a man displayed such a colour, to produce an utter disbelief of his testimony; or, when another has stood with his hand at the bar, the display of his party badge has mitigated the murder into manslaughter' ... 'With these Orange Associations I connect all commemorations and processions, producing embittering recollections, and inflicting wounds upon the feelings of others; and I do emphatically state it as my settled opinion, that until those Associations are put down, and the arms, taken from their hands, in vain will the north of Ireland expect tranquillity or peace'.

Once again in his charge Judge Fletcher returned to a hard-hitting condemnation of the magistracy and the injustice they pursued against the poor. 'Gentlemen, this subject brings me to a consideration of the magistracy of the country. Of these I must say, that some are over zealous, others too supine: distracted into parties, they are too often governed by their private passions, to the disgrace of public justice, and the frequent disturbance of the country.

Here let me solicit your particular attention to some of the grievous mischiefs, flowing from the misconduct of certain magistrates. One is occasioned by an excessive eagerness to crowd the gaols with prisoners, and to swell the calendars with crimes. Hence the amazing disproportion between the number of the committals and of the convictions, between accusation and evidence, between hasty suspicion and actual guilt. Committals have been too frequently made out (in other counties) upon light and trivial grounds, without reflecting upon the evil consequences of wresting a peasant (probably innocent) from the bosom of his family, immuring him for weeks or months in a noisome gaol, amongst vicious companions. He is afterwards acquitted or not prosecuted; and returns a lost man, in health and morals, to his ruined and beggared family. This is a hideous, but common picture.

Again, fines and forfeited recognizances are multiplied,

through the misconduct of a magistrate. He binds over a prosecutor, under a heavy recognizance, to attend a distant Assizes, where it is probable that the man's poverty or private necessities must prevent his attending. The man makes default, his recognizance is forfeited, he is committed to the county gaol upon a green wax process, and, after long confinement, he is finally discharged at the Assizes, pursuant to the statute; and from an industrious cottier he is degraded, from thenceforth, into a beggar and a vagrant.

Other magistrates presume to make out vague committals, without specifying the day of the offence charged, the place, or any other particular, from which the unfortunate prisoner could have notice to prepare his defence. This suppression is highly indecorous, unfeeling, and unjust: and it deserves, upon every occasion, a severe reprobation of the magistrate, who thus deprives his fellow-subject of his rightful opportunity of defence.

There are parts of Ireland, where, from the absence of the gentlemen of the county, a race of magistrates has sprung up, who ought never to have borne the King's Commission. The vast powers entrusted to those officers call for an upright, zealous, and conscientious discharge of their duty'.

Judge Fletcher then broadened his theme to fair administration of the law as the great remedy for the discontent of the peasantry. 'But there is one remedy, that would, in my estimation, more than any other, especially contribute to soothe the minds of the discontented peasantry, and, thereby, to enable them patiently to suffer the pressure of those burthens, which cannot, under existing circumstances, be effectually removed; I mean the "Equal and impartial Administration of Justice"; of that Justice which the rich can pursue, until it be attained; but which, that it may benefit the cottager, should be brought home to his door. Such an administration of justice would greatly reconcile the lower orders of the people with the Government under which they live; and at no very distant period, I hope, attach them to the law, by imparting its benefits, and extending its protection to them, in actual and uniform experience. Gentlemen, if you ask me, how may this be accomplished? I answer, by a vigilant superintendence of the administration of justice at Quarter Sessions, and an anxious observance of the conduct of all Justices of Peace. Perhaps, the Commission of the Peace, in every county of the kingdom should be examined. During a long war, in seasons of popular commotion, under Chief Governors (all acting, unquestionably, with good intentions, but upon various principles, and different views) it is not improbable that many men have crept into the commission, who, however useful they might occasionally have been, ought not to remain. The needy adventurer, the hunter for preference, the intemperate zealot, the trader in false loyalty, the jobbers of absentees, if any of these various descriptions of individuals are now to be found, their names should be expunged from the Commission, and if such a mode of proceeding should thin the Commission, vacancies may be supplied, by soliciting every Gentleman of property and consideration to discharge some part of the debt of duty, which he owes to himself and the country, by accepting the office of Justice of Peace'. He classed good clergymen from the established church as possible candidates, those who were charitable towards poor Catholics and worked for reconciliation. 'Some Clergymen there may have been, who, in a period of distraction, perusing the Old Testament with more attention than the New, and admiring the glories of Joshua (the son of Nun), fancied they perceived in the Catholics the Canaanites of old; and, at the head of militia and armed yeomanry, wished to conquer from them the promised glebe. Such men, I hope, are not now to be found in that most respectable order; and if they are, I need scarcely add, they should no longer remain in the Commission'.

As a climax to his charge, having reviewed the ills of the country and stated the necessary remedies, Judge Fletcher, gave his opinion on the renewal of the Insurrection Act and the passing of the Peace Preservation Bill. 'Gentlemen, two Bills, of importance to the public peace of Ireland, have recently passed both Houses of Parliament, almost, as I believe, without observation; and certainly without public inquiry into the state of the country. Having formed an opinion upon the causes of popular discontents, and public commotions in those counties, which I have, within these five years, visited, I thought it expedient, openly from this place, to state this opinion; hoping that my judgement being founded not upon secret whispering, or private communications, but upon the solemnity of public trials and the authenticity of criminal records, may have some weight towards suggesting the expediency of resorting to other means of tranquillizing Ireland, than those hitherto resorted to – banishment, the rope, and the gibbet. These expedients have been repeatedly tried; and have, by the acknowledgement of those who have used them, hitherto proved ineffectual. And here I must intreat, that I may not wilfully be mistaken and purposely misunderstood by any man or class of men. I mean not to question in the slightest degree, the prudence of the Irish government in introducing, or the wisdom of the legislature in enacting those laws; they may be suitable (for any thing I know to the contrary) to the existing state of things in some of these counties, where the discharge of my public duty has not yet called me. In others, although it may not be immediately necessary to put them into active operation, the notoriety of their existence in the Statute Book may be a wholesome warning to the turbulent and audacious ... With one of those Acts you have had a former acquaintnance. It is the old Insurrection Act, which, after having perished, is now revived and re-enacted for Ireland. The other is called the Peace Preservation Bill. The Insurrection Act consists, as you know, of a complete suspension of the English Constitution – of English law – of the Trial by Jury. Under these new laws, taken together, any seven magistrates may meet, and recommend the county or district to be proclaimed by the Lord Lieutenant as being in a state of disturbance. When the Proclamation has once issued, every person must stay at home after a certain hour. You are to have the assistance of a learned Serjeant from town, who may send abroad offenders in a summary way.

Gentlemen, I have seen times, when persons, who thinking the lives named in their tenants' leases were lasting too long have by the aid of such a law, found means to recommend a trip across the Atlantic, to the persons thus unreasonably attached to life; and thus achieved the downfall of a beneficial lease, and a comfortable rise of their income in consequence. Such things have occurred: I have known the fact.

Gentlemen, I may be told, that the state of the country requires its re-enactment. It may be so: I am not in possession of the secrets of the Castle. A desperate state of things calls for desperate remedies.

Gentlemen, the other Act of Parliament is the Peace Preservation Bill. It is a wholesome mode of administering the old powers, already vested by law in the magistrates. Any seven magistrates may recommend the application of this remedy; and either for the county at large, or any particular barony or district in the county. If their recommendaton should be acceded to by the Lord Lieutenant, this Bill comes into immediate operation. Now, you are to meet – a head magistrate is to be appointed, at a salary of 700*l.* a year; he is also to have a house and offices – his clerk is to get a salary of 150*l.* a year – the constables are to get 100*l.* a year each; any seven of your magistrates may get all this done. But listen to one thing more – the disturbed district is to pay the expense of the whole'.

Fletcher's candid reasoning, published in the *Annual Register* in abridged form, as it seems, did not please Peel who gave voice to his feelings in a letter to Lord Desart, 22 September 1814:

> Judge Fletcher's printed charge is a very inoffensive document compared to the charge which he really delivered, and of which I have an authentic copy. He is a shabby fellow for publishing a mutilated statement. One part of the real charge runs as follows:
> 'There is first an office of 700*l.* a year, a very good office for a *loyal* man, gentlemen, for a first-rate loyal man. There are three offices of 150*l.* for second-rate loyalists, and abundance of offices of 50*l.* a year for inferior loyalists. Oh most excellent Peace Preservation Bills, Oh! Mr Peel, Mr Peel, Oh![54]

To Lord Sidmouth, Peel reported a general opinion that 'it was a gross violation of the duty of a judge to animadvert, in the manner and language used by Judge Fletcher, upon Acts of the Legislature', and suggested that as some Irish member would probably bring the question before Parliament it would be well to consider what course the Government would be prepared to take. Privately he promoted the publication of a counter statement as 'an anti-dote to the poison'.[55] He returned to the subject in a long letter, 30 September 1814, to the Speaker (Abbot, who had been the first Chief Secretary after the Union) emphasising the generally improved state of Ireland:

> I never recollect such a cessation of outrage and disturbance as there has been for the last three months – it would seem presumptious to say since the passing of the two Acts of last session.
>
> It is impossible to advert to this without referring also to the oration delivered by Judge Fletcher. I will not say that it is disapproved of by all the friends of good order and subordination to the laws, but I may venture to assert that it has the unqualified approbation of every advocate for separation, and of every demagogue who flourished in the Catholic Board, who survived the periods of 1798 and 1803. The discretion of the judge has been greater than his candour, for he has omitted in the publication those parts of his speech which every loyal man heard with deep regret and indignation. I have supplied the omissions in the inclosed printed report from the original manuscript procured from the registrar.
>
> The obvious absurdity of inferring the tranquillity of a country from the paucity of committals (which may probably be the strongest proof of intimidation and general participation in crime), the ignorant exposition of those laws relating to the peace of the country which, whether wise enactments or not, were still the law of the land, and which as such should not have been condemned by one of its judges, are too obvious to require any comment. The sarcasms upon loyalty and loyal men are also too intelligible to be mistaken.
>
> Notwithstanding the charge, however, the country is much, very much less disturbed than it was a few months ago.[56]

The Speaker wrote to Peel from Kidbrooke, 17 October 1814:

> Mr Justice Fletcher's charge is reprinted at Bath, and circulated industriously throughout England. I am much obliged by the *variorum* edition which you have sent me. Our judges here do not deal in such political harangues, nor is it to be wished that they should, or else the Attorney-General should at all times have noticed, that he might attend and make a speech on the other side.
>
> The republication, which I have seen, contains a short biographical memoir of the Judge, stating him to be of no party, but promoted by Lord Fitzwilliam and the Duke of Bedford, and that his known friendship with Mr Ponsonby, Mr Grattan, and Mr Curran, prove him to be uninfluenced by any party spirit.[57]

Norman Gash in his book *Mr Secretary Peel* comments on the episode in the context of Peel's fair appointments without political consideration following the Peace Preservation Act: 'Peel was all the more incensed therefore when Fletcher, one of the Irish assize judges and a whig by connection, in the course of a long address to the Grand Jury at Wexford, satirised the new Preservation Act as a measure for providing jobs for government supporters. With considerable warmth and more than a touch of tenacity he was to show the following year over O'Connell, Peel not only busied himself with the publication of an elaborate counter-statement, but with the approval of the Lord Lieutenant and his advisers took up with the cabinet the question of proceeding against Fletcher in parliament. But Sidmouth and Liverpool were reluctant to engage in a party quarrel on such flimsy grounds, and though Whitworth feared at one point that Peel might go so far as to resign on the issue, in the end the mattter was allowed to pass over without any official action'.[58]

Six months later Judge Fletcher's charge still rankled with the government. The counter-attack mounted by other judges was in Gregory's opinion counter-productive. He wrote to Lord Whitworth from Dublin Castle, on 21 April 1815.

> The table talk and garrulity of those who should inspire confidence instead of increasing fear, adds much to the general consternation which prevails. Although the judicial charges from the Bench to the Grand Juries of Westmeath and Dublin are much admired, and are thought to act as antidotes to Judge Fletcher, I cannot approve of the wisdom of informing the Enemies foreign and domestic that the whole Kingdom is in the state of prepared Treason, that it requires only a spark to make it break into open Rebellion, this too when the alarmists are ready to believe that the whole Population is not only armed but disciplined and that Bonaparte has fleets and armies ready to send to their assistance ...[59]

Inevitably the vehement reaction of government with the threat of publishing the unexpurgated version, and the danger of being classed with demagaogues, forced Fletcher to mellow his criticism.

The first proclamation under the Peace Preservation Act was issued on 6 September 1814 declaring the barony of Middlethird in County Tipperary in a state of disturbance.[60] So also the second and third proclamations in 1815 involved baronies in County Tipperary. Gale E. Christianson in his article 'Secret Societies and Agrarian Violence in Ireland, 1790-1840' gives tables for those tried and convicted under the Insurrection Act by the courts of General Sessions (those presided over by an assistant barrister) for the six month period from September 1815 to February 1816. 328 were tried, 68 were convicted and 260 were acquitted. The disturbed areas were Tipperary, Limerick, Limerick City, Westmeath and King's County. Tipperary topped the table with 178 tried, 46 convicted and 132 acquitted. His second table gives statistics for the persons tried before the courts of Criminal Assizes for agrarian disturbances in 1815, the indictments being handed down by the Grand Jury. The areas included Westmeath, King's County, Queen's County, Roscommon, Longford, Tipperary, Waterford, Limerick, Louth and Clare. The offences were murder, attempted murder, and assembling in arms. In Louth two were tried for murder but not convicted and none was tried for attempted murder and assembling in arms. The statistics covered only those individuals brought for trial. Many others were not tried for lack of evidence.[61]

Peel wrote to the Prime Minister in January 1816 about Tipperary:

> In Tipperary we are ... making a terrific but necessary example under the special commission we have sent there. There have been thirteen capital convictions for offences amounting to little short of rebellion, and fourteen sentenced to transportation for the destruction of a barrack. All these sentences will be carried into execution without mitigation. We find convictions attended with so many difficulties that we are obliged to be very sparing in the extension of mercy. ... You can have no idea of the moral depravation of the lower orders in that county. In fidelity to each other they are unexampled, as they are in their sanguinary disposition and fearlessness of the consequences.[62]

In September as many as 12,000 troops were sent into the county.

On 12 March 1816, just a month before the first attack on Wildgoose Lodge, the barony or half-barony of Upper Dundalk, the barony or half-barony of Lower Dundalk, and the baronies of Ardee and Louth in the county of Louth, were proclaimed by Lord Lieutenant Whitworth, in a state of disturbance, requiring an extraordinary establishment of police. Samuel Pendleton, a former soldier, was appointed chief magistrate and Joseph Hanna clerk and James Lee chief constable. Major Richard Wilcocks had recommended Hanna as clerk. Wilcocks had been the first chief magistrate appointed, in the barony of Middlethird in County Tipperary in September 1816.[63]

A poster related to this measure has survived and there is a copy in the County Museum, Dundalk.⁶⁴ It reads:

> COUNTY OF LOUTH
> NOTICE
> Whereas, it has become necessary to proclaim several Districts of this County, in Consequence of the System of DISTURBANCE AND TERROR, that has shewn itself, and it appears that the said System is much Strengthened by Meetings at Public Houses, therefore the Magistrates residing in these Districts, do warn the Publicans therein against having their houses open after *Nine o'clock at Night*, being determined to deprive of their Licenses all such as shall be found offending this order. The Magistrates likewise declare to the Inhabitants of the Proclaimed Districts that they will not permit any MEETINGS, PATRONS or FOOTBALL MATCHES, until tranquillity shall be restored.
> Dated, March 19th, 1816

On 26 April 1816 Sir J. Newport, an Irish M.P. in the House of Commons and a member of the Whig party, sought the provision of documents, which would fully inform the members as to the state of Ireland, the causes of its existing evils and the measures which the executive and military might apply 'to rescue that fair portion of the empire from its present depression and disorganization'. Peel in his response explained the measures taken by the government. His analysis of disturbances in Ireland does not acknowledge any grievance on the part of the rural poor and indeed he believed that their motives were beyond rational comprehension. The *Annual Register* of 1816 reported:

> Generally speaking (he said) the north of Ireland was tranquil, no disturbance prevailing there except what arose from illicit distillation, and the consequent opposition to the revenue laws in certain districts. The extreme west, and the counties of Mayo, Galway, and Carlow were comparatively tranquil; and the same might be said of the south, of Cork, Wexford, &c. The last was likewise so far tranquil, that no application to government for extraordinary police had been made from these counties. The counties in which disturbances actually prevailed were Tipperary, King's County, Westmeath, and Limerick. The magistrates of King's County had requested the application of the insurrection act, but had since petitioned for its removal, asserting that tranquillity was perfectly restored. In Westmeath and Limerick a considerable improvement had taken place, but the insurrection act was still in force. The magistrates for Louth and Cavan had petitioned the government for the application, not of the insurrection act, but of the extraordinary police act. This was the general state of the country; but nothing was more difficult than to give a character of the precise

nature of the disturbances now agitating it. Formerly tumult and outrages might be traced to particular causes; but those which now prevailed seemed to be the effect of a general confederacy in crime – a systematic opposition to all laws and municipal institutions.

This debate took place on 26 April 1816, shortly after the first attack on Wildgoose Lodge. The situation in Louth was to deteriorate from then on. Louth, as we shall see, was placed under the Insurrection Act in 1817.

In 1817 Peel brought in the Irish Peace Preservation Bill to amend the act, 54 Geo. III, c.131. On 11 March 1817 he explained the changes in parliament. The *Annual Register* 1817 reported Peel's request for change: 'As the law at present stood, it was necessary on the appointment of a certain number of peace officers, to create a superintendent magistrate, who should act as the magistrate of the newly disturbed district. To prevent the accumulation of magistrates, he should propose, that different bodies of constables belonging to different districts, should be allowed to act under the same magistrate'. Expenses he proposed would be eased when costs were shared between the local district involved and public funds. He also proposed a considerable reduction in the army in Ireland from 25,000 men to 22,000, and the seven brigades of ordnance of 400 guns to be reduced to 200. These measures were accepted. John Mitchel, patriot and a leading human rights activist of his time, did not hesitate to continue his crusade against the coercion measures of the British Government in his *History of Ireland*. In his typical sardonic manner he speaks here for the oppressed:

> The men chosen for this office of stipendiary magistrate have been usually briefless barristers, or broken-down politicians in a small way, to whom the salary was a desirable livelihood; and as they have at least legal phrases at their command, a supposed acquaintance with the views of the Castle, and great self-importance of manner, it has been found in practice that these paid officials have really, to a great extent, controlled and managed the local administration of justice; which, in all conscience, had been bad enough before. ...
> In the year 1816, Sir John Newport moved in Parliament for a committee to inquire into the state of Ireland, which was then suffering greatly from scarcity of food. Sir Robert Peel steadily and successfully resisted the proposed inquiry. That prudent statesman had not been several years Chief Secretary of Ireland for nothing. He had no need of inquiry, being quite well aware of what was passing in Ireland, where

he knew that things were falling out exactly according to his calculations. If there was some extermination of starving wretches, it was because his cheap enactment laws were working well. If there was some disturbance and 'agrarian crime', he had his new police ready to repress it. Better than all, he had procured the renewal of the 'Insurrection Act' in 1814 – had caused it to be continued in 1815, and it was now (1816) in full vigour, filling the jails with persons who did not give a good account of themselves, and transporting men for possessing a fowling-piece. He felt that an assiduous Irish Secretary could do no more; and naturally, resisted Sir John Newport's medling motion for inquiry.

But, in truth, the low price of produce had made thousands of farmers unable to pay the rent; then they had been ejected; and then that lowness of price could not enable them to procure food, because they had no money. Then there was an occasional murder, or attempt at murder. Magistrates would meet, and write to the Castle for immediate proclamation of the county under the Insurrection Act. It is useless to go through the unvarying detail of torturing oppression which has continued and repeated itself year after year, and will never end while the British Empire stands. But in sad earnest, this year 1817, was a season of dreadful famine and suffering; and, of course, the Coercion Act of the year before was carefully renewed. The potato crop had failed; and although Ireland was then largely exporting grain and cattle to England, yet this good food was not supposed to be sent by Providence, for the nourishment of those who sowed and reaped it on their own soil ...

In that year (1817), ... the suffering from famine and typhus fever was already dreadful enough; and in the most fertile counties of Ireland, multitudes of people fed upon weeds of various sorts – some boiled nettles; others subsisted upon the wild kail, called in Irish, *prasagh*. All political movement was suspended for several years, both in Ireland and in England, and in 1819, Lord Sidmouth introduced and carried his celebrated 'Six acts', principally to quell the 'seditious' aspirations of English people. These acts imposed heavy penalties upon the possession of arms, and upon 'blasphemous and seditious libels' – meaning all plain and truthful comments upon the proceedings of Government. A horrible military massacre was perpetrated this year at Peterloo, near Manchester, by the onslaught of a body of troops upon a perfect peaceable meeting of the people to demand reform ... [65]

The Insurrection Act, due to expire in July 1817, was extended for another year. The debate in the House of Commons, which preceded the passage of the bill for the renewal of the act, reveals unease by some members at its draconian and arbitrary measures. The Insurrection Act was repealed in 1818.

The *Annual Register* 1817 reported:

On June 13th the order of the day being on the subject of going into committee on the bill for continuing the Irish Insurrection Act, *Sir Henry Parnell* rose to move that it should be referred to a committee for this day se'nnight, in place of this evening, for the purpose of the appointment of a committee to inquire whether there existed any necessity for such a measure. The chief secretary for Ireland had laid before the House, in the last and present session, certain documents referring to disturbances in Ireland, the latter of which mentioned outrages which had occurred in the county of Louth. It was upon the last of these documents that the right hon. Gentleman had called upon the House to continue these most severe and unconstitutional measures; but it was incumbent upon the House to exercise its inquisitorial powers, and to examine whether the disturbed state of the only four baronies in one county of Ireland was a sufficiently strong case for such an expedient. The law was one of uncommon severity; it went to create six new transportable offences; to enable the magistrates at sessions to proceed to trial without either grand or petit juries; and to sentence persons guilty of no greater crime than being absent from their homes after sunset, to be transported for seven years. But the right hon. gentleman, in palliation of his case, says, 'the law is not general; the House may depend upon the moderation of the magistrates in requiring its enforcement, and upon the forbearance of government'. But the occurrence in the county of Louth fully proved the disposition of the magistrates; for they were led to apply to government in consequence of a single outrage, which, though not of great enormity, had the effect of producing a compliance with their wishes. The continuance of the Insurrection Act appeared to the hon. member particularly objectionable, because it seemed to be one intended to complete the new system of the future government of Ireland. Though we were now in a state of peace with all the world, the right hon. gentleman had proceeded just as if we were in the midst of a war. He had first obtained an arms bill; he had then made his own particular law, the peace act, stronger than before; and he now aims at the continuance of the Insurrection Act.

The hon. baronet would not go so far as to say, that the facts produced showed that the Insurrection bill was not necessary; but they certainly proved the propriety of making some inquiry before the measure was adopted. If a committee were appointed, he should himself be prepared to point out some means for strengthening the civil power. He concluded by moving, 'that the bill be committed this day se'nnight.'

Mr V. Fitzgerald[66] said he could see no good ground for even a day's delay. The act had been passed by several successive parliaments, and no gentleman could be supposed ignorant of its contents; and being now near its expiration, it was thought necessary to revive it, lest the government of Ireland should be divested of its present powers. The government proclamation applied only to Louth, but the outrage was to be considered as coupled with the general state of the country. Every day produced fresh outrages; and at length there was an unanimous request from the magistrates, and from a county meeting, after which the proclamation was issued.

Mr Peel said, that he was led to attend to the county of Louth more particularly, because the disturbances which called for its exercise there, were more recently laid before the House, and the atrocities with which they were accompanied had made the deepest impression on the country. His argument was, that though the country was generally tranquil, yet if there was one part of it so disturbed that the laws could not be executed in their usual course, it was necessary to arm the government with this act, to be exercised on its responsibility when the emergency arose. The hon. baronet proposed that the bill should be suspended till farther inquiry should be made by a committee. If there was a measure brought before Parliament on which it was competent to decide, without the delay of a committee, it was the present. There never came before Parliament a case in which government had more clearly offered the grounds on which it called for permission to act upon its responsibility, and on which the House had received better means of judging whether it ought to be granted. The hon. baronet had said that the Insurrection Act was an evil, in which he (Mr Peel) fully concurred; but unhappily there was now only a choice of evils; and was it better to give to government the power of preserving tranquillity even by a severe measure, or to allow the country to be converted into a scene of confusion by withholding the present act?

Sir W. Burroughs entered into an examination of the several clauses of the act, and commented in strong terms on its severity. He particularly dwelt upon the great disproportion between the numbers apprehended and the numbers convicted in the several counties; and argued, that as it was to be presumed that the petty sessions had done their duty, therefore all those acquitted had been justly acquitted, and had consequently been wrongfully arrested.

After some further discussion, Sir H. Parnell's amendment was put and negatived. The House then resolved itself into a committee, when Sir W. Burroughs proposed to limit the duration of the bill to six weeks after the meeting of the next session of Parliament; which was negatived, and the duration was fixed at one year.

It does not appear that any further proceedings took place during the passage of this bill through either of the Houses.

By 1817 Judge Fletcher had picked up courage to deliver another charge tackling the practices of the Irish Grand Juries but concentrating in part on the swearing of oaths and the problem of perjury. As we shall see, directly opposing testimonies, generally between approvers and witnesses of the accused, are a feature of the Wildgoose Lodge trials. On 12 August 1817 Fletcher presided over the Crown Court at the Derry Assizes. The *Freeman's Journal*, Monday 23 August reported:

The enlightened and excellent Judge has delivered a charge at the Derry Assizes, in which we find several passages well entitled to attention:

He lamented the extent of the Criminal Calendar, which appeared to him to be unusually great for the County of Derry. He had just come from discharging a most painful duty at Omagh, where no fewer than twenty-six capital convictions had taken place. He was happy to find, however, that in his progress *he had not discovered anything tending to conspiracy against the Laws or Government.* The pressure of the times had led, in some instances, to the commission of crimes, but generally had given a pretext to the abandoned for the perpetration of all manner of wickedness. He noticed an Act, lately passed in the Imperial Parliament, for assimilating the practice of Irish Grand Juries, in the finding of bills of indictment, to the custom uniformally practiced in England, of which he highly approved, as tending greatly *to check the conduct of Magistrates, who either from ignorance, prejudice, or malignity, were too much in the habit of granting committals wantonly and, unnecessarily.* He also approved of another bill, which emanated from the one in question, which tended to the enforcing the penalty on forfeited recognisances ...

He lamented the extraordinary laxity of swearing which prevailed in this country, for which he attributed a variety of causes. He conceived they originated chiefly in the propensity of the lower classes to form *secret and illegal combinations,* which were generally bound together by an oath which frequently engaged them to the commission of all manner of atrocities. Such were the Hearts of Oak and Hearts of Steel – White Boys – Peep o'day Boys – Carders – Threshers, etc – *and latterly they have come to the colours of Orange and Green.*

In England actions were frequently brought against Sub-Sheriffs for non-performance of duty, but in this country the matter was managed by affidavits, the one party swearing directly contrary to the other, so that, to use a vulgar phrase, there was a complete swearing match between them; and for his part, when called upon to pronounce judgement, he has found himself completely at a loss whom to believe. He reprobated Attornies' actions as being attended with the worst consequences in this way; but he considered the present mode of administering the excise laws, if possible, still more pernicious. Contrary to the first principles and foundation of our laws, persons were admitted witnesses in their own case. Guagers were brought up to swear still-fines into their own pockets – others also interested were brought forward to disprove their testimony, and the jury, seldom to such cases free from bias, were sworn to decide – so that here was another swearing match.

He censured the present mode of swearing oaths in Courts of Justice, as wanting in proper solemnity; and suggested the propriety of having the various kinds of Clergymen in attendance on such occasions, whose presence he considered would be a check on their respective hearers.

Prosecutions for perjury were not pursued as they ought, nor were the punishments such as to correct the evil. He was afraid that the Sunday Schools and Bible Societies were not calculated to repress the general depravity – it was beginning at the wrong end. It would be necessary to begin with the parents first, in order to counteract the general depravity. He entered into a variety of other topics, and concluded by instructing the Grand Jury how to act upon the late law for examining witnesses before bills of indictment.

4
The First Attack on Wildgoose Lodge

THE LODGE

The first attack on Wildgoose Lodge, a raid for arms, took place on 10 April 1816. Anton, the soldier, gives a contemporary description of the lodge:

> Wildgoose Lodge was situated on a green knoll in a low marshy meadow, laid almost under water during the winter by the overflowing of the Louth and its tributary streams, which wend their last course through the fertile lands until they spread over the face of this meadow and form a considerable lake. It was owing to the insular situation of the house that it received the name of Wildgoose Lodge and the only approach to it in the winter season was by a narrow road or path on a ridge which extended from the verge of the meadow to the house.

John Mathews of the *Dundalk Examiner* describes it thus in 1881:

> The land surrounding the house is swampy and marshy. In the winter season, especially after heavy rains, the waters rise to a considerable height, and sometimes completely encircle the house. It thus became the favourite resort of winter birds, particularly wild geese, from which it derived its name. At the time of which we write Wildgoose Lodge, otherwise Carthill House, as it was sometimes called, was situated on the property of the late William Filgate, Esq. of Lisrenny. ... Beyond Reaghstown chapel, says a writer in 'All the Year Round,' the country gets very wild, and there is one very narrow swampy lane which horses can hardly traverse. There is one small farmhouse, Wildgoose Lodge, on a piece of rising land; in winter, almost surrounded by water; it is only approachable (except in a boat) by the narrow pass leading from the south side of Reaghstown chapel lane. The bog is a wild, mournful, desolate place ...[67]

The 1835-6 Ordnance Survey Map pinpoints the correct location of the lodge. This is the same location as illustrated by a photograph accompanying T. G. F. Paterson's article in the *Louth Archaeological Journal*. The photograph shows a partial ruin. Bassett's *Louth* (1886) under 'Edmondstown' recorded: 'Wildgoose Lodge, on the farm of Mr John Wildman, is a mile

Sketch of Wildgoose Lodge, thought to have been drawn by one of the children of Rev. Townley P. Filgate, rector of Charlestown, County Louth, and younger brother of William Filgate. Picture courtesy of the County Library, Dundalk.

Remains of Wildgoose Lodge, County Louth Archaeological Journal, xii, 2, 1950. *Courtesy of the Editor.*

and a quarter north-east of Edmondstown. ... Wildgoose Lodge stood on a slight elevation, and a small portion of one of its gables is still in existence'. According to Daniel J. Casey some residents of Reaghstown, in 1974, claimed (incorrectly) that the house was levelled by a succeeding occupier of the land and that it 'was located further down the hill and nearer the road'.

The house and land had been the property of Townley Patten Filgate as stated by his nephew William Filgate of Lisrenny, Ardee, County Louth, who as an old man recorded on 11 March 1867 the story of Wild Goose Lodge for his daughter Anne Henrietta Penelope Eleanor Filgate. The Filgate family is traced in *Burke's Irish Family Records*. William Filgate, the first holder of Lisrenny, is said to have been a Parliamentary officer who settled there on a grant of Cromwell. There followed two Williams in a direct line, and then Alexander (b. 1702) who was the father of William (b. 1740) and Townley Patten. This later William was the father of William (1781-1875) who figures in the present story. He was a justice of the peace in counties Louth and Monaghan, Treasurer of County Louth, and High Sheriff in 1832. He married Sophia De Salis in 1831. His uncle Townley Patten of Lowther Lodge, Balbriggan, County Dublin, and Drumgoolstown, County Louth, was a barrister-at-law. Details regarding William Filgate's personal experience of the outrage are interesting and one can accept a few of them as authentic but, unfortunately, he writes as an old man fifty years after the event and is mistaken in some important matters in the passage I quote here viz. he gives wrong dates for the two attacks, Terence Lynch's son was called Edward not James, one daughter of Lynch, not two, died in the blaze, the motive of the attack was a raid for arms and not an attempted abduction.

> Terence Lynch was huntsman to my father (as his father before him had been to my grandfather) and his son James (*recte* Edward), to whom my uncle, Townley Patten Filgate let Wildgoose Lodge, when he gave it up himself, was a very honest industrious farmer & weaver, had a bleach green & paid his rent to the day – to me, when I acted as my uncle's agent. Lynch had two daughters, one married to a weaver named Rooney, who lived at Wildgoose. The second was a very good looking girl, and the Louth Hall herd, a Ribbonman named Tierney [Tiernan], wanted to marry her but she would have nothing to say to him. He determined to carry her off by force, & with a gang of his fellow

Ribbonmen broke into Wildgoose Lodge, but Lynch and Rooney beat them off with pitch forks, wounding one of them. This was in 1814 [*recte* 1816]. Tierney [*Tiernan*] and two others, Shanly & Conlan, who also lived at Louth Hall, were tried for this outrage – convicted and hanged. The Ribbonmen vowed vengeance & Lynch got arms to protect himself, and a county constable (a frieze coated man, paid £10 a year for keeping the peace) slept in his house each night for a long time, till danger seemed over.[68]

William Filgate at the trial in July 1817 of Patrick Devan testified that he was a magistrate and lived at Lisrenny, that he knew Wildgoose Lodge, that it was a particularly retired situation and very difficult of access in the winter season. The Solicitor General opening the case for the Crown also said that the house stood on a morass, flooded almost all round in the autumn season of the year, and near to which a number of roads met. Amongst the Filgate papers in the County Library, Dundalk, is a drawing purported to be of Wildgoose Lodge with a comment that it was almost certainly done by one of the children of the Revd Townly P. Filgate, died 1822, youngest brother of William Filgate and rector of Charlestown, mid-way between Ardee and Tallanstown.

THE FIRST ATTACK

The first attack on Wildgoose Lodge occurred on Wednesday, 10 April 1816, and, as has been stated, the motive was a raid for arms by Ribbonmen. Being a hunting lodge it was a likely target. This is the only motive mentioned in the trial. Filgate in his late reminiscence ascribes a motive of abduction. The Ribbonmen would not have sanctioned such a cause. That story originated as local romantic lore and can be dismissed. Again, one daughter of Lynch died in the fire in the second attack, not two as Filgate states. Anton says that Lynch at first gave approval to the Ribbon association but later declined an offer to be a leading promoter and refused a request to make his remote dwelling available as a meeting place, thus incurring the wrath of the local association. D'Alton and O'Flanagan in *The History of Dundalk* (1864) maintain that a son of Lynch was solicited to join the Ribbonmen but refused. There is no contemporary evidence for these assertions. A number of men took part in the attack but only three were identified and brought to conviction in the first indictments, namely, Michael Tiernan, Patrick Shanley and Philip Conlon. Filgate says that Tiernan and Conlon lived at Louth Hall. The three men were tried at the Summer Assizes 1816. Sentences of death were passed on them on 27 July 1816.

The fate of the three probably caused little stir among the lesser gentry of Louth. Marianne Fortescue (1767-1849), daughter of John McClintock (d. 1799) of Drumcar, wrote in her diary:

> **C. Bellingham, July 26. 1816.** Sat at home all the morng after visiting Mrs Sweeney at the Miss Bellinghams – Emily Foster dined with us – we went on the jaunting car to Milltown Grange – found the ladies dress'd for a late dinner against the two Mr F Fortescues return from the Assizes – we stay'd to see them & came away just as they were going to dinner – had a pleasant drive & tea when we came home – Emily & I walk'd to the gate at Milestown with Emily Foster – all well thank God – a fine day but gloomy.
> **Saturday, 27th.** A very wet day – we stay'd at home, nothing new has occur'd.[69]

Alice Rispin, whose son James was burned to death in the fire at Wildgoose Lodge, gave a statement to Samuel Pendleton the following year on 2 April 1817, in which she said that she was in Lynch's house the night of the first attack. She gives a graphic description of the frightening outrage. Her son, as she was to testify in court at later trials, was taken by constables to Rosy Park to state to magistrate Fortescue and to other magistrates what he knew of the original 'breaking of Lynch's house' but was afraid to do so. She herself out of fear had obviously not come forward as a witness in the first prosecution for the first attack but having lost her son was willing to give information. In 1818 [Owen] Rickey (alias Matthews) and Patrick Waters were indicted on the burglary charge on her testimony; she said she was in the house the night of the burglary but had not testified before because of threats. Her testimony was inconclusive and both were acquitted. She testified also at the prosecutions for the burning and gave strong evidence against Hugh McCabe.

Statement of Alice Rispin, 2 April 1817:

> Information of Alice Moylan otherwise Respin [Rispin]when upon oath saith that her son James Respin [Rispin] was in the service of the said

[Thomas Rooney] for about a year before his house was attacked and [which was] on the Wednesday night before last Easter. That the [Deponent] was in the habit of being often backwards and forwards there and sometimes staying for a time for these sixteen years past; that she was there on the night aforesaid. She had been sent for by Rooney's wife to help her with spinning of some wool; she had gone to bed before the house was attacked; was roused by the noise at the door. The people outside were calling to them to give out the gun. They broke in the parlour window; it was in it Dep. had her bed. She saw a man [attempting] to come in of the window. He drew back and said to those without 'that he would not go in, maybe something might happen to him'. She then heard them breaking the door; it fell in and a number of men rushed in – can't say how many – they were tumbling on top of each other. She thinks there were not less than 20 men came into the house, and there were many withoutside that she knew did not come (these were the near neighbours who were afraid of being known at the first glance). When they came in she heard some of them say to Rooney 'not to be afraid, that they would not hurt him'. Rooney passed through the parlour then where Dept was to get into a closet where his bed was and went into it. She believes that the [sd Rooney] was employed about this time with Lynch. Rooney was not many minutes in bed when some of them came up to him and raised him out of bed, and told him he must go and take the pitchfork 'from that old rogue', meaning Lynch. They dragged him along with them. She heard the noise of some struggle and Rooney cried out that he 'was done for'. She believes that he was badly used and wounded at that time. Soon afterwards [some of] them came into the room called the Parlour aforesaid, in which Rooney's bed was, and in which Dept had her bed as aforesaid, and sniged with a knife the piece of linen that was in the loom. All this time Dept was lying on her bed. When the men who cut the piece of linen left the room she got up and went into the loom, and was either sitting or standing in Rooney's place there all the rest of the time. She saw Hugh McCabe and John Keegan both standing close by the window outside. They were in that place and close to her for a considerable time and she knew them both well, and is positively sure that she could not be mistaken in them. She saw Pat Waters (who lives at Wm. Hillard's Cross) backwards and forwards in the house with a candle in his hand. She saw one Butler, son of Butlers of Aclint, who lives next to Taaffe's. She does not know the young man's name, but believes it is the second son, and would know him when she saw him. He had a pitchfork in his hand and was one of them. She saw Owen Dicky and Ruck Sheenan; they were both of the party. She had them in view in the passage between the parlour and the kitchen. She saw them both and would not be mistaken in them. Dept is positively sure that everyone of the above 6 men was of the party who so broke and robbed [the house of] Ed. Lynch on the night aforesaid.

She saw another man who lives on the bog road facing Ruck Sheenan's [house]. He was of the party. She would know him anywhere but does

not know his name. There was another whose name she did not know but had a perfect knowledge of his person. He is first cousin of [?] McKenna and lives near Jemmy Smith's. He was one of the party aforesaid. After the party that was in the house had gone out those withoutside sent them in again 'that they did not do half damage'. When they came back again they broke everything before them. They had two candles lit when they were in at first. When they came back they had not any candle.
Given before me this 2nd April 1817.
Alice x her mark Respin [Rispin]   Samuel Pendleton[70]

Of the twenty-six men later apprehended for the burning of Wildgoose Lodge four were also indicted for this first attack – John Keegan, Hugh McCabe, Thomas Sheenan and William Butler. The County Louth Grand Jury Indictment Book[71] under 1816, Spring, lists those indicted for 'breaking into the house of Lynch and demanding arms', namely, Patrick Shanley, Philip Conlon, James Murray, and Michael Tiernan; bills were ignored in the case of Thomas Woods and John McDaniel but it is not clear if their case was connected with Wildgoose Lodge. At the Spring Assizes, 1816, Tiernan, Shanley and Conlon were convicted. The Indictment Book then states: 'There are other true bills against three others for stealing following these items. There is nothing to show whether they were connected with Lynch's house or not. Bryan Coleman, John Coleman, Bryan Durneen, for administering oaths to Terence Cassidy'. The case against these three does not seem to have come to court but Terence Cassidy became a marked man and as will be seen was murdered in July 1818. The Indictment Book, 1817, Summer, lists the following for 'assaulting dwelling house of Edward Lynch, breaking into house of Edward Lynch': Hugh McCabe, John Keegan, Patrick Watters, William Butler, Thomas Sheeran (Sheenan) otherwise Ruck Sheeran, Owen Rickey. Patrick Waters was indicted for the burglary on 3 April 1818 when he pleaded not guilty and was remanded until the next assizes. He and Owen Rickey were acquitted on 3 July 1818.

Lynch and Rooney must have reported the attack immediately for on 12 April 1816, Samuel Pendleton, chief magistrate of Louth, wrote from Dundalk to William Gregory, under-secretary in the civil department, Dublin Castle, announcing his success in apprehending suspects. He praised Edward Lynch, 'an old man', for his manliness in giving information. He also gives some idea of the disturbed state of Louth.

> I have the pleasure of informing you that my first essay here has been totally successful. I yesterday received information against six persons capitally charged. I have now five of them in the Gaol. You will perceive by the Examinations of which I inclose copies, that conviction is extremely probable as to all, but from different circumstances not immediately apparent, can hardly be doubted as to *three*. A few more each night would make this county quiet. It is however rather worse than I considered it when I last had the honor of mentioning an opinion to you. There has been since that time eleven houses attacked in this neighbourhood for arms. Several of the persons so attacked, and of the better class, who had signed the resolutions of Ardee & Louth, binding themselves to cooperate with Magistrates, to give information etc. etc. were of this number, and studiously kept back from all communication of it till it became matter of notoriety. I have summoned some of them, with the view of getting information if 1 *can*, or at all events to establish the fact, and stigmatise their inconsistency.
> In consequence of being informed by a person selling gunpowder here that a most unprecedented amount, and all in very small quantities, had been bought for some days preceding, I thought it not inexpedient to write to the different vendors of it in this district and neighbourhood, *recommending* that they should under the present circumstances not sell to any without a Magistrate's Certificate, otherwise that an application would be made to withdraw their licences, mentioning at the same time the cause of the admonition.
> The opinion as to the peaceable disposition of the vicinity of Ardee is so very much changed within the last few weeks, that I am now requested by the Magistrates immediately thereabouts to represent to you the necessity of ordering a detachment of Military there in the room of that lately withdrawn. From the well-known zeal and activity of those gentlemen, it is not likely that they would suggest such a want, if they did not *feel* it.
> I am also desired to mention that Edward Lynch, a copy of whose Examination I here inclose is an object worthy the attention of Government. He is an old man whose conduct and testimony have been most manly without appearing to be the result of any vindictive feeling. By exhibiting in strong colours the effects of such conduct contrasted with that of those who from fear or worse motives withheld important communications, the happiest consequences might be expected. In his present state I do not think the man safe. I offered him protection and support here. He preferred to venture himself at home, and has a constable in his house to assist him.
> There is a matter here on which I would be happy to receive a direction from the Attorney General. Will you allow me to solicit it through you, as I really feel too much fatigued and confused just now for a separate communication, and a quick decision is necessary? A man was

> committed last week on whose person papers were found, consisting of those treasonable articles, which I am sure you have often seen and other notices etc etc of a similar tendency. I have, on being applied to, advised that he should be held on for some days for further examination, (in fact to gain time for instruction) and intending for my own part to let him out on procuring security to a serious amount. I have no doubt he is a very bad person, but cannot of myself perceive the point in which he is at present tangible.
>
> Will you allow me to call your attention to the matter mentioned in the last letter I had the honor of addressing to you, as to the necessity of ordering another issue of money for this Establishment? There is no doubt it will be wanting before it can arrive, as you may perceive by the estimate I then inclosed you, and which is I am sure very much underrated.[72]

The official reply requested Pendleton to state in what way Lynch might be rewarded for resisting the attack on his house. Here are the Castle summary notes:

> 13 April 1816. To Samuel Pendleton Esqr. Acknowledging his letter of the 12th enclosing informations against 6 persons concerned in breaking into the house of Edward Lynch, 5 of whom he has apprehended. Requesting him to state in what way he recommends that Lynch should be rewarded for his conduct in resisting the attack on his house. With respect to the man on whose person threatening notices were found, informing him that there is no power to keep him in confinement, but his papers may be retained on matters of corroboration. Also that applications for Military should be made to the General of the District.[73]

Pendleton wrote again on 2 May 1816 saying that he had the witness Rooney in the police barracks. He suggested removing him to Dublin or Kilmainham for safekeeping.

> Dundalk. From Samuel Pendleton Esqr. Has in safe keeping in the Police Barrack the witness before alluded to, Rooney, on the business of Lynch's burglary, & McGahon who can identify the persons who broke his father's house on 21 ult., four of whom are in Gaol. Submitting the removal of the men (Rooney & McGahon) to Dublin or Kilmainham for safe keeping as he cannot think it safe to expose them again either to a repetition of the same acts or to destruction if they should seem disposed to resist them.[74]

A reply stated that Rooney could not be kept in confinement unless by his own consent.

> 4 May 1816. To Samuel Pendleton Esqr. Acknowledging his letter of the 3rd *(sic)* instant and requesting to be informed whether there are any charges against Rooney or McGahon, for if they are merely witnesses, they can not be kept in confinement unless by their own consent.[75]

A further letter to Pendleton, 23 May, acknowledged his observation that there was no need to retain Rooney except to prevail on him the necessity of remaining in some place of security.[76] It is clear from this correspondence that both the families and officialdom feared for the safety of Edward Lynch and Thomas Rooney. The witness McGahon was soon involved in an affray and there is a reference to the information of Terence Cassidy.

> Dundalk. 21 May 1816. From Samuel Pendleton Esqr. Alluding to the circumstances of a daughter of McGahon near Castlebellingham having been seduced by Mr Burr[?]m under circumstances of abominable aggravation and stating that Mr. B. has been daring enough to appear in different places thereabouts for these few days past, and on Sunday evening & yesterday he was at the Inn at Castlebellingham generally in a state of intoxication. This being imprudently told to McG. he went there in a frenzy accompanied by his two sons and a servant, rushed into the room where B: and others were, snapped one pistol and fired another at him, which happily missed, and was then arrested by a Constable but rescued by his sons. The Constable was severely wounded by one of them and a woman slightly in the arm by another. (N.A., Private Official Correspondence, 1815/16) 23 May 1816. To Samuel Pendleton Esqr. Acknowledging his report for week ending the 19th inst., and in reply to his observations relative to Rooney and the other witness, acquainting him that there is no need of retaining them except by prevailing upon them to remain in some place of security, but as he mentions Rooney's having a father in law and uncle who have expressed some anxiety about his safety, perhaps they might be induced to interfere by allowing them money for the subsistence of him and the other witness. Also acknowledging his letter of the 21st inst. relative to the affray at Castle Bellingham and of the copy of Terence Cassidy's information, the persons named in which should be closely watched.[77]

On 5 June 1816 Whitworth, the Lord Lieutenant, sent a long dispatch to Lord Viscount Sidmouth: 'A Statement on the Nature and Extent of the Disturbances which have recently prevailed in *Ireland* and the Measures which have ben adopted by the Government of that Country, in consequence thereof'. In it he expressed the difficulties and fears regarding the safety of prosecutors, witnesses and informers. His statement (with which Judge Fletcher would not be in full agreement!) has much relevance to the case of the prosecution of the first attackers of Wildgoose Lodge and the subsequent tragic fate of the witnesses Edward Lynch and Thomas Rooney:

> There may appear to your Lordship a great disparity in some cases between the number of committals and the number of convictions; and persons unaccquainted with the internal state of this country, may infer that committals too frequently take place without sufficient evidence of guilt against the parties apprehended. No such conclusions, however, (I mean so far as relates to the general practice of the Magistracy to commit suspected persons on slight and insufficient ground) ought to be drawn. The frequent instances which have come to my knowledge, wherein prosecutors and witnesses have been intimidated by the menaces of the friends of the parties deposed against; the experience I have had of the danger to which they, and even their relations, are exposed; of the necessity which in almost every case occurs, that they should quit the place of their birth and residence; of the odium which universally attaches to the name of an informer; compel me to consider the disproportion between the number of committals and convictions in many districts, rather as a proof of the disordered state of society, and of the impediments in the way of the administration of justice, than as a proof of undue precipitancy on the part of the Magistracy, in committing on the suspicion of criminality. I may be allowed here to add, that the danger attendant on the giving of information or evidence was so notorious, and so much impeded the conviction of the guilty at no remote period, that the Legislature found it necessary, with the view of deterring from the murder of witnesses, and of preventing the impunity of the parties against whom those witnesses had deposed, to enact, That if any person having given information upon oath of any offence against the Laws, should be murdered, or forcibly carried away before the trial of the person deposed against, such information on oath should be admitted as evidence on the trial.
> It has been necessary in the disturbed Counties (in most instances of persons having given information on oath, or intending to give evidence upon trial) on account of the serious danger to which such persons are exposed, to remove them to places of security previous to the trials, and ultimately to provide for their removal from their usual abodes. In many cases the witnesses for the Crown have, at their own request, been kept a considerable period prevously to the trial in the gaol of the County, as affording them the best means of protection; in other cases they have been protected in barracks, or brought to Dublin, where however, occasionally, they have not been safe from the hostility of the friends of the parties apprehended. (*Parliamentary Papers: Nature and Extent of the Disturbances in Ireland; Session 1 February 1816 – 2 July 1816*, Vol. ix)

TRIAL OF MICHAEL TIERNAN, PATRICK SHANLEY, AND PHILIP CONLON

Tiernan, Shanley and Conlon were tried at the County Louth summer assizes at Dundalk on 23 July 1816, at which Judge St GeorgeDaly presided. A printed proclamation announced the Grand Jurors:

> County Louth. At a General Assizes & General Gaol Delivery, held at Dundalk, in and for said County on Wednesday the 23rd July 1816. Before the Rt. Hon. St. George Daly, Third Justice, of his Majesty's Court of King's Bench. And the Hon.Robert Day, Second Justice of his Majesty's Court of King's Bench. The following Gentlemen were sworn Grand Jurors:
> 1. Rt. Hon. John Foster, Foreman. 2. Lord Viscount Jocelyn. 3. Rt. Hon. Thos. Henry Foster. 4. Blaney T. Balfour, Esq. 5. Sir Edward Bellew, Bart. 6. Hon. John Jocelyn. 7. Wallop Brabazon, Esq. 8. Matthew Fortescue, Esq. 9. Chichester Fortescue, Esq. 10. Alexander Filgate, Esq. 11. William P. Ruxton, Esq. 12. Nicholas Coddington, Esq. 13. J. F. Ruxton, Esq. 14. John McCintock, Esq. 15. Faithful Fortescue, Esq. 16. Henry Brabazon, Esq. 17. J. W. McNeale, Esq. 18. G. S. Eccleston, Esq. 19. Thomas Tisdall, Esq. 20. F. W. Fortescue, Esq. 21. Robert Thompson, Esq. 22. Philip Pendleton, Esq. 23. Thomas Wm. Filgate, Esq.
> Brabazon Disney Sheils, of Newtown-Darver, Esq. High Sheriff.
> Joseph Booth, of Darver, Gent. Sub Sheriff.
> Dundalk: Joseph Parks, Printer to the Grand Jury of the County of Louth, 1816.[78]

F. Elrington Ball summarises the career of Judge St George Daly in *The Judges in Ireland, 1221-1921*:

> 1801. **St. George Daly** was fifth son of James Daly of Dunsandle in co. Galway and Catherine, daughter of Sir Ralph Gore, baronet, speaker of the house of commons, and sister of Ralph, Earl of Ross; was born about 1757; matriculated in Dublin University 1773; graduated as bachelor of arts 1778; entered Lincoln's Inn 1781; was called to the Irish bar 1783; became member for Galway 1797; was prominent in promoting the union; became prime serjeant and a privy councillor 1799; was appointed a baron of the Exchequer 1801; acted as one of the judges in the trials at Dublin of the participants in Emmet's rebellion 1803; was transferred subsequently to the King's Bench; marrried his cousin, Louisa, daughter of Richard Gore, same year; was one of the judges in the trial of the King v. O'Grady 1816; lost his wife same year; tried Roger O'Connor at Trim, and O Connor's accuser for perjury in Dublin, and obtained an acquittal in both cases, 1817; resigned 1822; resided in Dublin in Rutland-square, and in co. Galway at Eyrecourt; died 1829.[79]

Edward Lynch could not identify any of them at the trial. Perhaps he held back through fear. His son-in-law Thomas Rooney identified three of the party. The *Belfast News Letter*, 2 August 1816, reported on the assizes:

> Philip Finegan, for stealing a bay mare, the property of Patrick Keenan, of Dunleer, on 16 October. Guilty. Death ...
> Michael Tiernan, Patrick Stanley [*Shanley*] and Philip Conlon indicted (under the White Boy Act) of breaking into the dwelling house of Edward Lynch of Rearstown (*Reaghstown*) on 10th April. It appeared by evidence of Linch that a number of persons came to his house that night with guns, broke in the door and asked for arms. Upon being told there were none in the house they destroyed a web in the loom and broke the furniture. Witness knocked one of them down and afterwards defended himself with a pitch-fork and one of them took a lighted coal out of the fire and attempted to set fire to the house. He could not swear to any of their persons. Thomas Rooney who lives with Linch said when the men entered he retreated up to the room where they followed him. He threw himself on a bed when one of them wounded him with a sharp weapon on the back. They then made him go up where Linch was and wanted him to take the pitch-fork from Linch, which Linch refused to give. They then attempted to get up on the loft where Lynch and witness were but Linch kept them down with the fork. Witness identified the three prisoners as being in the party. An alibi was attempted to be proved for the prisoners and it was sworn by their respective witnesses that they were otherwise employed on the night Lynch's house was attacked. Prisoners were all found guilty.

The *Dundalk Examiner*, Saturday, 24 May 1902 (also a summary in the same newspaper 8 October 1881), continuing a series of the 'Burning of Wildgoose Lodge', reprinted an early newspaper report of the trial of Tierney, Shanley and Conlon for feloniously and wilfully assaulting Edmund Lynch and breaking into his house.

> The following was the evidence given:
> **Edward Lynch**, lives at Reaghstown, in the barony of Ardee. Recollects the 10th of April – his being 'racked' on the night. The door was closed before he went to bed. A number of persons came to the house that night with guns, broke in the door, and asked for arms; and upon being told there was none in the house, they destroyed a web which was in the loom, broke the furniture of the house, and one of them said they would take the life of the old villain (meaning witness).
> Witness knocked one of the men down, and afterwards defended himself with a pitchfork. They threatened to set fire to witness's house,

and there being a lighted fire in the house, one of them took a coal out and started to set the house on fire, but was fortunately prevented by some person, as the mark of fire was seen next morning in the thatch. Cannot swear to any of the persons that was there that night.

Thomas Rooney sworn. Knows Edward Lynch – the last witness. Was there in the month of April last. Recollects the night when Lynch's house was attacked. Witness was in a small room in the house; heard a noise on side of the door about the middle of the night, by people wanting to get into the house; the door was broken open. About seven or eight men entered, there were more outside. One man had a bayonet, as he believed. They asked for arms. Witness then retreated up to the room, where they followed him, and witness then threw himself on a bed, and some of them wounded him then with a sharp weapon on the back. They then made him go to where Lynch was, and wanted him to take the pitchfork from Lynch, which Lynch refused to give. They then attempted to get up on the loft, where Lynch and witness were, but Lynch kept them down with the fork. They then proceeded to break the furniture (as described by last witness) and cut the web in the loom. Saw the prisoner Tiernan take a lighted fire in the tongs from the kitchen, which broke and fell from him before he could get it out. Did not hear them say what they would do with the fire. Saw prisoners Conlon and Shanly in Lynch's house that night, and identified them in court. Prisoner Tiernan had the bayonet. There was candle-light in the kitchen that night. Heard the men speak before they came in, knew the prisoner Tiernan's voice.

Here the prosecution closed.

The Defence

Thomas Tiernan sworn. Is father to the prisoner Tiernan. Prisoner lived with witness in April last. Does not know Edward Lynch; heard of his house being attacked on the day following – there was a market in Ardee the day before the attack. Prisoner Tiernan was at witness's house on the Wednesday night Lynch's house was attacked; having got a beating previous day at Ardee so as to render him unable to go out that day or night. Mr Filgate had witness's son arrested next day, Thursday; did not know what he was arrested for, was not told until next day. Witness was up most of that night, being ill of the cholic. His daughter was also up assisting him. His house consists of but one apartment, and his son, the prisoner, went to bed that night at 8 o'clock, and slept the whole night in the house. Witness's son had two black eyes, and his body much abused from the beating he got at Ardee. Was angry with his son for getting into a quarrel, and did not ask what he was taken up for. Thinking it might be for the riot at Ardee. Heard the offence was not bailable. Did not see his son until the Tuesday following. James Breen and Peggy Murphy came home with his son from Ardee the night previous to the transaction.

Thomas Rooney (being again called) described a second time he had seen prisoner at Lynch's house on the night of Wednesday, and did not see him have a black eye or any marks on his face.

James Breen sworn. Knows the night Lynch's house was attacked.

Recollects the day previous to the market of Ardee the prisoner Tiernan being attacked and very much beat and abused by a party of men on his leaving town, and would be beat worse were it not for witness's interference. Came part of the way home with prisoner that night; his face was much disfigured, and had two black eyes. Stopped with prisoner about an hour, at one Peggy Murtagh's where they parted.

Peggy Tiernan is sister to prisoner Michael Tiernan. Her testimony was the very same as that of her father's – in favour of prisoner Tiernan. This witness also proved her applying vinegar and sheep's liver to her brother's eye on his coming from Ardee, much abused as before described, and that she got the vinegar at Mr Reid's house.

Catherine Conlon sworn. Is sister to Philip Conlon, the prisoner; lives at Rathbody with prisoner, her brother. Recollects hearing of the racking of Lynch's house the day after, at about 12 o'clock. Swears positively the prisoner had slept that night in his own house with his wife and children. A stranger having slept in the house that night, and witness did not always on that occasion lock the front door and put the key under her head in the bed; that she did so on that particular night she positively swears, and that she was first up next morning; that her brother nor any other person could not go out without her perceiving him.

Peggy Cawlan sworn. Corroborates the foregoing testimony.

James Shanley was next sworn. Is father to the prisoner. Prisoner lives at Tallanstown with the witness. Has a wife and some small children. Recollects the night Lynch's house was attacked. His son was taken the Friday morning following. He swears that on Wednesday (being the night the mischief was done) his son had gone to bed between the hours of nine and ten o'clock with a young child belonging to him the (prisoner). This witness had been on the watch the whole night, lest his son (the prisoner) might hurt the child. That he (the witness) had called several times during the night without prisoner's knowledge. Lynch's house is three miles from witness's. Was present when his son was taken, but did not see him searched.

Rev. James Marron, PP, being called to give a character, said he knew the prisoners Shanley and Conlon, but did not know Tiernan. Knew Shanley for six years, and Conlon 14 years, and until this last Assizes never heard they had been charged with any crime, but always bore an honest, peaceable and industrious character.

John Reg came to give Tiernan a character; said he (the witness) is steward to Mr H. Foster, and knows prisoner a length of time, who, until this last business, bore an honest, peaceable, and industrious character.

After a long charge from the Judge, the jury retired a few minutes, and brought all the prisoners in guilty; and they were sentenced to be hanged; the sentence was subsequently carried out, and resulted in the burning of Wildgoose Lodge.

The *Dublin Evening Post*, 1 August 1816, stated that it was believed by Dundalk people that Tiernan and Conlon were innocent, that Shanley had sworn that they were not present with him at Lynch's house, and that Lynch wished to retract some of his evidence.

The Correspondent reported on 5 August 1816, 'The following sentences were passed this day (the 27th [July]): Michael Tierney [Tiernan], Patrick Shanley, and Philip Conlon, for the burglary at Wild Goose Lodge on the night of Wednesday the 10th of April, to be hanged. The Judge desired them to prepare, as they had but a short time to live'.

On 3 July 1818 Owen Rickey, otherwise Matthews, and Pat Waters, were indicted for attacking the house of Edward Lynch on 12 April 1816. Alice Rispin was the principal prosecuting witness and gave evidence in much the same terms as her statement to Pendleton above. On the night of the attack she slept in the parlour. The lower part of the house, she said, consisted of three apartments. She saw Rooney after the party left the house. He was wounded. Her evidence continues (account reprinted in the *Dundalk Examiner*, 12 November 1881):

> Identified the prisoners; the prisoner Waters had a lighted candle, and went back and forward through the house; witness was hid so that the party could not see her. When the party went out, they said they would go back and destroy all was in the house – came back and broke all the furniture in the kitchen. She would not lose her life, but did not care what became of her after her son was burned. Knew there were persons tried and convicted for the assault. The first information she gave was against people who threatened her, and when Mr Filgate took down their names, she told him there were four entered there, who were at the first attack on Lynch's house, but that she would not tell who they were till she would see what she could find out about her son.
>
> **William Filgate**, Esq., corroborated Rispen's testimony respecting the time she gave the information; he proved that he was obliged to meet her privately. He explained the situation of Lynch's house, to account for Rispen's being able to distinguish the faces of the prisoners and Lynch not being able to swear to them. He swore there might be a great many in the house who Lynch knew, and from the situation he was placed in, not be able to distinguish them.
>
> Mr Filgate was **cross-examined** at great length by **Mr Scriven** and **Mr O'Hanlon**.
>
> **John Woods**, the gaoler, was brought forward to prove the confession of Rickey, alias Matthews; he took the confession in writing, and gave

it to Mr Pendleton, which could not be produced; of course, the confession fell to the ground. (It should be remarked that it was not from any remissness or neglect in Mr Pendleton that the confession of Matthews could not be produced. Mr Pendleton handed the confession to Sergeant Joy, who conducted all the prosecutions, who, through mistake, took the confession to Dublin in the morning; nothing can, in every instance, be more correct than the conduct of Mr Pendleton has been, since he became chief magistrate of the police of this county.)

Water's brother swore that he was absent from the country for some time, but not in a very satisfactory manner.

The learned **judge** charged the jury at great length, said much in praise of the feeling manner in which Alice Rispen gave her testimony, which in his opinion was quite conclusive. He dwelt much on the steady manner she gave her evidence, and said that, to him, she appeared to speak the truth; at the same time, he said, her not coming forward for such a length of time, might operate against her credit, but that she accounted for in a very satisfactory manner, saying she was afraid of her life. He said if the jury had any doubt in their mind that she might be mistaken to the features of the men, they ought to acquit them; if not, they ought to find them guilty.

The **jury** retired for 58 minutes, and brought in a verdict of acquittal.
Counsel for the crown: Counsellors McCartney, Falls and Staples.
Agents for the crown: Messrs Gordon and Hamilton.
Counsel for the prisoners: J.B. Scriben, Esq., Patrick O'Hanlon, Esq.
Agent: Mr John Byrne.

In his account of the story of Wildgoose Lodge, Mathews, editor of the *Dundalk Examiner*, added some details in his paper of 27 August 1881 about the execution, although he does not give any documented source but quotes a tradition: 'They were hanged in Dundalk opposite the old gaol, now the Exchange. It is said that after they were sentenced Rooney repeated a rash oath he made with regard to the identity of one of them, and their counsel, Mr Perrin, afterwards Judge Perrin, endeavoured to obtain a commutation of sentence and for that purpose went to Downpatrick, where the Judge who tried them was then sitting, but he declined to sign the petition, so the unfortunate men were hanged and buried in the gaol yard; the three were thrown into one pit with nine barrels of lime'.[80]

It was inevitable considering the strength and purpose of the Ribbonmen that revenge would be taken for the hanging of these three men, two of whom, as rumour had it, were regarded as innocent. Any individuals who might offer or agree to give evidence against a member of an agrarian society on behalf of the state would be threatened with torture or death. Edward Lynch in face of threat faltered in giving evidence. Thomas Rooney persevered. The Lord Lieutenant despaired of the attempts on the part of the authorities to gather evidence or protect those who did from the violence of revenge. He wrote to Lord Sidmouth, the home secretary, on 5 June 1816 respecting the Whiteboys in Munster:

> It frequently happened that the sufferers of atrocities ... when visited by a Magistrate, would depose only generally to the fact of their having been perpetrated, and not denying their knowledge of the offenders, would yet steadfastly refuse to disclose their names or describe their persons, from fear of future additional injury to themselves or their relatives. Even where the parties offending were deposed against and apprehended, there was frequently the greatest difficulty in effecting their conviction, from the intimidation of witnesses, and in some cases, of juries ... I fear few instances can be found of late ... in which it has been possible for witnesses, having given evidence in favour of the crown on any trial connected with the disturbance of the Peace, to remain secure in their usual places of abode. ('Statement of the Nature and Extent of the Disturbances Which Have Recently Prevailed in Ireland, and Measures Adopted in Consequence Thereof,' 581).[81]

Lord Liverpool gave his opinion on the salutary effect of the emergency laws in a letter to Peel, 28 June 1816:

> I am happy to find that you have been so successful in your convictions under the special commission. Though it is deadful to think of so many executions as must take place in consequence, yet I am thoroughly persuaded there is no chance of peace for the country except by so extensive an example as cannot fail to strike terror into the minds of the disaffected. It is lamentable that the glory and success of the country, and the total discomfiture of our enemy on the continent, should not have had a sensible effect on the lower classes of the people of Ireland. In truth, Ireland is a political phenomenon – not influenced by the same feelings as appear to affect mankind in other countries - and the singular nature of the disorder must be the cause of why it has hitherto been found impracticable to apply an effectual and permanent remedy.[82]

A presentment of £20 0. 0. was made by the Grand Jury: 'To Edward Lynch and Thomas Rooney, for convicting Michael Tiernan, Patrick Stanley and Philip Conlan, for assaulting the dwelling house of Edward Lynch on the night of the 10th April last, and demanding arms from said Lynch'.[83]

5
The Burning of Wildgoose Lodge

THE BURNING

The burning of Wildgoose Lodge occurred at an early morning hour, perhaps between 1 and 2 a.m. on 30 October 1816. *The Correspondent*, 1 November 1816 and the *Belfast News Letter* of 5 November, reporting similarly and not quite accurately, were quick to put a finger on the motive for the attack and voiced the public revulsion:

> One of those atrocious acts of vengeance, the frequency of which bring shame upon the country, has been committed – under such tremendous circumstances as beggars all the power of words to describe the full enormity.
> A man named Lynchy, and who lived at a place within three miles of Ardee, in the County of Louth, had prosecuted, at the last Assizes for that County, three men who had broken into his house at night. Upon the testimony of Lynchy, and his son-in-law, Rooney, those malefactors, whose names were Tiernan, Shanley and Conlon, were convicted, and suffered death accordingly. Lynchy was aware of the danger to which his own life was exposed, by having brought those housebreakers to justice; but being a man of firm and intrepid character, he resolved not to change his residence, and to defend himself against any violence that might be offered him.
> On Tuesday night last, at the hour of midnight, a body of men, supposed to amount to forty, and well mounted, rode up to his dwelling, which they surrounded, and without a single compunction at the indiscriminate destruction in which they were about to involve so many, they set fire to this unfortunate man's house and destroyed in this diabolical deed, not only Lynchy and his son–in-law Rooney, but his wife, two children, two servant maids, and two young men!! Human nature sickens at the contemplation of such an act of horror, and language sinks under the task of expressing the emotions which it raises. One man is in custody on suspicion of being concerned in this deed of horror.

The Lord Lieutenant and council of Ireland, offering rewards for information, named in a proclamation the eight people who perished.

Whitworth.

Whereas it appears to us, from an Inquisition taken and held before HENRY MUNRO BLACKWELL, Esq., one of the Coroners of the county of Louth, on the bodies of EDWARD LINCH, THOMAS ROONEY, MARGARET ROONEY, PETER ROONEY, JAMES RISPIN, MICHAEL LINCH, BRIDGET RICHARDS and ANN CASSIDY, then deceased, that the same persons were burned to death by some person or persons unknown, having wilfully, wickedly and maliciously, set on fire the House of said Edward Linch, at Wild-Goose Lodge, in the said county, the night of the twenty-ninth day of October last.

Now we the Lord Lieutenant and Council, being determined in so far as in us lies to bring the persons concerned in the said most barbarous and most inhuman outrage, to speedy and condign punishment, do hereby publish and declare, that if any person or persons should, within Six Calendar Months next after the date hereof, discover any of the person or persons concerned therein, so as that he, she, or they be apprehended and prosecuted to conviction for the said offence, such person or persons so discovering the said persons, or any of them, shall receive as a reward the sum of TWO HUNDRED POUNDS for each and every of the persons so apprehended and prosecuted to conviction as aforesaid.

And we do further publish and declare, that if any person or persons shall, within the time aforesaid, discover his, her or their accomplice or accomplices, in the aforesaid outrage, so as that he, she, or they be apprehended, and convicted thereof, such person or persons so discovering shall not only receive the said reward, but shall also receive his Majesty's most gracious pardon for the said offence.

And we do hereby strictly charge and command all Justices of the Peace, Mayors, Sheriffs, Bailiffs, and all other his Majesty's loving subjects, to use their utmost diligence in apprehending the said offenders and every of them.

Given at the Council of Chamber in Dublin, the 18th day of November, 1816 Manners, C. Drogheda.   Norbury. Wm Saurin.   Wm Vesey Fitzgerald. Robert Peel.

God Save the King

The names of all the victims recorded above do not appear in the newspaper recordings of the trials. William Filgate, local landlord, testified in evidence at the subsequent trials that the nearest houses to Wildgoose Lodge were those of two men named Carroll and Halfpenny. Patrick Halfpenny, who lived in a cabin only eighty perches from the lodge, in his evidence at the trial of Patrick Devan identified the victims as follows: Edward Lynch; a son of Lynch [Michael]; Thomas Rooney his son-in-law and his wife Biddy Lynch [Margaret] and their baby son [Peter, variously said to be five and eight months old]; James Rispin, an apprentice to Thomas Rooney; two servant girls [one of whom was named as Biddy Richards by Alice Rispin, mother of James Rispin *i.e.* Bridget Richards, and Ann Cassidy].

John Foster wrote from Collon to Sir Robert Peel on 30 October:

> A most shocking murder of a whole family took place last night at Reaghstown in the Barony of Ardee, about ten miles from hence. Lynch who with his son-in-law Rooney gave testimony against three men, on which they were convicted at last assizes & hung after for breaking into his house & robbing it of fire-arms, were with children & servants, while in their beds, burned to death.
>
> I enclose a letter from the Coroner written to me in great hurry; he will be here in the morning, when I shall send you the Inquest & Finding. His brother, who came with it & was on the jury, tells me the verdict was "Wilful & Malicious Murder of the eight persons by being burned in their house by persons unknown".
>
> I am mortified & ashamed for the Country to have such a barbarity to state to you.
>
> As there is no Map of Louth on sale & you may wish at present to examine it, I take the liberty of requesting you to accept one enclosed herewith.[84]

Townley Patten Filgate, Lowther Lodge, Balbriggan, owner of Wildgoose Lodge, made a few entries in his diary:

> **Thursday October 31st** : I received a letter with an account of the murder of the Linchy family at Reaghstown eight in number, by burning them in their dwelling house Wildgoose Lodge on Tuesday night October 29th.
>
> **Monday November 4th** : I went to the County Louth in consequence of the murder of my tenants at Reaghstown and did not return until Thursday November 14th.[85]

Marianne Fortescue wrote in her diary:

> **Thursday, 31st Octr.** We sat at home all morng – Mr Thursby visited us - Doctr John is here and thank God we are all well – Emily's cold almost gone – we heard of Wild Goose Lodge being burned & eight souls in it - done maliciously – how truly dreadful.[86]

The evidence of William Filgate, Patrick Halfpenny, Alice Rispin and Dr Henry Munro Blackwell, physician and a coroner for County Louth, given on the second day of Louth Assizes, 21 July 1817, at the trial of Patrick Devan, a leader of the local

Ribbonmen, rings authentic. They give a picture of the situation after the burning. I have taken the account mainly from the *Belfast News Letter* of 25 July 1817 with extra detail from *The Correspondent* of 28 July:

At the trial **William Filgate**, esq., magistrate of the county Louth, said that he lived at Lisrenny, County Louth, and knew the farm-house called Wildgoose Lodge. He knew Edward Lynch the occupying tenant thereof. The house was in a peculiarly retired situation, difficult of access in winter, all the passages thereto but one being flooded. There was a trial at the summer assizes 1816 for a burglary and robbery committed at said house in the April preceding, when three prisoners, Conlan, Shanly, and Keenan [*recte* Tiernan] were capitally convicted of the robbery and burglary. He was present at the trial when Lynch and Thomas Rooney had been examined as material witnesses for the Crown. He was also present at the execution of those convicts. After that trial, the gentlemen of the neighbourhood gave Lynch, who was a brave old man, arms to protect himself. He knew Stonetown chapel, about five miles from Wildgoose Lodge to the north-west (NE Correspondent), and Kingscourt, in the county Cavan, about five miles in the opposite direction. The nearest houses to Wildgoose Lodge were those of Carroll and Pat. Halfpenny. Witness went to Lynch's house the day after the burning. Nothing remained but the walls. He saw the fragments of several dead bodies. The bodies were removed. Dr Blackwell, Coroner, held the inquest. On his cross-examination, he said that the former conviction had been for a common burglary. He was not a professional man and could not positively say that the objects he saw at Wildgoose Lodge next morning were dead bodies, except one, in which a small vestige of the human form remained.

William Filgate, reminiscing in an account for his daughter some fifty years later, wrote more colourfully on 11 March 1867. Some of the personal detail he gives of his visit to Wildgoose Lodge on the morning of 30th October is interesting. He has, however, mingled the story of the burning with false details from Carleton and he errs in the persons who died – correctly, one daughter of Lynch and two servant girls died.

Mr Philip [*recte* Samuel] (uncle to Mr Pendleton of Trim) was Resident Magistrate, & had under him 50 mounted police who kept vigilant guard. However, quite unknown to them, on the 16th October [*recte* 30 October] 1816, some 300 [!] Ribbonmen from Cavan, Meath, Monaghan & Louth met at the Reaghstown Chapel, & were sworn there, marched to Wildgoose, surrounded the house & set fire to it. Lynch fired out twice, but without effect. Mrs Rooney had a baby in her arms, & she threw it out of the house, imploring the wretches to save its life, but Devaun, the leader, flung it back into the flames on a pitch fork saying: "We'll burn the nit along with the lice".

The next morning, Bob Shiels my father's steward, came over from Lisrenny to Kiltibegs (Co. Monaghan), where I then lived, to tell me & I rode off at once to Wildgoose. The police had possession of the place by that time & had taken out of the ruin 8 bodies, of Lynch, his two daughters, Rooney & his two children, James Rispin, a servant boy and a young servant girl. They were so charred as to be past recognition, but James Rispin's mother identified her son by a mole on the right hip, the body being fallen on that side.[87]

The Correspondent 28 July 1817:

Patrick Halfpenny sworn –Lives in Reaghstown; knows where Lynch's house is; witness's house is about eighty perches distant from it; remembers the night of the burning; he was in bed; he was awakened by a man at the door desiring him to open it; he did so; and two men came in and asked if he had any fire in the house; he went over and rooted a coal out of the ashes, his wife attempted to prevent him, but they threatened her, and went away. In about two hours after he heard a noise of horses' feet passing; looked out of the door and discovered Lynch's house on fire; he went to his neighbour, Thomas Carroll, and told him of it; on his return a voice cried out, directed to both of them, to shut their doors, and they (the party) would not take their lives. Witness knew Lynch's family, which generally consists of Lynch, Rooney, James Rispin, a servant boy, Rooney's wife and child, two servant girls, and also a son of Lynch's. Rooney was married to Lynch's daughter; witness was acquainted with them all, and never saw any of them since that night. In about ten minutes after witness ventured out again; called his neighbour, and went to Lynch's house; all was burned, the roof had fallen in, and nothing remained, but the walls and a few old rafters. When people arrived shortly after, he saw some dead bodies carried out, but could not take on himself to say whose they were.

Cross examined – Was not in Lynch's house the evening before; only knew that the family generally consisted of those he mentioned; heard no shouts or cheers, only shots; his house, however, is eighty perches distant.

The version in *Belfast News Letter*, 25 July, adds that, when Halfpenny's wife refused to give out fire, one of the men told her he would drag her out of the house and kill her, if she should say one word; they set a guard on his house and desired him to go to bed; he heard a noise about the door, and sometime afterwards heard four shots fired, and subsequently heard the noise of horses passing by. He was the first to go to Lynch's house the next morning, with Kinahan; the house had been in a good state the day before, was continuing to burn when witness first went there the next morning.

> **Alice Rispin sworn** – James Rispin is her son; he is dead; he was bound to Rooney who lived at Lynch's house, for three years; he came home to her from Lynch's house after the first attack was made on it, and remained with her until about a week before the burning, when he returned; she went to the house the morning after the fire. And saw eight bodies laid at the door; knew two of them; one was Biddy Lynch, daughter to Lynch, and the other her son, whom, she said, she knew by some marks on his body from the time he was born, and which were at that time visible to her.

Belfast News Letter, 25 July: Her son had been bound to Rooney for three years; he came home to her about three weeks before the burning, and returned there the night of the burning; she saw eight corpses burned of which one was her son and Biddy Richards, a servant of Lynch's, another. Cross-examined: Lived about a mile from Lynch's across the bog; left her son on Tuesday morning, and found him dead next morning; knew him by his feet and a mark on his cheek.

> **Doctor Blackwell sworn** – Is a physician, also a coroner for the county; went to Lynch's house the morning after it was burnt; it was all in ruins; there were eight dead bodies lying in front of the house when he arrived; he had no doubt but one of them was Lynch – they had been consumed by the fire.

Belfast News Letter, 25 July (and *The Times*, 1 August 1817) gives the coroner's full name as Henry Munro Blackwell: he found the house burned; the fire was not entirely out; saw eight bodies and examined them all; knew Lynch long before this; saw him there dead; knew him and Biddy Richards.

Shock, fear and horror are expressed in the letters of the

magistrates to Dublin Castle.
Samuel Pendleton. Glyde Farm. 9 o'clock, Wednesday night, 30 October 1816.

> I have this day witnessed a most horrible confirmation of the opinion I had last night the honor to state to you of the disposition of the Barony of Ardee etc.
> In the morning I got from Mr Fortescue the note which I inclose; on my arrival at unfortunate Lynch's house, I found his report more than verified. *Eight* persons had fallen victims of this unexampled outrage; among them Lynch and Rooney, the rest the other members of the family; the house (as it seems) was surrounded by a large body of men, about 2 o'clock this morning; the family was kept in, and the house set fire to by large heaps of straw about it. The bodies are so far consumed as to be barely distinguishable from each other. Nothing material came out on the inquest. I have taken up Tiernan (the father of the man hanged) and a brother of his. There are some circumstances of suspicion which attach to them, and they are of infamous character. But from what yet appears, I fear that any evidence to affect them is rather to be hoped for, than expected.
> Nothing within my power to be done shall be omitted.[88]
> CHICHESTER FORTESCUE'S NOTE TO PENDLETON. GLYDE FARM. WEDNESDAY MORNING. 8 O'CLOCK:
> I have this moment been told by Robt. Shiels, Filgate's man, that Lynch's house has been burnt, and in it, Lynch, Rooney, his wife, two children and a boy!!!
> As to particulars, I have not time to ascertain them, but think it better to inform you at once.

Rev. George Lambart, Glebe Hill, also wrote on 30 October 1816, but it is clear that he had not as yet obtained the facts.

> As I am not certain that Mr Gregory may return to town tomorrow, I trouble you with this letter, to inform you that, the consequence of its having been reported that the Magistrates of this County had memorialed the Lord Lieutenant to withdraw the operation of the Peace Preservation Bill, has been, as I ever suspected, that last night the house of the person who prosecuted the three men who attacked Mr Filgate's shepherd's house last winter & who were hanged since at Dundalk was burned & seven lives lost but, fortunately the Prosecutor was not amongst the members.
> I thought it important to make this report to Government as soon as I could, in order to *meet* the memorial.[89]

On 31 October 1816 Foster in Collon forwarded to Peel copies of the verdict and examinations taken by Dr Blackwell, coroner at the inquest (N.A., SOC /1763/36). Unfortunately these are now missing from the files.

Peel, not yet briefed in the full facts, wrote in private from Dublin Castle to Lord Sidmouth on 1 November 1816:

> I do not often trouble you with the detail of individual outrages – but one has been committed in the County of Louth of so atrocious a nature that I cannot help reporting it to you.
> On the night of Tuesday last the house of a person who had prosecuted capitally to conviction three persons at the last Louth Assizes was set on fire by a number of armed men who prevented the escape of the inmates of it – and actually consigned to the flames a family of eight persons five of whom were children.
> This abominable outrage was committed in the barony of Ardee in the County of Louth. It is entirely to be attributed to revenge against the prosecutor – and is but one of many proofs of the wretched depravity and sanguinary disposition of the lower orders of this country.[90]

Pendleton wrote from Dundalk to Dublin Castle, 1 November 1816, regarding the confession of one, Kelly, giving names of people who had earlier plotted against Lynch, and narrated attempted escapes at Dundalk gaol.

> I have it not in my power to communicate anything material on the subject of my last. I am endeavouring by various clues to reach some . . . & in that may produce effect.
> One of the convicts (Kelly) whose confession I before submitted to you, has further informed me, that a few nights after I had apprehended the three men who were hanged for the original attack on Lynch, all the others who had been at it (of whom he, Kelly, was one) assembled together, and swore to each other that if they suffered, they would 'put to death the witnesses, and *burn them, and theirs to ashes*'. He has given me the names of all these persons. This is most material, though I must observe that this Kelly is not the man on whose confession I was disposed to rely. In a few days it will probably be expedient to have many persons apprehended on suspicion, or defective information. If a conditional pardon was held out, I think it would be likely to produce effect somewhere.
> The *fourth* attempt to break this Gaol has this day in part succeeded. Three of the convicts for transportation had taken advantage of an unguarded moment ... door, knocked down the gaoler and sentry, dreadfully wounding the former and taking his arms from the other, and got ... off. The streets were crowded from it being a Holy Day and the people favored their escape. They were all however taken, and brought back in ten minutes. One of them who had knocked down the soldier, and had his bayonet, was pursued by my servant *unarmed*, knocked down, and taken. The audacity of their conduct when

brought back is scarcely conceivable. This, added to the repeated and desperate efforts they have made, seems to call for serious example. And I would presume it will be proper to lay detainers on them to abide their Tryals for breaking of prison at the next Assizes. A Court Martial on the *two* sentries at the gaol door has very properly been ordered.[91]

On 2 November 1816 *The Correspondent* returned to the subject republishing from the *Newry Telegraph* of 1 April 1816 the account of the first attack and bringing its readers up to date with the latest news of the burning from the *Newry Telegraph*, which gave an accurate list (though without all the names) of those who died including a little detail on the unnamed farm labourer, 'a poor labourer who had been hired to assist in digging out potatoes.'

REACTION OF THE MAGISTRATES

As early as 16 December 1815 John Bourne, Clerk of the Peace, Dundalk, wrote to John Foster at Collon, summoning him to 'an Extraordinary Session of the Peace under the Statute of the 54th George III ... at the Courthouse of Dundalk'.[92] On 6 January 1816 he wrote again to Foster summoning him to a meeting of magistrates on 12 January 'to consider of that part of the County now apparently disturbed and to take measures accordingly under the Insurrection Act'.[93] On 12 March 1816 the Proclamation of Lord Lieutenant Whitworth was issued enforcing the Peace Preservation Act in the baronies of Upper Dundalk, Lower Dundalk, Ardee and Louth':

> (Signed) *Whitworth*
> WHEREAS by an Act of Parliament passed in the fifty-fourth year of His present Majesty, intitled, "An Act to provide for the better execution of the Laws in Ireland, by appointing superintending Magistrates and additional Constables in Counties, in certain cases", it is amongst other things Enacted, That it shall be lawful for the Lord Lieutenant, or other chief Governor or Governors of Ireland for the time being, by the advice of the Privy Council of Ireland, to declare by proclamation, that any county, county of a city, or county of a town in Ireland, or any barony or baronies, or half-barony or half-baronies in any county at large, to be therein specified, is or are in a state of disturbance, and requires or require an extraordinary establishment of police.
> And whereas it hath sufficiently appeared to Us, that the barony or half-barony of Upper Dundalk, the barony or half-barony of Lower

Dundalk, and the baronies of Ardee and Louth in the county of Louth, are in a state of disturbance, and require an extraordinary establishment of police.

Now We the Lord lieutenant, by and with the advice of His Majesty's Privy Council, by virtue of the said Act and of the powers thereby vested in Us, do by this our Proclamation declare, that the said barony or half-barony of Upper Dundalk, the barony or half-barony of Lower Dundalk, and the baronies of Ardee and Louth in the county of Louth, in this part of the United Kingdom called Ireland, are in a state of disturbance, and require an extraordinary establishment of police.

Given at the Council Chamber in Dublin, the 12th day of March 1816.

(Signed) Wm Downes   Manners, C.
          George Hewett   Erne
          Wm Saurin   Frankfort de Montmorency
          Castlecoote

GOD Save the KING

Attention has already been drawn to the long report, dated 5 June 1816, from Whitworth to Sidmouth on disturbances in Ireland, and printed in *Parliamentary Reports: Session 1 February 1816 – 2 July 1816* (Vol. ix). A small section deals with County Louth. It indicates that the Peace Preservation Act was enforced in those baronies of County Louth listed in the proclamation following a memorial from twenty-seven magistrates of the county. This memorial must have been drawn up at the meeting of magistrates on 12 January 1816. It states:

> In the course of the present year, the Insurrection Act has not been enforced in any new instance. In the month of March, in consequence of a Memorial from twenty-seven Magistrates of the county of Louth, a Special Magistrate with fifty Constables was appointed, for the purpose of assisting them to maintain the Peace in four baronies (Upper & Lower Dundalk, Ardee and Louth) of that County.
>
> Various acts of outrage were committed in these baronies about this period. In the course of one week, eleven houses in the neighbourhood of Dundalk were plundered of arms. The house and offices of a farmer, who had prosecuted some persons, by whom he had been robbed and nearly murdered, were wilfully set on fire and consumed. A party of armed persons, reported to be not less than two hundred in number, attacked the house of another individual, and entered it, after meeting with considerable resistance; after wounding very seriously the owner and two other inhabitants of the house, they compelled him to deliver his arms, and to take an oath that he would give up his farm.[94]

This report was followed by some statistics of crime in County Louth, which does not seem to be complete. In 1813 three people who had been involved with several others in attacking the 'Newry Fly' and killing the coachman and wounding others were convicted of murder. In 1814 of three people prosecuted for robbing arms, one was convicted and two were acquitted; one person was accused of attacking a house with others as White Boys and was acquitted. In 1815 two people were prosecuted for murder and were acquitted. In 1816 two people were prosecuted for murder and were acquitted; one person was convicted for attempted murder; one person was convicted of attacking a house with others as White Boys; one person was convicted of compelling a farmer to quit the land.

In August 1816 Peel wrote to Sidmouth informing him that Ireland was relatively tranquil and that there were fewer acts of violence though the condition of the 'lower classes' was no better.[95] By October 1816 it was thought that the situation had calmed sufficiently for on 15 October John Bourne at William Street, Dublin, wrote to Foster informing him that he had received a requisition to call a Session for 28 October 'to consider the State of the Baronies of Ardee and Louth'.[96] It is ironic then that on the day before the burning of Wildgoose Lodge on the night of 29-30 October 1816, a number of magistrates, no doubt unhappy with the local financial burden of the Peace Act, met at Ardee and directed a letter to the Lord Lieutenant requesting these baronies to be exempted from the Police Establishment, a withdrawal of the police on the grounds that peace had been restored. John Foster and Samuel Pendleton were not in agreement with it.

Foster wrote to the Rt Hon. Robert Peel:

> Collon. Oct. 28. 1816.
> A meeting of Magistrates was held this day at Ardee & I had the honor of taking the Chair as the oldest magistrate.
> I enclose in consequence a Memorial which you will have the goodness to lay before his Excellency the Lord Lieutenant.
> It was my misfortune from the sentiment I entertain of the state of the country, not to be able to persuade myself to join in the opinion it expresses or in the prayer it concludes with. My signature therefore is not to it; neither is that of Mr Jocelyn or Mr Henry Brabazon or Mr Samuel Pendleton who were also present.
> TEXT
> We the undersigned Magistrates of the County of Louth assembled at Ardee on Monday the 28th day of October 1816, pursuant to a notice

beg leave to represent to Your Excellency that it is our opinions that the Baronies of Ardee and Louth (except the parish of Louth, part of the said Barony of Louth) are restored to peace and good order and pray that the said Baronies with the exception as aforesaid be exempted from the Police establishment.

Edwd Bellew, W.P. Ruxton, John McClintock, A. Thompson, Chi: Fortescue, Jos. Wright, Fitzherbert Ruxton, Will: Filgate Jr, Faith: Fortescue, Phil. Pendleton, B. Balfour [97]

Samuel Pendleton, Chief Magistrate, Louth, wrote to Peel from Dundalk on 29 October 1816, reporting some outrages and also giving the background to the Ardee meeting of magistrates:

> I have the honor to report, that on Saturday night last a quantity of wheat in stack & also several cocks of hay, the property of Mr Neal McCann of Knockbridge, in the Barony of Louth, were maliciously destroyed by persons unknown. In the month of June last, a haggard of corn of considerable value, belonging to the same person, was maliciously burnt.
>
> I have further to inform you, that a Special Sessions of the Peace were yesterday held in Ardee, for the purpose of taking into consideration the state of the baronies of Louth, and it (;) Fifteen magistrates attended of whom eleven signed a memorial to his Excellency to exempt them (except the *parish* of Louth), from the effects of his proclamation.
>
> It is to be observed that Fourteen magistrates residing in the other baronies of the District and neighbourhood of Dundalk, not having received notice, did not attend. It is my duty to state, that although some parts of those Baronies, comparatively small however in their extent, have been free from actual disturbance, yet outrages to a greater number have taken place, and as far as I am capable of judging, a greater tendency to outrage now exists in them than in either of the other Baronies of which this district is composed.
>
> Of the six men capitally convicted here the last assizes, five were from the Baronies of Ardee and Louth. That the robbing of the house of Mr Atkinson of Channel Rock (on 26th Septr) for arms, and the matter at Knockbridge now mentioned, should be the only acts of outrage which have for some weeks occurred in them, I cannot consider a sufficient test of a return to peace and good order, while it is matter of notoriety that a considerable quantity of arms remains in their possession concealed; and while the original spirit of their association continues so strongly to actuate them, that no *young* man who is not a member of it, can venture to any of their publick meetings (patrons, funerals etc etc) or be out at night, without the probability of violent abuse. The conduct of this Establishment continues satisfactory. [98]

On Friday 1 November Foster wrote to Chichester Fortescue

informing him that he intended in the first instance to call a meeting of the magistrates 'to settle and arrange what should be proposed to a general meeting of the Gentry'.[99]

Meeting of Magistrates, 4 November 1816, Dundalk

On Monday 4 November 1816 Foster forwarded to Peel, from Collon, a copy of the memorial of a meeting of the magistrates of Louth.[100] The memorial expressed horror at the outrage at Wildgoose Lodge and listed subscriptions for obtaining information that would lead to the discovery and prosecution of 'those concerned in this terrific crime'. Marianne Fortescue was in Dundalk that day. She wrote in her diary:

> **Wednesday morning, 6th Novr.** On Monday Lady E. McC came about twelve oclock – she & I went to Dundalk in my carriage – there was a large gathering of magistrates here to talk over the horrid business at Wild Goose Lodge – Col. Foster & the two Faithfuls call'd here before I set out & a number visited the girls in my absence – Doctr John dined with J Woolsey yesterday. I sat working all day – the Foster girls visited & Mr Thursby - we dined at Drumcar – Sir Robt & Lady Trench are there – we got home safe a little after eleven – the weather very mild & fine.[101]

Foster wrote:

> I enclose a copy of the proceedings of the Magistrates this day & I have the satisfaction of informing you that there was no dissentient voice. Of those who signed the Memorial on Monday last, all except one, the Rev. Mr Wright, who was not present today, have joined in soliciting to continue the police in the Barony of Ardee & Louth, which they then wished to be discontinued. You will observe that they have desired a Sessions to be held under the Insurrection Act & we have desired the Clerk of the Peace to summon one for Saturday next. The object is to obtain a Proclamation for putting a part of the country under the Insurrection Act 54 G. 3 c 180 for which the disposition is very general. As to rewards you will see that our subscription has begun liberally & we mean to circulate it among all ranks that they may shew us their feelings.
>
> The anxiety for the Insurrection Act is much promoted by the language of numbers, who openly say the unfortunate men who were burned deserved their fate, & by the general belief that one at least if not two of our Magistrates are marked by the illegal associations for assassination.
>
> I wish much to know your feelings & that of Government on the subject before we meet next Saturday if you will entrust me with them in

CASTLEBELLINGHAM, *November* 4, 1816.

At a Meeting of the Magistrates of Louth, called by the Governors of the County.

Right Hon. JOHN FOSTER, in the Chair.

Lord Jocelyn,
Right Hon. Thomas H. Foster,
Honourable John Jocelyn,
Blaney Balfour,
Sir Edward Bellew,
Francis Tipping,
Wallop Brabazon,
John M'Clintock,
Robert Thompson,
Chichester Fortescue,
Lenox Bigger,
Mathew Fortescue,
Samuel Pendleton,

Fitzherbert Ruxton,
William P. Ruxton,
Reverend Doctor Little,
Alexander Dawson,
Neal Mc.Neal,
Hugh Moore,
James Read,
John Dawson,
George Evans,
F. W. Fortescue,
Faithful Fortescue,
William Filgate,
Philip Pendleton.

The following Resolutions were unanimously agreed to :—

THAT a Crime barbarous beyond the power of Expression, and scarcely credible to have been committed within the precincts of a Country deemed civilized ; appears to have been perpetrated at Reaghstown, in the Barony of Ardee, within this County, during the Morning of the 30th October last ; by the deliberate and systematic Assault, of a number of Persons upon the House of Edward Lynch, and the wilful burning of the same —consuming no less than Eight Persons, including three Women and one Child.

THAT it appears the same House had been attacked and broken into, in the course of the last Spring, and that the unfortunate Lynch, supported by the evidence of his Son-in-Law, Rooney, had appealed at the last Assizes to the Laws of his Country, for the protection of himself and Family, and had manfully discharged his bounden Duty to the Country that gave him birth ; in prosecuting to conviction, three of the Robbers that had attempted to plunder his House of Arms.

THAT this horrid and never to be forgotten Crime, staining the annals of our Country, has resulted from a system of illegal association, united by oaths of secrecy and obedience.

THAT it does appear the ordinary Laws of a free Country, calculated to be met and forwarded by a People impressed with a due sense of moral and religious Feeling, are not those adapted to contend with Crimes such as the present one ; unknown but to the savage Tribes of Indians when in open War.

THAT not having witnessed that general feeling of indignation, which such an atrocious act was calculated to call forth in aid of the Magistracy, a Special Sessions of the Peace be appointed to be held, in pursuance of the Insurrection Act, on the speediest day ; and that we solicit a continuation of the operation of the Police Act of the 54th of the King, within the Baronies of Ardee and Louth.

THAT application be made to the Lord Lieutenant, to offer such Rewards for the apprehending and convicting of the Persons concerned, together with such offers of pardon, as may by His Majesty's Government be deemed expedient.

THAT Subscriptions be immediately entered into, for the purpose of procuring such Information as may lead to a Discovery, and to the Prosecuting to Conviction of those concerned in this terrific Crime.

THAT the Right Hon. JOHN FOSTER, be requested to communicate to Mr. PEEL, the result of this Meeting.

JOHN FOSTER.

THAT the Sheriff be requested to call a Meeting of the County, for the purpose of communicating to them the foregoing Resolutions, on the earliest day most convenient.

JOHN FOSTER.

WE, the undersigned, severally agree to pay the Sums subscribed with our Names, in order to form a fund, for the purpose of obtaining Information and Prosecuting to Conviction the Persons concerned in the late horrid and atrocious Outrage at Reaghstown.

JOHN FOSTER,	£50	JOHN M'CLINTOCK,	£50	Rev. Doctor LITTLE,	£50	WILLIAM FILGATE,	£50
JOCELYN,	50	ROBERT THOMPSON,	50	ALEXANDER DAWSON,	50	PHILIP PENDLETON,	50
THOMAS HENRY FOSTER,	50	CHICHESTER FORTESCUE	50	NEAL MC.NEAL,	20	FITZHERBERT RUXTON,	50
JOHN JOCELYN,	50	FAITHFUL FORTESCUE,	50	HUGH MOORE,	10	NICHOLAS CODDINGTON,	50
BLAYNEY BALFOUR,	50	LENOX BIGGER,	50	JAMES READ,	10	HENRY CODDINGTON,	50
EDWARD BELLEW,	50	SAMUEL PENDLETON,	50	JOHN DAWSON,	10	TOWNLEY P. FILGATE,	50
FRANCIS TIPPING,	50	MATHEW FORTESCUE,	50	GEORGE EVANS,	20		
WALLOP BRABAZON,	50	W. P. RUXTON,	50	F. W. FORTESCUE,	50		

confidence.

I shall be in Dublin tomorrow to attend a Linen Board & remain next day & I will call at the Castle on the chance of you being in town and at leisure.[102]

This is the text of the meeting of the magistrates in Dundalk on 4 November 1816:

At a Meeting of the Magistrates of Louth, called by the Governors of the County.
Right Hon. John Foster in the Chair.
Lord Jocelyn, Right Hon. Thomas H. Foster, Honourable John Jocelyn, Blaney Balfour, Sir Edward Bellew, Francis Tipping, Wallop Brabazon, John McClintock, Robert Thompson, Chichester Fortescue, Lenox Bigger, Matthew Fortescue, Samuel Pendleton, Fitzherbert Ruxton, William P. Ruxton, Reverend Doctor Little, Alexander Dawson, Neal McNeal, Hugh Moore, James Read, John Dawson, George Evans, F. W. Fortescue, Faithful Fortescue, William Filgate, Philip Pendleton.
The following Resolutions were unanimously agreed to –
THAT a Crime, barbarous beyond the power of Expression, and scarcely credible to have been committed within the precincts of a country deemed civilized, appears to have been perpetrated at Reaghstown, in the barony of Ardee, within this county, during the morning of the 30th October last, by the deliberate and systematic assault of a number of persons upon the house of Edward Lynch, and the wilful burning of the same, consuming no less than eight persons, including three women and one child.
THAT it appears the same house had been attacked and broken into in the course of the last Spring, and that the unfortunate Lynch, supported by the evidence of his son-in-law Rooney, had appealed at the last assizes to the laws of his country for the protection of himself and family, and had manfully discharged his bounden duty to the country that gave him birth; in prosecuting to conviction three of the robbers that had attempted to plunder his house of arms.
THAT this horrid and never to be forgotten crime, staining the annals of our country, has resulted from a system of illegal association, united by oaths of secrecy and obedience.
THAT it does appear the ordinary laws of a free country, calculated to be met and forwarded by a people impressed with a due sense of moral and religious feeling, are not those adapted to contend with crimes such as the present one, unknown but to the savage tribes of Indians when in open war.
THAT not having witnessed that general feeling of indignation, which such an atrocious act was calculated to call forth in aid of the magistracy, a Special Sessions of the Peace be appointed to be held in pursuance of the Insurrection Act, on the speediest day; and that we solicit a continuation of the operation of the Police Act of the 54th of the King, within the baronies of Ardee and Louth.

THAT application be made to the Lord Lieutenant, to offer such rewards for the apprehending and convicting of the persons concerned, together with such offers of pardon, as may by His Majesty's Government, be deemed expedient.

THAT subscriptions be immediately entered into, for the purpose of procuring such information as may lead to a discovery, and to the prosecuting to conviction of those concerned in this terrific crime.

THAT the Right Hon. John Foster be requested to communicate to Mr Peel the result of this meeting.

JOHN FOSTER

THAT the Sheriff be requested to call a meeting of the county, for the purpose of communicating to them the foregoing Resolutions, on the earliest day most convenient.

JOHN FOSTER

WE, the undersigned, severally agree to pay the sums subscribed with our names, in order to form a fund, for the purpose of obtaining information and prosecuting to conviction the persons concerned in the late horrid and atrocious outrage at Reaghstown. [103]

All the magistrates present at the meeting signed the memorandum each giving a subscription of £50. Three others later signed it giving a like subscription, namely, Nicholas Coddington, Henry Coddington and Townley P. Filgate.

Subsequently advertisements appeared in the newspapers announcing the proposed rewards.

The Magistrates of the County of Louth offer the following Rewards, to be paid by John Stratton, Esq. Dundalk, Treasurer to the Fund, raised by Subscription for discovering and bringing to punishment the Perpetrators of the late horrid Murders at Reaghstown, in this County, on the 30th of October last.

A Reward of FOUR HUNDRED POUNDS, to the Person who shall give the first information against any one concerned in the late horrible Murders at Reaghstown, so as he be prosecuted and convicted thereof.

Four Rewards of TWO HUNDRED POUNDS each, to each of the four Persons who shall next inform against any Persons so concerned so as they be prosecuted and convicted.

A Reward of FIFTY POUNDS, to each Person who shall inform against any further or other Persons so concerned, after the foregoing five Informations shall have been made, so as such further or other Person be prosecuted to conviction.

Rewards of TWENTY-FIVE POUNDS each, for Private Information leading to the discovery, apprehension or conviction of any Person concerned in planning, concerting, or perpetrating the said Outrage and Murders, or being in any way accessory thereto, and a strict secrecy will be observed.

The Magistrates of the Head Office of Police, in Dublin, have given

> Notice by advertisement in the *Hue and Cry*, that if any Person shall within six Calendar Months, from 1st Nov. inst. apprehend and prosecute to conviction any of the Persons concerned in said Outrage, they shall receive a Reward of £50 for each so apprehended and convicted, and that they will give a further Reward of £20, for any Information leading to the apprehension and conviction of any of the Persons concerned.[104]

On 4 November Foster wrote to Brabazon Disney Sheils, High Sheriff of Louth, inviting him to a meeting of the magistrates and asking him to call a 'Meeting of the County on the earliest day most convenient ... '.[105] John Bourne promptly on 5 November sent out the necessary notice to call the Gentry session.[106]

Meeting of the Magistrates, 9 November 1816, Castlebellingham
Meeting of the County Gentry, 11 November 1816, Dundalk

A second meeting of the magistrates took place in Castlebellingham on 9 November. Twenty magistrates were present - John Foster, Jocelyn, T.H. Foster, John Jocelyn, John McClintock, Francis Tipping, W.P. Ruxton, William Filgate, Philip Pendleton, Chichester Fortescue, W. Brabazon, Faithful Fortescue, F.W. Fortescue, Charles Eastwood, Townley P. Filgate, Joseph Wright, James Forde, John Dawson, Fitzherbert Ruxton, Matthew Fortescue. They unanimously signed a memorial to the Lord Lieutenant calling for the proclamation of the four baronies of Ardee, Louth, Upper Dundalk and Lower Dundalk to be in a state of disturbance, thus evoking a measure of the Insurrection Act.

> We the magistrates of the County of Louth, summoned by due letter to attend an extraordinary Session of the Peace, to consider the state of this county, feel it our duty to lay before your Excellency by this Memorial signed by us, that we consider the Baronies of Ardee, Louth, Upper Dundalk and Lower Dundalk, to be in immediate danger of becoming in a state of disturbance; and we pray that your Excellency & Council may proclaim the said baronies to be in such immediate danger & we annex hereto many grounds & reasons of such our opinion.

Grounds and Reasons for our Opinion:

REWARDS.

The Magistrates of the County of Louth offer the following Rewards, to be paid by John Stratton, Esq. Dundalk, Treasurer to the Fund, raised by Subscription for discovering and bringing to punishment the Perpetrators of the late horrid Murders at Reaghstown, in this County, on the 30th of October last.

A REWARD OF

Four Hundred Pounds,

To the Person who shall give the first information against any one concerned in the late horrible Murders at Reaghstown, so as he be prosecuted and convicted thereof.

FOUR REWARDS OF

Two Hundred Pounds each,

To each of the four Persons who shall next inform against any Persons so concerned so as they be prosecuted and convicted.

A REWARD OF

Fifty Pounds,

To each Person who shall inform against any further or other Persons so concerned, after the foregoing five Informations shall have been made, so as such further or other Person be prosecuted to conviction.

REWARDS OF

Twenty-five Pounds each,

For Private Information leading to the discovery, apprehension or conviction of any Person concerned in planning, concerting, or perpetrating the said Outrage and Murders, or being in any way accessory thereto, and a Strict secrecy will be observed.

The MAGISTRATES of the Head Office of Police, in Dublin, have given Notice by advertisement in the *Hue and Cry*, that if any Person shall within six Calendar Months, from 1st Nov. inst. apprehend and prosecute to conviction any of the Persons concerned in said Outrage, they shall receive a Reward of £50 for each so apprehended and convicted, and that they will give a further Reward of £20, for any Information leading to the apprehension and conviction of any of the Persons concerned.

Having laid before the Lord Lieutenant, in March last, the state of four baronies in this county, His Excellency was graciously pleased immediately to take our request into consideration, & extended the provisions of the Police Act 54 G.3 c. 131 to them. Yet, notwithstanding the unwearied exertions of a most active, able & spirited magistrate, supported by a zealous, well-regulated police, of which he is the head, & vigorously aided by the resident magistrates, the tranquillity of the country has not been secured; on the contrary, the proceedings at a meeting of magistrates last Monday, which we annex hereto, shew that the spirit of insurrection has not been subdued, but still exists & we cannot but apprehend that the approach of the long nights of winter will encourage it to break out into encreased acts of violence & outrage. That we consider the Police Act to entrust the Government with very wise & salutary means of assisting the magistracy with extraordinary powers for supporting the laws; but it will be inadequate to restore the tranquillity of the country, & secure it against insurrection & disturbance, unless the provisions of the Insurrection Act 54 G. 3 c. 180 be also extended by Government to the four baronies where the Police Act is in operation.

That we cannot expect information to enable us to act with effect, nor evidences to come forward voluntarily, while the system of intimidation, which is one object of the illegal associations in those baronies, & many parts of the adjoining counties, not only exists, but must receive encreased strength from the late barbarous murder of a prosecutor Lynch, & his witness Rooney, with their families, unless we are enabled to counteract that intimidation & those associations by the provisions of the Insurrection Act.

(1) That this late outrage was committed by persons collected from various & distant quarters; that in one direction fifteen horses, each with double riders, were seen moving towards the place where Lynch lived, at a late hour of the night.

(2) That a considerable number of men had also approached from an opposite quarter by a boat.

(3) That after the perpetration of the act they had separated in small parties on their return to the places where they had assembled.

(4) That they were observed in different places, where they called for refreshment, to be armed.

That a general apathy has manifested itself in the mass of the inhabitants, on a transaction which must naturally be expected to excite horror, and call forth the exertions of every man to bring the perpetrators to justice.

That in some instances an appearance even of exultation has shewn itself.

(5) That a Magistrate has been cursed & threatened from an opinion of his active disposition against them.

(6) That there is reason to believe the bodies of Rooney, who gave evidence, and his child, were hindered by the influence of terror from been waked in the Roman Catholic Chapel, as the bodies of the other unfortunate sufferers were.

> That a Notice has been posted up in two different places, denouncing vengeance & destruction 'to any person who should pray for the souls of the "sufferers"'.
> (7) That this horrible murder appeared by the evidence taken before the Coroner & the Inquest, then found to have been committed under the influence & by the means of unlawful associations bound together by oaths for the purpose of outrage and assassination.
> That a part of the system on which they act appeared to be a determination to enforce secrecy & obedience to their rules by the terror of assassination & destruction of the property of those who either have or are suspected of having transgressed their regulations & to extend that terror to all who may shew, or be supposed to entertain any disposition to suppress them, or bring them to justice.[107]

A further nine magistrates added their signatures at a county meeting in Dundalk on 11 November. This frenzied activity brought forth a flurry of letters from John Foster and Samuel Pendleton to Peel.[108]

Foster to Peel. Collon. 10 November 1816.

> I enclose the result of our meeting of the Magistrates yesterday, - a Memorial to the Lord Lieutenant signed by every one present, 20 in the whole. When you recollect that 27 Magistrates at the meeting last Monday were unanimous in their determination to assemble yesterday at a Special Sessions, under the Insurrection Act, & are informed that three of those who signed the Memorial yesterday were not a part of the 27, you will not be surprised at my assuring you that the opinion of the country is in favor of the measure & that 30 Magistrates, there being not more than 31 resident, are clearly decided that nothing but the Insurrection Law, acted upon with moderation & firmness, is competent to put down the associations & guard the country against the murders & outrages on houses & property which threaten them. They are also firmly persuaded that the adoption of that law will effectively secure them.

Foster to Peel. Collon. 11 November 1816.

> I enclose a copy of the proceedings this day in the County Meeting assembled at Dundalk, & I am authorized & desired by the following nine Magistrates, who were prevented from being present at the Meeting of Magistrates on Saturday last the 9th instant, to add their signatures to the Memorial of the twenty Magistrates which I transmitted to you yesterday:
> Sir Edward Bellew, Wallop Brabazon, Bl. Balfour, Robert Thompson, Alexander Dawson, Neal McNeal, George Evans, Lenox Bigger, James Read.
> You will therefore have the goodness to lay before His Excellency their

concurrence in the said Memorial, & their request that he will be pleased to consider them as having signed it.

There are only three more resident Magistrates that I know of in the county, over & above these twenty-nine, viz. Dr Little, Mr Hugh Moore & Mr Alex. Rogers; the two first of whom, in signing the Resolutions of Nov. 4, already communicated to you by me, signified their concurrence in the sentiments of the 29; & the latter is confined with sickness.

You now have, my dear Sir, the express opinion of 29 Magistrates, the apparent concurrence of 2 more, & I will venture to say the probable concurrence of the only other resident Magistrate, all recommending & entreating the measure of the Insurrection Act. You have also the concurrence of a County Meeting convened by the Sheriff, without a dissentient voice, all joining heartily with the Magistrates, & furthering their concurrence by the substantial proof of a voluntary subscription for discovering & prosecuting the perpetrators of the late murders, & all persons who shall be guilty of any crimes tending to disturb the peace of the County, which we are all of opinion cannot be preserved without the Insurrection Act, & may be upheld with it.

A copy of the resolutions at the County Meeting accompanied Foster's letter to Peel:

> At a MEETING of the County of *Louth*, convened by the High Sheriff in the Court House at *Dundalk*, on the Request of the Magistrates, November 11, 1816.
> Resolved,
> THAT we feel with the Magistrates how unequal words are to express our abhorrence of the atrocious Murders, which have been committed at Reaghstown within our county, on the morning of the 30th of October.
> That we fully approve, and adopt as our own, their Resolutions, entered into at Castle Bellingham on the 4th instant; and that we pledge ourselves to each other, and to the Magistrates, that we will use our utmost exertions in discovering and bringing to punishment the perpetrators of that horrid crime, and of every other attempt to disturb the public tranquillity.
> Resolved,
> That a Subscription be immediately opened for the above purposes, to be placed at the disposal of the High Sheriff and Magistrates.
> Resolved,
> That the Thanks of this Meeting be given to the Magistrates of the county, for the example they have so promptly and unanimously afforded us of the course we should pursue.
> Also, that our Thanks be given to our worthy High Sheriff for calling this Meeting.

Pendleton also was observing the feeling at the meeting of the magistrates in Castlebellingham, 9 November, and the proposed 'meeting of the county' in Dundalk on 11 November. He wrote from Dundalk, 10 November 1816, to Dublin Castle:

> I have the honor to inform you that no act of outrage has occurred within this District for the last week. Many circumstances however concur to show, that an unusual ferment very generally exists amongst the lower orders, threatening letters of a savage tendency have been received by myself and others, and notices of the same description have been posted up.
> A Special Session of the Peace was yesterday held at Castle Bellingham, the proceedings at which are forwarded to you by Mr Foster. A general Meeting of the County to be held here is appointed by the Sheriff for tomorrow. I will remain here to observe what may occur at it, and propose waiting on you in the course of Tuesday, to receive such direction or communication as you may think proper to honor me with in the present state of this country. As it is intended immediately to send from hence the convicts under a rule of transportation, may I beg to suggest the experience of giving an order that *Berril* may be continued in confinement here, in order that the information he had given may be made available, should circumstances admit of or require it. The particulars with respect to him I have already had the honor of stating to you.[109]

The *Belfast News-Letter*, 15 November 1816, paints in the background of the magistrates at Castlebellingham on 9 November:

> Saturday last, a Special Sessions of the peace was held at Castlebellingham, under the Insurrection Act, 21 Magistrates present – the Rt Hon. John Foster in the chair – where it was unanimously resolved to memorial the Lord Lieutenant to proclaim the baronies of Ardee, Louth, and Upper and Lower Dundalk.
> Monday last, notwithstanding the severity of the weather, a very numerous and respectable meeting of all the rank and property of the county Louth, assembled at the Court house, Dundalk. The High Sheriff took the chair about one o'clock, and stated he called the meeting in pursuance of a requisition from the Magistrates who met at Castlebellingham on the 4th inst. The Right Hon. John Foster read the proceedings of that day, and commented in forcible language on the horrible murder of Lynch and his family, at Reaghstown.
> Thomas W. Filgate, Esq. in a short speech deprecated the diabolical transaction. The resolutions were read a second time and the Sheriff having put the question that they be adopted, passed unanimously. Thanks were then voted to the Sheriff for his readiness in convening the county.
> Among other resolutions adopted, one relates to a general subscription

in the county, so that even the poorest person may contribute, and others show the general abhorrence entertained of the shocking outrage that has been perpetrated and also show their determination to assist in restoring the tranquillity of the county ...

Foster sent the texts of the *county* meeting of the 'county gentlemen' which took place in Dundalk on 11 November and enclosed the document 'Grounds and Reason for our Opinion' which called for the invocation of the Insurrection Act as contained in the memorial of 9 November. That document gave vivid details of local reaction to the outrage.

The county meeting text read:

> At a meeting of the County of Louth, convened by the High Sheriff in the Courthouse at Dundalk on the request of the Magistrates Nov. 11th 1816.
> Resolved,
> That we feel with the Magistrates, how unequal words are to express our abhorrence of the atrocious murders which have been committed at Reaghstown within our County on the morning of the 30th of October.
> That we fully approve & adopt as our own their Resolutions entered into at Castlebellingham on the 4th inst. & that we pledge ourselves to each other & to the Magistrates that we will use our utmost exertions in discovering & bringing to punishment the perpetrators of that horrid crime, & of every other attempt to disturb the publick tranquility.
> Resolved,
> That a subscription be immediately opened for the above purposes to be placed at the disposal of the High Sheriff & Magistrates.
> Resolved,
> That the thanks of this meeting be given to the Magistrates of the County for the example they have so promptly & unanimously afforded us of the course we should pursue.
> Also that our thanks be given to our worthy High Sheriff, for calling this meeting.[110]

Peel marked a number of paragraphs, 1, 2, 3, 4 in the 'Grounds and Reasons' text and asked Pendleton for an explanation. Pendleton replied on 14 November 1816 giving his explanation and submitting the necessity for augmenting the military force:

> With reference to the communication with which I was yesterday honored by you, I am to observe, that the facts stated in the paragraphs marked by you, and now numbered 1 and 2 were taken on the

authority of Messrs Chichester Fortescue, W. Filgate, and myself, being the result of investigations separately made by us. These circumstances were not however stated upon oath, because we studiously avoided anything that could give the appearance of a formal examination, being convinced that no direct information could be at present expected, and that the best means of obtaining any clue leading to such, would be by carefully watching for what might unconsciously fall in an unguarded and apparently undesigned conversation.

The facts in 3 & 4 are stated on oath. The "exultation" alluded to in the following paragraph was taken on the authority of Mr Brabazon, who stated, "that on a property of his seventeen miles from the scene of the outrage, when the account of it was given to about thirty men working in a field, they received it with a shout of joy".

No. 5 was I believe inserted to mark much more particularly the bitterness of disposition among the people, but that being a matter of sufficient notoriety, the fact here stated seems unnecessary.

The truth of No. 6 is established on oath.

The conclusion drawn in No. 7 I conceive to be a direct, and necessary inference from the nature of the fact, appearing on the view, and established by the Inquest.

On consideration and comparison of circumstances it will be found scarcely possible to have been committed by any other means.

With respect to the degree of credit to which such reports as have reached me on this and other like occasions, may be entitled, I must observe that in the present disposition of the country, under the influence of a spirit of outrage on the one side, and a terror of it on the other, the Magistrates have no occasion to guard themselves against exaggerated rumours of aggravated crimes; their constant, and ineffectual struggle is, with the suppression of facts, and extenuation of offences. And under such circumstances, I believe their unanimous feeling is, that to enable them to act with effect, an extension of their present powers is necessary.

It does not rest with me to account for the apparent inconsistency of their two memorials. If the first was well-founded, certainly no single act of outrage, however atrocious, could be thought sufficient to justify the object of the second.

But I have reason to believe, that those who signed it, are fully convinced now, that the first was unadvisedly adopted, and on very partial, and imperfect consideration. They form a most respectable proportion of the Magistracy and are now loudest in the call for the Insurrection Act.

Whether it be the pleasure of Government to adopt that measure, or not, it is my duty to submit to you, that an additional military force appears to be necessary, to be disposed in such stations, and proportions, as may be judged best calculated for the preservation of peace, and security of the persons and properties of those, who are otherwise likely to become the victims of that ferocious spirit, which too generally, and palpably exists.

I would consider 200 men sufficient for the purpose, provided they are properly selected, judiciously stationed, and kept actively employed.

I would also suggest the expediency of having in that Country such Military only, as there is reason to know, have no local connections, or partialities, to interfere with the rigid and correct exercise of their duty. As you were pleased to mention to me the intended proclamation, I beg to mention that such an expression of abhorrence from the highest authority, is I know anxiously looked for. No act of such barbarous atrocity has, I believe, occured in this Kingdom since 1641 - the massacres of Scullabogue, and Saintfield, it will be recollected took place during the ferment of mutual animosity, and actual civil war. This, in all its other circumstances equally horrid, has the aggravation of being meditated for months, and deliberately executed.[111]

In his letter of 13 November to Dublin Castle Foster added the name of Hugh Moore to the list of magistrates who signed the Memorial of 9 November:

I have had the honor of your letter yesterday.

When I see Mr Pendleton our Magistrate of Police, I shall communicate to him for his explanation its contents, but I trust, he has already had an opportunity this day of seeing you on the subject as I understand he went to town yesterday.

I read with great satisfaction that part of your letter, which shows his Excellency to be in a state of convalescence & remain most truly yours. Mr Hugh Moore, one of our Magistrates, who was absent from the meeting of Justices the 9th has written to me this day authorizing me to mention his concurrence on the Memorial transmitted that day to his Excellency.[112]

Foster completed the toll of magistrates concurring with the 9 November meeting in a letter to Peel 15 November 1816:

I have seen Mr Pendleton this morning & am glad to find he had a long conversation with you on the subject of the reasons annexed to our Memorial, which I trust has proved perfectly satisfactory in removing the doubts you expressed.

A letter from Dr Little who was not at the meeting of Nov. 9 when the Memorial was signed, has this day signified his concurrence and his desire that I should add his name to it.

There now remains of the Resident Magistrates only one, who has been prevented by sickness from expressing his, & so the 30, who have joined in requesting the Insurrection Act. You know that Mr Pendleton, the Chief Magistrate of Police, adds the great weight of his decided opinion.

I have troubled you so much and so often on the subject, that I have now only to assure you of the sincere respect with which I remain yours very faithfully.[113]

Comment in the *Belfast News Letter*, 15 November 1816, gave strong approval to the measures adopted by the magistrates at Castlebellingham:

> The resolutions ... are possessed of no common degree of merit. They contain much useful observation upon the state of society that could give birth to so barbarous a deed, and trace the crime to its truest genuine source, a system of illegal association, which threatens a community with a repetition of flagitious acts.
>
> The object of the system is manifest; it is to put down law, and substitute the reign of terror. The offence of the unfortunate Lynch and of his son-in-law was that of having resorted to the laws of their country, for the protection of their property and lives. The conviction of three robbers, who had attempted to plunder their house of arms, was the consequence, and the punishment of the felons was considered as martyrdom to be expiated by the blood of their prosecutors.
>
> 'We can murder faster than you can try' was the recorded boast of the patriots in 1798, and the principle has never been abandoned. Committees of association still held their sessions, as is manifest from the cases of Mr Baker and the Lynches. It is melancholy to relate that, as to the former, none but the immediate agents have been as yet brought to condign punishment, or have been ever discovered. May this second attempt to enslave the country, under the worst species of tyranny, lead to the detention of the managers of the sanguinary drama, who have hitherto escaped, probably because, as was the case in the year 1798, the directors are not known to the tools that they employ.
>
> The 5th resolution, in language guardedly temperate, leads us to suspect that something like what took place at the murder of Mr Baker, in spirit, at least, if not in behaviour, was observable in the state of general feeling in the neighbourhood where the horrible occurrence has taken place. The authors of the resolution 'have *not* witnessed that general feeling of indignation which such an atrocious act was calculated to call forth to aid of the Magistracy'. No doubt – the fate of an *active evidence* was as little calculated to execute sympathy in the one instance, as that of an *active Magistrate* in the other.
>
> It appears, however, that the Magistrates of the county are not likely to be deterred by such an effective manifestation of the principle of *terrorism*. They have come manfully forward, in defiance of the tongue of malice, the dagger of the assassin, and the fagot of the incendiary. They enter into subscriptions in order to obtain information; they solicit the continued operation of the police act within the guilty baronies, and, in the spirit of true patriotism, they do not hesitate to declare that 'the ordinary laws of a free country, *calculated to be met and forwarded by a people impressed with a due sense of moral and religious feeling*, are not those adapted to contend with crimes, such as the present one, unknown but in the savage tribes of Indians – and that only *'when in open war'*.

BARONIES PROCLAIMED

After the meetings of the magistrates and the meeting of the gentry in November, one can sense a feeling of impatience among the magistrates at the slow action of the Lord Lieutenant in declaring the baronies named in a state of disturbance enforcing the Insurrection Act. Faithful William Fortescue at Milltown Grange wrote to Foster on 21 November reporting his discussions with the Attorney General and Robert Peel urging the early implementation of the Insurrection Act as requested. Fortescue commented: 'From my conversation with the Attorney General I expected the result (though I am pretty certain I caused him to waver) but from mine with Mr Peel *much the reverse*. He even asked me did I think one week earlier or later would be very much material'. Fortescue told the Attorney General, 'if it, the Insurrection Act, was not granted my feelings and those of the generality of the Magistrates whose minds I knew were to resign their commissions. Then he said if our opinions were so strong as to the necessity of the measure we had better again remonstrate and the thing would be done ... '. Fortescue feared that the government's refusal made it appear 'more merciful and tender in putting our tenantry and neighbours out of the Pale of the Constitution than we have been', and subjected the magistrates of Louth 'to more odium and danger if possible'.[114]

The magistrates had to wait. The baronies of Ardee, Louth, Upper Dundalk and Lower Dundalk were proclaimed in a 'state of disturbance' by the Lord Lieutenant and Council of Ireland on 4 February 1817. The text appeared in *The Correspondent* on 31 February 1817 (and also in the *Belfast News Letter*, on 19 August 1817). It was printed in the *Parliamentary Papers: Reports (Ireland), Session 28 January –12 July 1817 (Vol. viii)*: 'Papers relating to Disturbances in the County of Louth' :

> WHITWORTH
> Whereas, by an Act of Parliament passed in the fifty-fourth year of His present Majesty, entitled, "An Act to provide for the preservation and restoring of Peace in such Parts of Ireland as may at any time be disturbed by seditious Persons, or by Persons entering into unlawful combinations or conspiracies", it is Enacted, that it shall be lawful for the Justices of the Peace of any county, assembled at an extraordinary session of the peace summoned in manner by the said Act directed, and pursuant to the provisions therein contained, not being fewer than

seven in a county at large, or than three in a county of a city or town, or the major part of them, if they see fit, upon due consideration of the state of the county, to signify by memorial by them signed, to the Lord Lieutenant, or other chief Governor or Governors of Ireland for the time being, that they consider the county, or any part thereof, to be in a state of disturbance, or in immediate danger of becoming so, and the grounds and reasons of such their opinion, and praying that the Lord Lieutenant and Council may proclaim such county, or part thereof, to be in a state of disturbance, or in immediate danger of becoming so, and thereupon it shall and may be lawful, to and for the Lord Lieutenant, or other chief Governor or Governors of Ireland, for the time being, by and with the advice of his Majesty's Privy Council in Ireland, by Proclamation to declare such county, or any part of such county, to be in a state of disturbance, or in immediate danger of becoming so, as also such part as he or they shall think proper of any adjoining county.

And whereas twenty Justices of the Peace of the county of Louth, being the major part of the Justices of the Peace duly summoned and assembled, pursuant to the provisions for that purpose in the said Act contained, at an extraordinary session of the peace holden in and for the said county of Louth, on the ninth day of November last, and duly summoned pursuant to the said Act, have by Memorial by them signed, signified to His Excellency the Lord Lieutenant, that the baronies of Ardee, Louth, Upper Dundalk and Lower Dundalk, are in immediate danger of becoming in a state of disturbance; and the grounds and reasons of such their opinion; and have thereby prayed that the Lord Lieutenant in Council may proclaim the said baronies of Ardee, Louth, Upper Dundalk and Lower Dundalk to be in such immediate danger.

Now, We the Lord Lieutenant, by and with the advice of his Majesty's Privy Council, in pursuance of and by the authority to Us given by the said Act of Parliament, do by this our Proclamation, declare the baronies of Ardee, Louth, Upper Dundalk and Lower Dundalk, in the county of Louth aforesaid, to be in a state of disturbance, or in immediate danger of becoming so, and do hereby warn the inhabitants of the said baronies of Ardee, Louth, Upper Dundalk and Lower Dundalk, that they each and every of them be and remain within their houses at all hours between sun-set and sun-rise, from and after Sunday next, the ninth day of February instant, under the penalties by law established. And We do hereby further order and direct, that a special session of the peace for the said county of Louth, be held in the town of Dundalk, in the said county, on Monday next, the tenth day of February instant, for the purposes expressed in said Act of Parliament, of which all Justices of the Peace, and other Magistrates for the said County, and all others whom it may concern, are to take notice.

Given at the Council Chamber in Dublin, the 4th day of February 1817.
C. F. Hill, George Beckwith, St Geor. Daly, Wm Saurin, Manners, C., Erne, Wicklow, Frankfort de Montmorency, Wm McMahon.
GOD Save the KING

MILITARY STATIONS

A series of letters from Foster and Pendleton to Dublin Castle, from the middle of November 1816 to the end of the year, and a letter from Pendleton to Peel, outline the arrangements for military stations and patrols as requested in Pendleton's letter of 14 November, and mention several shooting incidents, cattle mutilation, robbing of arms, and arson. The main outrages I have gathered into a section below on the disturbed state of County Louth and bordering areas 1814-19. Patrols of police and military for the protection of individuals continued into 1817.

Foster to Dublin Castle. Collon. 17 November 1816. His list of military stations is not now with his letter but they are outlined in Pendleton's letter of 8 November.

> Mr Pendleton talked over with me last Friday the most desirable stations in the disturbed Baronies for troops and I enclose a list of some as occurred to us.
>
> I must hope from your desiring this list that you look to the Insurrection Act being in force, for I cannot see the use of troops for preventing outrage or insurrection, if we cannot patrol with them, keep people at home in the night time, pay domiciliary visits, search houses and take up arms. These are the weapons which that Act furnishes the Magistracy with & for the using of which with effect, the assistance of Military is necessary. What can the Magistrate do, by way of prevention? Without these powers he must wait for actual breach of the peace, for the commission of the outrage or information upon oath to authorize him to stir & I fear & so does every man, gentleman or farmer with whom I converse, that the long nights of the coming Winter, which we have repeatedly heard during the Summer, that the associations mean to work for, will produce many dreadful outrages, murder & demolition of property, if we have not the powers of the Insurrection Act, in time to prevent them.
>
> I send you now the desire of the only resident Magistrate who had not attended our meetings to be set down as concurring with our Memorial for that Act. Every Magistrate, 31 in number, join in the same request. The chief Magistrate has expressed to you his opinion of its expedience, the farmers & landholders, who are to pay the expence of it, concur with us, & they will have a cheap bargain, even if it exists till April, which I trust will not be necessary. We cannot calculate it for that time at more than $1^{1}/_{2}d$. or $2d$. an acre, but if it quadrupled that sum the security it would confer both at present & in future would amply compensate the expences. The present sums for losses by a few houses burned & stackyards burned would probably exceed them.
>
> I request your forgiveness for urging you so often with these sentiments. Determine as you may, my best exertions to enforce the law

shall never be wanting.

The magistrate whom I mention as wishing to be added to our Memorial is Mr Alexander Rogers resident in Lower Dundalk.

I have this day had an answer from my friend Mr Thos Forster about his son. We both concur in thinking his being under age & as undergraduate in the College, sufficient reason for declining to push him forward into the responsibility of being a Magistrate. At the same time if circumstances should unfortunately occur, to make his appointment desirable, his father will heartily concur in it. It was the young gentleman's offer of his service to Mr Pendleton & his excellent character & activity, which induced Mr Pendleton to mention him to you.[115]

Pendleton. Dundalk. 18 November 1816:

I have had the honor of your letter of the 16th. The stations I would propose as expedient for military detachments to be placed in are: 1. Louth, 2. Corcreagh, 3. Hackballs Cross, 4. Mansfieldstown and 5. Riverstown, at each from 30 to 40 men, with four or five of the police attached as peace officers. That the parties now in Ardee and Carlingford, should also be made up to at least 40 in each. That a night patrol by every one of these detachments should be vigorously insisted on, so that a continued circulation of it, might pervade the parts of the country most likely to be disturbed, from end to end.

As to their accommodations, it would be difficult in all those places, and could not be made comfortable in any. Billeting (if even possible) would not be safe, and would tend to make them less effective than if kept together. This effect I have reason to believe it has had already on those now in Carlingford and Ardee. I therefore conceive the only move to be, to take by the month, some sort of house, or houses, capable of containing them. As the quality of the accommodation would be inferior, the expence must be only proportionate. There is I know a considerable quantity of spare barrack furniture, in store in the Barrack of Dundalk, the indispensable parts of which might be issued by the Barrack Master there, on an order for that purpose.

I have delayed my answer till today, to take the sentiments of some of the principal Gentlemen of the County, whom I had not an opportunity of consulting before on this subject. They are satisfied of the expedience and necessity of the outline I have sketched, and differ with me only as to the possibility of the object being accomplished by so small a number. I have been influenced in the estimate by a consideration of the difficulty of procuring accommodation even for that number, and I hope that the zealous alacrity of those selected for the purpose, may supply such deficiencies. Any direction you may please to honor me with, as to preparatory arrangements, I will use my best endeavours to carry into effect. The Gentlemen who have properties in the neighbourhood of the places named, will, I know give every facility within their power.

A dwelling house, the property of a Mr Coulter near Cooly, within two miles of Riverstown in the Barony of Lower Dundalk, was last night maliciously burnt.

I am enabled to state from concurring authorities, of the correctness of which in substance I have no doubt, that unlawful assembling by night has recommenced in many parts of this District, and in some to a greater extent, than at any time since I have been in it.

Mr Forster whose desire to become a Magistrate I had the honor of communicating to you, is not yet (as I have found) of full age, however much the District in which he lives may require one, and however respectably qualified he may in all other respects be for the Duty, it is to be feared that his present period of life is not sufficiently mature, for the discretion necessary at this time.[116]

Pendleton to Peel. Dundalk. 6 December 1816:

In reply to your Letter of the 3rd inst. with which I am just now honored, I am to inform you, that the instructions given by me to the officers commanding the several Military Detachments in this County were:

"That Patroles of at least *one third* of each Detachment, should at uncertain hours, and in such directions as under circumstances might seem most expedient, be kept on foot *every night*; occasionally communicating with those of the next Stations, so that a continued circulation might actively pervade from end to end those parts of the County most liable to disturbance.

That such Patroles should be invariably attended by two peace officers. That the duty of the Patroles should be in effect similar to that of City Watchmen, merely to preserve peace and good order; not to enter houses in search of either men or arms; should persons at unseasonable hours, and under circumstances of such reasonable suspicion as to justify detention be met with, they are to detain them for examination etc. by a Magistrate in the morning; should they meet persons assembled in arms, or committing any unlawful act, no doubt (I presume) can be entertained of their legal competence to act against them under the authority of a Constable".

This I conceive to be the *routine* of their *ordinary* duty, made necessary from a strong conviction, that if the County is not kept alive by a lawful, it will be by an unlawful force.

Whenever a particular occasion shall occur "for calling out the Military" to act on special information, or in any way beyond the line I have here described, it is distinctly understood that both a Magistrate and the Military Officer are to be present. Circumstanced as we are, I am not aware of any other way in which the Military can be made active, and were they to remain inactive in their quarters until there should be an opportunity from *information* of calling for their assistance, they would be literally of no use.

If my conception of this matter is erroneous, or should I from misapprehension have been accessory to the possible misleading of others, I beg to be set right. It is a subject of too much importance for any doubt to exist on.[117]

A note is written on Pendleton's letter, 'I think that the arrangement proposed as to the Military is legal & may with propriety be acceded to. Wm Saurin, 9 December 1816'.

A few military reports give us an indication of the activity of the army before and after the new military stations were set up.

Report of M. Genl John Burnet. Armagh. 1 June 1816.

> Louth (part of). In the Barony of Upper Dundalk, several houses have been maliciously set on fire & a number of people have been apprehended in the course of last month by the Superintending Magistrate at Dundalk.

Report of Major Genl John Burnet. Armagh. Ist July 1816.

> Louth (part of). Several outrages have occurred in the Baronies of Dundalk in the course of the last month, perpetrated by a lawless banditti who attempt farmers & others from paying rent beyond the rate they fix upon.[118]

Robert Al. Dalzell, M.G. Commanding N. Dist. to Peel. Armagh. 1 January 1817.

> Louth (part of). From the Reports which I have received I am induced to believe that no disturbances of a serious or alarming nature have occurred in this part since last Monthly Report.[119]

Report of Lieut. Genl. Lord Forbes to Peel. Dublin. 1 January 1817.

> I have the honor to inform you that the reports from the several Military Stations in the Eastern District, state the Country to be in tranquillity, excepting that of Lieut de Rudyne's of the 62d Regiment commanding the detachment at Ardee, when the houses of two respectable farmers were robbed of arms; from which circumstances, coupled with the other robberies which the Lieutenant states to have occurred in and about Ardee, he considers that part of the Country to be in a disturbed state & no other symptom of disturbance has manifested itself in the neighbourhood, nor have the parties, which have been sent out very frequently to patrole for the preservation of the Peace, discovered, or apprehended any individuals concerned in the above acts of robbery or any others in breach of the Peace.[120]

Lord Forbes's Report to William Gregory. Dublin. 2 February 1817.

> I have the honor to state for the information of his Excellency the Lord Lieutenant, that, with the exception of the late outrage on the Grand Canal near Naas (which has been already reported to his Excellency) and the murder of a respectable farmer near Mansfieldstown in the County Louth on the evening of the 16th ult: (who, while sitting at supper with one or two friends, was fired at through his window & killed on the spot) no acts of insubordination or violence are stated to have occurred in the District under my Command since my last report.[121]

Robert Al. Dalzell. M.G. Commanding N. Dist. to Peel. Armagh. 5 February 1817.

> Louth (part of). The Party at Carlingford 83d Regt went in search of a wounded man with a view of discovering others who had assembled with arms on the night of 21st Jany at Grange 2 miles from Carlingford. The Mob entered several public houses & demanded whiskey which they would not pay for. They knocked down & abused a Coasting Officer in the head. They then went to Riverstown 3 miles distant, where they got more whiskey without payment & went to a Miller's from whom they took some trifling articles. The Magistrate who accompanied the Party swore several people who all denied any knowledge of the persons forming the mob.[122]

Samuel Pendleton was a former soldier but, in his new post as a police magistrate, he was prepared to maintain his civil authority as against any misconduct on the part of soldiers. Apparently he had trouble with some members of the 62nd Regiment who were stationed at Dundalk. They ended their term in March 1817 and were to to be replaced by the 45th Regiment. The affair caused some irritation with Lt Col. Goodridge of the 62nd Regiment who resented Pendleton's complaint. On 19 March 1817, Stewart King, a friend of Pendleton, wrote to him from Rutland Square, Dublin, advising conciliation and good will towards the highly esteemed incoming regiment. He ended his letter, 'I know that persons, high in rank and authority, have conceived that in the late transaction with Lt Col. Goodridge your communication had tended to irritate rather than conciliate the Military, and even an Enquiry would be injurious to you and certainly prejudicial to the peace of the country'.[123] Pendleton was extremely polite in his reply, 21 March 1817, but justified the action he had taken:

> I wish you had given me more advice, and had not thought of apology for it - I am more obliged to you for the interest you show in my concerns than it is in my power to express – I assure you I feel the full force of your observations and the propriety of attending to them. For myself I must also say that there are few men in the army who respect it more than I do, or would more seriously regret the possibilities of being involved in anything unpleasant with those belonging to it. The two field officers of the 62nd superior to Goodridge in command I can venture to say have acquitted me of any portion of the fault of what had occurred with respect to that Regt – one of them Col. Beckwith, on his resuming the command called on me to apologize for the misconduct which had caused me so much trouble, and it so much discredit. I have the highest opinion of the 45th and will follow your hints with respect to it and anything else you may offer therein.
> I will see you in Dublin on Monday – I write this with joy, rather in a hurry after a busy day.[124]

It is interesting to read Peel's reflection on 1816, the year of Wildgoose Lodge, in his letter, 25 December 1816, from Farnham Lodge, Cavan, to the Speaker (Charles Abbot):

> The internal state of Ireland I cannot help considering very satisfactory so far as the public peace is concerned, when I compare it with that of England, and reflect on the complicated difficulties of the present times – so satisfactory, indeed, that I have proposed to the Government of England a reduction, which I think they did not expect, to the amount of 3,000 men in our military establishment.
> There is, no doubt, the average proportion of murders and burnings and other atrocities, the acts of a set of human beings very little advanced from barbarism, unaccustomed to regard the law either as the protector from or the avenger of outrage, and subject, as far as the interests of society are concerned, to the pernicious influence of the religion they profess. It is quite impossible for anyone to witness the remorselessness with which crimes are committed here, the almost total annihilation of the agency of conscience as a preventitive of crime, and the universal contempt in which the obligation of any but an illegal oath is held by the mass of the people, without being satisfied that the prevailing religion of Ireland operates as an impediment rather than an aid to the ends of the civil government.
> There is, however, as little of disaffection towards the State as I have ever heard of, and less than I can remember ...[125]

By the end of 1817, as Tadhg Ó Ceallaigh comments in his article on 'Peel and Police Reform in Ireland, 1814-18', 'Pendleton had established a barracks in Dundalk, he had a party of nine men in a barracks at Riverstown, and he had also set up a barracks at Carlingford. His expense for the year included the costs of sending escorts and expresses to Drogheda, Dublin, Navan, Trim, Armagh, Monaghan and Newry'.[126]

6
The Disturbed State of Louth and Bordering Areas

EVENTS IN 1814-15

In Louth and its environs in County Meath, County Armagh, County Monaghan and County Cavan there were many indications of Ribbon and general criminal activity in the years 1814-19. Agrarian disturbances, spurred on by the economic depression, were already occurring in County Louth before the Wildgoose Lodge atrocity in October 1816 and indeed the heavy vengeance of the law did not bring disorder to an end. Lennox Bigger, ever an alarmist, wrote to Dublin Castle in July 1814 reporting the conviction of rioters in Dundalk. The 'Thresher'system, he said, was spreading in Louth and he had the offer of a person willing to enter the association and act as a spy.[127] In the same period disturbances were reported in Jonesborough, South Armagh, where houses were burned, horses mutilated and persons were intimidated from taking land. Chambre and McNeale, local landlords, appealed for the help of troops.[128] A provincial meeting of Threshers was reported in the summer of 1814 in Armagh.[129] In neighbouring Meath, J. Pollock wrote at this time, enclosing a copy of a new oath 'to destroy all heretics' being taken on the Meath-Cavan border, and asked that a military attachment be quartered at Moynalty.[130]

Three letters of McNeale of Faughart to Dublin Castle in 1815[131] emphasised spasmodic violence in the Dundalk greater area in 1815: 30 January, one Warnock murdered at Clermont Park because he was a Protestant and supposed Orangeman and an old soldier – vast amounts of arms being procured by the country people and secret oaths taken; 14 Feb. enclosed subscription lists for information as to the murder of James Warnock and an outrage on Robert Thomson's land; 22 Dec. Lord Jocelyn exhorted to restore order in Dundalk neighbouhood. The *Belfast News-Letter* of 1 September 1815 voiced the alarm of the landlords and clergy in an article from Dundalk, dated 20 August.

> In consequence of a requisition for that purpose, we had this day a numerous and respectable meeting of the Gentlemen, Clergy, Landholders, and Inhabitants of the Barony of Dundalk, held at the Court House, to take into consideration the disturbed state of this neighbourhood.
> The business was opened by the Hon. John Jocelyn – briefly stating the depredations that have recently been committed, and requiring the opinions and advice of the meeting, in order to put a stop to the refractory spirit that has appeared among the peasantry.
> Mathew Fortescue of Stephenstown, Esq., moved several resolutions, proposing that a fund should be raised by voluntary subscription, for the apprehension and prosecuting to conviction the perpetrators of the late outrages, committed in the neighbourhood – which were seconded by Francis Tipping of Bellurgan Park, esq. and unanimously adopted.
> Thomas Fitzgerald, of Fane Valley, Esq., read several resolutions, deprecating in strong language the houghing of Mr Denis Fitzpatrick's cows – and the destruction of poor Hearty's wheat.
> John Page, Esq., proposed that a reward of 300*l*. be given for prosecuting the offenders to conviction – and 200*l*. for private information that may lead to the same, for the above offence; and 100*l*. for the persons who destroyed the wheat – and 50*l*. for private information:- And that in case any of the persons concerned shall turn approver, that application will be made to Government for his or their pardon.
> It was also resolved that any persons in the slightest degree related to, or in connexion with the perpetrators of these disgraceful transactions, should not be continued as tenants or servants amongst them – and that every exertion would be made to prevent their being entertained as such elsewhere.
> On the motion of the Rev. E. Thackeray, rector of Dundalk – and approved of by the Rev. Doctor McArdle, P.P. of this parish, books are to be opened at every place of worship in the barony, where all the persuasions are invited to shew their abhorrence of these crimes, by subscribing from the smallest sum upwards, to the proposed fund.

Rev. Henry Stewart, Creggan, South Armagh, wrote to the Dublin authorities on 15 December 1815, reporting a burning by Threshers at Edward Hanlon's premises.[132] In the same month the *Belfast News Letter*, Friday 22 December 1815, reported the severe winter, the growing anxiety of the magistrates and landlords, and a further number of incidents in the Dundalk neighbourhood, County Louth:

> Saturday night there was a very heavy fall of snow, with a strong gale at N. W. A sharp frost ensued, and continued until 6 yesterday evening, when the wind veered to the S.E.with heavy rain. It blows a storm this day from the east with sleet.

> We this day have an extraordinary Session of the Peace, for the purpose of taking into consideration the state of the county, which was attended by the Right Hon. John Foster, Viscount Jocelyn, and an immense no. of the Magistrates and Gentlemen of rank and file of this County. As the statements were private, nothing has as yet transpired.
>
> Nine men brought in last night by Lord Jocelyn were admitted to bail, to appear the next Session, which is to be held here by adjournment on the 12th January next.
>
> A division of the Fifeshire militia, commanded by Major Rutherford, marched into our barracks this day.
>
> On Sunday night the 12th inst. Mr B. Duffy's stockyard was set on fire by some malicious evil disposed persons, and before sufficient help could be collected the fire had got to such an extent as almost to frustrate every exertion. However, by the assistance from Dundalk and neighbourhood, the flames were prevented from communicating to the houses, but between two and 300 barrels of oats and barley were consumed.

EVENTS IN 1816

Just before the first attack on Wildgoose Lodge, 10 April 1816, disturbances and highway robberies in Louth had increased. As has been stated, 'Ribbonmen' in these areas were akin to other agrarian associations such as 'Threshers' and 'Carders'. In January 1816 there were attacks on the house and property of Arthur Harrison at Camilly Ball, South Armagh.[133] The General and Brigade Major's Report of 1816 mentions an affray in Creggan, County Armagh, in 1816 between Dundalk police and 'persons assembled to pull down the house of a man paying high rent'. The same report mentions 'banditti' in County Louth intimidating people from paying rent beyond a fixed rate.[134] In February the home of Patrick Kirk in Inniskeen was attacked by 'Threshers'. He and his two sons, one of whom was called Tom, bravely defended it:

The *Newry Magazine*, 1816:

> On the 5th and 6th of Feb. Neal Mac Neal, and Lennox Bigger, Esqrs, searched the country from Dundalk to Carlingford for fire-arms, under warrants directed to them from the Lord Lieutenant, and succeeded in seizing a large quantity – they were joined at Carlingford by James Reid and Hugh Moore, Esqrs. From persons such as they supposed to be of a description not likely to use or lend their arms for improper purposes they merely took an account of them, assuring them they would be allowed to retain them until government should otherwise

order.

Lately, the house of Patrick Kirk of Ednagrena, parish of Enniskeen, was attacked by a large body of thrashers, who fired several shots into the house. They met with a most determined resistance from Kirk and his two sons, who wounded at least five of them with pitch-forks. The assailants however prevailed at last and wounded the Kirks severely ordering them to give up some land they had lately taken. Government have sent to L. Biggar, Esq. the magistrate £20 to be given to the Kirks for their gallant defence.

Chichester Fortescue, Faithful W. Fortescue, W. Filgate, Esqrs. Rev. J.Wright, J.P., J. Booth, B.D. Shiels, and J. Bell, Esqrs accompanied by an officer's guard, traversed a great part of the baronies of Louth and Ardee, on the night of Sunday 7th of April. About three in the morning when on the Carrickmacross road, a man was observed trotting towards them, whom they stopped on account of the late hour, and on searching his pockets found the form of an affidavit. The man said his name was Clark, and that he was going to his own house, but would give no further information respecting himself. Several copies of the oath were afterwards found in a box in Clark's house, with notices to be put on different farmers' houses.

The oath was principally directed against Orangemen, and was signed 'Bryan Clark, knight of St. Patrick'. Clark was lodged in gaol.

Lennox Bigger in February and August 1816 wrote to Dublin Castle asking for a reward for the Kirks for defending their home.[135] Ralph Smyth, Drogheda, 7 March 1816, reported two men apprehended in possession of 'seal and book' and in May related the presence of Ribbonmen in Ballymakenny, north of Drogheda. In June 1816 there was a serious riot at Clones fair in County Monaghan, where Protestants and loyal Catholics were attacked.[136]

Disturbances, as is clear from the accounts above, were often caused by land grievances. An anonymous letter, signed John [?Love], with post mark '1816' warns William Filgate of the consequences if he had anything to do with Pepperstown land:

> Your honour would be very much thanked if you would have nothing to do with Pepperstown and [Co. Louth] or not turn out the poor people out of their land ... You have got forgiveness for your doing at the time of the Wildgoose Lodge and do not renew the mind of the people against your self and your lady depend on it if you do you never see the hook going in to it or your lady along with you ...

Threatening letters[137] to Filgate informing him of plots to murder him were later to become a feature in his life: in 1820, one of them from a Mary Lynch or Mathews who had received information from a Biddy Campbell whom he had committed a few days previously for cow stealing; in 1821, one from a Patt Murry, Kilmainham Jail, Co. Dublin. Notes initialled W.F. of a confession, 5 June 1822, made by John Deery, a prisoner in Dundalk Jail, allege a threat by Ribbonmen on Filgate's life dating back to November 1816:

> In 1816 November 9th or 10th in Carrickmacross in a sheebeen House of Mary Clinton (met first in Barney Reilly's house) were sworn by Matt. Gilmore and Matthew McElroy who were Committee men (that is to say, Ribbonmen) – first sworn, and then sworn Patt Conlon of Ednarma, Larry Handlon about Inniskeen, Patt Curtis (thatcher) of Lonnett and Thomas Rooney of Ednarma, James Sheridan of Dromas now in Dundalk, John Deery of Gortin, Owen Hamill then of Gortin to take his - W.F. - life with stick, stones and shot and also his servant at first opportunity between Longford Bridge and Donamoin [Donaghmoyne] Church on Sunday. John McGraw was to be murdered as a pimp about the end of Harvest. About a year after at ... M.G. [Matt Gilmore] – J.D. [John Deery] - P.C. [Patt Curtis] – T.R. [Thomas Rooney], John and James Carroll also s[w]orn to secrecy and promised to make a party himself for the same purpose. Not to be in a hurry about the job – it was time enough when things would get quiet at any time in any year and the longer the better – I would be off my guard the more – Rooney and Deery - Rooney had Collon's blunderbuss. Disputed about their Arms – Tommy McMahon's pistol was to be taken from him – He had a gun, Jimmy Lennon got the gun – got James Hamill's Pistol. W.F.

It is clear that William Filgate, at least for a time during a very dangerous period, got some protection from the military. Lt Col. Ramsay to Gregory:

> Sunday 2 February 1817
> Has the honor of acquainting him that he communicated his wishes to Lieut General Lord Forbes relative to the two privates being stationed at the house of Mr Filgate in the Co. of Louth. His Lordship is desirous of the protection being afforded to that gentleman, and he has recommended the measure to the Commander of the Forces, whose decision on the subject Lieut Col. Ramsay will have the honor of communicating to Mr Gregory the instant it is received.[138]

Subsequently Lt General Forbes, Merrion Square, Dublin,

on18 February 1817, wrote to Dublin Castle, enclosing letters from Captain de Ravynet and Mr William Filgate, and enquired whether soldiers should be sent to protect property and not person of Filgate.[139]

A glance at the 'County Louth Grand Jury Indictment Book' gives an indication of the seriousness of the charges at the various assizes in 1816-17, aside from the Wildgoose Lodge crimes.[140]

> 1816. Summer: 'Combins. Confidn and agreed to form an unlawful society for seditious purposes' Bryan Clark and William Gernon.
> 1817. Lent: five highway robberies. Summer: 'murder' William Farley; 'assembling in arms' Patrick Sharkey, James Durnin, Thomas Breen, John Breen, James Goodman, Arthur McAneny, Patrick McAneaney, John Garagan, Nicholas Garagan, George McCabe, Laurence Tallon, Patrick Duffy, Philip Duffy, Patrick Mulligan, Patrick Brown or Brona.

William Foster of Barronstown, County Louth, swore a statement before John Foster, on 9 March 1816 who sent it to the Dublin Castle administration.

> Informeth & saith, That from information he hath received, and other circumstances. That there exits in this part of the country, a numerous association of persons, calling themselves Threshers or Carders, who have also taken an illegal oath, & who under that oath have committed many enormities, and intend further to commit (if not checked in time) various others of a more serious nature. That fearing their former system had been discovered, they have lately resolved to *reswear* each member, now making him pay a sum of money on his admission for the purpose (as he is informed & believes) of purchasing arms.
> That a man of the name of Charles McShane, and an other Michael McDaniel, both of the Parish of Roach, have been appointed to collect money, for the austensible purpose of feeing lawyers to prosecute some Yeomen, who are now in Armagh Gaol for an alleged murder, which as the informant has heard & does believe is not for that purpose, but to make up a sum of about five hundred pounds to compensate a man of the name of Able Magee for losses which he sustained in the support of the foregoing cause, and to enable him to defray his expenses as a grand delegate to Armagh & other places, where informant has heard & believes some of the heads of said association meet him.
> That in the instance of Owen Myers, a publican and black smith a tenant of informant having said he would not contribute money for any such purposes, notice was posted on Sunday the 3rd instant on the chapel of Sheelagh threatening destruction to any person who should deal with him. That a person residing near to him was for dealing with him severely beaten & the car of another person destroyed for the same

reason & in consequence of said notice – and informant has heard and believed, that they expect to be all *armed & ready* in about four or five weeks, if not persuaded by some very strong measures being adopted in the mean time. Informant's informations lead him to believe, that several persons connected in the same system residing in the County of Monaghan have committed outrages of a most serious nature such as destroying houses, haggards etc in the parish of Eniskeen & adjoining thereto & as he believes the Barony of Farney & in notice being given them have risen in large bodies, entered this county & been guilty of various nightly depredations & that he considers the same to be the case in the part of the County of Armagh adjoining the County Louth, & which his informations lead him to believe will be persevered in these counties, unless put a stop to, by the before stated means. [141]

A glance back to late 1815 indicates violence in South Armagh that continued into 1816. On 25 November a man was shot dead. The *Newry Magazine*, 1815, has the story:

> On the 26th November, an inquest was held on the body of Edward Hanlon, who was shot the preceding night, in the house of Hugh McMahon, on the road from Newtownhamilton to Dundalk. The finding of the jury was that the deceased came by his death by a shot fired from a gun, by an individual, who, with six others who were aiding and abetting, have been committed, to abide his trial at the assizes. A number of other persons were also committed to Armagh jail for a previous attack on some of the persons accused of the murder of Hanlon.

The *Newry Magazine*, No. 7, March & April 1816, reports two revenge burning outrages connected with prosecutions at assizes:

> The house, offices and stack-yard of Mr Treanor, near Ball's Mill, county Armagh, were lately set on fire, in revenge, as is supposed, for a prosecution carried on by him against some persons at the late assizes. He lost four horses and one cow. One of his children was scorched; and the whole family might have perished, if a neighbouring woman, who had been sitting up with a sick child had not observed the flames and alarmed them in time.
> One night in the latter end of March, a lighted turf was maliciously put into the thatch of a stable belonging to Arthur Harrison, of Camilly-Ball, the miller who lately prosecuted Car and McCosker, at Armagh assizes. Mr Harrison had providentially been sitting up, waiting for the return of a servant whom he had sent on a message; but he was badly burned in extinguishing the flames.

Patrick Thornton, who was to appear as a witness following the attack on Harrison's house was brutally murdered on 4 March 1816. *The Correspondent* of 19 March 1816 relates the story in graphic detail from the *Newry Telegraph*:

> On the night of the 4th instant, a dreadful murder was committed at Castletown, near Dundalk, upon the body of Patrick Thornton, miller, of which we took some notice in a former number. An inquest having been held before Lennox Bigger, Esq., Coroner, and a respectable jury, a verdict of wilful murder was returned. The circumstances attending it appear to have been these: Thornton returned from Dundalk market on the night of the 4th, as far as Castletown, and remained to drink in a public house until late, and finding a nephew of his who had been with him so intoxicated that he could not bring him with him from the house, he set off by himself, and had not proceeded many perches from the place, when, it appears, he was knocked down, and beaten so unmercifully in the head with stones, that both his eyes were driven out, and his skull fractured in several places, and being sent to the Louth hospital, he died there next day, about 12 o'clock. As two men have been lodged in jail on suspicion, we forbear giving further particulars, but we rest confident that the active disposition of the Coroner will not permit him to leave anything undone which can lead to the apprehension of all who appear to have been concerned in this brutal murder. Report says that Thornton was to have been a witness on a trial respecting an attack made upon the mill of one Harrison, in the County of Armagh, to prevent which he was murdered in a truly savage manner.

The *Freeman's Journal*, 19 March 1816, gave an account of a robbery as related in Newry papers:

> On Monday the 11th instant, as Christopher Gernon was returning homewards to Charleville, beyond Castlebellingham, he was met by two men at Haggarstown, two miles from Dundalk on the mail-coach road, between two and three o'clock in the day, who violently assaulted him and robbed him of bank notes to the amount of 21*l*. 5*s*. 4*d*.

The *Newry Magazine*, No. 7, 1816, also briefly related the murder of Thornton, and stated as a consequence:

> On the 12th of March, the barony or half barony of Upper Dundalk, the barony of Lower Dundalk and Ardee, in the county of Louth, have been proclaimed by the Lord Lieutenant and privy council, to be in a state of disturbance, requiring an extraordinary establishment of police.

At the Armagh Assizes, as reported in *The Correspondent* 14 March 1816, Baron McClelland, when he opened his Commission in the Crown Court on 17 February, spoke in earnest tones to the Grand Jury composed of the following:

> Charles Brownlow, Jun. Esq. Foreman; Joshua McGeough, William Blacker, James Johnston, Thomas Vernor, Nicholas G. Johnston, James W. McNeile, James Forde, Thomas Atkinson, William N. Thompson, John Ogle, Fathom, Jonathon Seaver, Arthur Irwin, Robert Harden, John Winder, George Robinson, Robert Livingston, Samuel Ball, William Loftie, Edward Courtney, Simon Langley, William Reid, and C. Woodhouse, Esqrs. William Irwin, Esq. Mount Irwin, High Sheriff.
> The learned Judge commenced his charge, by expressing his satisfaction, in finding from the information of the Sheriff, that this county enjoyed a state of comparative tranquillity. It was happily exempt from those offences which disturbed and disgraced the neighbouring districts, particularly the County of Louth – four, out of five, of its baronies, being at present under the operation of the Peace Preservation Bill and the Insurrection Act. And, although the Calendar was by no mans decreased, yet, it was, in great measure confined to that species of crime, which might naturally be supposed to grow out of the distress which the country every where laboured under. He exhorted the magistracy to observe the same vigorous regard to the public peace, which had hitherto secured to the county a state of tranquil subordination; and, as a means of deterring the population from joining in these mal-practices, to enforce on them, the enormous burdens they must undergo, if, from a contrary behaviour, it was found necessary to resort to extraordinary measures; for it was a fact, that in the County of Louth, the acreable assessment which was levied to meet the expenses incurred by special sessions, etc., was considerably heavier than the sum raised for bridges, roads, and other public works.

The hopes of Baron McClelland, who lived in Anaverna, County Louth, were not fulfilled. Generally disturbances in Armagh especially in North Armagh were of a sectarian nature. As has been previously referred to, in his own County Louth, after the proclamation of some areas following 'disturbance and terror', posters warning the owners of public houses against having their premises open after nine o'clock were circulated. Public houses were regarded as meeting places for Ribbon conspiracy.

The 'Abstract of Reports from General Officers and Brigade Majors of Yeomanry in Ireland on the state of their respective districts and boundaries' gives brief summmaries of disturbances.¹⁴² Here are some reports from the Northern District relevant to County Louth and its environs:

> April 1816
> *Armagh.* Major General Burnet reports that with the exception of an affray which occurred at a fair held in Newry on the 22nd , in which a soldier of the 61st Regiment was wounded and is since dead, the district under his command appears in a tranquil state.
> *Monaghan.* B. Major Hamilton. Some outrages had been committed in the Parish of Killanny near Carrckmacross – the Magistrates assembled at the Court House of Monaghan to enquire into the particulars and found that there were not sufficient grounds to induce them to consider the County in a state of disturbance.
> May
> Major General Burnet reports that, except in the Co. Donegal where two men who had acted as jurors in the trial of a man capitally convicted and executed, were much beaten at a fair held at Castlefin, and in the Co. Louth where several houses have been set on fire in the Barony of Dundalk, no instances of outrage have occurred in the several counties within the Northern District.

An interesting item in County Cavan, an example of robbery under arms, headed 'The Heroic Priest' is reported in the *Belfast News-Letter*, 12 March 1816:

> A few days since, a Roman Catholic Clergyman, in the county Cavan, was overtaken on his way home, by a man on horseback, who entered into conversation with him, and stating himself to be a stranger in that part of the country, requested he would direct him to some house in the village they were approaching, where he could be safely accommodated for the night.
> When they came to the village, the priest pointed out a house to him, and rode on towards his own residence some distance from the village; he had not gone far when he was again overtaken by the stranger, who told him he was afraid to stay in the house he had directed him to, as it was full of Orangemen; the priest told him he need be under no apprehension whatever, and advised him to go back, which he declined, saying he would rather be on the road at night. The priest then told him, as his apprehensions would not let him return, he would give him a bed and a place for his horse at his own residence, to which the stranger assented; after taking some refreshment they retired to their apartments. The man servant of the Clergyman, having occasion to go into the stranger's bed-chamber before he had gone to bed, observed under his great coat a blunderbuss.
> On quitting the room, which he did instantly, he went to his master and told him he did not like the appearance of his guest; that he was armed, and probably had bad intentions; his master, upon this statement, desired him not to go to bed, but to arm himself with a pitchfork, and

sit up in the kitchen, while he at the same time loaded a case of pistols, and sat up also reading to beguile the time. In the dead of the night the priest's door was opened, and the man whom he had sheltered entered the room, presented the blunderbuss, and desired him to deliver his money or he would shoot him; the Clergyman requested he would put down the blunderbuss lest it might accidentally go off, and that he would shew him what money he had; the priest then threw on the table a few tenpennies, saying that was all the money he had, on which the other replied, he knew he had plenty of money, and that he came for the purpose of getting it, and that if he had not brought him to his house, he would that night have broken into it; the priest then told him what money he had was in the desk that stood in the corner of the room, and putting his hand in his pocket, took out the key, which he threw on the table; during the time he had been in the room the ruffian was threatening him with immediate destruction; however, he took up the key, laid down the blunderbuss, and went towards the desk, when the priest drew out one of of the pistols, fired at him, and killed him on the spot. The moment the report of the shot was heard, the hall-door was forced in, and four men entered, and rushed into the room. The priest, collected for the worst event, took up the blunderbuss, when he heard the crash of the door, and firing amongst them as they entered, killed two, and a third with the reserved pistol; the servant attacked the fourth with the pitchfork, and inflicted a wound on his back, but he, unluckily, escaped.

Agrarian crime in Louth, in the wake of the first attack in April on Lynch's house, was by the summer time spreading to South Armagh. Samuel Pendleton, Chief Magistrate of County Louth, wrote to William Gregory from Dundalk, 22 June 1816:

> It is my duty to inform you, without waiting for the regular period of my report, of a matter which took place this morning. I had received information, the truth of which I did not confide in, but was determined to put to the test, that certain houses were to be attacked last night: it turned out to be accurately correct. After one o'clock, with a party of twenty-five men, I surprised them *in the act* of breaking the house of one McDaniel, of Glas Drummond in Armagh, about a mile beyond the border of Louth; they were twenty-two or twenty-three in number. We were not discovered till within about fifty yards of them, when they fired, and ran in every direction. One Murphy (whom I have reason to believe to be their captain) was killed; one Dullaghan (who is badly wounded) and three others, are prisoners; two of the police are also wounded, but not badly. The darkness, and their better knowledge of the country, enabled the others to escape; but from the tracks, and quantity of blood in many places, and other circumstances, I have no doubt there are seveal others wounded, and probably dead by this time. (*Parliamentary Papers: Papers relating to Disturbances in the County of Louth*)

The Times, 28 June 1816, reported the incident in similar terms, adding that the Chief Magistrate was accompanied by Charles Eastwood, Esq. and that this was the third house to be attacked by the party in the course of the night.

Other details are given in military 'Abstracts of Reports':

> June 1816
> *Armagh.* Major General Burnet reports the state of the District as follows. In the counties of Armagh and Louth several outrages have been perpetrated by a lawless Banditti who attempt to intimidate farmers and others from paying beyond a certain rate of rent. In one instance a number of persons assembled by night for the purpose of pulling down the home of a man who had paid a higher rent than the rate prescription, were met by a party of police, belonging to the Baronies of Dundalk and Ardee, who killed one, wounded many and took several prisoners – two of the police were wounded.
> July 1816
> Major General Burnet reports that except the extreme hostility to Excise officers on all occasions, by the lower orders, nothing occurred to disturb the tranquillity of the Northern district.
> August 1816
> *Cavan.* The vicinity of Mount Nugent has been rather disturbed. Some flax has been cut down and a house wilfully set on fire.

An incident is recorded at the Louth summer assizes before Judge Daly, 26 July 1816, and is reported by *The Correspondent,* 5 August 1816:

> Owen Shevlan, indicted for, that he, on the 2d of March last, did post on Darver Chapel, a notice tending to excite unlawful assemblies and combinations, and threatening the persons and property of John Moran, of Reddypenny. John Moran, the younger, endeavoured to prove the notice, so posted, to be the handwriting of the prisoner, but to the satisfaction of the Court, the prisoner was acquitted.

Lennox Bigger (1869-1857), a magistrate, wrote privately to Dublin Castle expressing his high fears, 30 August 1816:

> I beg to call your attention to a private letter which I wrote you a short time since mentioning 'that it was my opinion from the informations I had received that the people were well armed, and after a preparation of four years, at least, and a secretcy (*sic*) which rendered it almost impossible to obtain information in the usual way, they must soon break out openly'.
> I now feel it my duty to state that my informant has again been with

me & assures me that a rapid progress is making in arming the lower orders of the people and *that there will be a rising* and the *time fixed on* is *at the Tythe setting* after the Harvest is made up.
I fear I may be considered an alarmist yet I think I should be highly culpable if I kept this from Government, particularly as it is corroboration of what I before wrote you.
I take the liberty of suggesting the absolute necessity is for sending a number of persons amongst them who will find out *the particular time*, and also where the general places of keeping arms may be.[143]

Samuel Pendleton in a letter to Dublin Castle from Ardee, 15 November 1816, sums up the outrages in Louth in the period shortly before the burning of Wildgoose Lodge:

The number of outrages which have taken place in this District within the period you mention in your note of last night to me is so small, that I shall venture to state them from memory, without waiting for my return to Dundalk, particularly as you desire it to be done "without delay".
In the Barony of Upper Dundalk, one outrage only has occured - namely the cutting and maliciously destroying growing corn & potatoes, the property of a man who was suspected of having given information to me.
In Lower Dundalk *Fire* of the same nature took place. There was also a horse maliciously shot, and some other cattle mutilated and disfigured. There is reason to believe that the motive in these cases was a vindictive feeling in persons ousted of their farms, against those who succeeded to the possession.
In the Barony of Louth - the house of Mr Atkinson of Channel Rock was attacked and rob[b]ed of arms (viz. a gun, a blunderbuss, case of pistols & sword) on the night of the 26th Septr. Also a quantity of wheat & hay the property of Mr McCann of Knockbridge maliciously destroyed on the night of the 26th ult.
In the Barony of Ardee - the burning of Lynch & seven other persons on the morning of the 30th ult.
All these cases are stated on oath, and to be committed by persons unknown.[144]

A letter from 'An Armagh Catholic' in the *Belfast News-Letter* the following week, 22 November 1816, switched the scene from Louth to Dungannon but indicates a feeling for the use of coercion laws to bring about law and order.

Sir,
It is with great horror I tell you, that a more barbarous outrage (with the exception of the burning of Lynches' whole family last week in an

adjoining county) has not occurred in any of the proclaimed districts than was committed a few nights ago in another county adjoining this on the northern side, and in the most public street of the town of Dungannon, and at so early an hour as half past ten o'clock; it will not, I hope, prove so fatal in consequences, but none can be of a more atrocious nature nor proceed from a more dangerous principle – a principle which, if not immediately checked, will render it necessary, for the protection of our lives and properties, to extend the Insurrection Act to every part of the kingdom at once; and it appears to me the only way of protecting the well-disposed part of the Roman Catholics from being compelled to join in the revolutionary system of terror which evidently appears to be almost universally established, and from a motive almost universal in its influence, that of non-payment of rent, and that at a time when Government have released the lower orders from the payment of several of the taxes.

The unhappy sufferer in the present case, I am well informed, is a stranger in Dungannon, and his only crime was his loyalty to his King, while he was in the militia, and fidelity to his present master, Mr Davis, a Clergyman of the county Down, and the very first man of property in the neighbourhood of Dungannon who thought of relieving his tenants from the distresses arising from the late peace, and he did so in a way more judicious than any I have yet heard of; he then gave, and continues to give to every tenant who has not (contrary to a non-alienation clause in his lease) re-set his land for a profit, a quantity of lime, bearing a proportion of 20 per cent to the rent, who owe him two years' rent; and so well are these thrashers cemented, and so daring are they from their imaginary but united force, that I heard two of them, on a market-day on which I had occasion to be in Dungannon, say to Mr Davis's agent, a Magistrate of that town, with a constable at his elbow, that they would not allow themselves to be taken on any Sheriff's decree or writ; and though that Magistrate proposed giving any constable a guinea each for executing these and some other decrees, yet a man could not be got to do the business (so well is the system of terror established); and Mr Davis, in hope of showing the Magistrate that such relaxation of the law arose from the want of energy, sent Mr White, a confidential and spirited man, from the county Down, to have the decrees executed. This man succeeded in securing two of the tenants who owed most money, and who had re-set their lands for double the rent payable to Mr Davis, but in a few nights afterwards, that man was way-laid in the town of Dungannon, and by a most violent stroke given him on the back of head was immediately brought to the ground, and before he could recover himself so much as to speak or call for assistance, his head was battered almost into a jelly, in a most savage and brutal manner, upon the pavement, with a stone which a man held in his hand. In that state he might have remained until he had died by the effusion of blood, had it not been for some good-natured passenger who observed him and got assistance to take him to his lodging, and procured a surgeon, who had occasion to put ten stitches in the different wounds on his head.

A local magistrate, W. Murray, Dungannon, who features later in the Wildgoose Lodge story in relation to one of the informers, Thomas Gubby, replied on 25 November. His letter is printed in the *Belfast News-Letter*, 29 November 1816. Obviously stung by the criticism he challenged the full veracity of the story:

> Having seen in your paper of the 22d inst. a publication signed *An Armagh Catholic*, I feel myself called upon to state, that so much of that publication as relates to the peace and tranquillity of this town and neighbourhood is a gross misrepresentation; and if the author, who appears to be a person of no inferior description, will come forward and avow himself, I pledge myself to refute all he has advanced reflecting on the execution of the laws and the general tranquillity of this neighbourhood, which will probably be found to bear a competition with the most tranquil part of the kingdom.

October 1816:

> Monaghan. B. Major Armstrong states that there is every appearance of disturbances in the neighourhood of Tydavnet and Scotstown and Captain Wood of Ballylark has received threatening letters.[145]

Foster wrote to Peel, from Collon, 19 November 1816, a polite rebuke at the delay in the invocation of the Insurrection Act. He enclosed a letter of Paul Parks.

> It gives me sincere pleasure to receive from you the account of the Lord Lieut.'s advance towards recovery & I trust we shall soon hear that his Excellency is restored to perfect health.
> Be assured I shall always be happy in freely communicating every thing material which occurs & to convince you I begin this very post by enclosing a letter from the lower Barony of Dundalk which if that stated in it be confirmed, will remove one of his Excellency's occasions for postponing a final decision on our Memorial. You have given the Insurgents a long day. I wish you could give us the like.[146]

Paul Parks. Dundalk. 18 November 1816:

> I am extremely sorry to inform you, that an outrage was committed last night, in the Parish of Carlingford. Yesterday morning a Notice was posted up on the Chapple declaring, that if any person or persons, offered to take land, out of which any person had been dispossessed, or had left, that the person taking such land, his property would be consumed by fire, and his life taken the first opportunity. On that night, between 200 and 300 of these disturbers of the peace, marched through

the parish, and another party as large, was seen in the Lordship of Ballymascanlon. The end was, that a house was burned, the property of a Mr Coulter, on Mr Tipping's estate, in the parish of Carlingford. How promptly they put into execution, what they sett forth in their Proclamation. If the Insurrection Act is not introduced into this County and these fellows kept within doors at night, I fear many burnings will happen, and some lives lost. A tenant had left Coulter's land, another man became tenant, which caused these fellows to burn the house.[147]

In a short note to Peel from Collon, 19 November, Foster announced sending copies of Peel's official letter to him to the magistrates.[148]

Towards the end of 1816 Pendleton reported some more outrages to Peel:

Dundalk, 17 December 1816
I have the honour to inform you, that since the last communications from me, the houses of two respectable farmers named Eakins and Mullin, in the barony of Ardee, were attacked by night and robbed of arms, the latter also of money to the amount of about twenty pounds, by persons unknown and in disguise. (*Parliametary Papers: Papers relating to Disturbances in County Louth, Session 28 January – 12 July 1817 (Vol. viii)*

Dundalk. 22 December 1816
In obedience to your direction I enclose with this, copies of the depositions of Mullin and Eakins with respect to the attack and robbery of their houses on Monday last.
The circumstance of this being the first information given of a former attack and robbery of the house of Mullin, so long ago as the 3rd of June last, is strongly indicative of that system of terror which prevents resistance, or discovery.
This is further testified by my having only on Friday last, received *any* information (and even then not from the parties themselves) of the attack and 'racking' of three houses, on the night of the 8th inst. though within seven miles of this.
I also inclose the copy of an information of Jas. Feehan taken yesterday, as being more descriptive than *many* others of the same tendency, which I have, of the principle endeavoured to be established, namely - *That no change in the occupancy of land is to be suffered.*
It is to be observed that a dwelling house on another part of the same lands was burnt on the night of the 17th ult. in furtherance of that principle, as I have already reported.
As a specimen of the conduct of the Catholic Clergy, I inclose the deposition of P. Kirk. However he might have been disposed under the impulse of anger, to *give* the information, I have no doubt that the overwhelming influence of that Clergy would smother it, so as to make any prosecution for so gross an outrage ineffectual.

I have therefore neither acted on it, nor intimated to any one my having received it. Should I have erred in my view of this matter, I beg you will have the goodness to set me right.'[149]

Pendleton to William Gregory, Dublin Castle, dated Louth, 29 December 1816:

I have the honor to inform you that no act of outrage has occured within my knowledge in this District since my last report - except the maliciously shooting at a Mr John Reath by a person unknown, on the night of Sunday last. He is a wealthy farmer residing at Irishtown, near Ardee, and was in May last robbed of arms and money to the amount of about £200. One person was capitally convicted for it last Assizes; another had been taken up a few weeks ago by me on account of it; and Reath had been with me some days before to give additional information against others, which accounts for the attempt.
I am to request that you will have the goodness to have direction given, that a thousand pounds may be issued for the use of the Police Establishment, so as that it may be received by the *9th of Janry* on which day the former sum of same amount ordered on the *23rd of October* will be expended.'[150]

Pendleton's account of relative tranquillity towards the end of 1816 in Louth is supported by a military report:

December 1816
Major General Dalzell reports that the Northern District appears to be in a tranquil state. Instances occasionally occur of opposition to Revenue officers making gagues [gauges] and a disposition is manifest on the part of the lower orders to resist the law when exercised in driving cattle or making gagues [gauges] of rent.
Louth. Lieut. General Forbes reports that the Eastern district, with the exception of the neighbourhood of Ardee where several robberies have been committed, to be in a state of tranquillity.[151]

EVENTS IN 1817

Pendleton's first report to William Gregory in 1817, dated Dundalk, 7 January, had a hopeful note, which was soon to change in his subsequent reports to Peel:

This district has not been disturbed by any act of outrage since my last report, except the attack and breaking of another house in the barony of Ardee, inhabited by a brother of Mullin, whose information I had lately the honour of forwarding to you; it was not entered, the party being, as it appears, deterred by some symptoms of resistance from

within, and the approach of the patrole from Man[s]fieldstown.
(*Parliamentary Papers: Papers relating to Disturbances in the County of Louth; Session 28 January – 12 July1817 (Vol. viii)*)

Pendleton to Peel, dated Ardee, 14 January 1817:

> I have the honour to inform you, that since my last report the dwelling house of Arthur McCabe, a farmer in the barony of Lower Dundalk, has been assaulted and broke, and the corn in his haggard maliciously destroyed by persons unknown. This has been done in furtherance of the principle I have already mentioned: "The endeavour to control at their will the occupancy of lands". No other material act of outrage has occurred in this district during the week. It is considered that this is principally to be attributed to the system of night patroles, which has been steadily pursued. (*ibid*)

Then came the murder of John Reath whom Pendleton had mentioned in his letter to government at the end of 1816. Pendleton wrote to Peel from Dundalk, 17 January 1817:

> This county has been disgraced by another horrid assasination: Mr John Reath, an opulent farmer of Irishtown, near Ardee, was last night shot dead while at supper with his family. It seems to hav been done by a *blunderbuss* fired through the window, as his head was almost blown to pieces; shades of suspicion fall on different quarters: - *I* myself have little doubt that it has been done by the same person who fired at him before on the 23d ultimo, and for the reason I stated in my letter of the 29th. When I left that, at four o'clock this day, the Inquest had not been held; nothing is likely to come out on that; but any thing that may possibly appear, I shall have the honour of communicating on Sunday. (*idem*)

The Correspondent in its issue of 20 January 1817 reported the murder of John Rath [Reath]. The report was culled from the *Drogheda Journal*. On the previous Thursday Mr John Rath [Reath], 'a respectable and wealthy' farmer had the upper part of his head blown off by a blunderbuss fired through the window while he dined at 8pm with two friends. He had just returned from the Quarter Sessions of Ardee to his house at Irishtown on the Dundalk Road from Drogheda'. (Irishtown is a couple of miles north of Ardee on the Dundalk road). The immediate conclusion of the paper, an indication of the state of the county, was that this was an agrarian crime. There had been an attempt to shoot him on the night of Sunday 22 December 1816. The paper stated, 'At the last Assizes of Dundalk, Mr Rath prosecuted a man for robbery, who was convicted on the clearest evidence; Mr R. interfered in his behalf with the Judge, and his sentence was commuted to transportation. This act is a further proof, if any could be wanting, that there is a confederated society of villains, who sit in judgement on every man that has the boldness to support the laws of his country, and bring offenders to justice. The Magistrates in the neighbourhood will, of course, exert their usual vigilance to bring this monster and his associates to speedy trial'. The suspected 'monster' as it turned out was the victim's brother, Patrick Rath. The same newspaper reported on 29 January, 'Horrible as this crime must appear in the eyes of every feeling man, it is somewhat satisfactory to find, that it did not originate in the villainous system, which caused the destruction of Lynch, his family, and inmates, at Wildgoose-Lodge'. The trial of Patrick Rath for the murder of his brother John Rath, with whom it was alleged he was on bad terms, and sought to take over his farm, was reported in the *Belfast News-Letter* of 25 July 1817. He was found *not guilty*.

A correspondent of the *Belfast News-Letter* (31 January 1817) reported some more outrages from Drogheda on 29 January:

> On Tuesday night the 21 inst. Mr Learry's haggard, at the Mill of Louth, was maliciously set on fire, and three stacks of corn partly consumed. His *crime*, we understand, was, that his sons refused to join the confederated villains who infest the lower baronies of that county.
> Sunday night last, the home of Mr Read, guager, near Dundalk, was attacked by a party of villains, who demanded his fire arms, and being refused, they broke all the windows of his house. Mr Read, to insure the safety of his family, threw them one old pistol, upon which they retired.
> Same night, a constable and assistant of his, on duty near Knockbridge, were deprived of their arms, and ordered to return home by, it is likely, the same gang.

On 22 January 1817 Chief Magistrate Samuel Pendleton wrote from Ardee to William Saurin, Attorney General, to have John Berril pardoned that he might give indispensable evidence against others then in custody and enclosed his certificate of conviction 24 January 1817.[152]

One of the outrages in January 1817, which was reported in full in the newspapers, came before the County of Louth Assizes

Disturbances

in Dundalk on 6 March 1818. It throws light on the Ribbonmen and gives an insight into social life. The central character Michael McDaniel we have already met in William Foster's statement of 9 March 1816. Samuel Pendleton recounted the incident in a letter to William Gregory dated Ardee 27 January 1817:

> I am obliged to state, that since my last Report, the disposition to disturbance (of which I had no doubt of the existence, however tranquil appearances might be) has shown itself in an encreased degree in this district. In the Barony of *Lower* Dundalk, which *had* been so quiet that I took the liberty of suggesting the expediency of exempting it from the effects of the Police Bill, there have been latterly many acts of outrage reported by me. Within the last ten days I have taken information of the attack of eight houses in that part of the district: it also appears that large bodies assemble there by night, in arms. On Tuesday night last a revenue officer happened to fall in with a party of them near Cooly; he was assaulted and wounded by them; he fired among them and made his escape: it is *certain* that one of them is severely wounded by him, whom I am in search of; he is as yet concealed in the mountains. Last night the house of Mr Reed, near Dudalk, was attacked and robbed of arms by persons unknown. It is matter of notoriety, that *many* other outrages of a similar nature have occurred; but from the terror produced by the horrid acts which have been committed, the persons suffering will not give information voluntarily. The present state of this country I consider such as requires a more particlular detail than can be properly given by me on paper; I would, therefore (with your permission) wait on you on Friday next for the purpose. For the present I have applied the best means in my power to check the prevailing spirit. It being impossible, from want of accommdation, to fix a *military* party at Riverstown (in Lower Dundalk) as had been suggested and approved of, I have sent some twelve of the police, and two more to Carlingford to act as peace officers with the military patroles from thence, it appearing that the local constables were not competent. There are now fourteen only of the police in Dundalk; thirty-six are dispersed in the various out-stations, some at the distance of twenty-two miles from the others. (*Parliamentary Papers: Papers relating to Disturbances in the County of Louth, 28 January – 12 July 1817 (Vol. viii)*

The 'County Louth Grand Jury Indictment Book' lists those charged in the barony of Lower Dundalk:

1818. Spring: 'administering unlawful oaths' – Patt. Sheeran & Son,Thomas Matthews, McGuire of Riverstown, George McQuillan, Thomas Leonard, Brien McCluskey (a tailor), John Candillon, Richard O'Brien, John Rice, Joseph Martin, Thomas

Canny, John Millard, Patk. Sharkey, James Callan (a labourer), James McQuillan, Thomas Abraham; 'riotously assembling in arms' - Michael Monaghan (a tailor), Michael Magenis, Henry McDaniel, Michael McGrath, Michael Maguire, John McBride, Roger McGrien (?), Patrick McEnteer, James Rice; 'assembling by night in arms' - Michl. Daniel, John McBride, Michael Magrath, James Rice, Roger McGrene, Roger McGrehan, Michael Monaghan, Felix Monaghan. Patrick McEntere.[153]

Depending probably on the availability of a prosecuting witness those indicted seem to have been reduced to four. The following illustrative extracts are taken from the *Belfast News-Letter*, 10 March 1818 (also reported in the *Dublin Evening Post*, 12 March 1818):

> *Michael McDaniel, John McBride, Michael McGrath,* and *Patrick McInteer,* were indicted for a burglary and felony in the dwelling house of Charles Dullaghan, of Riverstown, on the night of the 21st of January 1817, and also for feloniously causing the door of the dwelling house of Loughlin Hanlon, of same place, to be opened by threats and menaces on same night; also for appearing armed by night, for a riot and an assault on John Grills.
>
> **James Dooley**, the first witness. Is a ribbondman, and has been so these some years. Last November he was bound to secrecy, and not to give evidence against a brother. Knows Michael McDaniel. It was he made witness a ribbondman. Remembers meeting one night about a fortnight before the police went to Riverstown. They met early in the evening. They proceeded to Templetown, and by that time there were one hundred persons assembled. McDaniel was among them. Witness saw him load a gun. Michael McGrath was also there, and called all the men at the Dundalk side of Riverstown No.5, and marched them off to the house of one Christy, which they searched for arms. They then went in search of an old woman who had been turned out of her house by her son because her and her daughter-in-law could not agree. They found her, and McBride and McInteer put her on witness's back, and they brought her to her house and left her there. Identifies all the prisoners as being of the party.
>
> They then proceeded to the house of one John Grills, in order to set it on fire. When they got there they cowed as they knew Grills had arms. His party had seven pistols and one gun. That of McDaniel's having left Grill's, they went to a public house and demanded whiskey. The man of the house gave them two gallons, which they drank and did not pay for. The publican's name is Larkin. Witness was the person who went in to demand the whiskey. It was McDaniel desired him, and gave him the gun for that purpose. When they had drank the whiskey a man passed by of the name of Grills, when one of the men cried out 'there is a damned dog', and Mc Daniel cried out 'follow him'. He was

followed accordingly and struck. When Grills turned round and fired and wounded one McCardle in the thigh. The rest ran off, but after they brought a grey horse and carried off McCardle.

Five of them went to the house of Loughlin Hanlon, of which number were three of the prisoners, McDaniel, McBride and McGrath. They rapped at Hanlon's and demanded two gallons of whiskey. It was some time before the door was opened, when McDaniel cried out they had money enough and not to be afraid. Hanlon in his shirt opened the door, and the party went into the cellar and got the whiskey, and brought it off.

Thy stopped at the house of one Dullaghan next, in order to get something to eat. Witness did not go in as he had care of the whiskey. The rest went to Dullaghan's. Saw them return with bacon. They brought the bacon to Michael McDaniel's house, and got potatoes boiled, and eat their supper of the bacon fried. Dullaghan the miller lives at the far side of Riverstown.

Witness was tried before Baron McClelland last assizes, and convicted, and sentenced to be imprisoned for three months; if the country remained quiet he was to be then discharged.

Evidence from Loughlin Hanlon, Charles Dullaghan, Riverstown, Cooley, and John Grills, revenue officer living in Cooley, followed giving details similar to that of James Dooley. James Corrigan, chief constable of police, gave evidence mentioning that McDaniel had sent for him while he was in the gaol of Dundalk and admitted being one of the party. Ann McDaniel swore that her brother with whom she lives never left the house the night of the disturbance. Mathew McGrath swore that he lived with his brother Michael in Ballymascanlon and the accused never left the house the night the miller was robbed of the bacon. Mary McGrath, wife of Mathew, deposed to like effect. Peter McBride, brother of John, swore that he lived in Rampactown (?) next to his mother's house where his brother lived; witness had a child dead and during the wake he was back and forward to his brother's house; his brother remained in the house all night. Judge Mayne summed up the evidence, the Jury retired for about half an hour and found Michael McDaniel guilty and the others not guilty. Sentence of death was then passed on Michael McDaniel. He was executed on Saturday 4 April 1818 at the front of Dundalk gaol. The execution is recorded in the *Belfast News-Letter,* 10 April 1818, an extract of a letter from Dundalk, 7 April [Reprinted in the *Dundalk Examiner* 5 November 1881]:

On Saturday last, McDaniel, who was convicted at the last Assizes, for burglary and other crimes committed near Carlingford was executed at the front of the gaol. Ever since his conviction he appeared hardened against all remorse, and persisted in denying the crimes of which he had been convicted. It was only on the day before his execution, that he could be prevailed upon to look into his prayer-book. At half-past one o'clock, he was brought out of the condemned cell, and the gallows was surrounded by the horse police, six dragoons and two officers. On mounting the scaffold he seemed much agitated and continued in prayer, with apparent fervour, for about 15 minutes. He inquired of the Rev. Mr Duffy, chaplain, who attended him till the last moment, if the gibbets which he saw hanging against the wall were for him? On being told that they were not, he replied, 'Well, I will die easy'. He inquired if his friends would get his body, and seemed much satisfied on being answered in the affirmative. He then stood up and addressing the few who stood round him, acknowledged his guilt, said he had been a Ribbonman, and that drunkenness and bad company had brought him to this untimely end, adding that he hoped his awful death would serve as a warning to others. Agreeable to his request, he was suspended so low that he could scarcely be perceived by the populace. He met his fate with much resignation, and died without a struggle.

Henry McClintock mentions the execution in his Journal:

Saturday 4th. Very fine day - C.[ustom] House – a man (McDonnell) was hanged in this town for a robbery near Cooley Point – I dined in the barracks with Matt Fortescue – James Forde, Henry Maxwell & Doctor Hinds were there.

Following shortly after his report on the murder of John Reath on 16 January 1817, Pendleton wrote to Peel on 7 February 1817 announcing another atrocity:

It is with much concern I have to report to you another act of horrid atrocity, which took place this morning at Channel Rocks, in the Barony of Louth – the malicious burning of the house etc etc of a James Burne, in which his daughter-in-law was also burnt to death. I inclose the information of the fact. The coroner's inquest is to the same effect. I was at first in hopes that the fire might have been accidental, but several circumstances have left no doubt in my mind of its having been as I have stated it. In the course of last night, in the same neighbourhood, there were two ploughs maliciously cut to pieces; one of them the property of a Neal McCann of Knockbridge, who, from the frequency of outrage comitted against him, seems an object of peculiar enmity. (*Parliamentary Papers: Papers relating to Disturbances in the County of Louth: Session 28 January 1817 – 12 July 1817 (Vol. viii)*

The Correspondent on 17 April 1817 carried an item that vividly illustrates the dire consequences of a breach of the Insurrection Act:

> At the Special Sessions which commenced last Thursday in Dundalk, two men were found guilty, and were sent off for transportation early on Friday morning. One of them was a publican who resided at Knockbridge; he had been found by the police patrole, in a public-house in Dundalk, after ten o'clock at night. Serjeant Johnston who presided, with Counsellor Macartney, the assistant-barrister, explained the insurrection law in a very clear manner, and stated that the prisoner had broken it in two instances, first, in being out of his house – and second, by being in a public-house, without being able to assign any satisfactory reason for being there. The other prisoner (a man named Dillon) had been found by the police, at a late hour, carrying away his neighbour's potatoes, which could not be proved a lawful occasion for being out after the prescribed hours – he of course received the same sentence of the Court.

On 1 March 1817 Walter Dawson, Carrickmacross, wrote to Dublin Castle saying that he had proofs of an illegal association of Ribbonmen of Corrybracken from information volunteered by Jacky Guilsnahan; there were outrages in the area and the Protestant clergyman was non-resident.[154] He then forwarded a letter to Pendleton outlining the method to be adopted by Pendleton in communicating with Guilsnahan.[155]

Lennox Bigger, Dundalk, wrote, 4 April, 1817 to Dublin Castle, to inform the government that a tenant on his lands in Creggan, South Armagh, was terrorised and his stable with its horses and cattle was consumed by fire.[156]

Pendleton, 6 April 1817, wrote from Ardee giving the grounds of his opinion that McKenna's stable and cattle were maliciously burnt.[157]

Report of Pendleton to William Gregory. 'General State of the District from 28 April to 4 May'. Dundalk. 5 May 1817:

> I have the honor to inform you that there has not any act of outrage taken place in this District since my last report.
> I am also to represent to you, that the sum of one thousand pounds ordered for the use of the Police Establishment on the 8th of March last, will be expended on the 18th inst. The new clothing for the men, to which they were entitled on the 1st of April, and with which they have been provided in the course of last month, has made a further issue necessary, about seventeen days earlier than it otherwise would.

> I trust you will have the goodness to give such direction as may make it available by this day fortnight.
> The conduct of this Establishment continues satisfactory.
> Louth. Weekly report of Duty of Police establishment. *Duty* etc etc. Monday the 28th to Sunday the 4th.
> In the course of this week the usual Patroles have been every night on foot (at uncertain hours) in the neighbourhood of their respective Stations.
> Pat Neary apprehended at Mansfieldstown on a Monday night has been committed for Tryal as an idle and disorderly person. Seven others brought in from different quarters have been discharged under recognizance for their good behaviour.
> No further material circumstance has occurred within the week.[158]

Part of nearby County Meath, which had supplied informers and some of the alleged participants in the burning of Wildgoose Lodge, was proclaimed in a state of disturbance in June 1817. The advertisement was still being printed in the *Drogheda Journal*, Wednesday, lst April 1818:

> And whereas it has sufficiently appeared to us, that the Barony of Navan, or as the same is known and denominated by the names of the Baronies of Upper and Lower Navan, or by whatever other denomination the same may be known or called; the Barony of Skryne, alias Skreen, and the Barony of Morgallion, in the County of Meath, are in a state of disturbance, and require an extraordinary Establishment of Police ...
> Given at the Council Chamber in Dublin, the 21st day of June, 1817.
> Manners, C. Thomond, Sligo, Erne, Frankfort De Montmorency, Chas. Kildare, Norbury, D. Browne, Mm. McMahon, George Beckwith.

Desmond Mooney in his article 'The Origins of Agrarian Violence in Meath 1790-1828' (*Ríocht na Mídhe*, Vol. viii, No.1) has described the acceleration of agitation in the greater half of the county, excluding only in his study some baronies in the east. He mentions the growth of Ribbonism in Navan in 1816 and the reported marching of 2,000 labourers through it. For the year 1817 he writes, 'Near Kells, raids for arms occurred, and notices were posted not to export food to markets outside the area. The property of those who refused to listen to these warnings was quick to suffer the consequences. In Curragha and Rathfeigh, raids for arms and food became commonplace. In Navan, mills were attacked, houses were ransacked for food while the military looked on and refused to interfere, saying they could do nothing unless ordered by the magistrates. At Athboy, the poor marched to demand work, while at Moynalty, robberies, house breakings and assaults occurred nearly every night. It was said that the poor were so united through oaths that even if a house was attacked, invariably no one was prosecuted. The country was in its worst condition since 1792-3. A petition by the poor was received by the magistrates, detailing want of employment or support as the cause of outrages, and promising it would get worse if their grievances were not redressed. The poor, the labourers and smallholders, were now beginning to see themselves as a social unit, repressed by an unjust system, and announced their determination to alter matters by their own efforts'.

EVENTS 1818-19

Some events refer back to previous years and indicate that disturbances and fears of outrages still continued in Counties Louth, Meath, and Monaghan and in South Armagh into the 1818-19 period. *The Correspondent*, reporting from Dundalk on 25 January in its 26 January 1818 edition, gives some more incidents connected with the Insurrection Act:

> On Friday and Saturday, the Special Sessions for the proclaimed district of Louth were held at Dundalk, pursuant to adjournment, before A.C. McCartney, Esq., King's Counsel, (who presided in the room of Serjeant Joy), Francis Hamilton, Esq., Assistant Barrister, and a bench of *eighteen* Magistrates. James Callaghan, Thomas McArdel, Richard Murphy, Patrick Byrne, Patrick Mills, Denis Harold, James Hagan, James White, John Haughey, Thomas Murphy, and Bryan McGeough, were convicted as 'idle and disorderly persons' and received sentences to be transported for seven years. The two last, however, were recommended, by the Magistrates, as fit objects for the clemency of Government. The remaining nine were ordered to be forthwith transmitted to Kilmainham, on their way to the place of embarkation. Five were acquitted, three put off their trials; and one, who was out on bail, forfeited his recognizance. Of those who were acquitted, two are detained under other charges, to take their trials at the Assizes.
> On the night of Saturday se'nnight, a dwelling-house on the lands of Tatebawn, in the barony of Dundalk, and adjoining the county of Armagh, from which a tenant of Robert Murphy, Esq. had some time ago been evicted, was maliciously set on fire, and destroyed. – This is the only outrage of that nature which has occurred in the county since the Insurrection Act was put in force.

Major General Beckwith in his report of 1 April 1818 recorded some houses burned maliciously in the barony of Tiranny and in May recorded Ribbonmen in County Monaghan 'traversing the country at night'.[159]

Pendleton, Dundalk, in a letter, 2 November 1818, to Dublin Castle, made an interesting comment that Ribbonism and outrages in County Meath seemed to be non-political and that disbanded soldiers and sailors were a contributing cause.[160]

The July 1818 election led to tension and disturbance in Drogheda with inevitable prosecutions at the assizes that immediately followed. The *Freeman's Journal*, 6 July 1818, gave this account:

> The Drogheda Election terminated on Saturday night, after one of the severest contests known for some years in this country. Mr Ogle has been returned by a majority of *nine*. A duel took place between Mr Wallace and the Recorder of Drogheda, in which two shots were fired on each side, but fortunately without injury to either party.

The *Belfast News-Letter*, 7 July 1818, reported the Drogheda Assizes and the comments of the Rt Hon St George Daly:

> His Lordship addressed the Jury at some length, and adverted, in strong terms of disapprobation, to the outrages which took place since the convenience (?) [convening] of the election. He said, that though he would make every allowance for the ebullition of popular feelings, and the constitutional freedom of election, yet that he would punish, in the severest manner, the perpetrators of such crimes. It had been proposed to him to adjourn the Assizes, in consequence of the state of fermentation in which the town was; but he would never consent to yield the dignity of his situation to the fury of a mob. In order that the polling should not be interrupted, his Lordship adjourned to the Mayoralty house. Bills of indictment were found against Christopher May for an assault during the election.

A military abstract for July 1818 covering the eastern command stated regarding Dundalk that through the exertion of Mr D. Hamilton a party of Ribbonmen had been broken up and several of them sent to gaol and information lodged against many more.[161]

Spasmodic robberies and assaults continued in north Louth in 1819. On 17 January, Pendleton, Dundalk, reported to Dublin that no steps had been taken for the disarming of the persons who burned Mr Tisdall's house.[162] He reported again on 10 March 1819 that in the case of Moore, Spear and Deal, who were set upon and beaten by 'banditti' near Dundalk, their recognizances might not be fulfilled for failing to prosecute.[163] James Dawson reported early in 1819 regarding a private of the 42nd Regiment who was not able to identify either of the men who had attacked him and added that a farmer's house near Dundalk had been broken into and robbed.[164] On 29 April 1819 Colonel Skeffington indicated in a letter to Dublin Castle that the Louth magistrates intended to hold a meeting to consider some plans for making the police more efficient.[165] Robert Page, collector of excise, Dundalk wrote to William Gregory from the Excise Office on 5 July 1819:

> There are two men now in Newgate, & are to be tried this week, for passing forged notes, who, I think, could give a vast deal of information relative to the disturbances & robberies, that have been going on in this county for some years & I think connected with gangs that are still going thro the country. Their names are James Dullaghan from Shortston & Pat Byrne of Canafanauge both places about three miles from this town. The former was concerned in the burning of corn which commenced in 1815 & fired at Mr Owen McKeone's steward the night that his corn was burned at Shortston & was very intimation (*sic*) with one Mallon, a very bad fellow who had been in the Louth Militia & lived at Tankardsrock not far from Shortston & is a taylor. Byrne sometimes went by the name of Wade (being his mother's name) but his real name is Pat Connolly born at Seatown, Dundalk, & took the name of Byrne from his nurse who would not give him up to his family, not having a son of her own.
> A week does not pass over without two or three robberies being committed & I think the men I have mentioned could give information against all the parties. By a letter from Dullaghan he appears to be much frightened & from some hints I got would tell a great deal.
> I think it my duty to communicate what I have done to you.[166]

On 20 July 1819 Frederick G. Bourns, Keeper of the Gaol of Newgate, replied to A. Mangin, Esqr., who must have made a similar inquiry, informing him that he had not these men in the prison nor at the period alluded to.[167]

7
Approvers and Arrests

ARRESTS

When one reads the accounts of the trials of those charged with the murders at Wildgoose Lodge, a serious question arises concerning the witnesses for the prosecution and the witnesses for the defence. Who is telling the truth? The state relied heavily on approvers who themselves faced prosecution or had already been sentenced for crimes and sought to escape the gallows. Their testimony is therefore suspect. The defence provided witnesses, generally relatives, neighbours or friends who acted as alibis and who for the most part had little respect for the truth.

Before unravelling the part played by informers in the Wildgoose Lodge case and the arrests that followed their information, one must turn to a chart or 'Return' drawn up by Samuel Pendleton, head of police and Chief Magistrate of Louth. It is an excellent guide to the arrests, the informers, trials and executions. Formerly it was a major task to sift through various newspaper reports for the facts and attempt even to ascertain how many men were executed. Pendleton lays it all out clearly.

There were five principal informers. Patrick Clarke gave evidence in the case of Patrick Devan only. He had been at the burning of Wildgoose Lodge and was classified by the police as a 'principal'. Thomas Gubby, a native of Cadian near Dungannon, was a notorious criminal. It was much doubted by the authorities if he had even been present at the Wildgoose Lodge murders as he asserted. He was a robber by trade, apparently also a Ribbonman acquainted with Ribbonmen in County Tyrone and County Armagh, judging by the many names he revealed in statements, but his knowledge of the Wildgoose Lodge incident was weak. He evidently gave information to save himself from hanging. Similarly Bernard Gilroy, Peter Gollogly and Patrick Murphy offered information to avoid the gallows.

Pendleton's Chart. It lists the 'prisoners names; when, where & by whom apprehended; by what witnesses identified; result of tryal etc; observations'. Those marked by a star he noted were leaders on this and many other occasions. It ends –'The above Return etc correct Sam. Pendleton Ch: Magistrate'.

RETURN OF ALL PERSONS APPREHENDED AND COMMITTED FOR THE BURNING AND MURDERS AT WILD GOOSE LODGE ETC.

Pat Malone (1)*, arrested 12th March 1817, Meath, by Mr Pendleton with his Servant, and 5 of the County Meath Constables; identified by Gollogly and Murphy; gibbeted at Louth, 12 March 1818.

Jas Campbell*, arrested 12th March 1817, Meath, by Mr Pendleton with his Servant and 5 of the County Meath Constables; identified by Gollogly and Murphy; gibbeted at Corcreagh, 12 March 1818.

Hu: McLarny, arrested 12th March 1817, Meath, by Mr Pendleton with his Servant, and 5 of the County Meath Constables, identified by Gollogly and Murphy; gibbeted at Louth, 12 March 1818.

Terce [Terence] Marron, arrested 12th March 1817, Monaghan, by Mr Pendleton with his Servant, and 5 of the County Meath Constables; identified by Gubby, Gollogly, Murphy; gibbeted at Corcreagh 12th March 1818; had solicited to be admitted an approver yet died declaring himself innocent.

Michl Kearnan, arrested 12th March 1817, Monaghan, by Mr Pendleton with his Servant, and 5 of the County Meath Constables; identified by Murphy; hanged etc. Dundalk, 4th July 1818; had been admitted an approver, when produced as witness denied his Confession – at the gallows admitted his Guilt.

Pat Meegan, arrested 12th March 1817, Meath, by Mr Pendleton with his Servant, and 5 of the County Meath Constables; identified by Gollogly and Murphy; gibbeted at Corcreagh 12th March 1818.

Jas Smyth, arrested 12th March 1817, Louth, by the Louth Police; identified by Gilroy and Gubby; hanged at Reaghstown 7th April 1818.

John Keegan, arrested 12th March 1817, Louth, by the Louth Police; identified by Gubby; hanged at Reaghstown 7th April 1818; also indicted for the *original* burglary on Lynch.

Hu: McCabe, arrested 12th March 1817, Louth, by the Louth Police; identified by Gilroy and Gollogly; gibbeted at Louth 12th March 1817; also indicted for the *original* burglary on Lynch.

Thos. McCullogh*, arrested 12th March 1817, Louth, by the Louth Police; identified by Gubby, Gollogly and Murphy; gibbeted at Louth, 7th April 1818.

George McQuillan, arrested 12th March 1817, Louth, by the Louth Police; identified by Murphy; admitted to bail 4th July 1818.

Edwd McQuillan, arrested 11th March 1817, Louth, by the Louth Police; identified by Murphy; admitted to bail, 4th July 1818

Thos Sheenan, arrested 12th March 1817, Louth, by the Louth Police, identified by Gubby; hanged at Reaghstown 7th April 1818; also incited for the *original* burglary.

Pat Craven*, arrested 16th March 1817, Louth, by the Louth Police;

identified by Gilroy and Gubby; gibbeted at Louth 12th March 1818; confessed his Guilt & named many others.
John Kieran, arrested 16th March 1817, Louth, by the Louth Police; identified by Gilroy and Gubby; gibbeted at Hackballs Cross, 12th March 1818; confessed his Guilt and named many others.
Pat Malone (2), arrested 16th March 1817, Louth, by the Louth Police; identified by Gilroy; admitted to bail – 4th July 1818.
Jas Laughran, arrested 31st March 1817, Louth, by the Louth Police; identified by Murphy; admitted to bail – 4th July 1818.
Pat McQuillan, arrested 31st March 1817, Meath, by the Louth Police; identified by Gollogly and Murphy; hanged at Reaghstown 7th April 1818.
Lawce Gaynor, arrested 11th April 1817, Meath, by the Louth Police; identified by Gollogly and Murphy; acquitted.
Owen Gaynor, arrested 11th April 1817, Meath, by the Louth Police; identified by Gollogly and Murphy; hanged at Dundalk 4th July 1818.
Jas Morris, arrested 11th April 1817, Meath, by the Louth Police; identified by Murphy; admitted to bail 4th July 1818.
Wm Butler, arrested 11th April 1817, Louth, by the Louth Police; identified by Gubby and Gollogly; put off his Tryal 4th July 1818; had been tried in March – the Jury could not agree, the Foreman stated that *one* only was for *acquittal*; is also indicted for the *original* burglary.
Pat Devan*, arrested 21st May 1817, Dublin, under Mr Pendleton's Warrant by a party of the Dublin and Louth Police; identified by Gilroy and Clarke; gibbeted at Corcreagh 24th July 1817; confessed his Guilt.
Michl Floody, arrested 1st July 1817, Monaghan, by Ch: Constable of Louth Police; identified by Gilroy and Gubby; gibbeted at Hackballs Cross, 12th March 1818.
Bryan Lennon*, arrested 8th October 1817, Monaghan, by Ch: Constable of Louth Police; identified by Gilroy, Gubby, Gollogly; gibbeted at Hackballs Cross, 12th March 1818; *pleaded Guilty*, named many others.
Hu: Tiernan, arrested 22nd December 1817, Louth, by the Louth Police; identified by Murphy; admitted to bail 4th July 1818; brother of Tiernan, hanged for the *original* Burglary.[168]

POLICE MEMORIALS

The police memorials seeking rewards for the arrests and convictions of suspects flesh out the information given in the table of Chief Magistrate Samuel Pendleton above.[169]

Thomas Hunter, Francis Davis, William Leary, John Robinson, Robert Hunter and Joseph Sillery of the Louth police gave the details of the arrests of 12 March in their Memorial to the Lord Lieutenant Charles Earl Whitworth, 14 September 1817, Dundalk:

> That your Memorialists are Constables of the Louth police, and were during the last Winter & Spring stationed in the village of Corcreagh.
> That on the night of the 12th March last and in the course of the following morning your Memorialists by the orders and directions of Samuel Pendleton Esqre, the Chief Magistrate, did apprehend twelve persons charged as principals in the burning and murders at Wild Goose Lodge.
> That ten of the said persons have been since indicted and are now in custody for the same.
> That Patrick Clarke another of those apprehended by your Memorialists has been since admitted an approver and as such gave material evidence on the trial of Patrick Devan who was tried and capitally convicted at the late Assizes of Dundalk for said burning and murders, without which evidence the said Devan could not have been found guilty, and by which it appeared that the said Patrick Clarke was himself a principal concerned in the said burning & murders for which your Memorialists humbly refer to the Honble Baron McClelland, before whom the said tryal took place.
> Your Memorialists further shew that your Excellency by your proclamation in Council of the 18th day of Novr last, and afterwards renewed, was pleased to offer a reward of £200 for the apprehending of each and every person concerned in said burning and murders.
> Your Memorialists therefore humbly submit themselves to your Excellency's consideration and pray that they may be allowed the benefit of said reward, to be distributed in such proportions as to your Excellency may think meet, and your Memorialists do as in duty bound will ever pray.
> Your Memorialists further beg leave to acquaint your Excellency that they have forwarded a similar Memorial on the 24th of *last month*.

Constables Thomas Hunter, Francis Davis, William Leary, Robert Hunter and Joseph Sillery presented another Memorial to the Lord Lieutenant on 21 January 1819:

> That your Memorialists are Constables of the Louth Police and were during the Winter and Spring of 1817 stationed at the Village of Corcreagh.
> That on the night of the 12th of March and in the course of the following morning your Memorialists by the orders and direction of Samuel Pendleton Esqre the Chief Magistrate, did apprehend the following persons viz. Thomas McCullough, James Smyth, John Keegan & Hugh McCabe, charged as Principals in the Burning and Murders at Wildgoose Lodge, who were at the last Spring Assizes of Dundalk tried, convicted and hanged for the same.

Constables Francis Davis & Robert Hunter presented a separate Memorial on 21 January 1819:

> That your Memorialists are Constables of the Louth Police and were during the Winter and Spring 1817, stationed at the village of Corcreagh.
> That on the night of the 12th of March 1817 your Memorialists by order and direction of Saml. Pendleton Esq. Chief Magistrate did apprehend Thomas Sheenan charged as a principal in the Burning and Murders at Wildgoose Lodge.
> That the said Thomas Sheenan was tried and convicted at the last Spring Assizes of Dundalk and underwent the sentence of the Law for the same, at Reaghstown on the 7th of April last.

Constables Henry Ogle and Richard Hopkins of the Louth police and Constables William Ogle Sillery, John Hopkins, Thomas Hopkins, Peter Halfpenny and Joseph Warren of the County of Meath forwarded a Memorial on 21 January 1819:

> That on the night of the 12th of March 1817 your Memorialists were called upon by Saml Pendleton Esqr Ch: Magistrate and accompanied him, and in the course of that night did apprehend the under-named persons viz. Patrick Malone, James Campbell, Hugh McLarney, Terence Marron, Patk Meeghan, and Michael Kearnan, all charged as principals in the Burnings & Murders at Wildgoose Lodge.
> That they have been all tried and convicted at the last Spring Assizes of Dundalk and hanged in chains on the 12th of March 1818.

Constables John English, Isaac McDonald and Henry Cunningham of the Louth police sent a Memorial 21 January 1819 on the arrests of 16 March 1817:

> That your Memorialists are Constables of the Louth Police and were during the Winter and Spring of 1817, stationed at the village of Louth; that on the night of the 16th of March 1817, they by virtue of a warrant received from Samuel Pendleton Esqr. the Chief Magistrate, did apprehend Patrick Craven and John Kearnan, charged as principals concerned in the burning and murders at Wildgoose Lodge.
> That the said Patrick Craven and John Kearnan were tried and convicted at the last Spring Assizes of Dundalk for the said Burning and Murders and hanged in chains for the same.

Constables Thomas Hunter, Henry Ogle, and William Leary, stationed at Corcreagh, forwarded a Memorial on 21 January 1819:

> That on the night of the 11th of April your Memorialists, by order and direction of Saml Pendleton Esqr, Chief Magistrate of the Louth Police, did apprehend Owen Gaynor, charged as a principal in the Burning

and Murders at Wildgoose Lodge.
That the said Owen Gaynor, was tried and convicted last Summer Assizes of Dundalk, and hanged for the same on the 4th of July last.

Constable James Corrigan outlined his arrest of Michael Floody in his Memorial on 21 January 1819:

> The Memorial of James Corrigan – Sheweth that your Memorialist was a Constable of the Louth Police and during the Winter and Spring of 1817 stationed at the village of Hackball's Cross; that on the night of the first of July 1817, he, by virtue of a warrant from Samuel Pendleton Esqr. the Chief Magistrate, did apprehend Michael Floody, charged as one of the persons concerned in the late Burning and Murders at Wildgoose Lodge; and also on the night of the 6th of October following, Bryan Lennon charged with the same. That the said Michael Floody, and Bryan Lennon, were tried and convicted at the last Spring Assizes of Dundalk, for the said Burning and Murders and hanged in chains for the same on the 12th of March 1818.

The fruits of the numerous arrests are visible in the lists of those indicted at the Louth Summer Assizes 1817 and named in the 'County Louth Grand Jury Indictment Book':

Patrick Devan: 'Murder of Rooney and conspiracy to murder. Burning Lynch's house. Burglary. Murder of Rispin'.

Hugh McCabe, John Keegan, Patrick Waters, William Butler, Thomas Sheeran, otherwise Ruck Sheeran, Owen Rickey: 'Assaulting dwelling house of Edward Lynch. Breaking into house of Edward Lynch'.

James Campbell, Owen Gaynor, Laurence Gaynor, Patrick McQuillan, Hugh McCabe, Thomas McCullagh, Edward McQuillan, Michael Kieran, Michael Fluddy, Matthew Clarke, Patrick Waters: 'Burning Edward Lynch's house. Murder of Edward Lynch, Thomas Rooney, James Rispin, assaulting the dwelling house'.[170]

APPROVERS

Patrick Murphy & Peter Gollogly

Patrick Murphy's information provided the breakthrough for the first arrests. *The Correspondent* of 19 March 1817 and a similar report in the Belfast *News-Letter* give us the background, 'The Assizes for the county of Meath commenced at Trim on Monday

(10 March) – Lord Norbury sat in the Crown Court. Five of the villains who robbed the house of Mr Sillery, of Carrickleck, county of Meath, and murdered his servant, on the night of the 19th ult., were capitally convicted, and ordered to be executed on Wednesday'. Patrick Murphy and Peter Gollogly were two of the five. They offered to give information on the burning of Wildgoose Lodge and were saved from the gallows. Their intervention on the day of their execution delayed the execution of the other three until Thursday morning 13 March. The *Belfast News-Letter* of 18 March said that 'one of them died in the most hardened manner, uttering curses the moment before he was launched into eternity. Three were convicted for administering unlawful oaths and for a conspiracy to murder'.

Murphy's information was taken on 12 March 1817. The affidavit of A.H.C. Pollock, Mountainstown, County Meath, 2 September 1817, outlines the circumstances of the taking of Murphy's statement:

> County of Meath to wit. I Arthur Hill Cornwallis Pollock of Mountainstown in the said County Esquire & one of his Majesty's Justices of the Peace for the sd County, do hereby certify that about the hour of seven o'clock in the morning of Wednesday the 12th of March last, whilst I was in bed in my lodging in the town of Trim, Mr William Ogle Sallery, Chief Constable of the Barony of Morgallion in the said County, in which Barony I reside, came into my bed chamber, and told me that Patrick Murphy, a convict then under sentence of death in the Gaol of Trim, was desirous of seeing me as soon as possible, in order to make a confession and disclosure of the part he and many others had taken in the Arson and Murders which had been committed some time before at the house of one Lynch at Wild Goose Lodge in the County of Louth. Whereupon I got out of bed, and went to the Gaol, and was there informed by William Smart the Gaoler thereof, that he the said Patrick Murphy had late the night before told him that he was one of the persons who had committed the said Arson and Murders at Wild Goose Lodge aforesaid, and requested him the sd Gaoler, to send for Mr Pollock, before whom as a Magistrate, he the said Murphy was ready to make a full confession. That he the said William Smart the Gaoler, had accordingly sent the said Mr Sallery to me, to request me to go down to the Gaol. And during this communication from the sd Wm Smart the Gaoler to me, the said Mr Sallery was present. I further certify that the said Gaoler then brought the said Patrick Murphy before me, and desired him to make such confession as he had signified his intention of doing, and accordingly the said Patrick Murphy did make a confession of his own guilt, and of the names, occupations, and

places of residence of many other persons whom he stated to have been present and acting in the said Arson and Murders at Wild Goose Lodge aforesaid, which confession was thereupon read to, and further explained by the said Patrick Murphy, and was copied out fair, and duly taken by me, and by John Pollock Esquire who was present and the same was signed by us in the presence of the said Patrick Murphy, and of the said Wm Smart and of Mr Dunn the Gaoler of Kilmainham, and was acknowledged by the said Patrick Murphy in the presence also of Samuel Pendleton Esqre who came into the appartment when the said Patrick Murphy was examined, shortly before the conclusion of his said confession, and to which said Mr Pendleton the said confession was delivered to the end that he, as Chief Police Magistrate of the said County of Louth, might take such proceedings thereon as might be proper, and to which confession I beg leave to refer.

And I further certify my full conviction that such disclosure and confession were obtained from the said Patrick Murphy by the activity and exertion of the said William Smart only.

Mountainstown. 2nd of September 1817. A. H. C. Pollock.[171]

Willam Smart the Gaoler in a letter from Trim, 3 September 1817, to the magistrates at Head Police Office, Dublin, requested receipt of a reward for his part in gaining Murphy's information. On receipt of his letter these magistrates passed his letter and the certificate on to Peel. Of course it must be remembered that it was Murphy who, within a short time of being hanged, made the first move.

In looking over the *Hue and Cry* of the Month of October last I see that there is a reward offered of £20 by the Magistrates of the Head Office for any information leading to the detection of any of the persons concerned in the Murder of the Lynches.

At the last Spring Assizes a man of the name of Murphy [was] convicted of another murder, and I suspecting he was one of the gang that was concerned in the sd murder of the Lynches, obtained from him the full particulars of that shocking outrage, not thinking of any consideration, unless that of bringing the guilty to justice. I am sure that you will be satisfied from the inclosed certificate that I gave the first information that lead to the discovery. Now as a reward was offered I hope you will feel me deserving of it. William Smart.[172]

Patrick Murphy's Information:

The Information of Patrick Murphy late of Meath Hill, County Meath, hackler, and now a convict under judgment of death in the Gaol of Trim in the sd County.

Says he was one of the party who burned the house of Mr Lynch at

Wild Goose Lodge in the County of Louth in harvest last. Patrick Malone of Meath Hill aforesd, weaver, was the first person who spoke to him about burning the sd house. The night before the sd burning Malone came into his house. Malone told him that one Lynchy of the County of Louth had prosecuted the boys at Dundalk, and asked him whether he would be one of a party who were going to burn his house? He said he would, if he got plenty of whiskey. There was a party then playing cards at Cammell's [Campbell's] house on Meath Hill aforesd near to his (witnesses) house. Malone left him, and soon after sd Cammell came into wits. house, and called him to the door, and asked him if he would join the party and go and kill or burn Lynchy. Said there would be lashings of drink. He said he would. Wits then went into Cammell's house to the party who were playing cards.

The party consisted of *Hudy McElarney*, of Meath Hill, labourer, the sd *Patrick Malone*, and *Patrick Meeghan*, Terence Marron of Drumban, Co. Monaghan, weaver, - [Michael] Kiernan, brother to a man who was hanged in Dundalk. The party remained about an hour or two and then went out in pairs on the door and they broke up for that night.

The sd Patrick Malone and Cammell appointed wits to meet the next night at the house that was formerly inhabited by Anthony Sallery, at Meath Hill. Wits accordingly went the next night to the said house where he met the sd Terence Marron, Kiernan who lives near Derry House (Mr Pendleton), the sd Hudy McElarney, Patk Malone, Patk Meeghan, - [Michael] *Kiernan*, who is brother to the man of that name who was hanged in Dundalk, and the sd Cammell. Does not recollect any more were at Sallery's old house. There were two jars of whiskey there. Does not know who brought them. They were there when he joined the party. The party went up the road as you would go to Drumbride, and picked up two or three horses from the adjoining fields. They proceeded and met another party above Drumbride near Crinaghan's. This last mentioned party came from below Kings Court and were about 10 in number. He did not know any of them, but Cammell and Kiernan knew them. The whole body then went on till they got near to Lynchy's house. Such of the party who met near Crinaghan's who were mounted, took, each, one of the men who were on foot, behind them.

The names of this party who met at Lynchy's house were, (1) the sd Patk Malone, (2) Hudy McElarney, (3) - [Michael] Kiernan, brother to the man who was hanged in Dundalk, (4) the sd Terence Marron, (5) Patk Meeghan of Meath Hill, (6) the sd Cammell, (7) Geo McQuillan, stone mason, and (8) Edwd McQuillan, hackler, both of Partnamuddagh near Louth, and (9) Kiernan who lived near Derry [House]. In all there were 14 men mounted, and each man had one behind him, but he did not know the names of any more of the party than he has mentioned.

This party rushed to the door of Lynchy's house. 4 or 5 of them called to Lynchy to open the door. There was a noise within the house as if the people within were propping the door inside. The party attacking the house were more or less drunk. 2 or 3 shots were then fired from the house. The sd Terence Marron then went to a small house near to Lynchy's, broke in the door with the but[t] of a gun and called for a coal of fire to be brought out, and threatened if any body should look out, he would blow the contents of his gun through them. Marron got the coal and ran to the back of Lynchy's house and set fire to the thatch, and then Marron brought the coal to the front of the house and set fire to the thatch there. Witness was employed when the fire began in carrying the flax from the haggard and throwing it into the flames to increase the fire. Saw Kiernan whose brother was hanged, busy about the flax. The roof of Lynchy's house soon fell in. The fire increased in the house, and the whole house and those within it were burned. The party then fired some shots about the house and then went to where they had left their horses and retired. Whilst the house was burning he heard a voice from within call out "I am the servant girl. I have no call to the house. Let me out". Some of the party answered, "You did not take warning in time". No person within the house escaped to his knowledge. When the party on their return got near Metcalf's new road, wits and the sd Pat. Malone, Pat. Meeghan, Cammell and Hudy McElarney, separated from the body and went to their own houses. The party knew one another by signs.

Trim 12th March 1817. J. Pollock   Saml. Pendleton   A. H. Pollock[173]

On the same day as he received this information, 12 March 1817, Samuel Pendleton moved quickly and made a series of arrests. As he outlines in his chart, Pat Malone, James Campbell, Hugh McLarney, Terence Marron, Michael Kearnan and Pat Meegan were arrested by him with his servant and five of the County Meath constables. Those arrested were all from Meath with the exception of Terence Marron who was from Monaghan. On 12 March also the Louth police arrested James Smyth, John Keegan, Hugh McCabe, Thomas McCullogh, George McQuillan, Edward McQuillan and Thomas Sheenan. The arrests did not go unnoticed by the newspapers. *The Correspondent*, 19 March 1817, reported from the *Newry Telegraph*: 'It has been stated to us that a considerable number of persons (twenty-five in all), said to be implicated in the horrid murder of Linch, of Wildgoose-lodge, have been taken prisoners and brought into Dundalk'. Further arrests were made in March and April, obviously a spin-off from Murphy's information. Details of arrests are given in the memorials of policemen seeking a share in the £200 that had been offered by the Lord Lieutenant's proclamation in Council of 18 November 1816 and later renewed. These memorials show that the police at Corcreagh apprehended twelve persons on the night of 12 March, ten of whom were later indicted. These included Thomas McCullough, James Smyth, John Keegan, Hugh McCabe, Thomas Sheenan, and Patrick Clarke, who became an approver and whose evidence, with that of Bernard Gilroy, was responsible for the conviction of Patrick Devan.[174] On 16 March the police at Louth village arrested Patrick Craven and John Kearnan.[175] Owen Gaynor was apprehended by the police at Corcreagh on 11 April.[176] The police stationed at Hackball's Cross arrested Michael Floody on 1 July and Bryan Lennon on 6 October 1817.[177]

We gain a little information on Gollogly and Murphy in the letters of the Rev. M. Wainright, inspector of the gaol of Trim. Wainright also took a statement from Gollogly.

> Trim. 10 April 1817
> I had the honor of yours & in answer beg to inform you, that it ever has been the custom in this Prison to permit the Wifes [sic] of Approvers to see their Husbands. If in Murphy's case there was any thing which ought to prevent that indulgence (which really I cannot see), Mr Pendleton ought on Friday last when he was here to have informed me of it. Murphy is by my orders kept in the Magistrate's Room separate from even the other Approver Gallagly who has given much information respecting the murder of Gosman and Sillery's robbery. These men are really named. I have received directions from Mr Pollock to procure for them some sort of covering & to provide for their Wifes & Children lodgings which I find difficult to obtain its being known to whom they belong, but I shall do the best I can & on the most reasonable terms. When everything is settled, shall inform you of it.[178]

Information of Peter Gollogly:

> Information of Peter Gallogly now a prisoner in the gaol of Trim who being sworn [before me] saith that Laurence Gaynor of Cornavon Co. Meath, came to Examinant whom he well knew, & told them (*sic*) that he and a large party had determined to burn the house of Lynch of Wild Goose Lodge in Co. Louth for prosecuting some friends of theirs at the Assizes of Dundalk who were executed – that Ext did agree to become one of the party, that Owen Gaynor of the sd Cornavon, Patrick McCullen of Carahaseiln (?), James Campbell of Meath Hill, Hugh MacLarnon of Meath Hill, Patrick Meighan of Meath Hill, were all of the said party with Patrick Murphy, now a prisoner in [the gaol of Trim] and many others to Examinant unknown, that the party set out and were met at the Chapel of Arthurstown by a number of people who were assembled there for the same purpose, that from the Chapel they proceeded to Lynch's house and left Examinant in charge of

Approvers and Arrests

several horses which they brought with them, which horses Examinant took care of at the end of a narrow road which led up to the former habitation of the said Lynch.
Peter Gallogly x his mark. Sworn before me this 14th day of April 1817.
M. Wainright

Trim. 21 April 1817. Private
I had the honor of yours respecting the purchase of clothes for the *Approvers*. I have done so on very moderate terms & in a few days shall have the honor of calling on you with the Acct. I am very sorry to inform you that this part of the County of Meath is in a very disturbed state. In this town it shall be necessary to augment the Military Force not only on acct of the *Prison* but also to enable me & one or two others to go out at night & endeavour to apprehend these villains. There are *one hundred & ten* this day in the Goal. I tell you in confidence that some Magistrates are not taking the proper method of getting hold of *principals*. They are dashing away without a settled plan. These men I remember the day when they wd not be entrusted with the commission of the peace. To you Sir I entrust *that secret* which is founded on truth. I must beg again to suggest that *forty men* will be necessary to protect this Prison and to enable the Magistrates to do some good.[179]

Trim. 10th Augt 1817
I have the honor to inform you, that three Men (Approvers) viz. Patrick Brady, Patrick Murphy & Peter Gallagly are left in this Prison without any order from the Clerk of the Crown or Crown Solicitor what is to be done with them etc. They are Prosecutors for the Crown. I beg leave to request your orders respecting their future keeping. I have the honor to inclose to you a Copy of the Resolutions of the Grand Jury of the County of Meath at the late assizes respecting the conduct of William Smart, the Keeper of Trim Prison. Mr Pollock's Testimony respecting this Transaction was very clear & acquitted Smart of any impropriety. I trust that to you Sir I shall appear equally so.[180]

A letter from Chief Constable Michael Farrell to the magistrate Head Police office concerning the same three men is filed with Wainright's letter.

Head Police Office, Augt 13th 1817
Gentlemen, Patrick Brady was examined as a witness in the Trial of three men for conspiracy to murder Mr Wade and Mr Rathroan (?) near Kells. The prisoners were acquitted. No one believed Brady, he having been under sentence of transportation for being convicted as a Ribbon man. Murphy is the person that gave information respecting the burning of Wild Goose Lodge, many of whom are in custody and not yet tried. I think that Gallaghly gave information to the same effect.[181]

Thomas Gubby

Thomas Gubby alias Hughes, native of Cadian, County Tyrone, but apparently living with his wife in Drogheda, was arrested by John Armstrong, chief constable of Drogheda, on Wednesday 9 April 1817.

Ralph Smyth, Deputy Mayor of Drogheda, certified the arrest on 28 July1817:

> I certify that Mr John Armstrong, Chief Constable of Drogheda, apprehended and brought before me on the 9th of April last a man called Thomas Hughes alias Gubby who has since confessed his guilt and become an approver on the part of the Crown against Patrick Devan and several other persons for setting fire to and burning the house of Edward Lynch and several persons therein at Wildgoose Lodge on the night of the 29th October last, and I have known Mr Armstrong for several years to be an active, zealous, intelligent & deserving peace officer.[182]

Armstrong states the arrest briefly in a memorial to the Lord Lieutenant of 26 July 1817:

> That your Memorialist on the 9th of April last apprehended at Drogheda a man called Thomas Gubby who confessed he was concerned in maliciously setting on fire the dwelling house of one Edward Lynch at Wildgoose Lodge in the County of Louth on the night of the 29th of October last, by which said Lynch with seven other persons were burned to death, and gave information before Ralph Smyth Esqre against Patrick Devan, Bernard Gilroy and several other persons as being accomplices with him in said barbarous and inhuman outrage, of which the said Devan was since convicted at the last Assizes of Dundalk and executed for the same. And your Memorialist on 22nd of May last caused the said Bernard Gilroy to be apprehended near Navan in the County of Meath and who also afterwards made a full disclosure of his guilt to the Chief Magistrate of Police Louth, and prosecuted the said Devan to conviction at the said Assizes.[183]

Sub-constable George Wright of the barony of Dungannon in a memorial in July 1817 gives the full story of Gubby's arrest, but does not name the Drogheda policeman who accompanied him, merely referring to him as 'a constable'. The memorial, on the request of Golding, a magistrate, was testified by a recommending letter of Lord Caledon, 25 July 1817, who stated in a letter to Peel that Wright was a man of excellent character and had acted as a constable in the neighbourhood of Caledon for several years with great zeal and integrity.

That Memorialist having received a warrant from George R. Golding Esqr. to apprehend some persons charged with felony, and having received information that said persons were concealed in some houses in the townland of Cadian in said County, went pursuant to said warrant on the night of the 8th day of April last to search said houses, that in one of said houses belonging to James Gubby he found a letter directed to Thomas - at Peter St, Drogheda, that conceiving said letter to be intended for Thomas Gubby against whom he knew there were charges of felony, he took said letter secretly into his possession, and the next morning brought it to George R. Golding Esqr the above named magistrate who on reading it sent Memorialist by the mail coach on the same day to Drogheda with a warrant to apprehend said Gubby. That Memorialist immediately proceeded to the house of Ralph Smith Esqr, Chief Magistrate there, and accompanied by a constable sent by said magistrate, did succeed in apprehending and lodging in the jail of Drogheda the said Thomas Gubby; that in consequence of his apprehension said Gubby, has, as Memorialist been informed and believes, confessed himself to have been concerned in the horrid massacre of the Lynches of Wild Goose Lodge.[184]

Gubby made six statements.[185] Those on the Wildgoose Lodge are vague, but his details on Defenders and Ribbonmen, which must be read with caution, are interesting, and, although alarmist and ingratiating in character, throw some light on Ribbonism and Defenderism. His two earliest 'informations' on Wildgoose Lodge are given here, along with one of the northern oriented statements which speaks of provincial meetings of 'Defenders'. I published the northern statements in the journal *Dúiche Néill* (No. 8, 1993).

9 April 1817. County of the Town of Drogheda to wit. The Information and Confession of Thomas Gubby of Cadian in the County of Tyrone, linen weaver, now a prisoner in the Watch House of Drogheda.
Informant being examined in the presence of Ralph Smyth, one of His Majesty's Justices of the Peace for said Town & County, states - that some time in or about the month of October last, informant, having then resided in the house of Manus Caulan at or near a place called Loughan in the County of Louth, he was called by one *Patrick Devan,* a schoolmaster, and weaver residing near said place, and who then kept a school in the Chapel at Stonetown in said County, and requested Inft to attend a meeting at the Chapel of Stonetown, in order to punish two men of the name of Lynch and Rooney, for having prosecuted three men to conviction at the preceding Assizes of Dundalk.
Inft. saith that he proceeded on said night to the said Chapel at Stonetown and there met the said Patrick Devan, Thomas McAnaney of Tully, in said County, labourer, James Smyth of Stonetown, or near it,

linen weaver, James or John Waters of near the same place, labourer, Bernard Gilroy, then a journeyman-weaver working with one Byrne at Feras in the County of Louth, a man called McKeever, and several other persons, whose names are now unknown to Informant who all met in said Chapel of Stonetown.

Saith that said Devan, and said man called McKeever, then and there proposed to the persons then present, to go to Wild Goose Lodge to punish said Rooney and Lynch, and it was also proposed and agreed upon to set fire to said Lynch's house and burn them therein.

Saith that said party remained in said Chapel for some time, waiting for a party of men to come to join them from Enniskeen, and who afterwards ar[r]ived at said Chapel about twenty in number. The said parties then considered it too late in the night then to proceed to Wild Goose Lodge and the intended attack was then postponed until the Tuesday night following.

Informant saith that on hearing said party intended to commit murder, he declined being concerned therein until he was threatened by several of said party, who declared they would put him to death if he refused to go with them as he had now known their secrets and intentions.

Informant saith that on Tuesday night after said meeting, he repaired at the desire of said Devan to the said Chapel of Stonetown, and there met sd Patrick Devan, Thos McAnaney, James Smyth, James or John Waters, Bernard Gilroy, - McKeever and several other persons unknown to Inft. being about one hundred men in the whole.

Saith that having then agreed to burn said Lynch's house and destroy him and said Rooney, and having settled the plan of attack, said party proceeded from said Chapel to Wild Goose Lodge aforesaid and set fire to said house from which some shots were fired and which were returned by said party, some of whom wished to save the lives of the children and servant maids then in said house, whilst others of said party declared – *that the nits should be burned & destroyed as well as the louse.*

Saith that said house was set on fire at four different places, and said Devan and Gilroy set fire to one part of the same, and were the first who went forward for that purpose.

Informant further saith, that at the time said house was set on fire as aforesaid he saw a living person therein, and he has since heard and believes, that eight persons were burned to death in said house, and he also heard the cries of several persons therein.

Saith that said party then retired from sd house or the remains thereof, and at a short distance therefrom, said Devan and McKeever swore Informant and the rest of said party to keep secret and not discover the names of any of sd party, and also to attend when & where called on, in order to put any person to death, who would make discovery of any of them.

Informant saith that he has now told the names of all the persons he knew at said meetings & burning according to the best of his recollection, but he thinks he may know the persons of some of the other persons concerned on seeing them.

Taken and acknowledged before me this 9th day of April 1817. Ralph Smyth.
Thomas Gubby. Witness present T. Armstrong.
12 April 1817.
Thomas Gubby took the name of Hughes having quit Tyrone for a Robbery laid to his charge - the plan of burning Wild Goose Lodge was first proposed to him by Pat Devan, schoolmaster at Stonetown. Says in addition to what he told Mr Smyth that the men who had settled with Devan the attack on Wild Goose Lodge on the Sunday morning, were of the party at Stonetown Chapel. Says he heard the people say in Stonetown that the boys near Wild Goose Lodge were to shun their homes that night, and be in procured places, to avoid being suspected. Believes it was about 12 o'clock on the Tuesday night, when he and the others got to Wild Goose Lodge - that Devan was the first to light the fire. He had fire closed in a little kettle from Stonetown and pulled the dry thatch and light (sic) the fire into it. They divided into two divisions and one went to each side and each end of the house. He supposes the party with him were from 16 to 20. Says the wind blew more upon the corner than the back of the house, and where Devan lighted the fire was on the wind side, so as to drive the blaze to the rest of the house. Was not a very windy night. Staid till the roof fell, and till the cries of the people within were a long time quelled. Saw a man in his shirt at a window, and all who were in sight of the window fired at him. Says there were many of the party without arms. These from Enniskeen had muskets and pistols & swords and long bayonets at the end of poles.
After the fire was completed and the house burned, they all went away and stopped at the bottom of the ditch and swore to secrecy and never to discover. And Devan and one McKeever swore them all. Says they divided then, and about one hundred Enniskeen and Stonetown boys were in the party with him returning, that they had parties as sentries, round the country, and left a party at the Mill of Louth for the purpose. Says he returned to one *Manus Callon* at nearly break of day in the town of Laughan. His wife was there. Says 6 or 7 weeks ago, he met one *Jemmy Laughran* in Drumgowna near Mullacrue, where he had a house taken. Laughran asked him what made him look ill? He said he had a trouble on his mind, and Laughran advised him to tell it to Captn. Murray, a Magistrate in Dungannon. He told said Laughran (who is a farmer of Reskmore near Dungannon) that he had been at Wild Goose Lodge, and stated in a letter he gave him to deliver to Captn Murray, that his conscience was struck, and he was determined to relieve himself by discovering all he knew. That Mr Murray went to Dublin before he could see him. He went to his place when he returned and took Laughran with him, was on yesterday sennight. Between the first time of his intention which was 6 or 7 weeks ago, and that day he heard of many men being taken up for the Burning at Wild Goose Lodge, which he stated in a letter, which he sent him before that day. Says Laughran told him that Mr Murray had written to a Gentleman in Dundalk upon receiving his letter, who he said had given him no

satisfactory answer, but requested him to come there on the business. Says he went with Laughran to Mr Murray's, but did not speak to him as Mr Murray did not call for him or desire to see him.

Says he never slept a right sound night's sleep since the burning at Wild Goose Lodge. Says that Thomas McAnaney, mentioned in his information to Mr Smyth, had a brother James. Says Bernard Gilroy mentioned there also was a native of Navan or near it, and had been in the Louth or Meath Militia, and by a letter Mr Smyth read to him, that he had lodged examinations against him for the robbery he was accused of.

Says that part *of the men* went on their way from Stonetown Chapel to a sort of Bleach where they heard *Rooney* used to sit up at watching yarn. Says his first acquaintance with Devan was his meeting him on the road, when Devan threw him a sign, which he answered. The sign was stroaking underneath his chin. The answer stroaking the back of his left hand. He then after some conversation produced to Devan a certificate the contents of which were that - I certify that Thomas Hughes (meaning himself) is a true made member of the Defender Society - after which were A.M.P., meaning member of Armagh Province Society - signed C.H. - meaning Charles Hughes - he (Hughes) is a farmer in good circumstances in the townland of Gort, and parish of Clonfeacle. Says this was in October last, and in about a fortnight after he asked him would he join to punish two persons, who hung three men at Dundalk? *Devan* has the certificate - says the same Charles Hughes swore him into the meeting. The oath he took was - I, A.B., in the presence of Almighty God and his blessed Son Jesus Christ, do swear that 1 will be true to my brother on all lawful occasions, and that I will not fight a challenge with my brother or see him struck, without espousing his cause, that I will attend when and where I am called by my committee, and spend what is just & proper on the occasion. That I will not hear my brother ill spoken of without giving him information, that I will not buy any article from a Protestant, while a man of my own religion has one at the same rates, that I will not drink to be drunk and I will not know a brother to be in distress without giving the aid of myself and my pocket.

Says that only the picked wicked men were appointed to come to the Chapel, that they were all of the Society he is - Defenders. Some call them Threshers, and Ribbonmen. Says that a stack of corn was pulled out of the haggard at Wild Goose Lodge, and thrown into the broken windows and door after the door fell in to assist the fire. Knows Owen McAnaney a poor man near Tully or Annamuna who has five or six children. Knows Pat McAnaney an old man in Feeras. Says the Enniskeen people brought the sledge which forced the door at Wild Goose Lodge. That he knows there is a smith near Corcreagh, but does not know his name. Has heard of a blacksmith in the neighbourhood of the name of Marron.

Taken this 12th day of April 1817 etc etc. (Copy).

In his statement of 21 April 1817, Gubby equates 'Defenders' and 'Ribbonmen' and reveals plans for a provincial meeting of delegates in Belfast. He gives the names of persons, who, he alleges, acted as delegates on former occasions.

County of the Town of Drogheda to wit
The further Information of Thomas Gubby late of Cadian in the Co. Tyrone given before Ralph Smyth Esq. Drogheda
Informant being further examined confesseth and saith that on or about the first Monday next there is to be a Provincial Meeting of Delegates belonging to the Society called Defenders at Belfast consisting of one Delegate from each of the following counties, Tyrone, Monaghan, Armagh, Down, Derry & Louth. Saith that he knows the following persons in addition to those already mentioned to have acted as Delegates on many former occasions, viz.

1	Wm or John Gormon	A Delegate for Louth, lived in the house now occupied by Woods a Constable on Mr Wm Filgate's land.
2	Mr Gartland	A Delegate for the town of CkMcCross, son to a Baker & Publican.
3	Frans. McNally	Publican Delegates for the town of Castleblayney
4	John Conelly	Farmer
5	Michl Kelly	A travelling Surveyor, is Delegate for a Parish in the neighbourhood of Castleblayney.
6	Thomas Donelly	Publican, Irish St, Armagh, a delegate for Armagh.
7	Michl Mullen	Weaver. Delegate for the Parish of Aughaloe.
8	John Donelly	A Delegate for the 13 townland Parish of Fintona, Co. Tyrone.
9	John O'Neil	A Delegate for the Parish of Errigle, Co. Tyrone.
10	Arthur Mc Guirk	A Delegate for Benburb. Do.
11	John Garland	A Delegate for the 7 towns Parish of Clonfecle, a cabinet maker by trade.
	Macklemeal	A farmer near Truoah or Mountain Bar. A Delegate for Co. Monaghan.
	Arthur Mc Cluskey	A Delegate for the Parish of Errigle Trua, Co. Armagh.
	- McKenna	Son to a wealthy respectable man in Monaghan. A Delegate for the town of Monaghan.
15	Pat Gafney	Horse Jockey. Carricklane &
16	Pat Cassidy	Farmer near the chapel of Deranoon near CBlayney are Delegates for that Parish.

Informant further saith that about seven weeks since he was much troubled in mind, and wrote a letter to Mr Murray of Dungannon Esqr, a Magistrate for the County Tyrone, the purport of which was as he now recollects as follows: That Informant had heard that there was a person in the Gaol of Trim, who had given information about the persons who had murdered Lynch, Rooney & family at Wildgoose Lodge, Co. Louth, that he heard a great number were in custody. That he did not know that he was sworn against also, *and was willing to do whatever his Honr would advise him*, which letter Informant put into the Post Office of Drogheda and the receipt of it ackbowledged by Mr Murray to John [James] Laughran of near Dungannon. Informant saith that not having received any reply to said letter he wrote another from his father's at Cadian, Co. Tyrone (on a Sunday) and sent it by James Laughran aforesaid. The purport was as follows, that he believed the chief part of the persons in custody for the burning etc. were innocent as they were getting out on bail, which they could not do, if they were charged with that offence, and that the persons who he could charge with being at that murder were not as he could learn in custody, and requested Mr M. to write to the Gentleman at Dundalk to know who was in custody or if there was a good information against them, which Mr M. (Laughran informed him) promised to do saying that he should wait the arrival of the mail from Dundalk on the Wednesday following. Saith that on said day Informant accompanied Laughran to a valley near to the house of Mr M. untill Laughran enquired from the footman if Mr M. was at home. He said he was at his mother's in Dungannon, to which place Informant & Laughran went. L. rapped at their door and was informed by the servant that he could not see Mr M. as he was in company. After waiting some time, Mr M. and another Gentleman came out and were followed by Laughran who (*in view of Informant*) stopped them and remained in conversation a considerable time. On his return to Informant he said Mr M. told him he had written to Dundalk to a Gentleman and had not yet any satisfactory reply, that the Gentleman wrote to on the subject would rather hold a conversation than commit it to paper. Mr Murray requested Informant would mention some particular transaction which he would mention in his next letter to Dundalk which he hoped would induce the Gentleman there to pay some attention to it. Saith that he desired the said Laughran to inform Mr M. that he could give information of every thing that passed on the night they conspired to murder Lynch, Rooney etc and up to the night the deed was done, and that as he wished to go to Drogheda to see his wife, if Mr thought proper to write to him on the subject (as Informant had every confidence that his Honr would not deceive him) direct to the care of Pat Hamil, Patrick Street, Drogheda, and he would immediately attend him at Dungannon, from which time untill he was apprehended and brought before Mr Smyth at Drogheda he was not favoured with any reply on said subject.

Informant saith that the Society of which he has given information are known by the names of Ribbonmen as well as Defenders. Informant saith that the object of said Society as he and others were sufficiently told by the *leaders* or *constitution bearers* of the Society, was that *they might be ready and know each other when some favourable opportunity would arise, to fight for their Religion and in Defence of their Faith, and to overcome, and put down all those who were oppressing and persecuting them, namely all enemies to the True Roman Catholic Religion, or Friends to a Protestant Monarchy.*

Saith that a meeting of Delegates was published to be held at Armagh on the second Tuesday in May next for the purpose of transacting the business of their Society. Saith that said meeting is to be attended by two Delegates from each of the before mentioned counties. Saith that said meeting was usually held at the House of Thomas Donelly, publican, Irish Street, Armagh, Terence Donelly, Market Street, Peter Donelly, Market Street and the House of a Widow Fields near the Shambles, Michl McBride, same street. The plan of meeting at Belfast was in a House near the Poor House, also in a Winetavern, or in Winetavern Entry, as he heard it mentioned by others but was not present himself. Informant further saith that the Charles Hughes mentioned in a former information collected and supplyd him with money when he was confined in the Gaol of Armagh on a charge connected with the said Society. Informant saith that the words & signs of said Society and the time and place of meeting are altered as occasion may require.

Taken and acknowledged before me this 21 day of April 1817. Ralph Smyth
Thos Gubby
Witness: Jn Armstrong

Looking at Pendleton's chart one can see that Gubby appeared as a witness in the cases of Terence Marron, James Smyth, John Keegan, Thomas McCullagh, Thomas Sheenan, Pat Craven, John Kieran, William Butler, Michael Floody, and Bryan Lennon. All with the exception of William Butler were put to death and Butler narrowly escaped. He was the sole witness in the cases of John Keegan and Thomas Sheenan. The magistrate W. Murray of Dungannon who was acquainted with Gubby's criminal past advised against the reliability of Gubby as a true witness. He tells us that he was a Captain of Ribbonmen locally in County Tyrone and mentions two brothers James and Michael who also seem to have been implicated in his robberies. The James Loughran, whom Gubby portrays as a rich farmer who can vouch for him, Murray dismisses as a scoundrel. Ralph Smyth of Drogheda thought his testimony valuable, although aware of W. Murray's opinion.[186]

Pendleton himself, Chief Magistrate of Louth, a few times

expressed his lack of confidence in Gubby as a witness. He did not use him to give evidence against Patrick Devan and yet used him as a sole witness in some of the trials in 1818. The most damning judgement of Gubby is bluntly expressed in Pendleton's letters respecting applications for rewards.

Peel wrote to Pendleton on 28 July 1817 requesting his opinion on the memorial of George Wright Sub-Constable who sought reward for apprehending Gubby.

Pendleton to Peel. Dundalk. 29 July 1817.

> In reply to your letter with which I am this day honoured, respecting the claim of Wright, a constable of Tyrone, to a reward etc etc I beg to submit that I do not consider any person whatever, under present circumstances, entitled to a reward for the apprehension of Thomas Gubby.
> There is no judicial knowledge of his having been concerned in the offence with respect to which the reward is offered. His own confession to that effect is of such description, that it was judged not only useless, but dangerous to produce him as a witness, nor has he been at all used as such.
> As his confession then has not (at least as yet) been available to the publick for any beneficial purpose, it ought not (I conceive) to be admitted for the purpose of aggravating expence by conferring a reward, more especially where the claim of it rests on *accident*, and is undistinguished by any circumstance of intrepidity, or address.
> I am to trouble you for an instruction as to the extent etc to which I shall be justified in going, for the care and maintenance of the wives and families of Clarke and Gilroy (the approvers who convicted Devan, and also who were pronounced by the Atty. Genl. to be the best witnesses of that description he had ever examined). Since their confinement I have given five shillings per week for the support of each. *That* is now very insufficient, as they are no longer admitted inmates into any house. They are for the present kept (and with much inconvenience) in the Police Barrack and if out of the way of protection would unquestionably be destroyed.[187]

Pendleton wrote again in the same vein, 23 September 1817.

> I do not conceive that any reward can yet with propriety be claimed for apprehending Thomas Gubby. Wright (the Tyrone constable) is misinformed as to having contributed by his testimony to the conviction of any persons. He has neither been used, nor *yet* admitted as an approver. It has not yet *judiciously* appeared that he was 'concerned' in the crime, neither is it certain that any publick advantage will *ever* be derived from his confession.[188]

Approvers and Arrests

In the following year, however, due to lack of other evidence Gubby was used as a witness. There is other correspondence that helps to highlight the dubious nature of Gubby's information. A note regarding the informer Gilroy on a letter dated 27 May 1817, signed J. I. Townsend, 31 May, reads: 'I am writing to corroborate Gubby as to the prisoner Gilroy, and as I understand Gubby is a convicted felon I don't think any man will be detained on his information'.[189] An undated letter of the Rev. M. Wainright, in the 1817 file, is probably a reply. Bernard Gilroy was arrested on 27 May 1817. Gubby had mentioned his name in his statement of 9 April 1817 and this information obviously led to his arrest. Wainright also comments on Gollogly.

> This day I had the honor of yours with the enclosed Informations of *Gubby*. I have gone through it very particularly with Murphy who declares that he knows not one of these People who are therein mentioned, not this *Gubby*. He states that on the very night of the Conviction of the three Villains at Dundalk, the plan was formed for the destroying of Lynchy & accordingly Notices were sent every where to the *Ribbon* Men to attend for putting it into Execution. As to numbers he agrees with this Man, but positively swears that they met at the Chapel of *Arthurstown* which from *Wild Goose Lodge* was but *two* miles, whereas Stonestown is *four*. I rather think this to be correct. Another fellow of the name of Gallagly who was also there & is become an Approver made Informations before me agst six (Mr Pollock has them) two of them of the name of Gaynor. He says that these two Men could give more Informations on this subject than any who were concerned in the diabolical act. I have this day taken Informations against *thirty-five* men who live in and about *Kells*, Crosakeil and Chamber's town - four of them rich fellows. I declare most solemnly that I believe this Country to be in a worse state than it was previous to 1798.[190]

Ralph Smyth, sub-sheriff in Drogheda, as stated, was impressed by Gubby's information, in particular his elaboration of his connection with Defenderism and a Louth/Armagh link up, not seeing it as a fleshing out on Gubby's part to hide his scant knowledge on Wild Goose Lodge. His information on the burning of Wild Goose Lodge could easily have been concocted on the general underground knowledge of the murders, the names of those already arrested and Gubby's inevitable knowledge of Ribbonism in Louth since he was connected with Ribbonism himself. Captain William Murray of Dungannon, a magistrate who already knew of Gubby's criminal activities in Tyrone, did not trust his evidence, being put off by Gubby's unsavoury character and the suspicious nature of contacts Gubby had previously tried to make with him.

Ralph Smyth to William Gregory. Drogheda. 14 April 1817.

> I beg leave to acquaint you for the information of his Excellency the Lord Lieutenant that on Wednesday last a man who then called himself Thomas Hughes, but who now appears to be Thomas Gubby, was apprehended and brought before me by Armstrong our Chief Constable, under a warrant which I had backed for a Robbery committed in the county of Tyrone. He was not many minutes under examination when he made a full confession of his having been one of the monsters, who burned *Rooney, Lynch & Family at Wild Goose Lodge*. He gave information against those of the party he knew, which I forwarded to Mr Foster of Collon, as it was a matter in which the county of Louth was much interested.
>
> Mr Foster & Mr Pendleton, the Chief Magistrate of Police, have been here to examine him also, & I believe have found him to correspond with other approvers, in some of the leading features of that melancholy business. Since which Gubby has given other information now enclosed respecting a widely intended and I conceive a very dangerous system of Organisation that has spread itself over the northern counties. He also states that Delegates attend their meetings at Armagh from the county of Louth, the names of which he hopes to recollect. There cannot however be a doubt that if those he has mentioned and their papers were seized it would be a death wound to this system and bring to light all the leading persons concerned.
>
> If any Gentleman is ordered from the Police Office to follow up these informations, Armstrong would have no objection in accompanying him. I believe he is worthy of any confidence that may be placed in him, on these occasions. Indeed we are indebted to his ingenuity & directions for this apprehension of Gubby who I hope will be extremely useful to the county.
>
> My particular friend Mr Balfour has undertaken to hand you this letter.[191]

W. Murray to Pendleton. Dungannon. 15 April 1817.

> I received your letter by late post, & in reply I have to inform you that a kind of confession was made to me by the person & on the subject you mention there: a man of the name of James Loughran. I had every reason for not acting upon this Information immediately & the principal one as the characters of the persons, namely Gubby & Loughran. They are men of the *worst description*. Since this business was first mentioned to me, I have been much perplexed as to how I should act & answer you. It has cost me much consideration.

However, as this proposal of Gubby has come thro another channel, I feel myself called upon to follow it up & give you any information & assistance in my power & for which I shall go to Dundalk on Saturday next when I hope to see you. I shall in the meantime see Loughran* & get as much information from him as possible & if I was to give an opinion it would be for you to rest on your arms till after I see you. Should you think it necessary that I should see Gubby I will with pleasure accompany you to Drogheda.

Note on this letter written by Pendleton:
Laughran whom he represented to me as a respectable farmer appears to have been for a considerable time concerned with Gubby and his Brother in horse stealing and was several times tried for his life.[192]

A further letter from G. R. Golding, Lime Park, written on 16 April 1817, gives more information on the background and crimes of Gubby.

In answer to yours of the 13th respecting Gubby I beg to state to you, that the first transaction in which he became known to me, was a charge laid to be made before me against him for taking up arms, but from knowing that the informant had before accused others of the offence I refused to take his information. It was however taken before another Magistrate, & he was tried for it at Omagh, & acquitted on my evidence. The next transaction which came within my knowledge was the one for which he is now in Jail & which I presume will be fully brought home to him, as the watch, coat & a quantity of yarn found in [Michael] Gubby's house, were fully identified by Dixon the man robbed.
There is also another reason to believe that he was guilty of stealing a horse from a person in this neighbourhood (since that time) of the name of Patk McSorley, as a mare perfectly answering the description has been sworn before me by the Kilroy aluded to in your letter, as having been in the possession of a brother of his who also fled at the time of Dixon's robbing, but who is now here & who I have had taken on this charge, & shall this day take heavy bail of, as I do not consider Kilroy's unsupported affidavit as sufficient cause for committing any person for such a length of time. The description of the mare stolen is as follows: light chesnut, hind legs white above the fetlocks, a white patch down her face, about 14 hands high, & 4 years old. She is still I believe in the County Louth. These are the only felonys I have ever heard laid to his charge. He is however well known as a Captain of Ribbon men & I have in my possession a Roll of his Company found in his breeches pocket after Dixon's robbing. A great part of the persons mentioned are well known to me as young men of the worst character. I had written so far when I was called to take bail of Michl Gubby, the brother whom I mentioned in the first part of my letter. After having done so he begged to speak privately to me, & then told me of a business which his brother in Drogheda wished much to make a full

confession to me, & that he would not make it to any other person, as he considered I had so much befriended him before. Now as I think it probable that it may be merely the confession you alude to in your letter, it would not be worth my while to take so long a journey to obtain a knowledge of what he has already made known. If you will therefore have the goodness to let me know the nature of his present confession I shall be guided by that as to my future measures.[193]

Ralph Smyth to Gregory. Drogheda. 20 April 1817.

I had the honor of receiving your letter of the 19th in reply to which I herewith send the original information given by Gubby, a copy of which I did not take at the time I forwarded them to Mr Foster, who sent them to Dundalk to Mr Pendleton & from whom they did not come to my hands until this night (11pm). As soon as you have copies taken of them, be so kind as to have them returned. I shall I hope by next post address you a few lines respecting some further information which Gubby has given whose removal to Dublin without delay would be in my humble opinion very advisable.[194]

W. Murray to Pendleton. Drumfields. 20 April 1817.

Since I had the pleasure of seeing you yesterday I have reviewed Gubby's case in every way that I am capable of doing and am still of my former opinion, that his testimony would not be believed. Should you think proper to take his Information what do you gain by it? Nothing that I can see. I enclose you a letter from him to me in which you will see that he says –"I believe all I know are taken" – you are the best judge, whether the men he is now willing to swear against were among those taken up* the time he mentions.
Note on letter from Pendleton:
None of them – except a Jas. Smith, which being a common name, cannot be relied on as the same, without a personal identification.[195]

Ralph Smyth to Gregory. Drogheda. 21 April 1817.

Every day furnishes fresh proof that Gubby may be a very useful man to the country. He has given forth information respecting intended meetings at Armagh & Belfast, which I beg leave to send herewith. I received a letter from Mr Pendleton enclosing the copy of a note from Mr Murray of Dungannon, from which it appears they are inclined totally to discredit his story. Gubby would therefore wish his letters on that subject to Mr Murray were produced, and as they were written and the proposal made at a time he was at liberty and not himself concerned he thinks it gives him some claim to credit.[196]

Gregory, suspicious of the validity of Gubby's statements,

must have written to the Rev. Wainwright, magistrate, Trim, seeking his opinion. The undated letter above marked 'private' from Wainright stated that Patrick Murphy, the approver in Trim Gaol, did not know Gubby or any of those Gubby named.

Bernard Gilroy

Bernard Gilroy (Kilroy, McElroy, McIlroy) was arrested on Thursday 22 May 1817. John Armstrong, chief constable, Drogheda, had published a description of him. Gilroy's information is not extant, but there are newspaper reports of his evidence in the trials of those charged with the burning and murders at Wildgoose Lodge. He testified in the cases of James Smyth, Hugh McCabe, Pat Craven, John Kieran, one of the two Pat Malones, Pat Devan, Michael Floody, and Bryan Lennon. There are some letters giving the background to his arrest and the evidence he was to provide. Gilroy was apprehended at the great flax mills factory near Navan by Mr John Shore, postmaster of Navan, in the presence of the portreeve of Navan, Francis D. Hamilton on the information of John Armstrong.[197] John Foster, Collon, in a certificate dated 27 July 1817, at the request of John Armstrong, gives the policeman a recommendation for his part in finding Gilroy:

> I have long known Mr John Armstrong, Chief Constable of Drogheda & Constable for Ferrard in this County, the Barony in which my residence gives me frequent opportunities of knowing his merit which is very eminent on all occasions for activity, great zeal, determined resolution & the most prompt & vigorous exertion accompanied with a sharp understanding & great moderation.
> I have reason to believe that he was very instrumental in finding out Bernard Gilroy's abode whereby he was arrested & appeared a most material witness in the late trial of Patrick Devan.[198]

Samuel Pendleton gave a like recommendation for Armstrong on 26 July 1817, referring to him as 'a most active and intelligent police officer'.[199]

Pendleton retains the name Gilroy in his summary chart of arrests and convictions. However he is variously named McElroy and McIlroy in the newspaper accounts of the trials. Although Shore was given the name 'Gilroy' for the suspect the police sought in Meath, he concluded from the description that the man he knew as 'Bernard McElroy' was one and the same person. It is noteworthy that on his arrest Gilroy told Hamilton that he was present at Stonetown chapel on one of the occasions when the murders were contemplated but was not present on the occasion of the murders. In his cross-examination in the case against Patrick Devan, Gilroy said that it was through the malice of Gubby that he was being charged, that he became acquainted with Gubby in Drogheda and that he heard of Gubby's arrest two days before he himself was arrested. In his evidence in court in the different cases in which he testified he gives a full story of being present at the murders. Gubby in his statement of 9 April 1817 names Gilroy as one of the perpetrators of the burning. Gilroy in his prosecution evidence against Patrick Devan admitted his part in the burning and said that he had also attended a preliminary meeting in Stonetown chapel with Gubby on 25 October 1816.

Rev. Francis D. Hamilton, Portreeve of Navan. Navan. 27 May 1817.

> I have the honor of informing you that in consequence of a communication from Mr John Armstrong Chief Peace Officer at Drogheda, Mr Shore the Post Master of Navan did this day in my presence apprehend a person named Bernard Kilroy (or Gilroy) and who upon his being told that he was arrested upon a charge of murder said that he knew it was upon a charge of being concerned in the (Horrid) outrage at Wildgoose Lodge.
> And I have also to add that this man was in a quarter of an hour after his being apprehended safely lodged by Mr Shore in the Jail of Navan where he now is protesting his innocence.
> The prisoner is a Weaver and was apprehended at the great flax mills near Navan.
> *Note written on letter in Dublin Castle:*
> I am writing to corroborate Gubby as to the prisoner Gilroy, and as I understand Gubby is a convicted felon I don't think any man should be detained on his information –J.L. Townsend. May 31. 1817.
> *Communicate* – to be admitted to bail.
> Mr Gregory wishes Mr Townsend to say if this statement is legal. The inclosed letter from the Portrieve (*sic*) of Navan, respecting the apprehension of a person concerned in the outrage at Wildgoose Lodge, was addressed to the clerk of the council, & received at the council office 28th of May.
> Delivered to W. Gregory Esq Dept same day.[200]

Hamilton to William Gregory. Navan. 5 June 1817:

> I have the honor to acquaint you for the information of his Excellency the Lord Lieutenant that Bernard Kilroy who was apprehended by Mr Shore, the Post Master of Navan, did soon after give me much important information on the subject of the outrage at Wild Goose Lodge, and also respecting a meditated attempt upon the life of William Filgate Esq one of the Magistrates of the County of Louth [h]as induced me, to send by letter to Samuel Pendleton Esq, Chief Magistrate of Police for the County of Louth, a written examination detailing the particulars. And he in consequence sent some of his Police Constables to escort him into the County of Louth for the purpose [of] occasional communication with Kilroy upon these subjects.
>
> Kilroy admits he was present amongst the party at the Chappel (*sic*) of Stonetown upon the occasion of one of their meetings to prepare for the accomplishment of the burning and murders but was not present at the perpetration of them, and wished to have disclosed the intended mischief, but was afraid, as he says, to be seen speaking to, or going near any Magistrate.
>
> And he certainly did soon after his return to his native place in this county immediately communicate by letter (tho' anonymous) to Mr Filgate the intended attempt upon his life and went to Slane in expectation of disclosing the particulars of *both transactions* to him
> Note *written on letter in Dublin Castle:*
> Mr H. was informed that he might admit Kilroy to bail on his own recognizance – from Letter 3 June.[201]

John Shore later sent at least four memorials (the last one dated as late as 23 June 1819) to the Lord Lieutenant seeking the £200 reward for the discovery and apprehension of Gilroy. In this extract from one of his memorials he describes briefly the part he played:

John Shore to the Lord Lieutenant.

> That about the 27th of May 1817 information was given by a letter from Mr Armstrong, Chief Constable of Drogheda, to Mr William Johnston formerly Chief Constable of Navan, that one Bernard Gilroy or Kilroy therein described and charged with murder generally was then lurking some where in the neighbourhood of Navan.
> That neither the name, residence or place of concealment of said culprit was in said letter with any certainty set forth.
> That Memorialist having a knowledge of one Bernard McElroy then living in the neighbourhood of Navan perceived that he was the person described in Mr Armstrong's letter and having made prompt and diligent inquiry discovered his place of residence and communicated same without delay to Mr Johnston.
> That Memorialist observing said Mr Johnston notwithstanding said communication unpersuaded, uncertain and undecided as to the

> identity of the said Bernard McElroy, Memorialist, began to fear for the consequence and that said McElroy would escape justice.
> That Memorialist thereupon communicated his fears to the Revd Mr Hamilton, Chief Magistrate of Navan and received from him immediate authority to apprehend said McElroy
> That Memorialist thereupon immediately on the said 27th of May proceeded to a place called the Factory about a mile from Navan and there apprehended and delivered into the custody of the said Magistrate the body of said Bernard McElroy.
> That said Bernard McElroy, having been transmitted to Dundalk, was at the subsequent Assizes admitted an approver ...
> That Memorialist is a very poor man with only a salary of £60 per annum to support a large family and owing a debt to the General Post Office which he has no other means of paying ...[202]

There are also letters from John Shore dated 12 December 1817 and 11 October 1818 begging payment of the reward.[203] He was then in straightened circumstances owing the Post Office money; he had to pay compensation following a robbery at his post office; he was threatened with replacement; his wife was sick. As late as 12 October F. D. Hamilton, Leighsbrook, Navan, wrote again in favour of his 'poor friend' Shore. Peel had asked Pendleton his opinion. Pendleton preferred to judge in favour of John Armstrong of Drogheda.

Pendleton to Peel. Dundalk. 28 July 1817.

> In reply to your letter of the 25th I have the honor to state that although I cannot presume to question on the accuracy of Mr Hamilton's statement respecting the apprehension of Gilroy, yet from my observation of Shore the Postmaster of Navan, I cannot well imagine *his* interference in such matters would contribute much to their success. Armstrong I know to be an intelligent and active peace officer, and attribute to *him*, what the other *might* have been actually instrumental in.
> From his Excellency's proclamation it appears, that the reward of £200 is offered "for the *apprehension of any person concerned etc*" etc. Should this be considered not to require *conviction*, but to extend to persons who appear from their own confession to have been concerned, there are already no less than *five* distinct claims for the reward, on precisely similar pretensions. The *County* rewards are "to the person who shall *prosecute to conviction*". If I may so far presume, I would humbly suggest that it might be most expedient to postpone for the present the consideration of any claims that may be made. The *general* development is as yet only *in limine*, and any determination that might now be made, liable to error from the imperfect view that can as yet be taken of the subject.[204]

Andrew Rooney

The information of Andrew Rooney who claimed kinship with the victim of the Wildgoose Lodge fire, Thomas Rooney, is included here for the sake of completeness. He names twenty-nine people in his statement to Samuel Pendleton as being present at the burning but his information does not seem to have been acted on and probably was not genuine and may even have been vindictive. It was given at a vital time when Pendleton was seeking more information and corroboration of the various stories of his approvers. It is interesting from a social history aspect.

> LOUTH TO WIT Andrew Rooney of Mountrush in said County, farmer, voluntarily came before me this day, and maketh oath, and saith - That at the time of the Quarter Sessions after last Christmas he was in the house of Geo Tierney, publican, in the town of Ardee - that there was a number of persons drinking in it at the same time - that a sort of quarrel or disturbance broke out among them, and in the course of it there were signs made to him, and questions put to him which he did not understand or know how to answer - that Bryan Malone of Stormanstown a near neighbour of Depts. interfered for him, and prevented his getting any ill usage - that they shortly afterwards left Ardee & went homewards together - that on the way the sd Malone told him that he ought to 'be up', thereby meaning to be 'a ribbonman' - that if he was one of *them*, no man would offer to say a saucy word to him.
>
> Dept. said that he had taken the freehold oath and that he was obliged by it, to be true to the King, and at the same time asked Malone, 'what great matters did ye (meaning the ribbonmen) ever do'? - 'Didn't we destroy Lynch and Rooney? (replied Malone) so that as long as the world lasts, there will never be a Stag in Ireland again'. - Dept. told him, 'they would be hanging each other for all that before the year would be out' - and mentioned 'that the very morning after the business was done, Jemmy Martin of Glack had spoken of it'. Malone said, that *he* (James Martin) knew nothing about it, whatever his brother *Tom* did and that whatever he told, it must have been from him (Tom) he heard it. Dept. told him it was little matter about which of *them* was there, but that it was a barbarous thing of *him* (Malone) to have any thing to do with such a business against his own flesh and blood - (he the said Malone being a near relation of Thos Rooney's who was murdered as is also Dept.). They talked of this all the way 'till they got home, and parted.
>
> Malone said he was never a day happy since it was done. He said he would do whatever Dept. would advise - and gave him to understand, that if he was sure he could save one of the party that was concerned in it, he would make a full confession about the rest. He did not name

the man whom he would wish not to discover of but Dept. has some reason to believe it was one Pat Runnaghan or Reynolds. Dept. advised him to go to Mr Foster and make the confession to him, and that he would go with him to Collon the next day for the purpose. He said he would go. It seemed that he repented of it, as he did not call on Dept. as he said he would - neither did Dept. ask him. He has very often since had long conversations with him about it. They never spoke of it but he seemed in great grief - used to cry bitterly and said he was very unhappy. He freely owned to Dept. that he was one of the party the night of the Burning, also two or three nights before when it was intended and put off. He never told Dept. that he was up *at the House* to burn it, but only that he was of *the* Party. Dept. believes that one quarter of the number that was out that night did not go up to the house, but there were many left to watch in all directions. He said the party he belonged to stopt on their way for some time in a field of Mr Filgate of Arthurstown, 'till they gathered - that they went on from that to the Chapel of *Reaghstown* where *all the parties met*. That Pat Durnan the publican there gave them drink in the Chapel, that Pat McGee was the man who set Lynch's house, and settled how it was to be done. Saith that in the several conversations they have had, he perfectly remembers him to have named as being of the party at sd Burning - (1) Richd Halfpenny (2) Thos Kelly (3) Owen McCabe, (4) Thos & (5) John Miles (6) Pat Runnaghan (7) Geo. Lamb (8) John Keelan (9) Thomas Sharkey (10) Thos Martin (11) Edwd Carlow (nicknamed the Fifer) (12) Bryan O Neil (13) Bryan Halfpenny (14) Peter Marron (15) Michl Duffy (16) Pat Branagan (17) Jn Bray the besom maker (18) Henry Flinn (19) Crawley the Yeoman (20) Pat Sheeran (21) Henry Sheeran (nicknamed the wrestler) (22) Jn Farrell (23) Michl Mohan who lived with Cooper Roony (24) Pat McGee (25) Pat Durnan of Edmondstown (26) Michl Smyth who is a servant of the Rogers's - and had a gun there belonging to *them* - (27) & (28) the two Hands blacksmiths, and (29) one of the Gargans. That there are some others whom he does not now recollect whom he perfectly remembers Malone to have often told him of being there and whose names and descriptions he more fully gave to Mr Filgate some time ago.

That Malone also at these times praised some of the persons for their bravery, or 'wickedness' they shewed. That Henry Sheeran, Michl Smyth, Michl Mohan and one Marron were distinguished by him in that way. That he told Dept. there was no man among those who were taken up, that was a *right* man for *'a Stag'* but that if Geo. McDonald the hackler was taken *he* would hang them all - that *he* had no friend to save in the country- being himself a stranger in it. Saith that he Malone informed Dept. that a different night from that on which the Burning did take place was first fixed on for the purpose, but that said Malone told him it was put off because some of those expected did not attend, and also for fear of one *Devan* who was one of their leading men and whom they did not think could be trusted, as he had got afraid. That on the said *first* night Dept. happened to be in his fields looking through his cattle and he saw a party of men with arms going across the fields in the same direction as said Malone told him he had gone. That on the night of the Burning he saw the same, but did not make much observation of it, as he had not heard of any mischief after the first party, and he was well used to see them going about.

Andrew X (his mark) Rooney   Sworn before me this 21st April 1817
Saml Pendleton.[205]

8
Arrest, Trial & Execution of Patrick Devan

ARREST OF PATRICK DEVAN

Patrick Devan, weaver, schoolmaster and clerk of the chapel at Stonetown, was regarded as the principal commander at the burning of Wildgoose Lodge. He is listed as one of the important leaders in Chief Magistrate Samuel Pendleton's chart. He is also the central character in the literary fiction that has grown from the episode. The story of his capture is clear in documents. According to a letter of H. Brabazon, Dundalk, written 27 July 1817 in support of Constable William Leary's claim to share the reward for taking Devan as against the claim of Chief Constable George Payne of James Street, Dublin, Leary went to Dublin with Pendleton who 'had full information derived by letters found in Devan's father's house here, where he was & what he was doing in Dublin and upon this information took him'.[206] Pendleton did not accompany Leary but he sent him and another policeman and followed them to Dublin the next day. Police constable Francis Davis found the letters in Devan's house on 20 May 1817 and went to Dublin and gave them to Pendleton. Devan's letters were made public at his trial and are published in the *Belfast News Letter*, 25 July 1817 (*The Times* 1 August 1817):

> Extract from Letter, dated 28th April [1817]
> Dear Father – I have been very ill off sometimes since I left home, but am in employment at present, and is in hopes of better, with the assistance of God. Write an answer to me by Biddy Cully when she is coming to Dublin; let no person know where I am unless Thomas Hasty and Pat McGough. Dear father, I will write in the course of a month, so no more at present from your loving and affectionate son. (Signed) Pat. Devan.
> *Direct your letter to Bridgefoot-street, No. 6, for Pat. Devan*
> Letter Dated May 4, 1817.
> Dear Brother – All the news you have sent me concerning I have been an informer is all false, thanks to God for it. Dear Father, I have travelled a very great deal since I left home, and never got any employment till I came to Dublin. I have been at the severest work, by all accounts, that ever was in Dublin. I am at wheeling a barrow in the

new docks these two weeks back, at the small wages of ten shillings per week; there was many a good man cast by my side in it. I expect a job something easier next week, and, in short, when I can buy a pair of shoes, I will seek for some sort of a place for teaching school in the county of Kildare. Dear father, I have often fasted on a pennyworth of bread in the twenty-four hours, so I was very happy to get work where I had got it, for I was very much in need of it. I was getting a very good place in the Queen's County for teaching, so as I would get a character from my Parish Minister, so I don't intend to write home till I travel more. No more at present from your dutiful son. Pat Devan.

The details of the arrest are given in an affidavit of Constable Leary:

> Louth to Wit. William Leary one of the constables of the Louth Police, maketh oath and saith, that he and John Burke, another constable of the same were sent to Dublin by Mr Pendleton on Monday the 19th May last, for the purpose of apprehending Patk Devan. That having ascertained that the said Devan was engaged in work at the Custom House Docks deponent & said Burke accompanied Payne the Chief Peace Officer, and two or three other peace officers or constables of the James's Street Police to said docks, on the evening of Wednesday the 21st of May, a short time before the men were to quit work. That Dept was informed by Payne, that he had examined the labourers acct book, that there was a man named *Devine* entered in it, but no Devan, and was told by the clerk that the man so named worked in Cody's squad. That when the bell rung for them to quit work, Dept went up to a man whom he thought to be Devan, but who was so much altered in appearance since he had seen him, that to be certain he wanted his own acknowledgment of it, and accosted him with "Devan Mr Cody wants you". He replied, "I'll go to him when I put by the shovel", that he did put by the shovel, and having done so was going off in an opposite direction from where Cody was. Deponent followed him and took him in the entry of a publick house near the gate, and brought him into a backroom in it. He was in about two minutes joined by Payne, and the others aforesaid. Further with that Mr Pendleton had given strict direction, that said Devan should be kept separate, and without having communication with any person that night and until he should examine him in the morning, and with that the peace officer of the night had free access to him whenever he thought proper. Willm Leary. Sworn before me this 15th July 1817 Saml Pendleton. 'Original now in the possession of Robt Hamilton Esqr.' (Copy).[207]

Leary in a memorial seeking reward for the apprehension of Devan on 14 September 1817 gives some varying detail to his first statement:

> That your Memorialist is a constable of police for the proclaimed District of Louth ... That on the 20th of May last, he and two other constables of the same were sent to Dublin by Samuel Pendleton, esqre the Chief Magistrate with his warrant, for the apprehending Patrick Devan for the Burning and Murders at Wild Goose Lodge.
>
> That said warrant was, on the day following, backed by one of the Magistrates of James's Street police force, and your Memorialist and the two other Louth constables were directed by Mr Pendleton to accompany Mr George Payne, the Chief Constable of the said James's Street office, to the Custom House docks, where he had information of the said Devan being at work.
>
> That your Memorialist did proceed there accordingly at the time of quiting work, on the evening of the 21st of May and having a knowledge of the person of said Devan discovered him amongst a very considerable number of men then engaged in work, accosted him by his name & followed him into a public house and there made him a prisoner; and had him in his actual custody in a back room of the same, where he was shortly afterwards joined by the two other Louth constables, by the said Mr Payne, and by two constables, or peace officers, of the James's street police ... that he forwarded a similar Memorial the 24th last month.[208]

The Louth policeman who accompanied William Leary to Dublin was John Burke. He swore before Pendleton, 21 July 1817, that he was the first person who followed Leary and Devan into the backroom of the public house where they secured Devan.[209] Some ill feeling was later caused when it came to claiming the reward. The chief constable at James's Street, George Payne, who attended Devan's trial and gave evidence, in a memorial of 14 April 1818 took full credit for the arrest of Devan and requested a reward.[210] He repeated his claim on I August 1817, and in a further letter and memorial 20 May 1819, the latter certificates subscribed by the magistrates of the Third Division of police, William H. Archer, John Graves, and John Tudor.[211] Pendleton had put the record straight in his letter on the application for rewards, 23 September 1817:

> It was not 'by any diligent search made by him through the city of Dublin' that the place of Devan's employ was discovered. The truth on the contrary is, that (having *previously fully ascertained both where he worked and where he lodged*) I had sent two of my own men who knew his person in Dublin, to have him and another person taken, and came myself the day after principally for the same purpose. I gave my warrant to *Payne*, that his being a known city police officer might prevent any attempt at rescue, when he should be arrested, and I

directed him to be at the Custom House docks shortly before the labourers there would quit work, where Devan would be surely found and identified by my men.[212]

TRIAL OF PATRICK DEVAN

The Assizes for the County of Louth commenced at Dundalk, the Assize Town of the County, on Saturday 19 July 1817 before Mr Baron McClelland in the Crown Court. The consideration of the Wildgoose Lodge burning was appointed for Monday 21 July. Bills of indictment were sent up against Patrick Devan only and on their being found by the Grand Jury, he was arraigned thereon and put upon his trial. There were several bills of indictment against him, three of them for the murder of Edward Lynch, Thomas Rooney, James Rispin and several men and women to the number of eight persons, and one for the burning of Edward Lynch's house at Reaghstown on 30 October 1816. Most of the trials for the Reaghstown murders took place in the temporary courthouse in the old Georgian Market House in Market Square. The new courthouse, also in Market Square, was ready for the assizes 3 April 1818 - 3 July 1818.

Townley Patten Filgate, owner of Wildgoose Lodge, records in his diary, Monday July 14th, 1817, 'I went to Lisrenny and did not return until Monday July 28th 1817'.[213] He obviously wished to be present at the trial and execution of Patrick Devan.

For a sketch of the career of the judge in this trial, Baron James McClelland, I refer again to *The Judges in Ireland, 1221-1921* by F. Elrington Ball.

> **James McClelland** was eldest son of James McClelland of Milmount in co. Down; was born about 1768; matriculated as a fellow-commoner in Dublin University 1783; graduated as bachelor of arts 1787; entered the Middle Temple same year; was called to the Irish bar 1790; married Charlotte, daughter of Acheson Thompson of Annagasson in co. Louth, 1797; became member for Randalstown 1798; supported the Union; was appointed solicitor-general 1801; became a baron of the Exchequer 1803; was the subject of several debates in the house of commns 1819; resided in Dublin successively in Temple-street and in Gardiner's place, and in co. Louth at Annaverna; resigned 1830; died at Annaverna in 1831; was buried in Ballymascanlon church-yard.[214]

Charles Kendal Bushe, the Solicitor-General, native of Kilmurry, County Kilkenny, was called to the Irish bar in 1790 and was member for Callan, 1797. He resigned his seat in 1799. He opposed the union and was author of a pamphlet against it, *'Cease your funning, or the rebel detected'*. He was elected for Donegal in 1800. He became third serjeant in 1805 and was appointed Solicitor- General in the same year. F. Elrington Ball says:

> [He] acted as one of the counsel for the crown in the prosecution of the Threshers 1806; was an advocate of catholic emancipation; took part notwithstanding in the prosecution of members of the Catholic Committee 1811; defended himself afterwards from a charge of inconsistency; appeared for the crown in the cause of the King v. O'Grady 1816; exhibited in his speeches, no less legal knowledge than forensic eloquence; resigned the office of solicitor-general after a tenure of seventeen years 1822; was appointed then chief justice of the King's Bench ... retired from the bench 1841; died near Dublin at Furry-park 1843.[215]

The *Belfast News Letter*, 25 July 1817 reported:

> The Assizes for the county of Louth commenced on Saturday the 19th instant, before Mr Baron McClelland in the Crown Court, and Mr Justice Osborne in the Civil.
> **Grand Jury.** Right Hon. John Foster, Right Hon. Lord Jocelyn, Rt Hon. T. H. Skeffington, Blaney Balfour Esq., Chichester Fortescue, Esq., Alexander Filgate Esq., Nicholas Coddington, Esq., Wallop Brabazon, Esq., John McClintock, esq., Wm Ruxton, Esq., John F. Ruxton, Esq., John Taafe, Esq., Faithful W. Fortescue, Henry Brabazon, Faithful Fortescue, esq., Thomas Tisdall, Esq., John Woolsey, esq., Thos. Fitzgerald, esq., Philip Pendleton, esq., William Filgate, esq., Thos. L[l]oyd, esq., W. Henry Richardson, esq., Turner Macan, esq., Sheriff.
> The consideration of the Wildgoose Lodge burning was appointed for Monday, when bills of indictment were sent up against *Patrick Devan* only, and, on their being found by the Grand Jury, he was arraigned thereon and put upon his trial.

The paper went on to say that in the course of selecting the jury the prisoner exhausted the entire amount of his challenges. *The Correspondent* of 28 July1817 reported (The report in the *Dublin Evening Post*, 29 July 1817, is similar):

> The Hon. Baron McClelland entered the court at a little after nine o'clock. The whole day was occupied by the trial. The following comprised the Jury:

William Foster, Henry McNeale, Malcolm Browne, Alexander Shekleton, (Pepperstown), John Baillie, Alexander Donaldson, Robert Wynne, John Scott, Lawrence Tallon, jun., George Eyre, John Corry and John Barrett, Esqrs.

Her Majesty's **Solicitor General, [Charles Bushe]**, (in his usual eloquent strain, in a speech which occupied the Court nearly two hours and a half) opened the case on the part of the Crown, stating that in April, 1816, before this murder was committed, an attack was made on Lynch's house, by a number of men who destroyed it; that he and his family had the courage to convict three unfortunate delinquents before the same Judge whom he now had the honour to address; and they suffered the sentence of the law at the last Summer Assizes. He continued to reprobate the spirit which prevails in this country, where, if a man comes forward to complain of the destruction of his family, he is execrated. I have, said he, known a widow to come forward and prosecute for the murder of her husband – a father to prosecute for the murder of his son; and, on their return from Court, they were obliged to be protected from the infuriated mob, by military interposition. It is in vain, said he, that the Judges are learned and impartial – that juries are upright and honest; whilst the present turbulent spirit prevails, a man must almost despair of the country. He then described the situation of the house, which stood in a morass, flooded almost all the year round in that season of the year, and near to which a number of roads meet; that the parties assembled at an appointed hour at that spot, with military precision; and they were so numerous, that some of them, when they met, did not know, and had never seen one another before that period. When the house was consumed, they gave three cheers, and took an oath of secrecy! What species of education these people had received he could not conceive, when, after having dipped their hands in innocent blood, they had the audacity to take a solemn oath to conceal their crime, in the presence of Almighty God.

The *Freeman's Journal*, 23 July 1817, gives an instant reporting directly after the trial and it adds some details to the opening speech of the Solicitor General regarding his emphasis on the validity of the approvers' evidence:

Extricated from the evening publication of yesterday ... Dundalk, 7 o'clock, Monday Evening.
Dear Sir, I think it may not be unacceptable to you to have the first news for your paper of the very important trials going on here. I have just come out of Court, where Patrick Devan's trial has occupied the whole day, on a charge of burglary and arson, which has been so much spoken of – The Solicitor General opened the case for the Crown in a speech of great liberality on all points, but particularly as to the scepticism with which the evidence of informers should be received. He said unless corroborated by other evidence or other circumstances no man's life ought to be taken on it. That in this case the most

extraordinary corroboration did exist. Approvers not knowing each other – not having ever had any knowledge of each other – one of them not even knowing the prisoner – had both concurred in the same particulars as to the prisoner, who was recognised by one of those persons the first instant he saw him. That if his instructions did not deceive him a doubt could not exist in this coincidence. The trial proceeded, and his statement was fully supported. ...

The evidence of William Filgate, Patrick Halfpenny and Dr Henry Munro Blackwell have already been related to describe the location and nature of the terrain around Wildgoose Lodge, the event of the burning of the house and the identification of the victims. Dr Blackwell had said that he had no doubt that one of the burned bodies was Lynch.

THE PROSECUTION

This report is taken from the *Belfast News-Letter*, 25 July 1817 with some additional pieces from the *Dublin Evening Post* (cf. *The Times*, 1 August 1817, *The Correspondent*, 28 July 1817, *Dublin Evening Post*, 29 July 1817):

Alice Rispin sworn: James Rispin is her son; he is dead; he was bound to Rooney who lived at Lynch's house, for three years; he came home to her from Lynch's house after the first attack was made on it, and remained with her until about a week before the burning, when he returned; she went to the house the morning after the fire. And saw eight bodies laid at the door; knew two of them; one was Biddy Lynch, daughter to Lynch, and the other her son, whom, she said, she knew by some marks on his body from the time he was born, and which were at that time visible to her.

Bernard McElroy (Gilroy), an approver: Knows the prisoner, Patrick Devan, whom he identified in court; knew him first in summer, 1816; he lived near Corcreagh; was a weaver, a schoolmaster, and clerk of the chapel of Stonetown. [Witness is a County of Westmeath man]. Witness lived in Farly, in the parish of Louth [since May 1816]; was in the county last October; remembers the burning of Lynch's house; was at it with the prisoner and Thomas Gubby; Thomas Gubby brought him to the chapel of Stonetown, on Friday before the burning (25 October); saw the prisoner there with four or five others. Prisoner said there must be a gathering as quickly as possible of the boys, to go and set fire to Lynch's house, for the purpose of burning him and his family, for prosecuting the three men at Dundalk; nine or ten more came from Inniskeen about 12 o'clock; they separated and went home; some of the party failed to meet on that night.

About an hour after nightfall, the night of the burning, witness again went to Stonetown chapel, and found some persons there, amongst whom was the prisoner. About half past nine, 40 persons who had assembled there left the chapel; prisoner divided the party into two divisions; witness and prisoner went with the first party straight to the Mill of Louth; they went within 100 yards of Lynch's house; 14 or 15 persons; they had fire in a small pot; they all stopped at the little swamp on the road until the whole body came, which had been joined by a great many strangers, and amounted to 100 and more; there were some horses but none belonging to his party; the ground was deep and greatly flooded; they received orders that some of them should spread themselves round the house to prevent Lynch or his family from escaping; the order was given by the prisoner. Witness was of the party, who went straight up to the house along the road; heard some of his party say that the people in the house were barring the door; heard a voice inside declare that the first person that should enter would be shot, and heard prisoner then say, 'Rooney, don't think it is old times, this night is your doom'. Witness was employed to carry unthreshed corn to the house to throw in, in order to add to the flames; saw and heard shots fired, but cannot tell whether any of them were fired from within; saw the door broke open with a sledge ('*A blacksmith, from Enniskeen, broke open the door with a sledge*'), and straw thrown in upon the fire.

While the house was burning, heard the cry of a woman and of a young child, and some persons interfered to have the woman let out, but prisoner cried 'Will you have the lives of all here endangered by letting any of them out?' Witness did not wait till the roof fell in.

Is a Ribandman, was made so in the Meath militia, in Captain Charleton's company. Witness sent a letter to Mr Filgate, the Magistrate, in April last, begging of him to meet witness in Slane; went to look for him to Slane, the Wednesday before May day last, in order to tell him all he knew about Wildgoose Lodge, but did not find him; heard at Slane that he had gone in the coach the day before to Dublin; was apprehended in Navan by the Rev. Mr Hamilton and Mr Shore; saw many persons in the town passing by the gaol; saw Mr Charleton; sent for him, and he came to witness, and he told him a good deal about Wildgoose Lodge; after that he was brought to Dundalk, and here made a full communication to Mr Pendleton and Mr Brabazon; knew Gubby had been taken up before the time that witness was taken up. Witness had written to Mr Filgate before Gubby had been apprehended.

Cross-examined: The people outside the house were armed; he had a pistol with intention to shoot the people, should they attempt to come out of the house; he dared not refuse to do so, or he would be probably shot himself; he was obliged to go for the straw, and admitted that he brought straw to add to the fire after he heard the cries of the people inside; he did not think it harmless to do so, but he was obliged by his party; he lived near the place; got his pistol between Friday and the night of the burning; he could not have stayed in the country if he had not gone to that business; it was want of work brought him to the country; he would have quit the country but might not have gotten work elsewhere if he had quit it; did not tell sooner because he was afraid of being destroyed if he should be seen speaking to a gentleman; he was sworn under the pain of the same fate as Lynch's, not to discover; they were all sworn to that, and the whole party were very closely watched by one another; got acquainted with Gubby in Drogheda; heard of his being taken up two days before witness was taken up by Mr Hamilton. When made a Ribandman, it was an obligation he made on his knees, and not on a book; the oath was, to aid and assist our brothers, not to deal with a Protestant if they could get what thy wanted from a Catholic, and to assist the cause with person and pocket; was sworn to secrecy after the burning. He wishes to do justice; he expects nothing, and has no motive but to tell the truth; does not know whether it will save his life or not; does not come for a reward, but would take a situation if protected; has been confined in the gaol.

Mr Filgate proved the letter, which he marked 30th April; it is dated the 20th of April, but Mr Filgate did not receive it till the 30th; he was from home.

Francis D. Hamilton, Esq., Sovereign of Navan, apprehended McIlroy on Tuesday the 27th May at the factory, a mile from Navan; on their going to jail, witness told him that he had been taken on a charge of murder; McIlroy replied he knew what the charge was; it was for the burning and murder committed at Wildgoose Lodge, and said he was sure it was through Gubby's malice that he had been charged with it; and he declared his innocence.

James Charleton was Adjutant of the Meath militia; knows McIlroy; he called witness from the street into the jail of Navan [on the 28th of May], and told him he had been at a conspiracy to burn Lynch's house, and destroy him and Rooney, but had not been at the burning. He begged witness to send immediately to Mr Filgate by express; to be guarded, lest he [Filgate] should be murdered that night, that he was present at a conspiracy to murder him; cannot say whether he ever admitted to witness that he had been at the burning or not [He (witness) sent for Mr Hamilton, sovereign of Navan, on the next day, and they took down his evidence on paper] .

Patrick Clarke, an Approver. Remembers the night of the burning; he lived at Churchtown, between Ardee and Wildgoose Lodge; was called out of his house that night by the party; when he had gone with them about ten perches from his house, he asked where they were going - they answered he should soon know, and gave him a book, and swore him not to tell; they then went on, and he again asked where they were going; when he was told they were going to punish Lynch and Rooney, and that he must go; [There was, he believed fifty in his party when they came to Reaghstown; when they were all assembled, he thinks there were upwards of 100 people]; they proceeded to Wildgoose Lodge, where they met a number of persons; about a hundred were concerned, many of whom he did not know; heard a voice inside the house cry out, ' he would shoot them if they should enter'. Identifies prisoner, whom he had not till that night seen, and did not know his name. Prisoner belonged to a different party from witness's; some of the people wanted to let the girls and child out, but prisoner refused, saying, it would be running too great a risk; and he asked, 'Did they want their lives to be taken, by letting any out to inform against them?' Witness was ordered to hold five or six horses at the end of the house; heard prisoner call out to those in the house, it was the last night they had to live; when set on fire there was a great uproar in the house; three shots were fired outside, and one from the house; most of the party had arms; they gave three huzzas when all was over; was taken prisoner after last assizes, and confined in Dundalk gaol; never saw the prisoner after the burning, till he saw him on Wednesday last, in the jail of Dundalk, and there knew his person immediately, although he was mixed with several others.

Cross-examined: When holding the horses at the end of the house, heard three shots fired about the door, and a great shout within; some people of the party carried flax and straw to the house; did not see the door broke, but it might have been done without his knowledge; it was the prisoner who ordered some of the party to take the horses from witness; never saw the prisoner before that night, but took great notice of him on account of his activity; knows Pat. Murphy by sight these seven years; was not much surprised at being taken up; never was before judge or jury, or charged with any thing before this; never heard that Murphy swore against him; never spoke to the prisoner about Lynch's business; he kept his mind to himself; does mot know a man named McIlroy; heard of such a man being in jail, but don't know him, nor ever spoke to him to his knowledge; did not know McIlroy was to be a witness on this trial.

Samuel Pendleton, Esq. Chief Magistrate of Louth: Recollects a communication made by a man of the name of Clarke – one had been made before that on the 13th March, by one Murphy, to Mr Pollock and Mr Arthur Pollock; Clarke made his about the 18th or 19th March, and at that time no person had communicated intelligence that Clarke was there; the notice was given by Clarke through the jailer, and witness took him into the jailer's room, and took down his confession in substance, as this day delivered; he did not then name Devan, or know him; the 20th June was the earliest period he received McIlroy's communication; witness never asked Clarke or McIlroy any leading questions; the instant McIlroy was taken, he had Clarke removed to the police guard-house, and they have not had any intercourse with each other; on Tuesday or Wednesday Devan was removed from Kilmainham to Dundalk; Clarke never mentioned any thing respecting Devan, nor did Murphy make any charge against Clarke; witness directed a search to be made for Devan – and one Davis, a police man, delivered him in Dublin two letters, when he directed Paine, a Dublin peace officer, and one of his men, to look for Devan; Clarke was taken up under no particular charge; never heard Murphy was a relation of Clarke.

The *Correspondent*, 28 July 1817 (and *Dublin Evening Post* 29 July 1817), adds some detail on Pendleton's evidence and that of the policeman Patrick Corrigan:

> **S. Pendleton.** Did his duty as well as he could; recollects having a number of persons arrested on the night of the 12th of March; Clarke and Murphy made communications to him, on the morning of the 12th of March; Patrick Clarke represented himself as being implicated in the affair of Wildgoose Lodge; knows Churchtown, about two miles SW of Wildgoose Lodge, and Stonetown Chapel, exactly in an opposite direction. In the communication Clarke had with him, Clarke did not at all implicate Devan; Mc Elroy made a communication to him (witness) about the 28th of June, not by any suggestions from him; witness took precaution to keep the two informers (Clarke and McElroy) apart. Up to Devan's committal to this gaol, Clarke did not implicate him, but McElroy did.
>
> **James Corrigan:** Is a police-man of the county; got charge of the prisoners (Clarke and McElroy) after their communications to Mr Pendleton; he was desired to keep them asunder, which he did placing one in the gaol, and the other in the guard-room; was present in the gaol, the other [*also*] when Devan came in; mixed Devan with a number of prisoners in the yard; Clarke immediately came to him saying, 'There is a man that was at the burning of Wildgoose Lodge!'; he knew his features but not his name.

The *Belfast News-Letter* report, 25 July 1817, continues:

> **Charles Henry Silliery:** Is confined in the gaol for debt; remembers Clarke being brought to the gaol; witness walked away from Devan and the other prisoners with the police constable [Corrigan]. When Clarke returned, he said he knew that man, who was very active passing from front to rear, and gave orders to put plenty of flax and sheaves to burn; and that when a person interfered to save the woman, it was he who replied, 'Would you have the lives of all of us in danger by letting any of them out?' and instantly ordered the fire to be put to the house; witness never saw McElroy and Clarke together.
>
> **Francis Davis [police constable]:** Was directed, about the 12th or 13th of March, to take a number of persons, nearly 20; searched Devan's house, but could not find him; went again on the 20th of May, searched the house and found two letters, which he identifies; went to Dublin and gave them to Mr Pendleton.

Devan's letters, the text of which I have already given in the account of his arrest, were read in court.

The *Correspondent*, 28 July 1817:

Thomas Woods: Knows Devan, the prisoner, these four or five years. There were two letters produced, which witness identified as prisoner's writing. They were found in prisoner's father's house. [*The Correspondent* quotes a few lines and mistakenly quotes the opening of a letter as 'Dear Brother' for 'Dear Father'.]

The *Belfast News-Letter* 25 July 1817 (*The Times*, 1 August 1817):

George Paine: Chief constable of the 3rd division of the Dublin police; received a bench-warrant to execute against Patrick-Devan, the prisoner [he took two of his men, and two of his town Policemen, who came up for the purpose]; went to the custom-house docks about 6 o'clock as the men were quitting work; saw prisoner going into a house; he said his name was Pat. Divine, and denied that he was Pat. Devan; said he was from the county Meath, and denied that he was from Louth [took him to Police-Office, James's street].

Here the case for the Crown closed.

THE DEFENCE

Belfast News-Letter, 25 July 1817 (extra details added from *Enniskillen Examiner & Erne Packet*, Thursday 31 July1817).

James Devan: Is brother to the prisoner, who was a weaver, and a schoolmaster betimes, and parish clerk – the spring is not a good season for the school. [did not weave this while back – received very little benefit from his station last spring, the family were in hard circumstances – had not a spot of ground]. Prisoner lived with witness's father; recollects when Lynch's house was burnt; prisoner was at home that night; slept with witness; could not have been absent without his knowing it.
Cross-examined: Never heard his brother was charged with the crime until he was arrested; never was afraid of being taken for it; they went to bed about seven o'clock they were scutching flax that evening [discoursed with his brother going to bed – twice in the night, and going to work in the morning]; his brother was ill; he went and bought physic for him; he was confined better than a month; was not fit to teach school; the times were very hard; he thought it better to go to the county Kildare; cannot tell why he (the prisoner) was called an informer, or what was the reason of writing that he was not; heard he was called so but cannot tell why; witness can't write; got a boy to write for him to his brother; the people told him his brother was an informer, but can't say who told him so.
[*The Correspondent*, 28 July 1817 and *Dublin Evening Post*, 29 July 1817– The Judge at this period suggested the propriety of producing the medical person, in Carrickmacross, who sent the medicine to prisoner;

the prisoner mentioned that, so far as we could hear, that he thought it unnecessary].

Philip Devan: Father to prisoner, lives at Corcreagh; his son lived with him; remembers the burning of Lynch's house; he was at home with him that day, and slept with his brother that night [witness shut the door himself when they all went to bed]; had been some time ill, and had taken physic; went to Dublin after the 11th March [about 18th March, through pecuniary wants]; cannot tell why he was called an informer, or where he did hear he was called an informer; he left him very ill; was a school-master, used to teach in the chapel [Stonetown]; had the care of the key of the chapel.

Rev. Mr[Thomas] McCann: Parish priest of Stonetown Chapel; says he knows the prisoner upwards of five years; always considered him a well-conducted peaceable young man; never heard him of his being concerned in riots or trouble; he acted for him as parish clerk; does not know McElroy; prisoner kept a school, a very poor one; his duty was to attend the Chapel; never got any reward, or was ever paid for such duty, either by him or his congregation; was apprised if prisoner did not come back in a fortnight to provide himself with another; the key of the Chapel was entrusted to his care.

The Correspondent added that witness was at great pains to keep his flock from mixing 'in these troubles'. Fr Thomas McCann, parish priest of Louth 1799-1822, was a native of Knockbridge which at this time was part of Louth parish. He was a brother of Dr Matthew McCann who served in Dundalk 1817-1836. Fr Thomas McCann is credited with building St Mary's Church in Knockbridge in 1811. Following the death of Fr Patrick Bannon in July 1858 Louth was divided into two parishes, Knockbridge and Louth.

Case closed.

Dublin Evening Post said that the trial occupied the Court the whole day and gave a summary of the Judge's address:

> The Learned Judge, in his charge to the Jury, which lasted one hour, took the opportunity of cautioning them not to be carried away by indignation, at the atrocious circumstances which formed the features of the case, and should rather operate in making them more scrupulous and slow in their verdict to the Prisoner – he also took occasion to express his abhorrence of illegal Associations in reference to the Ribandmen's oath, which had been given in evidence, and which appeared to be an obligation 'to stand by each other, and not to deal with Protestants'. It was a feature in the state of this Country, of the most lamentable description, that Associations of exclusion of different religious descriptions existed. That they were alike illegal, whether Protestant or Catholic, equally deserved reprobation, and should

equally be made to feel the vengeance of the law. He said he had long looked for and wished to see the abolition of party feuds, which so much distract this unfortunate Country – that we all worship the one God, and expect redemption through the same Saviour; and that both Protestants and Catholics received equal protection from the laws, and when brought before him he would equally inflict on offenders the justice of those laws which they dared to transgress.

The *Freeman's Journal*, 23 July, reported Baron McClelland's 'very luminous and acute charge' in similar vein. The *Correspondent* reported that after an able charge from the learned Judge the Jury retired for about eight minutes and returned a verdict of guilty against the prisoner Patrick Devan. The *Belfast News Letter* says that the jury did not remain one minute out, that he was ordered for execution on Wednesday the 23rd of July to be hung at Corcreagh, near Stonetown Chapel, where he was to be gibbeted in chains. It reported: 'He has made a full confession of his guilt, and has conducted himself with great resignation and devoutness; he has been attended by the Priest of the jail and another'.

The *Freeman's Journal*, 28 July 1817, adds (cf. *The Times*, 1 August 1817):

> After the very impressive address of Baron McClelland to the prisoner, previous to his passing the awful sentence of the law, in which he exhorted him to atone to his country etc by making a full discovery of his associates etc, and after the dread sentence was pronounced, which Devan heard wholly unmoved, except when the Baron pronounced the words, 'The Lord have mercy on your soul', he was seen to raise his eyes, as if to say, 'Amen'. Devan, on retiring to the inner part of the dock, said very audibly, 'He wants me to disclose my secrets, but he is mistaken if he thinks I will'.

The day Devan was convicted, 21 July 1817, the Solicitor-General, Charles Bushe, wrote to Mr Harker, the Attorney General, from Dundalk at 7.30 p.m.

> Devan was at six o'clock found guilty after a long trial by a verdict which has left no doubt of his guilt on any man's mind. He appears to have been the principal commander and a most ferocious character. Since the trial the counsel for the Crown & Pendleton have had a long consultation upon the most prudent course to be now pursued and we have come to the resolution of not bringing forward any other case at present, but of selecting those cases which we think strongest &

> applying to the judge to postpone the trials to the next Assizes without bailing the prisoners, upon his judicial knowledge that the approvers have in this day's case been corroborated & the probability that other corroborating evidence (without which we cannot go to trial) may be procured in the interval.
> Tho' this may appear a strong measure, I think the judge will be fully warranted in complying with the application from the particular circumstances of the extraordinary case this day disclosed. If he should hesitate to grant it we shall apply to him for an adjournment of the Assizes until the close of Downpatrick Assizes, & perhaps even in that interval something may turn up in consequence of the spirit of the confederacy being much broken by this conviction of their leader.
> You cannot conceive a more useful and powerful charge or a more impressive & awful exhortation on passing sentence than Baron McClelland's but the wretch was not only unmoved but displayed a firmness which nothing can account for except the persuasion, which I am convinced he feels, that he is to die in support of a just cause & that the burning the house & family of an informer was not only not criminal but meritorious. I hope to be in town tomorrow evening.[216]

According to the *Dublin Evening Post*, 24 July 1817, twenty-seven persons were arraigned on Tuesday 22 Juy, for the Wildgoose Lodge outrage, 'but the Crown not being ready, the trials were postponed to the next assizes; and under the circumstances of the case and the state of the country, the Crown would not allow them to be admitted to the bar'.

EXECUTION OF PATRICK DEVAN

Henry McClintock, one of the local gentry who lived in Dundalk, County Louth, was present at the execution of Patrick Devan. His remark that no regular soldiers attended the execution is noteworthy. He wrote in his diary:

> **Wednesday 23rd [July 1817].** Very fine day. I attended a Yeomanry Parade at eight oclock in the morning & at ten we escorted a prisoner (Patrick Divan) to Wildgoose Lodge at Rheastown [Reaghstown] in this county, where he was hanged inside the walls of Wildgoose Lodge from a board that was placed on the two chimneys of the house – his crime was being the commander of a party of near a hundred men who on the night of 31 of October had set fire to Wildgoose Lodge & burned eight people in it – men, women & children – he fully confessed his guilt on the gallows – after he was hanged his body was put into iron chains & conveyed to Corcria [Corcreaghy] (about four miles from Rheastown) & hung there on a gibbet – Corcria was his native place &

a party of soldiers are stationed there which will prevent the gibbet being taken down – this Divan was a school master clerk to the Popish chapel at Stonetown very near Corcria – this chapel was the place where he & his associates met at night to plan their diabolical act – almost every gentleman in the county attended the execution – Mr Foster, Lord Jocelyn, Lord Louth, Mr Balfour, &c, &c – no regular soldier attended the execution, merely the different Yeomanry Corps & the staff of the Louth Militia – the Dundalk, Collon, Louth & Castle Bellingham Corps attended & also some of the police – we did not get back to Dundalk 'till ten oclock at night when we (the officers of the Dundalk Corps) dined with our captain Lord Jocelyn – our officers are Joe & Willy Purcell, Alexr. Shekleton & myself – I rode all the day.

His sister Marianne Fortescue also made a reference to Devan's execution in her diary:

> **Thursday, 24th [July].** On Sunday I expect seven from Stephenstown at dinner – the day was so wet only four came. Monday was tolerably fine – Le Blanc visited our new curate Mr Magee for me & invited him to dinner, he came & in the eveg Lady E McC, Miss W & six children came to tea – they left us about eight. Tuesday tolerably fine – Lady E McC & two boys dined here – Mr Magee drank tea & John came from the Assizes a little after ten - & went home with Lady E. Yesterday was a lovely day – Le Blanc & I went to Stephenstown for Emily – all at home except Matt who had gone to an execution where all the country were assembled (the man who was hang'd was the principal person concern'd in the horrid burning at Wild Goose Lodge past Reastown) –we visited Mrs Fitzgerald on our way & Miltown Grange also – I wrote to Mrs Salvador – we walk'd to Lady Bellingham's garden after dinner. – this morning is not fine – my hay is finish'd – we are well thank God.[217]

More detail of the ceremonious nature of the execution is given in the newspaper accounts. A huge, apparently sympathetic crowd, attended, as also was the case at other executions for the Wildgoose Lodge murders. The *Belfast News-Letter*, 29 July 1817 reported (some details added from *Dublin Evening Post*, 29 July 1817; accounts of the execution is also given in the *Freeman's Journal*, 25 July 1817):

> **Execution of Patrick Devan.** Wednesday morning [23 July] about nine o'clock the High Sheriff, the Dundalk yeomanry commanded by Lord Jocelyn, and Louth police under S. Pendleton, Esq. [accompanied by the Right Hon. Hen. J. Foster, and Townley Filgate, Esq. on whose property the Lodge is situated] assembled in front of the jail for the purpose of escorting Devan to Wildgoose lodge, the scene of his crime,

for execution.

About ten o'clock all the arrangements were made; two carts with the gibbet and apparatus for execution in front, and the right of the Dundalk corps under Lord Jocelyn – next, the prisoner dressed in black, attended by the Rev. Mr Duffy, in a cart [Chaplain to the County of Louth Gaol, continued during the journey to administer to him spiritual advice and comfort] – the executioner in another cart surrounded by foot police – the left of the Dundalk corps, under Lieut. Skekelton [*Shekleton*], and the horse police, brought up the rear.

The whole moved off at a solemn pace. At Louth they were joined by the Louth infantry under Col. Fortescue; on the hill of Mullacrew by the Ardee corps under Lieut. Young; on the hill of Arthurstown by the Collon yeomanry under Lieut. Skekelton [*Shekleton*], and the staff of the Louth regiment under Capt. Rickaby, the county constables and sheriff's bailiffs also attended.

As they proceeded, they were joined by the Grand Jury, and a great number of the gentry of the county.

[Devan behaved with great firmness, but on the arrival of the cavalcade in Tallanstown, he for a minute showed signs of trepidation. However he soon recovered his firmness.]

About four o'clock they arrived at the ill-fated spot. Within the walls of the house, a beam was extended between the chimneys, to which the culprit ascended by a ladder. He addressed the people around him in an audible voice, and said: 'Good people, I die guilty. I forgive my prosecutors – [good Christians], pray for me'. After which he was with some difficulty launched into eternity (having got hold of a rung of the ladder). After hanging half-an-hour, he was lowered down and the body fixed in chains made for the purpose, and suspended from a gibbet, near thirty feet high at Corcreagh.

He appeared between 25 and 30 years of age, about five feet seven inches high, stout made, with a forbidding countenance.

The *Freeman's Journal*, 28 July 1817 (cf. *The Times*, 1 August 1817), reported:

He asserted his innocence to the very moment of his going out on the cart, at which time he fully acknowledged his guilt; he was seated in a dray, with the priest, preceded by another carrying the chains, gibbets etc. and appeared to pray with the utmost fervency, but with great firmness. He was clothed with a long loose black stuff gown, and cap of the same. When he arrived at the house, the scene of the horrid outrage, he retired to one of the rooms (being that in which the unhappy Lynch and family slept) and prayed long and fervently. The two chimneys of the house being still standing, a beam was thrown from one to the other as a gallows, and on his coming out of the room, he coolly looked up at the beam, and turning to the executioner, said, 'How am I to get up there?' He was informed by a ladder, and on going up the ladder the lower part of his gown caught his feet and impelled his progress; he very deliberately stooped down and lifted the gown high enough up not to prevent his proceeding; at last, having gone up several steps of the ladder, he asked, 'Am I high enough?' He was desired to proceed two steps more; which when he did, he again acknowledged his guilt, the justness of his sentence, forgave his prosecutors, and said, 'he died in charity with all men'. He evinced not only the most cool and steady firmness all through, but the utmost degree of piety and resignation. The only thing that gave him concern was being gibbeted opposite his father's door, and asked, 'Would not a fortnight be long enough to remain on the gibbet?'

The *Dublin Evening Post* added on 29 July 1817 that after Devan's body 'had been hanging for about twenty-five minutes it was cut down and carried to the cross-roads of Corchna [*Corcreagh*], being there gibbeted on a long pole, the feet of the body being fifteen feet above the reach of any man.' An 'immense concourse of spectators lined the road and at the place of execution, and on the surrounding hills not less than thirty thousand spectators were present'. A great sympathetic crowd watched the spectacle of the procession of Devan to his death. One cannot be certain of the accuracy of numbers. In his account written on 11 March 1867 William Filgate alleges, 'to the last moment Devan expected a rescue, but, though immense crowds were collected on the surrounding hills, no attempt of the kind was made'.

It was inevitable that Devan of the 'forbidding countenance' would be the subject of legend. His close connection with the church lent a sacrilegious tone to stories told. When Judge Fletcher at a later trial criticised the Catholic clergy for not showing enough opposition to agrarian crimes, letters to the contrary were sent from respectable individuals in Dundalk to a newspaper in Dublin. *The Times* of 27 March 1818 copied them from the *Weekly Freeman's Journal* of Saturday 21 March (published also in *The Correspondent*, 24 March 1818). One of these letters especially recounted the action of the parish priest of Louth, Fr Thomas McCann, on the Sunday after the outrage. Fr McCann gave evidence at the trial of Patrick Devan.

> Murder of the Lynches. We have some letters from respectable individuals in Dundalk and its vicinity, on the subject. We shall extract one passage, to exhibit at once the unparalleled obduracy of the desperados over whom it was so strangely imagined that their Priests

had an unbounded influence, and the ardour with which these Priests did all that lay in their power to subdue the hellish passions of these miscreants, and give them a due impression of the enormity of their offences:- 'It as known that Devan was clerk of the chapel of Stonetown. Mr McCann, the parish priest, occasionally officiated there. On the Sunday after the burning of the Lynches, he proceeded to that place of worship, penetrated with the most indescribable horror and concern. He ascended the altar, robed in his vestments, and with accents which will never leave my ear, cursed the author, abettor, and assistants of the crime! He then came down from the altar, took from his feet his shoes and stockings, desired his congregation to follow him, and he and they went in procession round the chapel, calling aloud to heaven for vengeance on the murderers. Guess who was next the minister of religion in the awful procession? Devan, the clerk! - the planner, - the instigator – the mover – the commander in this horrible transaction! And, of the whole congregation, he appeared to be the person who reiterated Amen with the most vehement devotion!'

Since Fr Patrick Duffy, O.P. of Dundalk was chaplain of Dundalk Gaol and attended the prisoners in the gaol and at the executions, it would be appropriate to sketch his career. He studied at Holy Cross, Louvain, in the latter half of the 1780s, since he received all orders from tonsure to ordination to the priesthood at Malines, Belgium, between February and May 1790. He was probably the Duffy who attended one of the Dominican provincial chapters in 1808. He is described in a letter of Archbishop Richard Reilly to his Vicar General at Dungannon, Fr Henry Conwell, 2 April 1811, as 'chaplain to the Military Gaol, with permission of Dr McArdle PP'. Within the Dominican Order he was a 'son of Carlingford', meaning the priory there, from which the Dominicans had departed by c.1727 to take up residence in Dundalk. He was, it seems, the only Dominican in Dundalk. His position there became vacant on his death, shortly before 12 June 1827. In documents in Propaganda, Rome, one finds him in January 1819 described as 'prior of St Malachy. Carlingford', though resident at Dundalk. Again he is mentioned, October 1818, as being present in Drogheda with other friars supporting Matthew McCann for the see of Armagh. Fr Duffy was a friend of Henry McClintock of Dundalk who mentions him frequently in his journal. He dined there often and indeed McClintock dined at the friary on a few occasions.[218]

Alice Rispin, mother of the victim James Rispin, figured in

another case at the Summer Assizes in Dundalk. The *Dublin Evening Post* reported it on 30 July 1817 (apparently from the *Newry Telegraph*). It is of interest because of the light it throws on the continuance of 'Whiteboy' activity locally despite the executions for the first attack on Wildgoose Lodge. Alice Rispin, one of the prosecution witnesses, appears as a resolute woman uncowed by the murder of her son. I also include the account of the trial of some South Armagh men and a local family for a robbery in Rathneestan, a townland in the parish of Tallanstown.

ROBBERY AT RATHNEESTAN

Dundalk, July 22. Owen O'Heire, Lawrence McDonald, John A. Montgomery, and Mary O'Heire, stood indicted for burglary and robbery on the house of Edward Byrne, of Rathneesan, in April last.

Owen O'Heire, and Mary O'Heire, also stood indicted for receiving said property, knowing it to be stolen.

Edward Byrne sworn. Lives in Rathneestan; on Easter Monday night last (1817), a number of people came to his door, and said they were the police, and desired him to open the door; he did so; one of the party bid them secure him, which they did, by tying his hands and feet, and leaving him on the floor in his shirt – they then tied his wife in the same manner, and a labouring man that was in the house; there appeared to be five or six of the robbers; and one of them, he thinks, had his face blackened. They then proceeded to take all his money, about 30*l.*, some of which was of gold; they also took a quantity of meal, eight or nine shirts, a pair of breeches, a web of frize, two watches, a calf-skin, his wife's gown, pork out of a tub, some bacon out of the chimney; they remained in the house, he thinks, about two hours.

Mary O'Heire, about 18 years old, sworn. Is daughter to the O'Heires at the bar, who are her father and mother; her father is tenant to Edward Byrne; recollects four men coming to her father's house last Easter Monday night, two of whom were the prisoners, Montgomery and McDonald – the latter of whom is her mother's brother; they said they were going to rob Byrne; they eat eggs and potatoes, and remained about half an hour; heard them go out; they staid away a good while – and when they returned told her father and mother that they had found Byrne's two watches, and his breeches and money in them; they went out again, and came back with meal and bacon with them; it was dark, and she only heard them say they had those things – she saw them next day – they said they would borrow her father's mare, to secrete the meal.

Cross-examined by Mr Scriven. She said she knew the prisoners by their voices – could swear to their voices – her mother spoke to them by their names, and they answered her; she (witness) now said they had a light when they were eating the potatoes and eggs – she then saw their faces.

Peggy Byrne sworn. Is wife to E. Byrne; remembers Easter Monday night when her house was robbed; was very much frightened; it was in the dark; she could not now identify them; missed the property already mentioned by her husband; the day or two after the robbery a policeman brought her one of the shirts from O'Heire's house.

James English sworn. Is a police-man for this county; went to O'Heire's house in search for Byrne's property; found a shirt round the body of Mary O'Heire, the prisoner, (he identified her); he brought the shirt to Mrs Byrne, (the last witness); she said it was her husband's; found some bacon hid in a hole near the fire; this happened on the Wednesday after Easter Monday; he also discovered a quantity of linen in a cradle, and went out to tell Mrs Byrne; there was, in his opinion, about seven yards of linen in the cradle; on his return there was about thirteen yards; he searched further and discovered the remainder of the linen, exactly corresponding, and appearing to be freshly cut – (he produced the linen).

THE DEFENCE

Redmund McDonald sworn. Is father to McDonald the prisoner; he lives at Jonesborough, about 10 miles distance from Edward Byrne the prosecutor; recollects Easter Monday night; that his son slept in the house with him; and that he had not been absent any night for three weeks before or after Easter Monday.

Catherine McDonald sworn. Is daughter to last witness; slept on Easter Monday night in the house with the O'Heires, (the prisoners); did not see either him or Montgomery at O'Heire's house on Easter Monday night; there was nothing brought into that house that night; saw her brother (the prisoner) in Dundalk at the market on Easter Monday, and went with him part of the way home over the bridge of Dundalk. There often was bacon in O'Heire's house, but acknowledged that there was none at this time.

James English again examined. Said Catherine McDonald was in O'Heire's house the time he found the bacon; she could not but see him, as the house was all composed of one room.

Lawrence McDonald and John Montgomery guilty of of the burglary and robbery. Mary O'Heire and Owen O'Heire not guilty of the robbery, but guilty of receiving stolen goods well knowing them to be stolen.

This party had come from Jonesborough, for the purpose of robbing.

Riot and Assault

James Darley and Michael Byrne stood indicted for assembling with a riotous mob, on the 5th of June last, and assaulting Charles Kennon (a baker of this town) on his way from Balbriggan, with a load of flour. Guilty. Imprisoned a month, and to give a good security to keep the peace.

'Whiteboys'

Patrick Sharkey, Thomas Breen, John Breen, James Goodman, Michael McAneany, John McAneany, John McNamee and James Durnan, stood indicted for appearing in arms at night (under the Whiteboy act) to the terror of his Majesty's subjects, under the common law (two indictments).

Alice Rispen examined. Says she knows all the prisoners and identified them particularly, except James Durnan, who she insisted was not the James Durnan she knew, and she thinks, and is almost positive she saw in the gaol; though she did not get a full view of his face there; she had a good right to know him, as he was the captain of the party, and always exercised them, and was the only man she saw with fire arms – they exercised as soldiers do, marching, etc. etc. She often, say ten times, saw them employed two or three hours before day; and said it was in consequence of her and her son's dread of remaining in their house; she was sometimes close to them, say within two perches; and saw them from behind ditches and potatoe fields where she lay; she said her son was one of those burned with Lynch's family, and being cross-examined, she said it was not through malice or revenge she swore against these men, as God was kindly merciful to her, and she was enabled to bear her misfortune with fortitude, but she considered it could have been a mortal sin to have hid it on them. She gave her evidence in the clearest and most affecting manner.

James Durnan, not being identified, was acquitted.

Patrick Sharkey, Thomas and John Breen, Jas. Goodman, Michael McAneaney and McNamee, were sentenced to one year's imprisonment, and all, excepting the younger McAneaney, to be whipped three several times during that period, through the streets of Dundalk.

The sentences were given in the most impressive manner by the Hon. Baron McClelland – and the prisoners evinced the greatest joy, by repeated thanks to the Court.

Michael McAneaney being a very young lad, Baron McClelland extended to him the mercy of the court, by ordering him to be discharged ...

Twenty-two prisoners were remanded on an application from the Crown, until next assizes charged with being concerned in the burning of Wild-goose Lodge, at Reaghstown.

Tribute to Samuel Pendleton, Chief Magistrate of Police

Following the execution of Patrick Devan, the Grand Jury and John Foster, personally, moved to congratulate Samuel Pendleton, Chief Magistrate of Police for the county of Louth. It was published in *The Correspondent*, 28 July 1817, together with a short correspondence between Foster and Pendleton.

We, the Grand Jury of said County, assembled at the Summer Assizes of 1817, having witnessed not only the ability and perseverance by which you have succeeded in bringing to justice, a principal perpetrator of the horrid murders at Reaghstown, but also your judicious and indefatigable exertions in all the other duties of a Magistrate, deem it incumbent on us, publicly to express our approbation of your conduct, and the high opinion we entertain of your talents, which have been so fully displayed in this County.

It is to a continuance of your exertions we look for a speedy restoration of tranquillity; and, should our hopes be realized, we have no doubt, in whatever situation you may then be placed, that the same eminent qualities that have distinguished you here, will contribute to confirm to the public, the justice and propriety of the high opinion which your condition in this County has impressed on our minds.

Dundalk, July 22, 1817

John Foster, Jocelyn, Matthew Fortescue, W. P. Ruxton, Thomas Lloyd, T. H. Skeffington, Chichester Fortescue, John Taaffe, John Woolsey, Wallop Brabazon, Thomas Fitzgerald, B. Balfour, Faithful Fortescue, Philip Pendleton, William H. Richardson, Thomas Tisdall, Alexander Filgate, T. H. Fortescue, H. Brabazon, William Filgate, John F. Ruxton, N. Coddington, John McClintock.

COLLON, JULY 24, 1817

My Dear Sir, - It is a great and sincere gratification to me to have the honour of transmitting to you, as Foreman of the Grand Jury at the late Assizes, the enclosed Address. No man can feel more strongly than I do, what the country owes to your unwearied exertions, supported by your very distinguished talents and legal knowledge; nor is any man more sensible of the good fortune of this County in the choice which Government has made, in placing you at the head of our Police Establishment.

Believe me, my dear Sir,

With every feeling of regard and respect,

Your most faithfully, John Foster

PENDLETON REPLIED TO FOSTER. DUNDALK, JULY 25, 1817

My Dear Sir – I have had the honour of your Letter, enclosing an Address to me from the late Grand Jury of Louth. I find it impossible to express how peculiarly gratifying it is to me, that my conduct, as a Magistrate, has been so highly distinguished by the notice, and sanctioned by the approbation, of those most capable of appreciating its merits, and most interested in its result. I hope to preserve their good opinion, by a steady perseverance in the same course which obtained it. For having so far succeeded, I am materially indebted to the suggestions of your eminently superior knowledge and experience, and to my having always before me the example of your energy and decision.

I have the honour to be, my dear Sir,

With the highest esteem, and most sincere respect,

Your faithful Servant, Samuel Pendleton

The Arbitrary Insurrection Act

The year 1818 was to see the trials and executions of the seventeen other men for the Wildgoose Lodge raids and murders. Meanwhile a letter to the *Dublin Evening Post*, from 'An Inhabitant', Dundalk, 28 February 1818, and published 3 March 1818, gives us an insight into the working and effect of the arbitrary Insurrection Act. It is prefaced by a commentary from the editor:

> Upon the general policy (under existing circumstances) which dictated the Insurrrection Act, it would be now, perhaps, superfluous to speak. That it is a very severe law is acknowledged, and the framers only justify it by the necessities of the Country. Whatever our own opinions may be as to the nature of these necessities, or the adequateness of the remedy which this Act applies, it must be acknowledged that among Country Gentlemen, generally, there exists a strong conviction, that it has proved salutary in its operation. Withour meddling, therefore, for the present, in the question of its constitutionality, there can be no question, we believe, that many of the benefits derived from the Law may be marred by the mode of its execution. The following statement, which we give from most respectable authority, will exemplify our meaning better than a mere descriptive and unappropriated detail. From the temper of the present Irish Administration, we feel quite persuaded, that the mischief and inconvenience to which the Town of Dundalk is subjected will be removed, when the Lord Lieutenant shall have the statement corroborated, as no doubt he will, by the proper authorities. Mr Gregory is a working and efficient man – he knows what the gentry as well as the People are made of – and he will be able to derive his information, not alone from the local authorities, but from *indifferent* persons. We will venture to say that the result of his investigation will prove favourable to the People of Dundalk. Let this be made only apparent to the Lord Lieutenant and Mr Peel, and the good folks of that town will be suffered, in a few weeks to proceed on their business, or to take their recreation, without the fear of black holes, or Police Magistrates.
>
> *To the Inhabitants of the Town of Dundalk*
> Fellow Townsmen – Fifteen months have now elapsed, since the Magistrates of the County of Louth, by their application to Government, have subjected your Town (that has ever been conspicuous for peace and good order) to all the rigour of the Insurrection Act.
> If abuses were committed in a remote part of this County, by the very dregs of the Peasantry, and that the Insurrection Act was deemed by the Magistracy a salutary cure for the improvement of their morals, I cannot conceive, why your Town should suffer for the atrocities perpetrated by these ignorant and misguided men, more than the

Barony of Ferrard, which has been exempted, although lying as near the scene where one of the most flagrant acts has been committed, that has stained the annals of this County – I must only conclude, that the Hon. John Foster, who answered for their peace and conduct, while the first Town in the County, possessing, as yours does, all the advantages of trade, with a population of 12,000 souls, who have ever conducted themselves in the most exemplary manner, had not, at the Board of Magistrates, one *fostering* hand held out, to preserve inviolable the Liberties of its Inhabitants.

I feel pain in being obliged to reflect on the conduct of the representative of a Noble Family, who both by inheritance and election should have been the Guardian of your Liberties – he should have paused, before he would surrender his Native Town to all the misery and degradation the Application of this Act had brought upon it. He is not, however, suffficiently long amongst you, to judge in person, the peaceable demeanour of your Town – matters may have been represented to him in a very different light to what they really were, and your own silence, in not soliciting him to have the burden removed, may have confirmed him in the opinion, that there was a necessity for it.

In enumerating the many grievances this Act has brought upon you, the most conspicuous in the list is the loss your trade has sustained; before its introduction, it is true, that trade had been declining here, as well as in other parts of this Kingdom, caused, in a great degree, by the County's quick transition from war to peace – but although it has recovered in some degree in other Commercial Towns, yours has received such a mortal blow from the Insurrection Act, that it has rendered it irrecoverable; add to this, the authority vested in every Peace Officer belonging to the Police Establishment, to arrest your persons, if found out of your dwellings after nine o'clock at night – the meanest Police Officer in that Establishment may enter your houses, and disturb your families by nocturnal visitations, on the most frivolous pretences. These, and many other restrictions which the Act imposes on you, render it even more intolerable than the Suspension of the Habeas Corpus Act, nor can parallel be found in British History, unless the reader seeks it in the dark pages of the Norman Conquest, when that despotic Usurper, William the Conqueror, after overthrowing the Liberties of the Natives, drove them out to repose by the sound of the Curfew.

Mr Peel himself appears to be sensible of the many grievances the Act imposes on the inhabitants of any district to which it may be applied, and during the last Session of Parliament, when he introduced a Bill for the renewal of the Act, it was warmly opposed by one of the first Lawyers in England (Sir Samuel Romilly) on the ground of its being unconstitutional, he Mr Peel pledged himself to the House of Commons, and to the Country, that the Irish Government would use the extraordinary powers vested in it with the greatest clemency. How that pledge has been redeemed, inasmuch as it relates to your Town, by those persons appointed to administer this Law, within the proclaimed Districts of this County, it is now full time to explain. Mr Pendleton, the Chief Magistrate of Police, that watchful guardian of the peace of your Town, has taken more than ordinary pains, on several occasions, to impress on the minds of many of your Fellow-Townsmen that the Act makes no distinction as to persons, and in this he is perfectly correct; but will he, or can he say, with truth, that he and those connected with him, have not made distinctions? Have not the fashionable circles of the Town and Country been as much frequented as ever, and in these circles are not some of the idlest of the community to be found? Was there no distinction made in this Town on the 12th of July last, when the bacchanalian orgies of an Orange Society were celebrated by a bonfire, and a band of music, by firing, and acclamatiuon, and by perambulation through your streets until nearly day-light the following morning? It will hardy be believed that these excesses would be permitted in a Town where the Insurrection Act was in full force and vigour; but it will appear incredible to every person but those who actually witnessed it, that the majority of the police stationed in your Town attended in procession this very lawless Assembly, and joined in all their excesses, to the utter annoyance of every peaceable inhabitant. It would, of course, be expected that those Police Constables, who had so flagrantly broken that peace, which it was their duty to preserve would be instantly discharged from the establishment; but, on the contrary, they have been, since that period, taken more into notice and favor, and entrusted with more important situations.

To convince you that distinctions have been made, it will be only necessary for me to mention one or two facts which speak more than volumes of assertion, and, in order to do so, I must reverse the picture. A respectable Physician of your Town who has grown grey amongst you, and whose profession should have protected him, if his venerable locks, his situation in life, and well known peaceable habits did not, has been incarcerated (in leaving his friend's house in the act of proceeding to his peaceable mansion) in a damp prison for the night, and was not dismissed until late the following morning, with severe injunctions, that if he was again found out of his dwelling, he would be committed to Gaol.

On another occasion, when a Police Officer, in a state of ebriety, had taken into custody eight or nine of your inhabitants, respectable from their situations as men of business, or professional occupations in life, they consider and feel that they have suffered more from the 'insolence of office', displayed by the gentleman, charged with the distribution of the Law here, than if they were felons charged with the most enormous crimes; they were detained in the miserable black hole, nor were they discharged until they entered into recogniszances to keep the peace, (as if they had committed any breach of it), some in sureties of £50 each, and *one* in sureties of £150. True, this person had the spirit to repel the most base insinuations thrown out by Mr Pendleton against his character.

I know not what the views of Mr Pendleton may be, but if he means to hold a situation of vast emolument, it is not the way to do so by holding a sword of terror over the heads of men who have as much respect for the Laws as he possibly can have, and who have, from their intercourse with the lower orders, done more real good by their advice in improving their morals, than all the terrors that he and a Police Establishment could visit a People with.

The Spring Assizes for the County, will be held in your Town on Tuesday next, and with them a full Meeting of its Magistrates. I therefore recommend you to present to them, or the Grand Jury, a strong remonstrance, requiring to be relieved from the burden of the Police Establishment, in as much as it relates to your Town, and I have no doubt but that your request will be treated with the desired effect, and that your patience, under such grievances, will urge both them and the Government to break the chain with which your privileges have been so long fettered; and that you will be allowed to enjoy the blessings of an invaluable Constitution.

9
Trials and Executions (1)

Thirteen men, as has been previously stated, were arrested on 16 March 1817 in Louth by Louth police. On 31 March two more were arrested by Louth police, one in Louth and one in Meath. On 11 April three men from Meath and one from Louth were arrested by Louth police. Then on 21 May came what was looked upon as a major coup – Dublin and Louth police arrested Pat Devan in Dublin under Pendleton's warrant. On 1 July, 8 October and 22 December 1817, three men were arrested by the Louth police, two in Monaghan and one in Louth. Subsequently ten men were tried at the Spring Assizes in Dundalk, 1818. Familiarly as in Devan's trial, William Filgate, Alice Rispin, and Patrick Halfpenny appear again as witnesses giving similar evidence as to the some details of the background of the case. Bernard Gilroy [McElroy], the approver, who testified at Devan's trial, appears again, and also the approvers Patrick Gollogly, Patrick Murphy and Thomas Gubby who identify various members of the accused. Inevitably there is repetitive evidence from the witnesses for the prosecution but often there are new details and new nuances to be gleaned from it.

The opening of the Louth Assizes on 3 March 1818 is reported in the *Drogheda Journal*, 4 March 1818:

> The Hon. **Judge Fletcher** appeared on the Bench about ten minutes before eleven – and shortly after the following Grand Jury were sworn:
> Right Hon. John Foster, Foreman
> Rt Hon. Viscount Jocelyn, B. Balfour, Esq., Mathew Fortescue, Chichester Fortescue, A. Filgate, W. P. Ruxton, Thomas Lee Norman, John McClintock, Turner McCann, John Taaffe, F. W. Fortescue, Henry Brabazon, Robert Thompson, Esqrs, Sir Wm Bellingham, Bart., G. S. Eccleston, B. D. Shields, Mathew O'Reilly, Thomas Wm Filgate, Henry Chester, Thomas Tisdal, J. W. McNeale, Thomas Fitzgerald, Esqrs
> The learned Judge addressed the Grand Jury in nearly the following words: he commenced by stating, that this was the third time he had the honour of travelling the North-East Circuit; that with deep regret he had to state, that the Calender was one of the most frightful that ever came under his notice – crimes of the most dreadful nature were there charged against a numerous list of prisoners, which certainly proclaimed this County in a very bad state. He being a stranger, could not know as well as they from whence this proceeded; but it was

shocking to learn, that four Baronies out of five, in one County, were proclaimed as disturbed in a most serious manner, and which this Calender of Crime, against prisoners now in custody, strongly corroborated. From the state of this County, they were called upon to use every exertion to discover the causes – that causes of a local nature exist is evident, otherwise effects could never be produced. He then enlarged upon the mode of proceeding adopted by our laws, viz. that of a Jury to examine the indictments before the accused were exposed to the ignominy of a trial, proceedings which had the most salutary effect. He afterwards pointed out the duties incumbent upon them as Jurors; if, then, they discharged those duties faithfully, the consequences would be most salutary. He spoke of the objections urged against this mode of trial, but declared that he ever felt himself an advocate for it. Sometimes men were indicted upon frivolous pretences, and whom, when brought to trial, no person appeared to prosecute; that although they were acquitted, yet such was the tenacity of the Irish Nation, that this was ever after an indelible stain upon their character. Often had he heard a Counsellor say to an unhappy man brought forward, "were not you indicted at such a time, for such and such". - Suppose a person really guilty, and, through the inattention of the Jury, suffered to escape, he went away more confirmed in wickedness than ever, believing that those laws, enacted to check vice and immorality, were not all so calculated. He once knew the Gaol of Tipperary to be full of prisoners, and he himself discharged them in two days – this was the effect of trial by Jury. The unhappy men had been committed to Prison by rash and unadvised Magistrates, and when their indictments were examined, they were found to be of so trivial a nature, that they were considered not liable to trial. He then stated what he conceived to be sufficient evidence for them to determine upon, and conjured them to make every possible investigation before they submitted any man to trial by Petit Jury. The Learned Judge concluded his Charge, with ex[h]orting them to have, for the benefit of the County, a fever hospital erected, and stated, that they could, at every Assizes, claim £250, to that purpose.

We have received reports of the trials of other prisoners yesterday, which we shall insert on Saturday. The important trials of upwards of twenty persons concerned in the horrible murders at Wildgoose Lodge will not come before Friday.

All the prisoners who were brought before the Special Sessions, under the Insurrection Act, on Saturday last, were discharged.

Faithful Fortescue, of Corderry, Esq., is appointed to the office of High Sheriff for the present year.

TRIAL OF HUGH McCABE, JOHN KIERAN & JAMES CAMPBELL

The *Dublin Evening* Post, 9 March 1818, *Faulkner's Dublin Journal* of 3 March (reprinted in the *Dundalk Examiner and Louth*

Advertiser of 17 and 24 September 1881), and the *Belfast News-Letter* of 6 March 1818 reported the trial of Hugh McCabe, John Kieran [Kiernan], and James Campbell on the second day of the Assizes, Wednesday 4 March 1818 before the Hon. Judge Fletcher. Counsel for the Crown were Serjeant Joy; Arthur Macartney; A. Hamilton; Thomas Staples; John Hall; James, W. and John Bell, Esqrs. Counsel for the Prisoners was Mr Slack.

The court sat a few minutes after nine o'clock – the following gentlemen were sworn on the **Petit Jury**:

Messrs Bernard Duffy, James Johnston, Robert Moritz, James Boyle, Robert Sheddan, Benjamin Atkinson, Joseph Parks, Henry Hale, William McKittrick, Nathaniel Milling, Nicholas Norris, Robert Getty.

Hugh McCabe, John Kieran, and James Campbell were indicted for an assault on the house of Edward Lynch, of Wildgoose Lodge, on the night of the 29th, or the morning of the 30th October, 1816, and also of being aiders and abettors in setting fire to the house, and cruelly burning therein eight persons, viz. Edward Lynch; his son-in-law, Rooney; two other men, inmates of Edward Lynch; three women, and one child.

The prisoners pleaded *Not Guilty*. The prosecutor in the case was Serjeant Henry Joy, youngest son of Henry Joy of Belfast, owner of the *Belfast News-Letter*. According to F. Elrington Ball who outlined his career in *The Judges of Ireland, 1221-1921*: 'he signed a requisition for the bar-meeting to protest against the Union in 1798; was afterwards allied with the tory party; became king's counsel 1808, third serjeant 1814, second serjeant 1816, and first serjeant 1817; was appointed solicitor-general 1822; became attorney-general 1827; was appointed chief baron of the Exchequer 1831; died 1838'.

Belfast News-Letter account, 6 March 1818:

The Crown Case

Serjeant Joy stated the case – He adverted to the original attack on Lynch and his manly defence, and the subsequent prosecution and conviction of three persons. Religious fanaticism, he said, was not intermixed in this transaction, which arose entirely from a detestation of the law, and a wish to obstruct its operation. He dwelt much upon the unparalleled atrocity of the crime with which the prisoners stood charged, and indeed his whole address was eloquent and pathetic beyond any thing that we have heretofore experienced.

The first witness, **William Filgate, Esq.** said, he is a Magistrate of the county Louth; attended the Louth assizes of summer 1816, and was present at the trial of Tierney, Conlan, and Shanley, at that assizes, for breaking the house of Edward Lynch and Thomas Rooney, prior to that date. On that trial Lynch and Rooney were examined in support of the prosecution. The three persons then tried were convicted and executed in Dundalk. Knows the situation of Wildgoose Lodge, late the residence of Lynch – it is peculiarly situated on a small rising piece of land, which in the winter season is almost an island, having only a bad narrow pass to it from the south side of the high road near the chapel of Reaghstown – witness described the relative situation of Wildgoose Lodge to Stonetown Chapel, Grimskeen, the Mill of Louth, and King's Court, all of which places lie in different directions round Wildgoose Lodge, and by and from which the several parties had proceeded. He was at the spot the morning after the house had been burned.

Alice Rispin said, she knew the late Edward Lynch and James Rispin, who was her son – Rispin was in the house of Lynch when it was burned, with Lynch and six others, all of whom were known to her when living. Thomas Rooney's son, a boy of five months old, was the youngest of the sufferers. Witness went to the house the morning after the fire, and saw the remains of eight human bodies that had been consumed in the flames – two of them viz. her own son and Biddy Richards, a maid servant of Lynch, she was able to identify – the others were so disfigured and consumed she could not identify them; tho' from her intimacy with the family she knew well enough whose remains they were.

Bernard McIlroy [Gilroy], an approver, remembers the burning of Lynch's house on the 15th October 1816. Witness was there as an accomplice. He met a party at Stonetown Chapel that night, about an hour after night fall. Pat Devan, who was tried and executed at last assizes was amongst that party. Devan was a schoolmaster and clerk to the chapel. The party that ultimately gathered together at the chapel that night consisted of about forty men, armed with guns, pistols, and pitch-forks. Devan divided the whole number into two parties, and witness was of the first party. They marched from the chapel by the Mill of Louth to Wildgoose Lodge. They met no person till they came about midway on the lane leading from the high road near Reaghsto[w]n chapel to Lynch's house. They met about twenty persons, who had fire in a small pot. Both the parties joined, and then spread right and left round the hill on which Lynch's house was situated, to prevent the family from running out of the house down to the water. The party set fire to the house as quickly as possible – heard the family securing the hall-door at the inside; and heard a person from within threaten to shoot any one that would offer to enter the house. Devan called out with a loud voice *'Rooney, these are not old times – this night is your doom.'* Witness was stationed at the front of the house. He was employed in adding unthreshed straw to encrease the fire. Saw the door broke open with a sledge, and unthreshed straw was thrust into the door way to encrease the fire, and prevent the people from getting out. Heard cries of women and children in the house. The cries did not continue long. The destruction was soon accomplished. Witness identifies John Kieran, one of the prisoners at the bar, as having been present. Kieran was blasted in the face that night with gunpowder – he had his hand up to it, and was bemoaning the accident. He also identifies Hugh McCabe, another prisoner at the bar, as having been also present. Witness left the house with the first party after the burning was complete. None of the persons in the house escaped. All were consumed. Witness thinks there were above a hundred persons at the conflagration. He went home to Faris, about three miles from the scene of action. Went to Slane the latter end of April to meet Mr Filgate, in pursuance of a letter which witness had previously (about 20th April) written to Mr Filgate, requesting to meet him there. He wrote the letter from Navan, where he put it into the post-office – witness enquired for Mr Filgate at Navan, but he did not come there. He was told he had gone to Dublin on the coach a few days before.

Cross-examined: Witness was lodged in Navan gaol before he gave any information to a magistrate. He had been apprehended, as he supposed, upon a charge of murder, respecting the transaction at Wildgoose Lodge. Witness had a pistol with him at Lynch's, which was charged. He helped to set fire to the house with lighted straw. As soon as witness got an opportunity he expressed his desire to state all he knew about the business, and he did so to Capt. Charleton. Witness was forced into the business by Devan and others, and was afraid to refuse. Admits that he heard the cries of the people in the house, before he thrust the straw into the burning house, to add to the fire. Witness had been a soldier in the Meath militia.

Mr Filgate again examined: Proves his having received the letter alluded to by McIlroy about 30th April, on his return home. He had been absent for some days. When he received the letter alluded to, the day appointed therein for meeting the witness at Slane had passed by, which was the reason he had not attended in pursuance of it.

Michael Kiernan [Kearnan], an approver: Knows nothing of Wildgoose lodge, except what he has heard. Has been a year in gaol. A police man had told him he would be hanged in front of the gaol, if he did not discover. Another offered him money. He has seen Mr Pendleton before, and told him a false story in his examination lodged before him, which implicated the prisoners. Witness was not of the party at the burning. McIlroy, a prisoner, put him up to saying he knew of the circumstances of the business. He told witness to be led by him, and they would get a great deal of money, which they would divide, and go to distant countries. McIlroy told him what he should say about Kieran's being blasted in the face, and Bryan Lennon breaking in the door with a sledge. McIlroy told him that the reward was £7,000, a great part of which they would get.

Peter Galogly [Gollogly], an approver. Used to reside in the county of Meath. Remembers the burning of Lynch's house. He was one of the party. He joined a party at the cross roads of Correcklick, went from that to the cross-roads of Ballynavorneen, and from that to the cross-roads of Drumbride, at each of which several places they were joined by others. Amongst these was Jas Campbell, one of the prisoners at the bar. From Drumbride they proceeded to Churchtown, where one man only joined them. The footmen went from Churchtown to Reaghstown Chapel, the near way across the fields. The horsemen went by the road at Reaghstown. There were a large number assembled and they got whiskey there. The person who seemed to command the Reaghstown party said that he had a party that he could depend upon, and swore to Campbell, that if any of his party should flinch, he would blow their brains out. The whole party then proceeded together from the high Reaghstown road by the lane in front of Lynch's house. Witness was left to hold some horses in this lane, at a distance from the house. He saw the house on fire. When the fire became somewhat abated, he heard huzzaing, and before that heard some shots fired. After the fire, the first man he heard speak was the prisoner, Jas. Campbell, who said that they had burned the little as well as the big, and had left no person to tell the story. Witness and Campbell rode home on one horse together, towards Meath side.

Cross-examined. Came from the gaol into court. He is charged with Sillery's murder, and the burning of Wildgoose lodge. He was induced to depose his knowledge of the circumstances through a desire to save his life, and do public good. He admits that the desire to save his life was the most predominant incentive.

Thomas Gubby, an approver. Remembers going to Stonetown Chapel, on the night that Lynch's house was burned; he met there a number of people. Some of them had come from a place called Enniskeen. They proceeded together to Wildgoose Lodge. When witness advanced part of the way, he saw others of them stopping at a house near Wildgoose Lodge to get fire. There could not be less in number in witness's party than 50. There were additional numbers at Wildgoose Lodge who had arrived there from other quarters, before witness's party had come there, and witness was stationed at one of the corners of the house. Devan seemed to have a great command. Fire was immediately set to the house. He heard people making a noise within. He identifies John Keeran, the prisoner, as having been there, heard him complain that he had been blasted in the face in the course of the night. Witness remained till the cries ceased. The party declared that they would show the country that there should be no more informers allowed in it.

Cross-examined: Came from the gaol into Court. Was here last assizes, but was not produced as a witness against Devan, against whom he conceives he might have been a good witness. Does not know the reason why he was not used as a witness on Devan's trial, but supposes it was because they could do without him. Has been charged with different robberies etc, but he was only at one, viz. Dickson's. He was tried and acquitted of another for robbery of arms. Never belonged to a Drogheda gang of robbers. Devan brought witness into Lynch's business. When witness was apprehended, two notes that were said to be forged were found on him.

Patrick Murphy, an approver. Remembers the burning of Lynch's house. He was present at it. Witness saw McCabe the prisoner at Arthurstown that night. Malone enlisted him to be of the party. He met a party at James Campbell's, the prisoner's house, the night before the burning. On the night of it, they went together to the cross-roads of Drumbride. They then met a party had come from below King's Court. Malone knew some of them, and Campbell knew others. The party consisting of 16 or 17 proceeded to Churchtown. Witness was on horseback as well as some others. The mounted party went round by Tullykeel. The foot people went another shorter way across the fields. At the chapel of Arthurstown they had some drink. He there again saw Campbell. The party went forward to Lynch's house. Before reaching it, witness went with another person to a house at this side of Lynch's, in the lane, for fire, which he obtained. The man who was along with witness had a gun. He threatened the people of the house that if they would look out, he would blow the contents of the gun through them. Witness and his companion broke open the door and got the fire, which was applied to some flax, and the flax, burning, was put up to the thatch of the house, which was consumed by fire. Jas. Campbell was positively one of the party that burned the house, and he also saw the prisoner McCabe there. He first got information of this transaction in Trim gaol. He was then under sentence of death for the robbery of Mr Sillery. Witness told the gaoler to go for Mr Arthur Pollock, a magistrate. Mr Pollock came to him next morning. He then declared to Mr Pollock what he knew about Lynch's burning.

Cross-examined: Was under sentence of death, but did not know his deposing as to Lynch's murder would save his life. Was concerned once in a robbery at Harkfords, near Carrickmacross. Became approver on that occasion, and was examined in the trial which followed. The persons tried then were acquitted. For Sillery's robbery and murder an approver was examined against witness, etc and he (witness) was convicted. Does not know where he is to be sent after his trial. Knows Galogly. He was with him at Sillery's robbery, and also at Lynch's murder. Witness knew that the party intended to destroy Lynch and Rooney.

Arthur Pollock Esq. Is a magistrate of the county of Meath. Recollects Patrick Murphy, a prisoner in Trim Gaol, sending for him by the gaoler. Murphy had been apprehended on witness's warrant, and afterwards committed to gaol by him for the murder and robbery at Sillery's house. Witness on Tuesday night received a message, from Smart, the gaoler at Trim, to come to Murphy. He went accordingly the following morning, and received his confession respecting the Wildgoose outrage. The man expected to be hanged in half an hour, and did not express the least hope of reprieve, nor did witness hold out any hope to him; he seemed much affected when giving his information, and when told afterwards by Mr Pollock sen. that he had got a respite of a few days for him, he fainted away.

Pat Halfpenny. Lives at Reaghstown, in a house next Lynch's. Remembers the night that Lynch, with his house and family were destroyed. Some people came to witness's house and rapped at his door. Witness opened it. Two men walked in and took out fire in a little pot. Witness's wife was unwilling to let fire leave the house at that hour of the night, and so expressed herself, to which they said if they should hear a word from witness or his wife, they would drag witness out. After the fire was taken a sentry was left on his house for some time. He soon after heard a noise and people on horseback passing after the party, who from the noise they made must have been numerous. Had retired, and the sentry had been withdrawn. Witness came out and saw the ruins of Lynch's house on fire. The next day he saw the burned bodies.

Cross-examined. On opening his door to go out after he thought the party had dispersed, and call up his neighbour Carrol, he heard a voice desiring him to shut up his door, or he should be shot.

Alice Rispin. Called up again on the part of the Crown. She says she knows Hugh McCabe, one of the prisoners, a long time. Remembers hearing McCabe say after the three men had been hanged for the original robbery of Lynch, that it should be avenged. Witness's son, who was among the murdered at Lynch's house on the night of the fire, had been brought forward before a Magistrate as a witness against the persons accused of the original robbery. He had been much threatened in the country on this account. Witness heard McCabe say if her son's oath had been taken, that by his Maker he would make him dance in the fire with Lynch and Rooney yet, and this expression of McCabe's came very forcibly into her mind on the morning when she was viewing the dead body of her son, with Lynch's and the others.

Owen Reilly. Resided at John McKinlay's, about four miles from Lynch's house. Was up early on the morning after the burning. Heard voices on the road and on hearing people outside the house at such an early hour, he barricaded the door. Some rapping took place. He was unwilling to open, but the people insisted on it, and assured him no harm was intended to any in the house; that they merely wanted to eat and drink. They opened the door and some men entered; they called for a farral of oaten bread, which they got with some milk. They seemed tired. One of them had a black hurt or mark on his face. He afterwards heard of what had happened at Lynch's house.

Henry Brabazon, Esq. A Magistrate of this county, remembers being present when John Keeran, the prisoner, was examined shortly after his apprehension. The prisoner was asked as to the black mark on his face. He said he had been shooting at a mark with a man of the name of Lennon, and that it was in that way he got the mark. The powder had hit him in the face. Has since heard the prisoner examined touching the business of Wildgoose Lodge, upon which occasion he acknowledged his having been at the burning of the house, and admitted that he received the injury and mark on his face by means of a shot fired from within the house of Lynch on that night. Points out the prisoner Kieran as the person alluded to by him.

Here the prisoner Kieran declared that he had been at the burning. He did not wish to deny it. That there were only about 25 persons

concerned in the burning. The 100 persons had been stated by the approvers to have been there, and in this respect, he said, they had sworn falsely.
Here the case on the part of the Crown closed.

EVIDENCE FOR THE PRISONERS

Bryan Greenan. Knows the prisoner McCabe. Remembers the burning of Lynch's house. Witness saw McCabe the Monday before the burning, which happened on Tuesday. McCabe had a sore knee which disabled him from moving. Witness saw the knee – it had a lump exactly on the cap of it. The country people called it 'a touch me not'. The next time witness saw McCabe was some time about ten days after the burning, and then he appeared to be well.
Cross-examined. Witness went to McCabe's about some turf which he had bought from and left in the charge of his (McCabe's) father. Witness often saw McCabe since, but it was a good while after. Went to Liswinny [Lisrenny] on the Wednesday after the burning, to tell Mr Filgate of it. Witness told Mr Byrne, the Attorney for McCabe, of the circumstances of the sore knee at the general assizes.
Peter Keenan. Knows McCabe. Not seeing McCabe at the gathering about Lynch's house the next morning after the fire, he went to see what ailed him. He found him complaining of his knee. Witness first thought his ailment might be a wound that McCabe had perhaps received at the burning, but at looking at it he found he had a boil on it, which the country people call a 'touch me no[t]'.
James McGahan. Remembers the burning of Lynch's house. On the Sunday before, witness saw McCabe with his knee tied up.
Owen McCabe. Knows Wildgoose Lodge. Witness's house is near it. Prisoner is witness's son. At the time of the burning the prisoner was lame with a boil on his knee. Witness did not hear the noise at Lynch's on the night of the burning. The back of witness's house looks towards Lynch's house. The prisoner was not able to work for some days before or after that period.
Alice Rispin again called. She saw McCabe on Friday after the burning, coming across the fields, and vault over a ditch very actively. He did not appear either lame or blind. She stated on Sunday last to a lawyer, who examined her, and whom she did not know, that she had never seen McCabe lame.
James Coleman. Has known the prisoner McCabe a long time – never heard any thing to the prejudice of his character before this.
Margaret Donaldson. Knows Campbell the prisoner. He came to her house about five miles from Lynch's, at half past seven in the evening, and went away on the next morning at seven o'clock. There was a wake of a child at witness's house. She can be particular to the hours, as she examined a neighbour's watch, both at the time of prisoner coming and going from her house.

The *Dublin Evening Post*, 10 March 1818 gave a more detailed account of the conclusion of the trial:

> This trial lasted six hours, the **Learned Judge**, addressing the Jury exactly one hour, commenting upon what the several witnesses that had come forward had deposed. He entreated them to divest themselves of that natural wish to punish the perpetrators of such horrid crimes, that must exist in the breast of every honest man, to take every circumstance into their most serious consideration, and if they had not a rational doubt but that from what had been deposed, the Prisoners at the bar were guilty, to bring in their verdict accordingly; but, on the contrary, if they had a doubt founded upon rational grounds, it was then their duty to acquit the prisoners. He had entreated them from the beginning to take notes themselves of the trial, as he foresaw, from the length of time it must necessarily occupy, and the confined place where he sat to administer justice, that his strength would not permit him to comment upon the evidence, in the copious manner he could wish.
>
> The **Jury** retired, and it being now five o'clock, the Court adjourned for one hour. A few minutes before seven the Hon. Judge again appeared, and the Jury having agreed, returned to their box. *John Kieran, Patrick McCabe, and James Campbell*, were found Guilty, and being set to the bar and the Verdict read, with astonishing effrontery cried, 'We are innocent; our Prosecutors are all false and perjured'; even *Kieran* who confessed his guilt, said the same. The obduracy of these wretched men astonished all present; their hardiness appeared to be of the most unconquerable nature; and the Judge with marks of indignation and astonishment addressed them:
>
> 'Wretched men, I am sorry to say, that you appear to be the most obdurate and hardened miscreants that ever came before me - I thought I should not be able to pronounce the Sentence of the Law upon you – I feared that my feelings would not be able to sustain the task my duty imposed upon me; but your obduracy has strung my nerves, and I do feel myself now able, without any feeling for your fate to pronounce the awful Sentence of the Law that awaits you'.
>
> The Learned Judge then pronounced the awful Sentence of the Law in a solemn and impressive manner, imploring them to employ the short time allotted to them in this world, in fervent supplication to Almighty God, to have mercy on them, and forgive them their offences. They were ordered to be hanged on Friday, and their bodies sent to the County Infirmary for dissection. The wretched men heard their sentence with apparent indifference.'

A further note to the above report in the *Belfast News-Letter*, 10 March 1818, taken from the *Drogheda Journal* of Saturday, 7 March, states that the three men who were to be executed at Wildgoose Lodge on Saturday, 7 March, received a respite until

Monday, 9 March, when they would be executed with Terence Marron, Patrick Craven, and Patrick Malone found guilty of the same crime at Dundalk assizes on Friday 6 March.

TRIAL OF TERENCE MARRON, PATRICK MALONE (1), & PATRICK CRAVEN

In the account *Dublin Evening Post* of 11 March 1818 and the *Drogheda Journal* of 7 March, it is stated that Terence Marron was from Carrickmacross, Patrick Craven from Castlering and Patrick Malone from Meath-hill. The trials of 20 accomplices in 'this abominable catastrophe', it said, were put off until next Assizes.

The trials of the following eight men are reported in *The Correspondent*, 11 March 1818. Judge Fletcher was again the trial judge.

> **Louth Assizes. Friday, March 6.**
> The Hon. **Judge Fletcher** entered the Crown Court a quarter before ten o'clock. Patrick Craven, Terence Marron, M[ichael] Floody, M. M'Clarney [Hugh McLarny], Laurence Gainer [Lawrence Gaynor], Patrick Malone, B[ryan] Lennon, and William Butler, were indicted for arson at Wildgoose Lodge, and burning of eight persons therein, on the 30th of October 1816.
> Patrick Craven and B. Lennon pleaded guilty, probably under an idea of being admitted as approvers; but after an admonition from the Judge, they agreed to take their trials. The following culprits were then put to the bar: Patrick Craven, Terence Marron and Patrick Malone.
> **The Jury.** In forming the Jury, the challenges were so frequent, that the panel was nearly exhausted. At last a most respectable and truly impartial Jury, consisting of the following Catholic Gentlemen, was sworn: Hugh McSherry, Thomas Byrne, J. Hampton, Philip Boylan, John Norris, Bernard Duffy, Arthur Sherry, James Caraher, John Coleman, John Carroll, N. Coleman, jun., Joseph Kelly.
> **Serjeant Joy** opened the case on the part of the Crown, in a short but animated speech; and explained the proceedings of the sanguinary mob on the above lamentable occasion.
> **William Filgate, Esq., sworn**: is a Magistrate of the county of Louth. Remembers the time Rooney prosecuted to conviction three people at the Summer Assizes at Dundalk, 1816. Recollects the time Lynch's house was burned, which was in the month of October, after the Assizes; saw the house on the day after it was burned, and nothing but the walls remained – the roof fell into ashes.
> **Alice Rispin sworn.** Recollects the night on which Lynch's house was burned; she then mentioned eight persons who lived in the house, among whom was her son; she knew all the inmates. Witness went to

the house the day after the burning, and recognized her son and Biddy Lynch, but could not recognize any more of them, they were so dreadfully burned. She perceived the track of straw carried from an adjoining hagyard to the house.

Bernard McIroy [McElroy, Gilroy] sworn. Was one of the party at the burning of Wildgoose Lodge. He and others collected at Stonetown Chapel, to the amount of forty persons; they left that for Wildgoose Lodge, at about half-past nine o'clock. Patrick Devan, who was executed last Assizes, formed the party into two divisions; Devan took the command of one of them, and they proceeded to the Mill of Louth; then to Reaghstown where they were joined by about fourteen or fifteen persons more, who were armed and waiting for them, and had fire in a small pot. They stopped there for some time, till the whole party collected, when they amounted to one hundred; saw some people holding horses. Their reason for going to burn Lynch and Rooney, was, for hanging three innocent men at the Dundalk summer assizes before. They then got orders to completely surround the little hill on which Lynch's house stood, to prevent any of the family escaping; they then closed to surround the house as fast as possible; he heard a noise inside the house, as if bolting the door, and a voice like a man's saying, if any man came in or out, he would shoot them. They then set fire to the house, and witness was employed carrying unthreshed corn to assist the flames; his station was in front of the house; he waited till the house was enveloped in flames, and heard the cries of men, women, and children.

Witness identified the prisoner, Craven, as being one of the party. He, witness, was taken up in May 1817; previous to which he wrote a letter to Mr William Filgate, dated the 20th of April, and posted it in Navan post-office, requesting him to meet him at Slane the following Wednesday, and that he had a communication to make to him relative to Wildgoose Lodge. Witness went to Slane accordingly, but did not meet Mr Filgate there. He was armed the night of the burning, he supposed, with the half of a barrel of a gun placed in a pistol stock.

William Filgate, Esq., re-examined: He received a letter from McIlroy, on the 30th of April last, at Lisrenny; it was dated on the 20th, but he was not then at home.

Peter Gologly sworn. Lived at Carricklick, county of Meath; remembers going, with a party of men, from his side of the country, to burn Lynch's house, for prosecuting three men in Dundalk to conviction; on their way they met another party at the cross-roads of Drumbride, on horse and foot, which joined them; they then proceeded to Wildgoose lodge, by way of Churchtown; at the latter place they were joined by a man on horseback of the name of Patrick Malone; when they arrived at Reaghstown, they were about one hundred in all. They proceeded to Wildgoose lodge, up the lane; at a part of it that was very boggy, he (witness) was left holding horses; a short time after he heard shots, and saw a blaze of light in the direction they went. Shortly afterwards the party returned, and witness heard James Campbell, who was convicted yesterday, say, that they burned the little ones, as well as the big ones, and left no one to tell the story. At Reaghstown on their return home, he heard a man, named Terence Marron, called, who immediately answered, but knows no man of that name. Witness identified Patrick Malone.

Thomas Gubby sworn. Was at the burning of Wildgoose Lodge; went to Stonetown Chapel that night where he found twenty-five or more people there before him. They then proceeded on by way of the Mill of Louth, and had an advanced guard before them, that they might not be surprised. When they reached Wildgoose lodge they amounted to about one hundred; witness was stationed at the corner of the house; he saw fire brought to the house and thrust in. Identified the two prisoners Craven and Marron, as being present.

Patrick Murphy sworn. Was one of the party that burned Wildgoose Lodge; witness lived at Meath-hill; at that time Malone, the prisoner, came to witness's house, and told him that he, and a good many others were going to burn Lynch and Rooney, for prosecuting the three innocent men at Dundalk. Prisoner told witness he would have plenty of drink; on which he, witness, agreed to go; the prisoner and witness lived opposite each other at Meath-hill, and, consequently, were well acquainted. Witness then identified Malone. They went to provide horses the night before the burning; they proceeded to Reaghstown, and he, witness, was ordered by Malone, who was what may be called Captain, to hurry a party that was behind them. When they arrived at Lynch's house, they thought to force open the door, but in vain; they then retired, when some shots were fired out of Lynch's house. Malone then ordered witness and Marron, another prisoner, to go to a house at a small distance, and bring fire, which they did; they got some flax at the back of the house, which witness lit, and thrust into the roof, and set fire to the thatch; the roof was falling in as they departed. The party then fired some shots, took off their hats, and huzzaed, wishing Lynch luck of his hot-bed. Malone, witness, and another, when going away, said, all was well now if they had Mr Filgate.

Arthur Pollock, Esq., sworn: Recollects the last witness (Murphy) sending for him to the gaol of Trim, the day before his execution was to have taken place, and confessing to him that he was at Sillery's robbery. The next morning he was sent for again, and went to him about a quarter of an hour before he was to die, and Murphy acknowledged that he was at Wildgoose lodge. Murphy appeared to him very weak, and seemed not to have the most distant idea of a pardon.

Mr Wainright, Inspector of the gaol of Trim, sworn: Recollects Galogly being in Trim gaol, in April, 1817, and making a communication to him of being at Wildgoose Lodge.

William Smart, gaoler of Trim, sworn. Remembers Galogly making a communication to Mr Wainright, after which Galogly and Murphy were put into one room, but could have had no communication up to the time of the confession.

Patrick Halpenny sworn: Lived very near Wildgoose Lodge at the time of the burning, and recollects the night when two men came to his door and rapped; when it was opened, they demanded fire, which they took out of the house in spite of him, in a bit of a pot which they found at the fire place. They bid him go to bed, that it was the [right] place for him; he shortly after heard four shots, fired at intervals, and then the tramping of horses passing by; he went to the door, and saw Lynch's house on fire; he went to call his neighbour Carroll, but was desired to go to bed again, or they would have his life. When he arose in the morning, he found Lynch's house burned to ashes, and crowds of people collected round it.

James Corrigan, Chief Constable of Police, sworn: Identified Craven at the bar, and said, he had acknowledged to him in gaol, that he was at the burning of Wildgoose lodge, and desired him to communicate the same to Mr Pendleton.

Craven pleaded guilty when brought forward for trial.

Here the prosecution closed.

The defence established nothing towards the acquittal of the prisoners.

The learned **Judge**, in a copious and able charge, recapitulated the evidence. The Jury then retired for about half an hour, and brought in a verdict of *Guilty* against all the prisoners.

A scene of horror now ensued. The convicts, regardless of the awful situation into which their crimes had plunged them, burst forth into outrageous clamour, and evinced the most obdurate and remorseless spirit. Scarcely could they be pacified, or induced to listen to his Lordship's pathetic address, which was twice interrupted by the poignancy of his feelings. At last he pronounced the solemn sentence of death, which was not finished, when one of the convicts, (Malone), seized the book, which happened to be within his reach, and proceeded to swear that he was innocent. The crier, however, snatched it from his grasp. Ungoverned rage, vented in execrations against the police, the jury, &c., now ensued and struck the spectators mute with astonishment and horror.

Sentence of death was then very feelingly pronounced against them. They were to be executed on Monday the 9th instant, and their bodies delivered over to the surgeons for dissection.

Marron and Malone were clamorous in declaring their innocence to the Court, and on their way to the gaol.

Pendleton in his chart notes that Terence Marron 'had solicited to be admitted an approver yet died declaring himself innocent'.

TRIAL OF MICHAEL FLOODY, PATRICK MEEGAN & HUGH McLARNY, AND BRYAN LENNON

Reported in *The Correspondent*, 11 March 1818 (and in the *Dublin Evening Post*, 12 March 1818):

Saturday, March 7.

Michael Floody, Patrick Meighan (Meegan), and Hugh McElarney (McLarny), were indicted for the burning at Wildgoose Lodge, &c.

The following Jury were sworn: Henry McNeale, William Cairns, Robert Dickie, John Morgan, James Dickie, John Henry, William Hale, Owen McKenna, John Young, William Reid, Paul Parks, and James Crawley.

Serjeant Joy, as before, opened the case on the part of the Crown.

Alice Rispin sworn: In addition to what she adduced yesterday, she said, that Rooney was found sitting by his wife, his child between his knees, as if sheltering the infant from the devouring flames; saw tracks of straw through the garden, and flax all around the house, when she came over next morning.

The four informers, who prosecuted yesterday, came forward again, and agreed in their testimony against three prisoners.

Bernard McIlroy [Gilroy], in the course of his evidence, said, that a voice, when they attempted to break open the door, exclaimed, 'The first that should come in or out, he would shoot him'. Devan answered, 'Don't think it is old times with you, Rooney; this night is your doom'. Identified Floody, the prisoner.

William Filgate's testimony was the same as before recorded.

Thomas Gubby said, they saw the appearance of a man at Lynch's window, and Devan gave orders to fire, which was done; identified Floody. When returning from Wildgoose Lodge, within twenty perches of it, they swore never to disclose what they had seen to any one unworthy of it.

Peter Galogly deposed, that he was left holding horses at a boggy part of the lane, which they could not well pass; McElarney, the prisoner, was asked to hold them, but he refused, saying, that he was as fit to go to the burning as any man there.

On his cross-examination he said, that there were parties at the burning, from Louth, Cavan, Meath, and Monaghan; that he was joined in a Committee; and they were sworn to do what they were commanded, even to the committing of murder. He took the oath willingly.

Patrick Murphy, on his cross-examination, said that he was sworn to obey his brethren, to the utmost of his power – he would, if at liberty, do the same again, under similar circumstances.

Messrs Smart, Pollock, Halfpenny, and Wainwright, were called and sworn as before.

Marcas Callan, James Kisley, and Hugh Quin, made an attempt to prove an *alibi*, for two of the prisoners, but totally failed.

When the evidence was completed the judge in a lengthy speech criticised the Catholic clergy for not using their influence with their flocks in preventing such atrocities. This created some controversy in the aftermath of the trial. His remarks and the sequel to them are dealt with after dealing with the sentence and some reaction to the trials.

SENTENCE

The Correspondent of 11 March 1818:

> His Lordship then exhorted the jury to consider the whole business dispassionately and maturely. If they entertained any doubt, the prisoners at the bar were to have full benefit of that doubt. Such is the beneficial spirit of that law, which the wretched and infatuated people who perpetrated the crimes in question, have sought to destroy.
> He conjured the Jury not to permit their minds to be biased by the indignant expressions which he had uttered to the bye-standers. God forbid, that, by describing the atrocity of the crime, he should excite prejudice against the accused. He had merely sought to impress on the minds of the people, a conviction of the dreadful consequences which must result from the malignant spirit too prevalent in the country.
> The Jury retired for a short time, and returned a verdict of *Guilty*.
> An indescribable scene then ensued. The most dreadful imprecations burst forth from the wretched prisoners. McElarney [McLarney], an old and malignant convict, vented his rage, by cursing the Counsel who had pleaded against him, and by frequently interrupting the Judge in pronouncing the awful sentence of death. "I don't care", " I don't care what you do with me!" was the incessant cry of the hardened and inhuman miscreant.
> In the morning, one of the prisoners, named *Lenan* [Bryan Lennon] had pleaded guilty; the Judge had admonished him, and given him time to consider his plea. He persisted, and was sentenced with the other three. The 9th of March was the day appointed for the execution of ten of these offenders. Their bodies were to be delivered over to the Surgeons for dissection.
> Fifteen yet remain in Dundalk gaol untried, whose indictments were read to them on Saturday morning. Thirteen of these culprits said they were ready for their trial.

EDITORIAL REACTION IN *THE CORRESPONDENT* TO THE TRIALS

On the same day, 11 March 1818, as it reported the trials of Craven, Marron, Floody, McLarny, Gainor, Malone, Lennon, and Butler, the 'evening correspondent' of *The Correspondent* commented:

> Fifteen (*recte* 11) of the persons arraigned at Dundalk Assizes for the horrid crime of burning Wildgoose Lodge, and all its inhabitants, *eight in number*, have been convicted upon the clearest testimony, and sentenced to suffer death. The trial has exhibited as melancholy an instance of deep depravity and wickedness, as has ever come under our observation. The same ferocious and inhuman spirit which

instigated them to the commission of an act of almost unparalleled cruelty, displayed itself at that awful moment, when the Law exacted a terrible retribution for the abominable act they had been guilty of – and, instead of being impressed with the slightest sense of sorrow or contrition for what they had done – or with the fear of God, or of his eternal and immutable justice – or with a shadow of religious or moral sentiment, they broke out into blasphemous imprecations, and horrible curses, against their accusers, and all those who had been in any manner concerned in their prosecution. The solemn tone and aspect of the Judge, in passing sentence, had no effect upon them – they continued in the same obdurate disposition, unawed and unaffected by their fate, all the time his Lordship was passing the fearful denunciation of the Law upon them, and even after they were taken out of the Court to be remanded to the gaol, until the period of execution. The mind recoils from the contemplation of such a scene as this – and it is made even worse, by the recollection, that it has sprung out of a diabolical combination among persons, from various parts of the County Louth, to pursue with sanguinary vengeance, all who may thwart or obstruct the plans which they had conceived, in the demoniacal spirit of outrage and villainy. There was a sad example in the course of the trial of this latter fact – one of the witnesses who belonged to these misguided conspirators, having declared, that he felt himself bound by the oath of association he had taken, no matter what it enjoined him to perform.

Where such things occur, the Magistracy, and the loyal and orderly portion of the community, cannot be supine or indifferent to the duty which they owe to society. Such a system of atrocious co-operation as that which united the barbarians who burnt Wildgoose lodge, must be broken up effectually – and care must be taken, that, if it have any ramifications, or extends beyond the part of the country where it has first displayed itself with such horrible effects, it must be followed, vigorously and unceasingly, until not a link of it is to be found, or a trace of it suffered to the peace of society.

There are fifteen more of the persons accused of the burning of Wildgoose lodge, yet to be brought forward for trial – making the entire of those whom the power of the Law has reached for a share in that nefarious transaction, thirty in number.

JUDGE FLETCHER'S CRITICISM OF THE CATHOLIC CLERGY

Judge Fletcher was a supporter of Catholic Emancipation. It is evident that leaders of the movement consulted him. Sir Henry Parnell in a letter from Emo Park, Queen's County, 7 January 1816, to Daniel O'Connell wrote: 'As the responsibility of giving advice in so very important a measure is a very heavy one, I hope

I shall be excused in suggesting the propriety of showing the amended copy (draft of an address – 'perhaps a draft of the address to the Prince Regent which the Catholic Association later resolved, 16 March 2826, to entrust to Sir Henry Parnell') to Judge Fletcher before it is acted upon'.[219] His outburst of criticism of the Catholic clergy in neglecting to instruct their flocks on the problem of agrarian violence is all the more remarkable in the light of his general favour towards Catholics. As in his Wexford speech there seems to have been two versions of his speech and following some public criticism he toned down the strength of his remarks.

The Correspondent, 11 March 1818:

> When the evidence had terminated, his Lordship addressed the Jury at considerable length, and with much animation. The crime with which the prisoners stood charged, was, perhaps, the most enormous that had ever come before him in his judicial capacity. How it was proved, it was for them to decide. He knew, he said, that they would fully discharge their duty. Then addressing himself, with much energy, to the crowd which filled the Court, he said, that the madness of enthusiasm or religious bigotry had no part in producing these monstrous crimes. There were not here two conflicting parties arrayed under the banners of orange and green; not Protestant against Catholic, nor Catholic against Protestant – no! It was Catholic against Catholic.

[Some more detail of the speech is given by the *Belfast News-Letter*, 13 March 1818, and is inserted here:

> 'Lynch was a Catholic, and those whom he had prosecuted to conviction were Catholics; with increased warmth, his Lordship called out – 'Where are their priests? Why do they suffer such wickedness to proceed among their people? If they knew of it, why do they not interpose their authority? – if they know it not, why are they so inactive, why are they not roused to act like men zealous for the honour of the Catholic name? If they be dead to every sense of their duty, in the name of God, where are their Bishops? Where are the Catholic Bishops of the dioceses, where these enormities are committed ? Why not use the authority with which their Church has invested them, to rouse their lazy priests into action? Where was it these ruffians met for the purpose of concerting their hellish schemes? In a chapel. Who was their principal leader in this most diabolical outrage? The clerk of a chapel. Can any one suppose that this was unknown to their priests? Impossible! We all know what opportunity the Catholic priests have of knowing what passes among their people, by means of confession.' He did not know if there were any priests in his hearing; he did not

care. He hoped that what he was saying would be published; he knew it would. Those who were acquainted with his character knew that he was not partial to any party or sect, but administered justice to the extent of his knowledge. When Catholics complained, he was one of the first to advise their grievances to be redressed. He only spoke from an honest indignation – a zeal for Catholic honour. The honour of the Catholic name is stained by these outrages against the laws of their country. And what laws do these infatuated people oppose? A code that for mildness has no equal. He declared that the priests of Louth, Monaghan, Cavan, and Meath, were called upon to come forward and vindicate their sacerdotal character.]

Why do not the Clergy exercise their power over these people? We all know, said the Learned Judge, that, by means of confession, the Catholic Clergy possess much information of what is transacting in the country. Why, then, do they not perform their duty, and deny the rites of the church to all who participate in such crimes, or who refuse to discover the conspirators? Can a combination, extending over four counties, be yet a secret to all the Catholic Clergy in those counties? They, at least, see its effects, and it is their bounden duty to investigate the causes of those effects. But if they will remain inactive surely the Bishops should exercise the authority with which the Church had invested them, and stimulate the Priests to a discharge of their duty.

Where was the diabolical scheme planned and matured? In a chapel. Who conducted it? The clerk. Catholics were the agents and perpetrators of the crime. Catholics the miserable sufferers. Why did they suffer? Because the unfortunate Lynch and Rooney had resisted a mid-night attack upon their house with manly fortitude, and had afterwards prosecuted to conviction, those miscreants who were since hanged for the crime. Yes, their offence was simply, that they had appealed to the mild and beneficent laws of their country for redress and protection. It was incumbent on the Catholic Clergy of Louth, Monaghan, Cavan, and Meath, to vindicate the sacerdotal character. He knew not whether any of that order was then present, nor did he care, but he was desirous that what he was now saying should be published. It ought to be widely promulgated. He was known to be no party man, and he spoke only from the impulse of an honest indignation. It was his peculiar study to fulfil his duty to the utmost extent of his knowledge and ability. He was always an advocate for the Catholics, and sincerely sought to have their grievances redressed'.

This account of Judge Fletcher's criticism of Catholic priests caused a stir, and perhaps Judge Fletcher was not happy with the above summary for *The Correspondent* returned to the subject on 13 March with further comment and a 'Correct Abstract of the Judge's Charge'. It was also published as a broadsheet, a copy of which is in the Royal Irish Academy, Dublin, and is reproduced here after the comment of *The Correspondent*:

The Address of Mr Justice Fletcher to the hardened criminals, on whom it became his duty to pass sentence at Dundalk, is an extremely important Document; and should, or, at least that portion of it, which bears upon the horrible system of fraternization, that led to their guilt, be generally disseminated. If the Learned Judge has pronounced justly on the influence which the Roman Catholic Clergy possess over the humbler classes of the people, and has taken a right view of the duties which their sacred functions have imposed upon them (and we believe few will be found to doubt that he has done both), that Body is called upon to pursue a more useful course in Society, than it would seem they have done in those districts, where the abominable project of burning Wildgoose Lodge, and all its inmates, was organized. There are very many instances on record, where the Clergymen of the Roman Catholic Church have acted as became good citizens of the State, and with moral and religious energy, for the prevention of crime – or its punishment, when committed; but, it appears, from what the learned authority in question has advanced, that much more is required from them, than partial examples of a determination to support the Laws, and to maintain the peace of the country – and, we trust, that he has not invoked them in vain, to do all the good they are capable of, as men of enlightened minds, and Ministers of the Christian Religion. We give a part of this Address, especially applicable to the purpose we point out, in a more correct form than it has appeared in the proceedings arising out of the trials for the burning of Wildgoose Lodge; and we are most anxious to impress upon our countrymen of an humble condition, and who are most exposed to the snares that are laid by villainy to corrupt and debauch their morals, and to lead them to the perpetration of crime of a terrible magnitude – to rebellion against the Law, and all who are in the administration of it – the concluding words of the Learned Judge Fletcher, on this important occasion:-

'And what are the Laws they labour to subvert? I know something of the Laws of *other* countries, and I have grown old in the study, the practice, and the administration of the Laws of *this* – and *I tell you all, there is not a country upon Earth, whose Criminal Code is founded upon principles so humane and so benevolent; -there is no country upon Earth but this, where the first duty of the Judge is to act as counsel for the Prisoners!*'

Correct Abstract of the Charge of Mr Justice Fletcher, on the conviction of the persons charged with the burning of Wildgoose Lodge.[220]

'I will take this opportunity of making some observations on facts that have come out on these trials; they do not actually bear on this case, nor are they intended for the particular observation of the Jury. I address them *to all who hear me*, and especially for the consideration of all those of the *Catholic* Religion who are now in this Court. I particularly allude to the conduct of the *Catholic Clergy*. If the Priests of this and the neighbouring counties, where this horrible conspiracy was hatched and formed – possessing, as they do, and as *everybody knows they do*, the most unbounded influence, and means of information respecting the conduct of their several Congregations – had done their duty, *it is impossible* such a conspiracy could have existed, without coming to their knowledge.

The prisoners already convicted of these diabolical murders (I am saying nothing as to those now at the bar) after the most serious consideration of their cases, and the solemn verdict of a Jury, with a hardihood of guilt, which, long as my experience as a Barrister and as a Judge has been, I never saw paralleled, have flown in the face of their God, and by a declaration of their innocence, attempted to disprove that guilt, of which no man, endowed with the smallest portion of reason, could, for a moment, entertain a doubt. Can it be supposed that men in their situation, who must, within a few hours, appear in the presence of that Judge, to whom not only their actions, but their thoughts are known, if they were influenced by a proper sense of their religion, or if they were instructed in any, the smallest particle of religious duty, would have obstinately and impudently persisted in such a declaration, and gone out of this world with a lie in their mouths? I say, *if the Priests* of this, and of the neighbouring counties, had properly exerted that influence which the rituals of their Church give them, not only over the actions, but the secret sentiments and opinions of their flocks – if they refused the performance of these rites, to such as did not make penitence and a disclosure of their crimes, the condition of their pardon – I *say if the Catholic Clergy* had not slumbered on their posts, we should never have witnessed such conduct as was yesterday exhibited in this Court.

It appears that the monster, *Devan*, (who now, on a gibbet, pays the forfeit of his crimes) was clerk to the Catholic Priest; he was, it seems, the parish schoolmaster too. It was to this *wretch* that the forming the morals and the minds of the rising generation was committed. The Chapel of Stonestown, (at whose altar he assisted in administering) was the place of meeting for the party of which he was the Leader. Another Chapel (that of Reaghstown) was the general rendezvous of all the parties of this [diabolical] confederation. If the Priests of these parishes had done their duty, could these meetings have taken place without coming to their knowledge? And if the Catholic *Priests* do not do their duty, where are the Bishops? Do *they, too*, sleep upon their posts? Why do they not pour upon their Clergy the censures of their Church – censures, with which, we know, they have the power of visiting them in the severest manner.

I know not whether any Catholic Priest now hears me, nor do I care; what I speak is for public benefit and I wish it to be publicly known. I respect the Ministers of *every christian Communion*, who conscientiously discharge their important duties. The friendly feelings I have borne to the Catholic Religion are well known; my character and my conduct in that respect are known and established. I therefore call on its Clergy, of *every* description, *Bishops* and *Priests* to come forward and exert the authority they possess. I call on them by every obligation, as Ministers and as Men, to come forward, and vindicate their sacerdotal character, by an active and sincere performance of their duty. I have seen cases, where religious, and those political differences (if they can be called *political*) which have distracted this unfortunate country, have caused much animosity between parties – I have seen cases between Orangemen and Ribbonmen; but this is no case of party zeal or religious fanaticism – *here* was Catholic against Catholic – here we see a wide extended conspiracy – men from *all* parts, East, West, North, and South – from the Counties of Meath, and of Monaghan, and of Cavan, and of Louth, bound by oaths, for the commission of *any crime* to which their leaders might conduct them – and these leaders selected for their determined and desperate characters – joining in a diabolical scheme for the destruction of an unfortunate man and his family, against whom it does not appear that any of them felt *personal* animosity – most of them had never seen him. What was the *offence* that called for the extinction of this man, and of every *living creature* that composed his family? He had the audacity to defend his property, when it was attacked by a band of nightly robbers; and when appealed to the Laws of his Country for redress, he brought *three* of these robbers to condign punishment. Do the deluded people of this County consider to what their conduct tends? I will tell them, it will drive from it every man of property – every man of mild and peaceable disposition – every man of kind and humane feeling; all those who, by their property, or from inclination, would be likely to improve it, or ameliorate their condition; in short, every man who is not boldly determined to risk his safety, to set them at defiance, and stand ever watchful, and on his guard. To this wretched state would they reduce this country.

And what are the Laws they thus labour to subvert? *I* know *something* of the Laws of *other* countries, and I have grown old in the study, and the practice, and the administration of the Law of *this*; - and I *tell you all*, there is not a country upon earth, whose Criminal Code is founded on principles so humane, and so benevolent; - there is no country on earth but this, where the first duty of the Judge is to be of Counsel for the Prisoner'.

The *Dublin Evening Post*, 14 March 1818, summarised Judge Fetcher's speech but also politely criticised it:

> We believe *The Evening Post* will not be readily accused of volunteering any hostile remarks on the conduct of Judge Fletcher. When this learned Personage was made the theme and topic of abuse by the Castle Scribes, this Journal, the first to publish his Charge, was also the foremost to repel the attacks made upon his personal and political conduct. Having seen little to alter our opinions, and still feeling that the Honorable Judge was justified in most of his statements, we look back to this period of our labours with sentiments of satisfaction. It is therefore with great pain that our duty compels us to impugn certain

doctrines promulgated by this excellent Magistrate on a recent occasion...
His Lordship's wish, as expressed in the course of the Charge, has now been fulfilled. His sentiments on this occasion are promulgated through every part of Ireland. It is now laid before such of the English nation as take an interest in the affairs of this Country. All the objects which he could desire from publicity are now attained, and all the Catholic Clergy in Ireland will read, mark, and inwardly digest them. It is their bounden duty to do so. The high rank of the man, his unimpeachable public and private character, his constant advocacy of the Catholic Claims, all will ensure the most serious and general attention to whatever sentiments he deems it his duty to give utterance. Indeed it is the first duty of the Catholic Clergy to vindicate themselves from the aspersions, we use the mildest word that occurs to us, which this Charge, in no very guarded language, flings upon their character. What, in a word, is the amount of these aspersions? Only this, that the Catholic Clergy *might*, if they had done their duty, have prevented the horrible catastrophe that occurred at Lynch's house at Wildgoose Lodge. Might have prevented the roasting alive of so many innocent creatures, if they pleased – might, and did not!! We know not whether such another horrible charge was ever yet made upon a man, or a body of men, before this. Sir Richard Musgrave, in his volume of fanaticism and falsehood, never ventured so far as Mr Justice Fletcher, the Friend of his Country, and of Catholic Emancipation. Such a charge must be supported by very grave evidence indeed. What is the evidence? The honest indignation of the Judge! He was shocked – who would not be shocked at the horrible murder of Lynch's family? He was shocked, and who would not, that the miscreants who perpetrated that inhuman act, which, can be only paralleled by the atrocities of the American Savages, was planned in a Temple devoted to the worship of Almighty God! But by the association, which, it appears, was irresistible in the mind of the Learned Judge, he immediately pours the phial of his wrath upon the Catholic Clergy of the District, and infers, at a jump, that if they had done their duty, the Murder would not have been committed. Good.
Now we would ask Judge Fletcher, is it likely – is it within the compass of possibility, that nefarious Ruffians, such as these Murderers were, would consult the Clergy, not as to the guilt of committing Murder – for to do the Learned Judge justice, he does not say so – though a Sophist might infer the fact from his declaration – but does he really think, that men, whose minds had been indurated to such a degree of infernal wickedness, would consult their Pastors upon any moral theme whatever? Again, does he think, that if any Priest, however vicious, had an inkling of what was about to be perpetrated, he would not have taken measures to prevent the crime? He must answer these questions, as every man of sense will answer them.
What, then, does the Honorable Judge's *indignant* accusation amount to? But it is idle to follow up the question.
As to the vindication of the Catholic Clergy, they shall have none from

us – *they want none*. Their lives, their labours, their virtues, furnish a shield of proof which has hitherto resisted all the assaults of their enemies, and which will serve as a panoply against the attacks of their friends.

On 16 March 1818 the *Dublin Evening Post* returned to the subject of Judge Fletcher's charge and his time published this extract from the *Weekly Freeman's Journal*:

> We are somewhat limited in space this day, but we cannot suffer our Sheet to go forth to the Public without a few remarks on some extraordinary passages which we have read in what is termed 'A Correct Abstract of the Charge of Mr Justice Fletcher, on the conviction of the persons charged with the Burning of Wild Goose Lodge', and which is ostentatiously published in an Evening Paper of yesterday, as an 'extremely important document', and one which should be 'generally disseminated'.
> In this report the Learned Judge is made to accuse the Catholic Clergy of the district in which this atrocious and savage act occurred, of a criminal neglectfulness of duty, asserting, that if they had not 'slumbered on their posts', it is *'impossible'* that such a conspiracy as that of which the unfortunate Lynches were victims, could have existed without coming to their knowledge. '*I* say', observes the Learned Judge, according to this authentic abstract, '*if the Priest* of this, and of the neighbouring counties, had properly exerted that influence which the rituals of their Church give them, not only over the actions, but the secret sentiments and opinions of their flocks – if they refused the performance of these rites to such as did not make penitence and a dislosure of their crimes the condition of their pardon – I say, *if the Catholic Clergy* had not slumbered on their posts, we should never have witnessed such conduct as was yesterday exhibited in this Court'.
> We recollect a time when the Journal to which we are indebted for this correct report, the dissemination of which is considered so important to society, had made very strenuous efforts to prove Judge Fletcher an indiscreet, foolish, perverse old man – a propounder of idle theories, a favourer of factious projects, and, in short, a person who compromisd the dignity of the Bench by his intemperance and blunders on all questions which had any relationship to politics. If this Journal happened to think as we do respecting the recent exhibition, we would not be desirous that it should, in giving expression to its sentiments, revive any portion of its ancient vituperation against a man who will be allowed, at all events, to be honest and well-meaning; but, we could heartily join it, if it had said, that the Learned Judge, through some fatality which is not easily to be accounted for, had been betrayed into a line of observation as singularly erroneous, and unsustained by the fact, as ever was heard in a Court of Justice.
> The Learned Judge has spoken of the influence of the Catholic Clergy, and he demands, in effect, why they had not called the miscreants in

question before them; made them pour out their blackened and demoniacal hearts; and turn aside from their evil courses? Doubtless, a Catholic Clergyman might summon every human being in his diocese to the confessional, as he might 'call spirits from the deep', but does it follow that they would 'come'? He has no means of obtaining information except through confession, or controuling (sic) the bad passions unless by exhortation. Suppose the atrocious conspirators against the lives of the unfortunate inmates of Wild-goose Lodge had not presented themselves at either mass or confession, were regardless of all the exhortation he could address to them, and were just as ready to rob or murder him as any individual in the community, if his life or property could be made ancillary to the attainment of any end, however trivial, would it be contended that he merited censure? That the murderers of the Lynches were persons of such a stamp we need only refer to the words of his lordship, and the descriptions of the Paper to which we have alluded, to be fully convinced. His Lordship has said, that long as his experience has been, both as a Barrrister and Judge, he has never met such hardened and impenetrable miscreants. Their conduct in the dock, even after conviction – after all hopes of mercy had vanished – after their existence in this life had been limited to a few fleeting moments, was more like that of fiends than beings in human shape. Their trials were solemn. The detail of the wholesale sufferings of which they had been the authors, was sufficient to move all that were not sunk to the lowest ebb of obduracy. They were found guilty and they cursed the Jurors. They received sentence, and they scoffed at the Judge. The gallows was presented to their view, and they appeared only to regret that it left them no chance of vengeance. Remorse or compunction, or feeling for their situation, were visitings to which, to the last moment of life they remained utter strangers. The very terms they could not comprehend the meaning of. Yet these were beings upon whom it was expected that their Priests could work miracles. These were the docile and tractable people who would have been snatched from disgrace, punishment and infamy if the Catholic Clergy of their district had not 'slept on their posts!'

Oh, but Devan, the leader of the murderers was Clerk to a Catholic Chapel – how could he err, if his master were not in some respect criminal? If the question be a justifiable one, we may be allowed to impeach the integrity of the very founder of our religion himself, for amongst his Twelve Disciples there was found a traitor and a delinquent. Perhaps, however, it will be admitted to be a circumstance somewhat remarkable, that the conspirators assembled in a Catholic Chapel. We see nothing extraordinary in the occurrence. It was a better rendez-vous place than a barn, because it was more detached, and because there was easy access to it, Devan having custody of the key. It was better than a cabin, because it was more private and commodious. The fact of all the parties directly interested in the horrid league, the conspirators as well as those conspired against, being Catholics, keeps the circumstance of the meeting in the chapel free of all the importance which is sought to be attached to it. It could only borrow interest from a difference of religion existing between the murderers and murdered. That there was no difference is attested by Judge Fletcher. His words are (and similar expressions were used by the Council [sic] for the prosecutions, Serjeant Joy): 'I have seen cases where religious, and these political differences (if they can be called *political*) which have distracted this unfortunate country, have caused much animosity between parties – I have seen cases between Orangemen and Ribbonmen – but this is no case of party zeal or religious fanaticism – *here* was Catholic against Catholic'.

In fine, there is no view which we can take of the extraordinary imputation upon which we have thought it our duty to animadvert, that does not strengthen our impression of their being wholly uncalled-for, without any foundation, extremely ungenerous and equally impolitic.

There have lately been some horrid, and apparently gratuitous, murders in England. Persons' throats have been cut, and sculls battered to atoms, as far as people can judge, for the mere luxury of man-slaying and butchery. It would, we dare say, be pronounced a very atrocious slander to connect these abominations in any manner with the mode in which the Protestant Clergy think fit to discharge the duties which devolve upon persons in their stations. A Methodist Preacher was convicted some time of a murder and robbey perpetrated in open day, and of which two defenceless females were the victims; and Haitch, whose enormities still cause a shudder, wherever they are mentioned, was a constant attendant at some lately established Meeting-house, convenient to the scene of his atrocities. It would, doubtless, be considered an act of great injustice to denounce the sects to which these wretches belonged, because individual members turned out to be the most detestable culprits of the whole race of Christians. Just of a piece with such denunciation, in candour, equity, and reason, do we pronounce the aspersions under consideration.

The report then quotes the account from the *Newry Telegraph*, 14 March 1818, where some of the prisoners had laid violent hands on the prison chaplain – 'Is it credible, that any of these wretches had ever explained the nature, or even hinted at the existence of the conspiracy under which they had systematically acted, under their infernal leader, Devan? By no means'.

The *Drogheda Journal*, Wednesday 18 March 1818 (extract in *The Correspondent*, 19 March) came to the defence of the priests:

The Honourable Judge's zeal for Catholic honour, led him into a warmth of language, that his cooler judgement, would have revolted at. No rational man will entertain a thought, that any Roman Catholic Clergyman knew of the infernal plot, devised and brought into action by that monster, Devan. We are acquainted with three of the Clergymen who reside in the neighbourhood of Reaghstown, and do not believe there are better, or more zealous and pious men in any part of this country. They have, in every instance, and at personal risk, endeavoured to break down the spirit of insubordination to the laws, which was visible in some of the peasantry; and if their laudable admonitions could not effect that desirable object, they surely are not accountable for the misdeeds of infatuated and vicious men.

Judge Fletcher moved on in his circuit from the Dundalk to the Armagh Assizes where he presided at the Crown Court on Thursday 12 March 1818. There he made it his business to allude to the evil of agrarian and sectarian crime in Ireland, condemning the supiness of magistrates in the past and specially their failure to protect Catholics against the Peep of Day Boys and the Orangemen in County Armagh, a failure he hoped would be remedied by the new Act of Parliament where Petty Juries would decide whether there was ground for prosecution. He concluded by emphasising his friendship towards Catholics. This pleased the *Dublin Evening Post* and this time, amends having been made as it would seem by Fletcher, it rushed to defend him against criticism and praised him for his balanced stance in opposition to religious and political animosity and in particular for divorcing the Wildgoose Lodge atrocity from sectarian conflict:

> The Court sat shortly after 10 o'clock. The following Grand Jury was sworn:
> Hon. H. Caulfield, Walter McGeough, Roger Hall, Nicholas A. Cope, Wm Blacker, James Johnson, Thomas Verner, William Irwin, Jos. Atkinson, Jonathan Seaver, Robert Harden, George Ensor, James W. McNeale, James Forde, John Winder, William Reid, William Loftie, Henry McVeagh, Arthur Irwin, Curran Woodhouse, W. N. Thompson, Hunt. W. Cambre, John Cross, Esqrs.
> His Lordship commenced his charge to the Grand Jury, by calling their attention to the provisions of the late grand jury act, and pointed out with great cleverness and perspicuity, the benefits which resulted from it over the former laws, for the grand juries. He noticed the distress which had been felt by the different counties through which he had passed, and of the scandalous practices that had been committed, arising from party feuds, etc. These, and other causes, which he had enumerated had demoralized this kingdom, and had opened a way for deluges of perjury, etc. He then expatiated at considerable length, and with great animation, on the evil consequences which resulted from party feuds and combinations. The mischiefs they produced were, he said, incalculable. They arrayed one portion of people against another, and produced the most dreadful effects through society. All these factious parties, whether known by the name of Orangemen, or by

other denomination, were noxious and illegal – as such, he should always set his face against them and mark them with his strongest disapprobation. He had witnessed their melancholy and deplorable effects in various parts of the kingdom – in the counties of Cavan, Tyrone, Donegal, etc. In some instances petit juries had even inquired what colour the prisoners wore; a plain proof this, how widely the poison of these societies was diffused through the community. All combinations of party-men, to aid and protect one another, all secret and sworn associations, whether Orangemen, ribandmen, or any other denomination of partisans – were equally hostile to the laws of the land, to social order, and to the good government of the country.

He next adverted to the late dreadful outrage at Dundalk, which, he said, was totally unconnected with any party – and concluded by calling on the jury and on the clergy of all denominations, by their example and conversation, to use every exertion in their power, to put down such unlawful combinations and confederacies, as there was no saying to what evils they might lead, or where they might terminate.

The charge was considerably long, and was chiefly levelled against the dreadful effects of parties bound together by unlawful oaths, which far surpassed any thing that could be conceived. For God's sake, said he, crush the sleeping dragon. He remarked also, in the course of his charge, that he had been always friendly to the Catholics.

The *Dublin Evening Post*, 17 March 1818 (and some repetition in the issue of 18 March 1818) gave a further commentary on Judge Fletcher's address to the Grand Jury at Armagh along with a more complete text.

> It was easy to foresee that the attack contained in Judge Fletcher's Charge on the Catholic Clergy of Louth and the adjoining Counties would have been seized upon with avidity by those men who pander to the worst prejudices of the People.
> Accordingly an Evening Paper, notorious for its slander as well as for its stupidity, has repeated, in feeble echoes, all the objectionable and injudicious portions of the learned Magistrate's Address, and has strained its little modicum of understanding to prove that the Catholic Clergy, if not accessaries before the fact, are, at least, guilty of misprision of Treason for not having prevented the catastrophe at Wildgoose Lodge. It would be an idle waste of time to follow the dull diatribe; and we mention the circumstances only to show that there is still a lurking wish to plunge the Country into all the heats and horrors of faction, by endeavouring to make these cruel proceedings to originate in a Popish plot. It will not do, however; the time is past when such a war-whoop could be raised with any prospect of success. No Orangeman, however determined and enfuriated, will be made to believe that the fatal events grew out of religious animosity and the learned Judge himself seems anxious to guard against any such inference; for he expressly and repeatedly declared, in the course of his

Charge, that the Murders were perpetrated by Catholics upon Catholics; and that no perversion of ingenuity could make it a party concern. That no possible doubt may remain on the subject of his sentiments on this occasion, we shall proceed to lay before our Readers a summary of his Charge to the Grand Jury of Armagh. *This* Charge does credit it his heart and understanding. It should be engraved upon the hearts of his Countrymen, and, bating a few expressions, to which, however, we do not deem it necessary, at present, more particularly to refer, it will be read with mixed feelings of pleasure by every friend of Peace and of Ireland. It comes in too, at this period, and on this occasion, with particular aptness and effect.

ARMAGH ASSIZES

These Assizes commenced on Thursday, and terminated on Saturday evening. In the Civil Court, where the Hon. Mr Justice Mayne presided, there was but little business, and in the Crown Court where the Hon. Judge Fletcher presided, the calendar exhibited but that list of ordinary accusations, which no state of society can be expected not to give rise to. There were no party quarrels, no rackings, no burnings, no murders – but few Trials for capital offences, and no capital convictions. On the Grand Jury Panel being called, there were many defaulters, owing to the great severity of the weather, which detained some of the first Gentlemen of the County from attending. Of this number were Mr Richardson, one of the Knights of the Shire, and Mr C. Brownlow his avowed opponent on the approaching Appeal to the Constituency – both were storm-staid, we understand at Holyhead – the Hon. Mr Caulfield, brother to the present, and son of the late illustrious Earl of Charlemont, was Foreman of the Jury. On th routine of the arrangement being completed, the incorruptible and constitutional Judge Fletcher addressed Mr Caulfield and his Fellow-Jurors in nearly the following words:

'Gentlemen, You have been constituted the Grand Inquest of this County. On the important duties which you have to perform, it is not necessary that I should go into detail, aware as I am, that they are familiar to you and trusting, as I do, to your conscientious conception of them. But it is proper that I should revert to a recent Act of Parliament, which regulates your Proceedings, in the consideration of such Indictments as may be sent up to you. I do not know how the late unconstitutional practice became prevalent, nor can I conceive why that anomaly should have distinguished this Country, while the uniform practice of the Sister Island, now made imperative on us by the wholesome Statue to which I allude, has been coeval with all we know of what is pure or excellent in the British Constiution. That admirable system of jurisprudence, under which it is our good fortune to live, requires that no man should be put even to answer on any criminal charge, until a Jury of his Country, on their oaths, see sufficient grounds for subjecting him to Trial on the accusation. It is, therefore, that it is required that twelve of your number should agree to every

Indictment, ere it can be returned to this Court as a True Bill. But hitherto you had not the means afforded to form a judicious decision; the only evidence placed before you was the examinations taken by the Magistrates – and you must all of you, Gentlemen, be aware how fallacious these may often be. We all know how greatly the heat of passion – the first feelings of resentment – the ignorance of some – the fraud of others, must necessarily discolour objects: the incapacity of the Magistrate – often his prejudice or malice, or party feeling, mixing with or thwarting his reason, and his sense of justice. If these, or any of these, have had any thing to do in originating the accusation, their mischievous evidence will be stopped by your conscientious examination of *civa voce* evidence. You can now have no other – you ought never to have had any other. It ought to have been so without the enforement of an Act of Parliament – but habit is inveterate, and I do not wonder that doubts were entertained by country Gentlemen, of the expediency of assimilating our practice, in this respect to that of England, when I know that doubts existed amongst the Gentlemen of the Bar, and in no small degree amongst the Judges themselves. It is my Boast never to have been of this number, and I have experienced much pleasure in contemplating the happy operation of our amended practice. You can only have evidence *for* the Crown, and it is only necessary that you should be satisfied by the testimony of one Witness swearing from *his own knowledge*, to the criminal act, to justfy you in sending the accused to his Trial before a Petty Jury. I say *of his own knowledge – belief* is made up of conjecture – of hearsay – indeed there is no saying what belief is – it may, perhaps, be best defined by calling it 'the opinion of the circle in which we live'; a thing of too vague and uncertain a nature on which to subject any one to a serious accusation. The evidence before you ought to be such as would justify you, if not contradicted, in finding the accused party Guilty – if you were a Petty Jury. This is enough, gentlemen, on this subject.

Gentemen, I find with great pleasure, that the Calendar laid before me exhibits but that kind of catalogue of accusation which, perhaps, no state of society can be expected to be free from. I do not find in it any evidence of the existence of party feuds. From personal inspection I know nothing of your County, this being the first time I have borne his Majesty's Commission in it; but I cannot be supposed ignorant of the unhappy state of society which it presented at a period not remote. You Gentlemen, must know, much better than I possibly can, the extent of the mischief *locally*. You must have witnessed the misery inflicted upon thousands of the King's onoffending subjects, by the ruthless persecution which drove a large portion of the Population of the County from all the dear (however humble, still dear) delights, sympathies, and associations of home, to wander where they could; or, in the language of the Russian Faction, to wander '*to Hell or Connaught*!' But, Gentlemen, if you have had better opportunities of viewing the deserted, or destroyed habitation – the melancholy and desponding Family bereft of its little all, and flying, with hasty and disordered steps from the spoiler, you have not had better opportunities than I have had of of tracing the fearful consequences of the persecution. The emigrants from this County carried into every district of the island, a fearful tale of the persecution they had fled from – they bore testimony of their sufferings, and of the cruel inflictions *of your Orangemen, or Break-of-Day men.* And artful persons availed themelves of a melancholy and frightful truth, to originate and spread an Association, which sought afterwards, in its maturity, to overthrow our Government, and destroy our Constitution. Thus, may the late rebellion, the atrocities which marked its progress, the shocking tale of Scullabogue – all, all, be traced to the Armagh persecutions – wanton, as they were unprovoked. The cruel and pitiless warfare of an infuriated populace waged against a defenceless people, while the Magistrates, who ought to have been their protectors, looked on, it is said (you can best judge it truly), quiescent, if not approving. It may not be *mal-apropos* that I should mention a circumstance related to me by a Gentleman, with whom I had the honour to have a considerable degree of intimacy – a Gentleman of great worth and intelligence, Mr Hume, the Member for Wicklow: In the County of Wicklow, at least in two Baronies of that County, where he had great and well deserved influence, and in which his estates lay, he learned that for many nights the Roman Catholic Inhabitants had deserted their dwellings, and had lain in the fields, under the apprehension of being massacred by their Protrstant neighbours. He found an artful Emissary of Rebellion had used the too true and too cruel story of Armagh persecutions to work upon the fears of an industrious and simple Peasantry, with a view to bind them, while under the panic of expected suffering, in illegal associations. My friend was fortunate (thus we understood the Learned Judge, who spoke throughout in rather an under tone) to discover and trace this incendiary, and to bring him to justice and deserved punishment. But you see, Gentlemen, in his anecdote, the train of mischief which flows from an encouragement of any faction. *Association naturally begets counter-associations.* There is no knowing where the evil will end – no tracing its malignant ramifications – no saying to it in the language of Omnipresence, 'thus far shalt thou go, and no farther'.

Gentlemen, I am happy to find Faction sleeps in your County – smother the Monster, I entreat you! Let him never resuscitate. I trust the People of this industrious and populous County will never again be deceived, either by their own inflamed prejudices, or the artful instigators of any sordid and short-sighted politician, to conceive that any good can accrue to them from the persecution of their neighbours, who may believe a little more, or a little less, or who may worship God in a different temple, or with different observances. Let them never again be so deceived, as to their happiness, or their duties. For myself, I think it right for me to say to you, Gentlemen, that I regard all these associations as illegal. I care not what the badge, whether Green or Orange, nor what the pretence, nor what the profession – all are illegal, and when any indictment against either comes before me, so shall I charge the Jury. The law knows no difference, regards no distinction of

colour or pretension, and it is the Judge's duty to administer the law.
Gentlemen, I have come from a county of whose politics I know as little personally as of yours. There, a most atrocious and abominable crime was perpetrated, for which a number of unhappy wretches have paid the forfeit of their lives. There, however, no Religious feud existed; the Sufferers and the Perpetrators were all of the same Religion – all were Roman Catholics. A brave man had defended his House successfully against the Assault of midnight rufffians, and he afterwards appealed to the laws of his country for their deserved punishment. Hence he became the object of a wide extended combination for vengeance, which was wreaked upon him, and upon all his family, under circumstances of horrible atrocity. There is no effect without a cause, and it were much to be wished, that we could trace the source of so foul a conspiracy against the peace and security of social order.
One subject remains for me to say a few words to you on. An Act of Parliament introducing a New System regards County Presentments was expected t be now in operation – but the Legislature for the present suspended it. This Statute was perhaps faulty in making too much to depend upon the integrity and good judgement of the Engineer – it is, however, obvious the System cannot remain as it is. The most enormous abuses grow out of it - and to it, perhaps, more than to any thing else, are we to attribute the but too general disregard of the Sacred Obligation of an Oath, which is the security of life, of property, and of honor. To borrow a foreign expression, hence the 'demoralization' of the People. No sacrifice would be too great to fetch us back to simplicity and truth. I know not, Gentlemen, if you have any Jobbing in this County – I come amongst you, as I ought in my Relation to come, without leanings, without partialities, or dislikes – but in some Counties I know of the grossest proceedings in Presentment Business – blank affidavits sworn to - and other, the most shameful violation of integrity. The wisdom of the Legislature will, I hope, devise a remedy, for it is obvious, as I have already said, that the present System cannot go on.
Gentlemen I will no longer detain you from the exercise of your important duties'
O si sic omnia –

The subject of Judge Fletcher's criticism of the Catholic clergy at Dundalk was taken up again in a lengthy polemical letter signed *Poplicola* which appeared in *The Correspondent*, 21 March 1818, after executions for the murders at Wildgoose Lodge. It should be the duty of Catholic clergy, it maintained, as a preventative measure in combating atrocities, to teach their uncivilised flocks proper moral principles. This would be the real emancipation, and not to sit in the Lords or Commons.

Sir,

I have lately seen in the Newspapers two Charges, said to have been delivered by the very Learned Judge Fletcher, at the Dundalk and Armagh Assizes. They are so jumbled together, and are set so much at logger-heads with each other, that, perhaps, it might not be unacceptable to the various critics who are so much puzzled about them, to attempt to reconcile them to each other.

Every one must certainly agree with this able and well-meaning Judge, that it is to the Roman Catholic Pastors (and not to the Legislature) that our Petitions should be addressed for Emancipation, as it is called. And, if the statement in the English Papers be correct, about Haitch the murderer, that he was not only a Secretary, but came out of a Conventicle to commit the murder, and returned to it shortly after 'the deed was done', we might also Petition the new Sects likewise, to infuse into their Congregations less hostility to public order and the laws; a better temper, together with sounder opinions, as a *pre-disposing state of mind* for becoming good, or, at least, inoffensive members of society.

So we should join, one and all, in conjuring the Roman Catholic Powers to endeavour to eradicate, if possible, from their Congregations, hatred, envy, resentment, and determined hostility to the Established Church and State, to the Laws, to the Bishops and Clergy of England, to the customs and manners of England – its very language even – in short, to every thing that is English.

The worthy judge is represented to have broken out, in his Charge at Dundalk, into the following expressions of an honest and virtuous indignation: - 'I have come from a County where a most atrocious and abominable crime was perpetrated, for which a number of unhappy wretches have paid the forfeit of their lives. A brave man had defended his home, successfully, against the assault of midnight ruffians; and he afterwards appealed to the laws of his country for their deserved punishment. Hence he became the object of a wide-extended combination for vengeance, which was wreaked upon him, and upon all his family, under circumstances of horrible atrocity. There is no effect without a cause, and it were much to be wished, that we could trace the source of so foul a conspiracy against the peace and security of social order'.

This cause is, very fortunately, to be discovered in the same Charge, a little higher up, where the Learned Judge is made to say, that the cause is Faction. '*Association*', he says, '*naturally begets counter-association*'. That every sect, whether religious or political, and whether of the more ancient errors (as the Roman Catholic one), or of the more recent ones, sprung up in the Conventicles and Coffee-houses of our day, form an organised and very active Association against the Established Church, there can be no doubt. Some late Statutes, since the era of 1782, in a moment of division and faction at home, and of weakness abroad, have rendered this Association, for the time, a legal one. But, as 'Association naturally begets counter-association', and as the Legislature have not enacted that this one should be without its due offspring, it follows, that something like a "counter-association" (call it Orange or Protestant, or what you please) is thereby become a necessary consequence of those very Statutes.

There is little doubt, that if any of those conspirators in the county of Louth (one hundred in number, at the least) had disclosed to their Roman Catholic Pastor their intended murder, the latter would not have lost the honour of communicating it, instantly, to the Civil Power; and he would have taken great credit to himself for such a service. But it is also the predisposition to think of outrages against all laws and religion, that it is the Pastor's duty to do away; and, perhaps, Judge Fletcher's reproof is pointed against the not attempting, with sufficient earnestness, to remove the predispositions. Every body must know, and the Roman Catholic Clergy amongst others, how frequently the people are told, by the public Speakers, and by the writers of the day, who affect to be in their interests, that the Law is not their friend – that it is their oppression, if they are not immediately *Emancipated*, as it is called. Mere religious worship is not sufficient to counteract the effects of so much pernicious zeal, or to lull the evil and rancorous disposition which such excitements tend to provoke in the minds of an ignorant and irritable people - something more should be done, because it is obvious, that something more is wanting to qualify the people for the *Emancipation* which they are pursuing. This must be the Christian Pastor's task. He should instruct and civilize them. It is needless to explain, that these words are meant in the sense taken by Protestants; which must, at bottom, have been the good Judge's meaning, as we know he is a sound Protestant in his heart; otherwise, indeed, he could not have been a Judge. This alone gives any sense or meaning to the word *Emancipation*. But, when we daily read (in the Newspapers) of midnight Roman Catholic banditti beginning to roast a man at the fire, to make him confess what money or arms he has, and where he had hid them – knowing him to be a Roman Catholic, as well as themselves – and when, at Wildgoose Lodge, the whole country actually consumed with fire, a family of eight persons, in the hour of night, we would ask, whether such people are in a condition to address the Lords and Commons to be admitted to a seat among them?

The people are so mistaught, and so utterly confounded in their moral and intellectual principles, that it is common for them to load with bitter imprecations the Judge and Jury after the plainest conviction – a conviction confirmed, afterwards by their own voluntary confession of guilt upon the scaffold. Such a temper of mind as this the Roman Catholic Pastor should labour to reclaim; and his powerful influence would be nobly employed in contending against so monstrous a condition of depravity, and in subduing it to the purposes of civilised society.

The *immediate* cause of all the disturbances in Ireland is, doubtless, as this upright Judge has proclaimed, a spirit of Faction. I heartily join with him in praying that that 'monster', as he calls it, may be crushed; and I have to congratulate the county of Armagh, that this triumph of reason and loyalty is to begin *there*. But really, from the year 1782 to

1788, inclusively, we have, instead of advancing in reformation (that is, civilization) been gradually dismantling and pulling down both Church and State – the head and principle and foundation of all our civilization. We have been de-civilising, unreforming and un-protestantising the people here, instead of reclaiming them. The absurd result of all our reasoning and public acts, wrested from us by the above Faction, is that, besides the Police being broken up in so many Baronies – what with the idleness, drunkenness, and visionary dreams of the people, our streets, suburbs, and cabins swarm with beggars; and to the inversion of all logic and common sense, as well as Police, Faction is, at the moment, thundering with these hosts at the Bar of the House of Commons, as if all those things were qualifications for insisting upon fundamental changes in our Civil and Religious Constitution.

We are informed, by the Newspaper of *Newry*, that this barbarism is beginning to explode, and to become dissipated. It appears (if this account be true, and I do not vouch for it) that the convicts fell upon their own Priest, and, if not prevented, would have strangled him. And these Newspapers go on to say, 'remorse or compunction were visitings to which, to the last moment of their lives, they remained utter strangers. *The very terms they could not comprehend the meaning of'*. But whence arose this shocking and singular outrage, and this deplorable want of information? Their spiritual teachers or pastors are the most proper persons to pursue *this* charge, which I leave, therefore, *to them*. There were one hundred people present at the burning. They had previously concerted the plan in the Roman Catholic Chapel, having for their President the Clerk or Schoolmaster of the Parish; but, yet, it is insisted that the Roman Catholic Pastor might not, and did not, know of what he was doing. Be it so; but is not the Learned Judge justifiable in asking what the Pastor had been about – and in reproving Pastors generally 'for being asleep at their posts'.

How many baronies of Ireland are now under the operation of the Insurrection Act? The whole landed property must, at length, be put under a *custodiam* to answer to the King for the peace of the country. What is the state of opinion in the minds of a large portion of the people? What are the topics the Press daily groans with against England, because it cannot carry, by sapping, or by storm, the citadel of Religion? If the population of Ireland be divided into three parts – two of these are against the Established code, in Church and State; but the three thirds are almost unanimous against the Revenue. May not all this furnish a reasonable presumption, but there is, if not a general co-operation or connivance, at least a most lamentable *unguardedness* somewhere in the great body of the people, and those by whom they are influenced, as to any atrocity, provided it is levelled only and distinctly against Established Order?

Is this worse than Pagan persecution at Wildgoose lodge – this *Auto da Fé* to which the supplicants to the laws have been subjected – is this to be palliated (as the Newspapers attempt to do) by the trite plea 'that there are good and bad of all religions - that there are exceptions to every rule – that there was a traitor even among the twelve Disciples?' Such desperate hostility to English institutions – to the Laws, purely as Laws – to civilization, as such – this, in Ireland, is not confined to one, or to one thousand instances. It is general – it is fast becoming universal: these are not the exceptions, but the very rule itself. If such practices, or any thing like them, were general, or even common in England, no doubt the Protestant Clergy, as Teachers, would be blameworthy. Whereas in England enormities are not the rule, but the exception only.

It is clear, that an ultimate remedy must soon be resorted to. These enormities, for the honour of human nature, for its very existence even, must not, and will not, be suffered to continue. The Roman Catholic Clergy, doubtless, do much good; but it is quite obvious that Judge Fletcher conceives they may do much more, and the whole community sanction this opinion. They should lose no time in endeavouring to win from this learned and enlightened Judge a less qualified panegyric than he has been pleased to bestow upon them. They should, in good earnest, set about reforming the people – first rectifying any French or Italian bias, which a foreign education may have given to their own minds, imperceptibly. It is to their Teachers only the people can look for Emancipation, and not to the Legislature. POPLICOLA

One recalls the letters sent from Dundalk to the *Weekly Freeman's Journal* in March 1818 recounting the extraordinary condemnatory reaction of Fr Thomas McCann of Louth parish after the Wildgoose Lodge murders, in the tradition one might say of the Church's steadfast opposition to the violence of agrarian secret societies initiated by Bishop John Troy in 1779 when bishop of Ossory. The reaction of the Dublin press must have influenced Judge Fletcher to speak out once again in favour of Catholic Emancipation. In Armagh and in two later trials in Dundalk he went out of his way to praise priests whom he acknowledged were not versed in the detailed secrets of a secret-bound society. He especially lauded them for their attitude towards the approvers Thomas Gubby and Patrick Murphy.

EXECUTION OF HUGH McCABE, JOHN KIERAN, JAMES CAMPBELL, TERENCE MARRON, PATRICK MALONE (1), PATRICK CRAVEN, MICHAEL FLOODY, PATRICK MEEGAN, HUGH McLARNY AND BRYAN LENNON

The following ten men were condemned to death at the Spring Assizes in Dundalk in 1818. They were executed on the hill of

Reaghstown three at a time on Monday 9 March 1818. After they were cut down they were sent for gibbeting on 12 March 1818, three to Corcreagh, three to Hackballs Cross, and four to Louth.

PAT MALONE. Gibbeted at Louth.
JAMES CAMPBELL. Gibbeted at Corcreagh.
HUGH McLARNY. Gibbeted at Louth.
TERENCE MARRON. Gibbeted at Corcreagh.
PATRICK MEEGAN. Gibbeted at Corcreagh.
HUGH McCABE. Gibbeted at Louth.
PAT CRAVEN. Gibbeted at Louth.
JOHN KIERAN. Gibbeted at Hackballs Cross.
MICHAEL FLOODY. Gibbeted at Hackballs Cross.
BRYAN LENNON. Gibbeted at Hackballs Cross.

Two newspaper accounts of the Executions
The *Dublin Evening Post* of 11 March 1818 reported the execution of the ten convicted men under the title 'Extract of a Letter from Ardee'. March 9 [Monday]:

> I am this moment returned from Reaghstown after beholding a most tragic scene. Ten wretched victims have been immolated on the altar of offended justice, namely, Marron, Fluddy, Campbell, Malone, McCabe, Craven, Kieran, McLarney, Gaynor [*not executed in this group – mistaken in the newspaper for Patrick Meegan*] and Lannin [Lennon]. On the scaffold Craven, Lannin [Lennon], Kieran and Campbell confessed their guilt; but the other six unfortunate beings declared, in the most solemn and impressive manner, that *'They were as innocent as the child unborn, of the crime for which they were about to suffer; and that they never in their lives were at the burning of Wildgoose Lodge; and that they forgave their Prosecutors, and all the World'*. They were apparently very penitent, and some of them met their fate with a fortitude worthy of better men. Prior to their ascending the fatal platform, they prayed most fervently, although I was astonished to find they were not accompanied by a Clergyman. I enquired the cause, and was informed, that the narrow prejudice of the unlettered minds of two magistrates dictated the uncharitable policy of preventing the attendance of several respectable Catholic Clergymen on the unfortunate Prisoners, who, with laudable zeal and piety, offered their spiritual services. Even in a Court of Justice they could not refrain from the 'Insolence of Office', and the enlightened and liberal Judge Fletcher felt it his duty to reprimand them, by designating them 'Intermeddling Under-Strappers'.
> But to return to my subject. It is true, that the Rev. Mr Duffy, the Catholic Chaplain of Dundalk Gaol, was attending on the Prisoners in his spiritual capacity; but it was morally impossible for him to administer spiritual consolation to ten wretched victims. There were

on the ground a concourse of twenty thousand persons, who assembled for the purpose of beholding the melancholy spectacle. There are three of the victims to be suspended in gibbets at Corcreagh, four at Louth, and three at a place called Hackball's Cross, on the road leading from Dundalk to Castleblayney'.

The Correspondent, 14 March 1818, and the *Belfast News-Letter*, 13 March 1818, also reported the executions and provide other details. Fr Duffy was present but that does not contradict the *Dublin Evening Post*. The point made was that the presence of one priest was hardly sufficient for the spiritual needs of ten men. The *Dublin Evening Post*, 17 March 1818, published an extract from a letter addressed to it 'by an intelligent and well-informed friend at Ardee':

> If they have the effrontery to impugn the truth of my Statement, I shall cause three Catholic Priests to make an affidavit of their being prevented by Mr Fortescue, the High Sheriff and Mr Pendleton, the Police Magistrate, from attending the Prisoners. It is a fact that canot be denied, that on Monday morning last, when *the Rev. Mr Duffy visited the Prisoners for the purpose of joining them in Prayer, that some of them attempted to lay violent hands upon him* – it was for suggesting to Serjeant Joy the propriety of objecting to respectable Catholic Jurors, that the Hon Judge Fkletcher indignantly observed 'he did not blame the Law Officers of the Crown for objections, but he was determined not to suffer the suggestions of little intermeddling Under-Strappers to have any influence in the Court'. He therefore ruled, that the Jury should be composed of the very Gentlemen set aside by the Crown, who were all Roman Catholics. The impartiality and justice of Judge Fletcher have 'won golden opinions' from all ranks.

The Correspondent, 14 March 1818 (same account in the *Dublin Evening Post*, 16 March 1818):

> Execution of McCabe, Keirnan, Campbell, Marron, Craven, Malone, Floody, Meahan, McElearney and Lenon *(who pleaded Guilty)*.
> A little after six o'clock on Monday morning, the above convicts were taken from the gaol of Dundalk, pinioned, and seated in two sociables, attended by the Rev. Mr Duffy, R.C. Chaplain, Colonels Baker and Bretherton, and an escort of the 14th Light Dragoons, Samuel Pendleton, Esq., and the Horse Police of Dundalk, the Staff of the Louth Regiment, the High and Sub-Sheriff and the Gaoler and Executioner. Notwithstanding the inclemency of the morning the Right Hon. John Foster and the Lord Viscount Jocelyn, most of the Grand Jury and several Gentlemen of the County attended. This awful procession moved off at a quick pace for Reaghstown - the road to Wildgoose

Lodge being impassable, or they would have suffered within the walls of the house. The hill of Reaghstown looks down on Wildgoose Lodge. These unfortunate wretches were executed three at a time. After they were cut down, three were sent to Corcreagh, four [recte three] to Hackball's Cross, and three [recte four] to Louth, to be hung in chains. Keirnan, Craven and Lenon submitted to their fate, and acknowledged their guilt; and just before the latter was launched into eternity, he said he well knew that seven of his unhappy companions were guilty.

When taken out of the gaol, Malone, Meaghan and Campbell conducted themselves in the most disgraceful manner. Mr Duffy intreated [sic] of them by the sufferings of their Saviour, to confess their guilt, and not to leave this world with a lie in their mouths. His admonitions had no effect and these miscreants endeavoured to inflame the minds of the populace by declaring their innocence.

At the place of execution, their conduct, with the exception of Lenon, Keirnan and Craven, was equally hardened. They prayed with apparent devotion for a short time, but, on ascending the scaffold, they burst out into their former exclamations against their prosecutors, and declaring their innocence. The Rev. Mr Duffy during this trying scene patiently and fervently implored the wretched men to meet their God as penitent sinners, and to forgive their prosecutors; he acted in every way becoming his sacred profession, and deserves every praise.

On Sunday morning (the very day previous to their execution) when the Rev. Mr Duffy, Chaplain, visited them, to administer spiritual consolation and exhort them to prepare for the great and awful change they were to meet, two of them laid hold of him, and, had it not been for assistance that instantly came to his relief, they would have strangled him.

This last incident was reported in the same words in the *Drogheda Journal*.

We can get a view of the other world of the local lesser gentry during during the March Assizes. Henry McClintock of Dundalk wrote in his journal:

Tuesday 3d There was frost early, then heavy rain & the day very stormy – C. House – the Assizes began here – Bessy, Louis & I dined with my mother & sister Fortescue, my brother John dined there also.

Friday 6th Very fine day – C. House – Bessy & I dined at home – we drank tea with my mother, sister Fortescue & Emily – my brother John was there – the Assizes are not over yet – six men are already sentenced to be hanged & gibbeted for burning eight persons in the house at Wild Goose Lodge last October twelve month.

Saturday 7th March Very showry – I was in the Court House most of the day hearing the trials of more men for the burning of Wild Goose lodge – four more are sentenced to be hanged on Monday next, the ten men are all to be hanged at Rheastown [Reaghstown] which is quite

> close to Wild Goose lodge – Justice Fletcher is the judge that tried all these fellows – Bessy, Louis, Marianne & Louisa & I dined at home.
> **Monday 9th** Hard frost & snow – C. House – the ten men were hanged at Rheastown –Bessy & I dined at home – I rode out.
> **Tuesday 10th** The ground quite covered with snow, day pretty good – C. House – Bessy & I dined with my mother, sister Fortescue & Emily.
> **Wednesday 11th** Smart frost in the morng, day soft with snow showers – C. House as usual – Thomas Filgate of Lissrenny dined with us & slept also, my mother dined with us also and Henry Maxwell came in the evening.
> **Friday 13th March 1818, Dundalk**. Very fine day – I went out hunting with Wolfe McNeale's hounds at Castletown – had pretty good sport, killed one hare – Fortescue (of the barracks) and Friar Duffy sat for an hour with me after dinner and took some punch – I went to a Charity Ball at the Free School & Jocelyn, my sister Fortescue & Emily, Colonel Brotherton, Mr Wilton & Mr Hammond all of the 14th Lt. Dns., Matt Fortescue of this town & Mr Horner all came home & supped with Bessy & me.
> **Sunday 15th.** Fine day – Bessy, Louis, Marianne & I went to church – I rode to Stephenstown with Matt Fortescue of this town – George Forster & Friar Duffy dined with Bessy & me.

Townley Patten Filgate recorded briefly in his diary, Thursday March 10th: 'Six men were executed at Wildgoose Lodge for the murder of my tenants'.

After the executions the *Newry Telegraph*, 14 March 1818, commented:

> Ten of the inhuman murderers of Lynch have been executed. Of these some acknowledged their crimes and died penitent. Others denied their guilt and exhibited even till the last moment of their existence the same remorselessness and vindictive spirit, which had struck the spectators of their trial with astonishment and horror. In the gaol some of these wretches had endeavoured to murder the Roman Catholic pastor, who sought to awaken them to a sense of their most deplorable situation. Now, if on the awful moment preceding their execution, this rev. gentleman found it impossible to elicit from them a confession of their crimes and to humble them to repentance, is it reasonable to suppose that a conspiracy planned and executed by such hardened miscreants had ever been divulged to the Roman Catholic clergy of the country, or to any of them? That all who suffered at Reaghstown, on Monday last, were guilty is indubitable. Some confessed their individual guilt, and one of the convicts declared that he knew seven of his fellow-sufferers to be participators in the crime. Is it credible that any of these wretches had ever explained the nature, or even hinted at the existence, of the conspiracy under which they had systematically acted, under their infernal leader, Devan ? By no means.

A letter to the editor signed 'A Louth Catholic Priest' subsequently followed the *Newry Telegraph* reports:

> Sir, I have with much satisfaction read the very correct impartial statement, which your paper of the 10th ult. contains of the proceedings at the late assizes at Dundalk. Whilst every friend of humanity must feel horror struck at the very idea of the inhuman crime with which the culprits stood indicted, it is highly gratifying to every unprejudiced mind, to read the candid and dispassionate comment you make on that part of Judge Fletcher's address, which reflects on the *imputed supineness* of as loyal a body of men as breathe Irish air, I mean the Roman Catholic Clergy.
> Your liberality in this instance does you credit, as an ingenuous unprejudiced journalist, and calls for the warm acknowledgement of those, whose cause you so ably defended, and in whose name I beg leave, thus publicly, to return you sincere thanks. Would to God that every conductor of public prints, were actuated with the same impartial spirit! were as ready to soothe as to irritate outraged and insulted feelings, on similar occasions! We would be no longer a divided, distrustful people – the demon of discord would no longer interrupt our happiness, or blight the germs of concord; we would be what the true spirit of religion dictates, of one heart – of one soul.
> It has long been the misfortune of unhappy Ireland to afford a wide field for misrepresentation, as well to her avowed enemies, as to those, who unwilling to take the trouble of making proper inquiry, treat of her affairs and character, upon the mere *ipse dixit* of those who feel little interest, and less inclination, to furnish correct intelligence on any thing connected with her interest. I would be sincerely sorry to rank the honest, unbiased Fletcher with either class: his fair even handed distribution of justice, without favour to person or sect, since he first stepped into office, has invariably distinguished him as an upright, incorruptible judge, as a friend to virtue, and a foe to vice, in whatever shape he may meet either, in his judicial capacity. But as praise or censure, from such high respectable authority, is apt to make a lasting impression, I have to regret that he was no better acquainted with the character and exertions of the Roman Catholic clergy of this country before he would, from the bench, in a court of public justice, brand them with such a sweeping charge as to their suffering the public peace to be disturbed, for want of their performing their duty. Although, as you properly observe, when deluded Catholics are bent upon entering into any illegal association, or perpetrating a less appalling deed than the horrid outrage committed at Wildgoose Lodge, their designs are industriously concealed from their spiritual directors. Priests, long before the burning of this place, saw the gathering storm and cautioned their respective flocks to guard against it. Although Judge Fletcher accuses them of sloth and indolence, they lost no time in communicating their alarm to their bishops, who with that steadfast loyalty which has ever distinguished them, even in the time of

remorseless persecution, unsheathed their spiritual sword, and reprobated their nefarious system, by passing their ecclesiastical censures on any person connected with such associations. Happy would it be if the magistrates had aided them with more promptness. Had Judge Fletcher made proper inquiry he would find that the bishops carried their zeal so far in this business as to make it a reserved case to have any connection with riband-men, and that no priest had power to absolve them without special application to the bishop and the person making an unconditional promise of immediately withdrawing from such associations.

It is a well known fact that the disgraceful catastrophe of Wildgoose Lodge was accelerated, if not occasioned, by the active and zealous interference of the Rev. Dr Marron, the parish priest of that place. Whilst remonstrating with his flock from the altar, on Sunday, whilst admonishing them to keep free from party, to guard against those who would attempt to bring them into any illegal combination, which he said was creeping into the neighbourhood, but which had not, he hoped reacted his charge, Lynch stood up and told him, 'he was much mistaken, that the greater part of his auditors were sworn riband-men'. This imprudent, bold declaration was the cause of all the misfortune which has ensued and disgraced our county. It drew upon Lynch the vengeance of the disaffected; they meditated revenge; his place was shortly after broken into and racked, for which three men, Tierney, Shanly, and Conlan were executed at the following assizes in Dundalk. Rooney, who was son-in-law to Lynch and joint prosecutor against the above mentioned three people, felt a remorse of conscience for what he had sworn, [and] between the time that the unhappy convicts received their sentences, and the period destined for their execution, he communicated his uneasiness, and expressed a wish to retract his testimony, which he afterwards refused doing. This prevarication incensed the friends of those who died, and prompted them to enter into the inhuman resolution of acting as they have done, of setting fire to the house wherein Lynch, Rooney, and their family lived. This is a brief account of the particulars that relate to the burning of Wildgoose Lodge, and shows clearly that the Catholic Clergy were not inactive or indifferent spectators of those disorders. Had Judge Fletcher reflected on the acknowledgement made by one of the approvers in this cause, when he said that although he had been at confession, he concealed his being connected with this business from his confessor, and said that 'he was sworn never to disclose it to Priest or Magistrate', he would not be surprised that outrages would be committed by nominal Catholics without the knowledge of their priests. I fear, Mr. Editor, that I have trespassed too much on your columns and patience. However, as this affair concerns the reputation of a body of men whose moral worth you so kindly and liberally defended, I will take the liberty of stating another fact which alone will be sufficient to remove the stigma unintentionally, I hope, thrown on the Catholic Priesthood, and hierarchy of this country, by the Hon. Judge Fletcher.

At the time that disturbance made its first appearance in the county of

Louth, the magistrates and respected landholders assembled in various parts of the country, to take into consideration the disturbances which then existed, and to adopt the most effectual measures to secure order and tranquillity. After mature deliberation and inquiry into the nature and cause of these disorders, and the exertions of the various pastors in the cause of loyalty, and endeavouring to bring their deluded flocks to a sense of their duty, it was resolved without a dissenting voice, 'That the zeal and activity of the Roman Catholic Clergy deserved the thanks of every friend to order and discipline'. This is a fact that every magistrate in the county can bear witness to, and which if known to Judge Fletcher would, I am sure, draw forth from him the same expression of approbation.
I am with respect and esteem,
Your obedient, humble, servant

The re-publication of this letter in the *Dundalk Examiner* (5 November 1881) received a query from 'an Old Inhabitant' as to the identity of the priest who wrote it. The editor in the 19 November 1881 edition confessed he did not know, as it was a reprint from the *Newry Telegraph*.

10
Trials and Executions (2)

TRIAL OF JAMES SMYTH, PATRICK McQUILLAN, AND LAWRENCE GAYNOR

The trial of James Smith, Patrick McQuillan and Lawrence Gaynor took place at the Louth adjourned Assizes at Dundalk, Tuesday 31 March 1818. **Counsels for the Crown**: Serjeant Joy, Bell, Staples, Hall and McCartney, Esqrs. **For the Prisoners**: Hamilton, and McNally, Esqrs. Leonard McNally (1752-1820) was called to the Irish bar in 1776 and to the English bar in 1783. He had once been a member of the United Irishmen and had defended Napper Tandy, Wolfe Tone and Robert Emmet in court. He turned informer and received large sums from the secret service at the same time as taking fees to defend the United Irishmen whose confidence he betrayed. His duplicity was not discovered until after his death. The trial is reported in the *Drogheda Journal*, Saturday, 4 April 1818:

> The Adjournment of the Assizes for the County of Louth was held at Dundalk on Tuesday, the 31st ult. The Hon. **Judge Fletcher** took his seat on the Bench a little before ten o'clock.
> The following Gentlemen were sworn on the **Grand Jury**: Right Hon. John Foster, Foreman; Lord Viscount Jocelyn; W. Blayney Balfour; Matthew Fortescue; Alexander Filgate; J. McClintock, Drumcar; Faithful W. Fortescue; Henry Brabazon; Robert Thompson; Philip Doyne; Matthew O'Reilly; Fitzherbert Ruxton; Matthew Fortescue; Thomas W. Filgate; William H. Richardson; Thomas Tisdall; Thomas Fitzgerald; James W. McNeale; John Woolsey, Esqrs
> James Smith, Patrick McCullen [McQuillan], and Laurence Gainer [Lawrence Gaynor], were indicted for the murder of Edward Lynch and his family, at Wildgoose Lodge.
> After numerous challenges the following Gentlemen were sworn on the **Petit Jury**: Neal Coleman, junr; James McAlister; John Martin; Lawrence Tallon, junr; Patrick Hill; Philip Boylan; Owen McKeown; Joshua Harris; James Carrol; Peter Sandys; David Williams; James Hampton.

THE PROSECUTION

> **Serjeant Joy** opened the case in a speech of some length, stating the duty which the Jury were called upon to discharge; they were called

upon to sit as Judges upon the lives of three of their fellowmen, accused of crimes of the most diabolical dye that ever disgraced a civilised country – to discharge that duty, every man, possessed of the feelings of a man, is called upon to discharge to his fellow-mortals; they were also called upon, by their country, not to suffer the perpetrators of such enormous crimes to escape the punishment which the law inflicts. The Learned Serjeant then proceeded to state the facts which took place, viz. that the unfortunate Lynch, of Wildgoose Lodge, and Thomas Rooney, his son-in-law, had prosecuted to conviction three men in Dundalk, for assaulting their house, in 1816; that for this daring to appeal to the laws of their country for a redress of injuries, a conspiracy of a most extensive kind was entered into for their destruction; parties came from the counties of Monaghan, Cavan, and Meath, as well from the county Louth, for the express purpose of sacrificing to their resentment these unfortunate men, with the whole of their family. One party assembled at Stonetown Chapel, and proceeded to Arthurstown, and were there joined by parties from the different counties alluded to; and then being assembled, to the number of about one hundred men, they proceeded to the house of Wildgoose lodge, some on foot, and others on horseback; before they reached the house, they spread themselves, lest any of the family should escape; having procured some fire from a cabin in the lane leading from the road to Lynch's house, they surrounded the house, set fire to it in several places, and, in order to increase the flame, threw lighted flax and unthreshed oats into the house – in short, they consumed the house, with all its inhabitants, and completed the scene of horror with three huzzas. He then enlarged upon the necessity, in cases of this kind, of having recourse to the testimony of approvers. As every individual of that unfortunate family were destroyed, it must be naturally suggested that the testimony of accomplices must be reverted to, in order to bring the perpetrators of this most nefarious deed to condign punishment; in such cases, when the testimony of accomplices is supported by incontestible evidence, the law allows such testimony to be sufficient to rest a verdict of guilt upon. After some further observation upon this distressing subject, he concluded, and the trial proceeded.

Note: The *Belfast News-Letter,* 7 April 1818, adds a detail in Joy's speech that the child of Thomas Rooney and his wife Biddy [Lynch] was eight months old.

Alice Rispin sworn. Remembers the burning of Wildgoose Lodge; lived then in that neighbourhood. Saw the house the Sunday before. Saw it on Wednesday. Saw it the day after. It was burned on Tuesday night. Saw it on Wednesday. It was all consumed but two small sticks. Saw some bodies all burned. Did not know them. Knew the body of James Rispin, her son, and the mouth and nose of a servant maid, who lived in Lynch's, called Biddy Richards; her son was an apprentice with Thomas Rooney; had been with her for some days, but had returned the day before the burning. Knew him by a mark under his left shoulder. Saw sheafs of flax scattered about the house, and straw. Saw a sledge upon the grass near the road side, a little distance from Lynch's house.

Bernard McElroy [Gilroy] sworn, examined by Mr Bell. Knows Stonetown Chapel. Remembers the night of the burning of Wildgoose Lodge. Knew Devan. Was at a meeting on Friday previous to the burning. A few had met for the purpose of proceeding to Wildgoose lodge. Waited until 11 or 12 o'clock at night. The whole party did not come. Met again on Tuesday night following. In all about forty, for the purpose of burning Lynch. All had arms, some guns, some pistols, pitchforks, &c. Witness was armed with what he thinks was a piece of a barrel of a gun in a pistol-stock. They proceeded to the mill of Louth in two divisions, to escape a watchman stationed at the mill. Proceeded to Reastown. Did not meet any more there. Met some afterwards, about fourteen or fifteen. Waited then until the whole party came up, about 100 men; saw some on horseback. Spread themselves round the hill, lest any of the family would escape. Set fire to the house. Witness was stationed in the front. Heard a noise as if securing the door inside. Heard a voice threatening to shoot any man that would attempt to enter. Was answered by Devan –'Think not, Lynch, that it is old times – this night is your doom'. Saw fire in a pot; it was used to set fire to the house. Saw the door broke open with a sledge. Saw unthreshed corn brought and thrust in. The house was fired in several places. It was all consumed. Witness did not wait until the roof fell in. He points out James Smith, the prisoner at the bar. Saw him there, is positive. Was assisting him to carry the oats. Knew him before that night. Saw him at a foot-ball. Knew him about three months. Witness went home. Lived then at Faris. Remained there until April. Went then to Navan. Wrote a letter from Navan to Mr William Filgate; the purpose was, to meet him on the Wednesday following at Slane, and to bring Mr Pendleton with him, to tell him about the burning of Wildgoose Lodge, and to take care of himself or he would be murdered. Wrote this letter the 20th of April [the letter here produced – he acknowledges it]. Witness went to Slane, but did not meet Mr Filgate. Went on the very day and hour he had appointed. Was apprehended on the 26th of May.

[Note a detail from the *Belfast News-Letter* that the party was divided into divisions by Devan.]

Cross-examined by Mr McNally. Has given an accurate account of the murder. Had assisted in it. Had no malice, no revenge to gratify. Had no remorse at that time. Did assist without having any ill-will to the sufferers. Did not know Lynch. Never saw him. Never heard of him before that time. His motive was, he could not avoid it. If he had refused, he would have been himself murdered. Could not leave the country, had no money to take himself away. Assisted to burn eight persons rather than hazard himself or leave the country. Was not dragged to it, did not attempt to shun it. Had arms, yet was afraid to refuse. Could not avoid going. If he did not go he would be killed.

Could not leave the country. Was unemployed and the times bad. Knew of it before that night, and did not run away. This is the only crime he was charged with, thank God. Does not thank God for this. Did not know whether this would save his life or not. No promise was ever made to him. Does not know what will be done to him. First gave his information to Capt. Charleton, of the Meath militia. Had never deserted, had not the King's pay. Had no support, had been disembodied. Had no compunction of heart. Dare not shew a partiality to any of the persons murdered, or he would be murdered himself. Knows Smith. Knew him before, saw him near Tallanstown at a football. Was a stranger before to him. Saw him in the cell, saw him before. Was not told by any person that he was there. Knew him himself. Never said that he did not know him. Never brought to the cell where he (prisoner) was. Was not told it was to identify a man. Knew prisoner whenever he saw him. Does not know any more of that name in the country.
[Note a detail added in *Belfast News-Letter*, that he had known Smith a quarter of a year before the burning. Re-examined on the part of the Crown - had mentioned Smith's name in his examination long before he came to the gaol. The *Dundalk Examiner*, 22 October 1881, reprinting an account of this trial presumably from *Faulkner's Dublin Journal* as in its previous reprints, states that he was re-examined on the part of the Crown by Mr Bell.]

William Filgate Esq. sworn. He proved the burning of the house and receipt of the letters, &c.

The *Belfast News-Letter* adds, 'Identified the letter by the last witness; he was from home at the time the letter was written, and did not receive it till after the day appointed in it to meet at Slane; there was no name to the letter'.

The *Dundalk Examiner* account 22 October 1881, records the cross-examination of Filgate by Mr Hamilton: 'It was well-known in the country at the time that a man of the name of Murphy had been apprehended for Sillery's robbery, and that several people had been taken up on his informatiom'.

Peter Gilogley [Gollogly] sworn, examined by Mr Hall. Was at the burning. Points out McCullen, and Gainer. Remember[s] Gainer telling him what was to be done. Told him they were making a party to punish Lynch for prosecuting three of their brethren. Appointed to meet at the cross roads of Carrickleck. Met Patt McCullen there. Proceeded to Bal[ly]navoran. Met 12 or 14 more, some on foot and some on horseback. Does not see any of them in court, 2 on each horse. Patrick McCullen was with him at Drumbride. All assembled at Arthurstown, about 100 in all. Proceeded to Lynch's house by a bye road. Witness held 7 horses at a boggy place. Some horses went on. Saw a great blaze in the direction that the party went. Were more than an hour away. Heard shots. Heard shouts when fire was over, and more shots. Pointed out Gainer and McCullen, as going on from him to the house. Gainer asked him to hold horses. [Here the prisoner

Gainer asked liberty to put some questions to witness as he had no counsel, which was granted.] He (prisoner) represented that he was at the taking of this witness for Sillery's robbery, and that he now prosecutes him through malice. It appeared afterwards, that it was not this witness but Murphy, as witness (Gilogley) was not taken for Sillery's robbery at all.

Note: The *Belfast News-Letter* mentions 'Carolan and two others' as those prosecuted for the first attack on Wildgoose Lodge, but this is an obvious error for 'Conlon and two others'. Account in the *Dundalk Examiner*, 22 October 1881:

Saw the two prisoners Gaynor and M'Quillan, the night before the burning - Gaynor told witness they were making up a party to burn Wildgoose Lodge; upon which witness consented to go, and they were to meet the next night at the cross-roads of Drumleek; witness accordingly repaired to Drumleek the next night where he met M'Quillan and Gaynor; they proceeded to Wildgoose lodge – when arrived at Ballynavoran there were about fourteen of them; they met other parties at Reaghstown.

Cross-examined by Mr McNally. Was at Sillery's robbery where a murder was committed, but did not see the murdered man. Had no arms himself, therefore he could not commit the murder. Was taken but not tried. Because he gave evidence supposes it was that saved his life. Swears now to save his life and do good to the public.

Note: *Dundalk Examiner* account 22 October 1881, 'To a question by Mr Bell witness said the burning of Wildgoose lodge took place before Sillery's robbery'.

Thomas Gubby sworn, examined by Serjeant Joy. Remembers the night of the burning of Lynch's house. Was one of the party. Met that night at S[t]onetown Chapel. Remembers a number of persons meeting also. Had met a few nights [in the same place – *Dundalk Examiner*] before for the same purpose. Proceeded in two parties to the mill of Louth. Went on to Wildgoose lodge. Met other parties. Party stopped at a cabin near Wildgoose Lodge. Did not know why, heard some of them say it was to get fire. Surrounded the house, fired it, made use of unthreshed corn and flax to encrease the flames. Witness was placed in the rear of the house. Could not see the front. Heard a noise as if breaking the door. Heard shots, heard men speak inside. Did not wait until the roof fell in, but waited until the cries ceased inside. Saw fire brought in a piece of a pot, that was used to fire the house. Points out James Smith at the bar. Saw him there, saw him carry corn to increase the flame. Did not see the door broke, saw a sledge with the party, heard it was for that purpose, saw it after the house was consumed.

Cross-examined by Mr Hamilton. Was apprehended in April. Lived then in Drogheda, which is not his native place. Had lived before that in Louth. Had left his own country [Tyrone] for having been charged with a robbery. Was tried upon another charge but was acquitted. Never saw Lynch, never heard of him before. Would not have murdered him if he could have avoided it. Would be murdered himself if he refused. This was before he went to Drogheda. Was at a meeting previous to the murder at Stonetown. Had requested to be excused when he heard for what purpose they had met. Was told that he would be the first man that would be murdered if he refused. Could not give information then. Was afraid of his wife being murdered. (Questioned by a juryman) – first saw Smith carry oats, was placed at the corner of the house within sight of the rear, could not see the front, did not see the flax, but it might be at the other end.

Note: The *Belfast News-Letter* adds that he had left his own county, Tyrone, on a charge of robbery, that 'Devan had caused him to attend a meeting at Stonetown Chapel'. *Dundalk Examiner* account, 22 October 1881, on cross-examination by Mr Hamilton 'previous to that charge he was tried in Omagh for taking up arms at night, but acquitted'.

Patrick Murphy sworn. Examined by Mr Macartney. Remembers the burning of Wildgoose Lodge. Came from Meath-hill. Met several parties from Carrickleck, more from Kingscourt , more from Co. of Monaghan. Some on foot and others on horseback, in all about 100 men. Witness was one of those sent for horses, took them from the fields and the road sides. Knows Arthurstown Chapel, had some drink there. The party had arms. Witness was one of them sent for fire. Went to a cabin on the side of the lane. Got it. The man that was with him carried it in a pot. Witness used some of it to light flax, and applied it to the thatch of the house, to set it on fire. Heard some voice saying '*let out the innocent*', was answered '*that they had not taken warning in time*'. Heard shots from the inside. Tried to break the door but could not at that time. Believed it was done afterwards. Saw the roof fall in. House all consumed. Was present when they took off their hats and huzzaed, wishing Lynch joy of his hot bed, and fired a couple of shots. (Points out Gainer and McCullen) is positive that they were there. Remembers Sillery's robbery after this murder, was at that robbery and murder, was taken for it and tried, was condemned. First gave his information to Mr Pollock; he sent for him.

Note: *Dundalk Examiner* account, 22 October 1881, 'Lived at Meath-hill, in the County Meath, and went to Wildgoose Lodge the night of the burning with a party from that part of the country; they were joined at Drumleek, by a party from the Co. Cavan; a little further on by a party from the Co. Monaghan.

Cross-examined by Mr McNally. Was an old acquaintance of his. Had seen him at Trim. Had been sentenced to die, was pardoned. Was very active at Lynch's murder, was one sent for fire, knew why it was wanted, assisted in lighting flax and thrusting it into the thatch. Was very active. Did hear people inside cry, was one of those who huzza'd. Could not avoid being there, would rather murder than endanger himself.

Note: *Dundalk Examiner* account 22 October 1881, 'was tried before Lord Norbury, at Trim, for Sillery's robbery and condemned, notwithstanding all he (Mr McNally) did for him to save him. At the time witness was reprieved he was on the point of going out to be hanged'.

Arthur Pollock, Esq. sworn. [Examined by Mr Bell]. Knows Murphy the last witness. Remembers him in Trim Jail. Gave information to him, first on Tuesday, concerning Sillery's robbery. Afterwards sent for him on Wednesday, and gave information concerning Wildgoose Lodge. Had held out no promises to him. He (Murphy) seemed to be much affected, so that they had to give him water. Fainted when he heard he was reprieved.

Cross-examined by Mr McNally. Gave him no hope, does not believe he had the least expectation of a pardon, does believe him a very bad character.

The *Belfast News-Letter* adds the testimony of Pat Halfpenny [examined by Mr Staples], which is the same evidence as in previous trials.

THE DEFENCE

Defence for Smith [Smyth]

Lord Louth was called on to give a character of Smith, but did not know much about him; knew his father.

Note: The *Belfast News-Letter* reports, 'as to the character of Smith, of which he gave a favourable account; so far as being apparently a sober orderly man and regular in attending as a mason'. *Dundalk Examiner* 'Lord Louth ... said he knew the prisoner Smyth's family for a considerable time, and he believes it to be a very honest one; always heard so. Prisoner and his father wrought mason-work for him often'.

Robert Hamilton, Esq. Knew prisoner and his father very well. Had wrought for him, and considered them very good characters. [*Dundalk Examiner* 'they wrought mason-work for a considerable time, five years ago'.]

Lawrence Smith sworn. Examined by Mr McNally. Knows the prisoner, Smith, his son. Remembers the burning; his son was at home that very night. Are stone-masons, had been working that day with Lord Louth. Prisoner was in his house all that night, remembers it very well. [*Dundalk Examiner* 'they both went home straight that night from their work; he saw his son eat his supper and go to bed at 10 o'clock'.]

Cross-examined by Serjeant Joy. Was at home that very night. Was in the habit of rising before day-light. Saw his son in bed. Went to take some sticks from under his bed, to light the fire, and saw his son in bed; remains of sticks that had been used to make a cure, got them from a neighbour; will not tell his name (after long prevaricating, said it was one Brennan). Lives at Arthurstown. Did not hear any noise that night. His house is a perch from the road.

Belfast News-Letter adds, 'saw both his sons in bed; had seen them go to bed the night before'; *Dundalk Examiner* 'prisoner did not go to work that day but staid at home to beetle flax'.

Patrick Smith sworn. [Examined by Mr Hamilton]. Is brother to prisoner. Slept with him that very night in his father's house. On being cross-examined, he stated that the sticks were under his bed, were some brush that was cut off their own ditches.

Belfast News-Letter account: 'Patrick Smith, is brother to the prisoner James Smith. They both slept together on the night of the burning in their father's house. His father slept in a separate room. His father was up first and lighted the fire. He called them both. The fire was lighted. There was some ash sticks under the bed in witness's room; some of them were used as firing. His father's house is in Arthurstown , about a perch from the road. He was not so fast asleep that night but he could have heard the noise of cars; but could not hear the noise of foot-people. His brother never left him the whole night'.

Dundalk Examiner account: **Cross-examined by Mr Bell.** 'His father got up the morning after the burning, before he and his brother, and had the breakfast ready when they arose; witness was employed on that day beetling flax with his brother'. This witness, as well as his father, prevaricated some during their cross-examination.

John Coleman sworn. Gave Smith a very good character.

Belfast News-Letter adds, 'knows James Smith; his character stood as fair as any other boy's in the county till this business. Has known him since he was a child. He and his father worked for him as masons and were always diligent and orderly. **Cross-examined:** Has heard of ribbond [*sic*] men; has often warned Smith and his father from joining them, and they seemed impressed with what he said'.

Defence for McCullen [McQuillan]

Mr Sillery sworn. Knows prisoner many years; has worked for him. Remembers the night of the burning of Wildgoose Lodge, prisoner was working for him that day and the day after. Left his work at dark, and was there as soon as any other man that morning. Knows Murphy, the approver. Believes him to be a villain who would say and swear any thing. Prisoner was at the taking of Murphy, for his brother's robbery. It was at night, there were eight of the party, only two of whom went into the house to seize him. Prisoner lives at the mearing of his land.

Cross-examined by Mr Staples. Believes he had time enough to go to the murders, and be with him next day at work if he liked it.

Belfast News-Letter version: 'John Sillery, lives in county Meath, knew McQuillan [McCullen], worked with him eight or nine years; prisoner worked for him at the [*time of the*] burning of Wildgoose Lodge; worked that day till dark; don't know where he lay that night. Lives seven miles from Lynch's; had a good character, worked for him next day also. Knows Murphy well, he would either say or do any thing; he is a noted rogue. Prisoner was aiding witness in taking Murphy. Wm Murphy was with witness and McQuillan at this time.

Cross-examined: [*Dundalk Examiner:* Lives about 2 ? miles from Meath-hill] Prisoner had time enough to be at the burning after he quit work. Murphy was taken at Kilmainham, near Nobber, in the evening about dark; eight persons came to Murphy's to take him.

Defence for Gainer [Gaynor]

Philip McGuire, sworn. [*Dundalk Examiner*]: Examined by the clerk of the crown, by desire of the prisoner Gaynor, who had no counsel employed. 'Lives one mile beyond Carrick. Gaynor lived with him'.] Says that the prisoner was in the house the night of the burning. Slept there. Was up that night until 12 o'clock; a tailor was making him a pair of breeches.

Cross-examined by Mr Hall, and continued in the same story [*Dundalk Examiner*].

The **tailor** [**Patrick** Ward] came forward, and swore that the prisoner that night was with him while making the beeches, and afterwards slept with him (prisoner) and his wife.

McGuire's wife swore to the same effect.

The *Belfast News-Letter* gives a fuller account and gives the witness's name as 'Patrick':

Patrick [Philip] McGuire: Saw Gaynor after nightfall at witness's house. He slept there that night, and had been there from the commencement of the night till the morning. His wife lived with him, and had done so for two years. His house is about seven miles from Wildgoose Lodge. There was a tailor in witness's house making small cloaths for prisoner Gaynor; they sat up late at night; and had candles, to enable the tailor to work long. The tailor slept with Gaynor and his wife that night. Witness was up at different times that night watching his master's turnips. Witness and prisoner are married to two sisters.

Patrick Ward: Knows Gaynor. Remembers the night of the burning. After digging potatoes all day with Gaynor, witness set about making a pair of small-cloaths for him after nightfalling. They sat up till past twelve o'clock on Wednesday night. The night was dark, and he lay in the bed on which Gaynor and his wife lay. She was ill. He completed the breeches by twelve o'clock, save putting strings on the knees. [*Dundalk Examiner,* 'was working for former witness (McGuire) digging potatoes the day before the burning, and on that account did not begin the breeches till about 8 o'clock'.]

Biddy McGuire [wife of Philip McGuire]: Knows the prisoner Gaynor. His wife was hired to her and her husband for two years. Gaynor and a tailor he had employed sat up late the night of the burning. They lay down on the bed in which Gaynor's wife was about eleven o'clock. She was smoothing linen till four o'clock in the morning for Tom Murran her master. She sometimes has had to do so when hurry requires exertion. Remembers the next day hearing of the burning having taken place. [*Dundalk Examiner*: 'She swore that Gaynor lay in their home the night of the burning of Wildgoose lodge, from which place they live a distance of seven or eight miles. On her cross-examination she said the reason she remembered the night of the burning so well, was on account of the great alarm that was raised in the country the day after'.]

Dundalk Examiner **adds,** 'By a motion from a juror – Arthur Pollock Esq., was again called, and asked by the juror (J. M'Alister) if Murphy, when making the disclosure to him, had mentioned the names of any of the three prisoners at the bar. **Mr Arthur Pollock:** He mentioned McQuillan but none of the other two.

The *Drogheda Journal* **continues:** When the evidence on behalf of the Crown, and the prisoners' defence concluded, the Learned Judge recapitulated the whole in a clear and satisfactory manner, making comments as he proceeded, which occupied an hour and a half.

The Jury retired about 4 o'clock, and the Court adjourned. About 10 o'clock the Learned Judge resumed his seat – and the Jury having agreed, brought in a verdict of *Guilty against Smith and McCullen, and acquitted Gainer.*

During the time the Jury were considering on the verdict, the Court remained very full, and some of the friends of the prisoners were permitted to speak with them. One of them who was said to be sister to Smith, *charged him to die hard, if he was found guilty – never to forgive his prosecutors – and, dead or alive, to have revenge. She conjured him not to let any thing that the Clergy could say, have any effect upon him, nor ever persuade him to confess his guilt – and, when going to be hanged, to throw off his hat.* She was proceeding in this diabolical way, when the Sheriff had her turned out with the others.

The *Belfast News-Letter* reported similarly on 3 and 7 April and added that the Jury 'remained closed for about three hours'.

Pendleton in his chart notes that Lawrence Gaynor, arrested on 11 April 1817 in County Meath, was acquitted in April 1818.

TRIAL OF THOMAS McCULLOGH

The trial of Thomas McCullogh, a well-to-do Catholic farmer took place in Dundalk on 1 April 1818. Henry McClintock in his journal announces the renewal of the Assizes:

Tuesday 31st [March]: Very fine day – the second Assizes (in the month) began here to try the remainder of the Wild Goose men before

Judge Fletcher – two were found guilty out of the three that were tried & sentenced to be hanged on Thursday next – my brother William dined & slept at my house – he, Bessy & I drank tea with my mother, my brother John was there - I was in the Court House all day.

Wednesday 1st April 1818, Dundalk. William breakfasted with us – the day very fine – I went to the C.[ustom] House for a short time & then to the Court House to hear the trial of Thomas McCullagh who was convicted of having been a leader at the burning of the Wildgoose Lodge & was styled captain there & a decent well dressed man – Bessy, William Louis & I dined with my mother, my sister & Emily & my brother John were there.

Thursday 2d fine day – Wm. Breakfasted with us & then went home to Stonehouse – I stayed in the Court House nearly the entire day – two men more were found guilty of the burning at Wildgoose Lodge & sentenced to be hanged – Bessy & I dined at home – Marianne & Louisa with us – Friar Duffy sat for an hour with us in the eveng.

Friday 3d Very fine day – the Assizes ended here – four men having put off their trials & the others having been let out on bail –C. House – we dined at home.

Thursday 16th April 1818, Dundalk. Fine day - I went to the Custom House – Friar Duffy dined with Bessy & me – Surgeon Noble attended Caroline.

The *Dundalk Examiner*, 22 October 1881, begins its account of the trial of Thomas McCullogh, 'The Hon. Judge Fletcher entered the court at half-past nine o'clock. Thomas McCullough was put to the bar for the burning of Wildgoose Lodge, and the murder of Lynch, and seven persons therein contained'. The report that follows is taken from *The Drogheda Journal*, Saturday 4 April 1818, with a few added details from the *Dundalk Examiner*:

This day [Wednesday, 1 April] a most important trial took place. Thos. McCulla, a man of most interesting appearance, possessed of considerable property was set to the bar. He is six feet in height, well-proportioned, and though like a country man, was genteely dressed. After a few challenges, a most respectable jury was sworn, composed of the following gentlemen:
Malcolm Brown, Dundalk; Henry McNeal, Stranfield; Robt. Thompson, Ravensdale; James Johnson, Water-Lodge [Falmor]; John McNeal, Mountpleasant [Ballymascanlan]; M. B. Taylor, Redbarns [Dundalk]; Laurence Tallon, sen. Dundalk; Robert Getty, Dundalk; Robert Sheddan, do; Ben. Atkinson, Mount-Balie [Dundalk], N. Coleman, jun. Dundalk; Alexander Donaldson, Philipstown [Dundalk], Esqrs.

THE PROSECUTION

Serjeant Joy opened the case in a short speech. He remarked that it would not have been necessary for him to take up the time of the court, but that the prisoner at the bar was different from all those who had been indicted for this most nefarious transaction. He was a man possessed of a considerable property. He could not plead what many of the wretches that had appeared before them on former trials might do – ignorance – his situation in life gave him an opportunity of knowing better, and if he was found guilty it would considerably aggravate his offence. He then proceeded to detail in a brief manner the transaction of that horrid might. He stated that incontestable evidence would be produced that the prisoner at the bar was not only of the party who murdered the unfortunate Lynch, but that he took a most active part, that he was particularly remarkable not only to those acquainted with him, but to those who had no knowledge of him before. After some further remarks upon the important duty the Jury were called upon to discharge, he concluded and the trial proceeded.

Alice Rispan [Rispin] sworn. Deposed as on the former trials. [Cross-examined at some length by Mr McNally but without effect.]

Patrick Murphy was sworn to answer such questions as should be put to him.

Mr Murray one of the prisoners' counsel asked him if he had not been convicted of a murder and robbery at Trim. He answered that he had. Was asked if he was pardoned. He answered that he believed he was.

Counsel demanded that the record be produced.

Mr Pollock, clerk of the crown, was called but not appearing, much altercation took place and points of law debated, the prisoner's counsel objecting to his evidence, having said that he was under sentence of death and having only stated his belief that he was pardoned, they required his pardon to be produced. Mr Pollock shortly after came into court and the record was produced and read. Some debate ensued whether the conviction was for the murder only, or the murder and robbery. The pardon formerly produced was for the murder only. His pardon was now produced and read by the Clerk of the Crown; a new pardon for all offences whatever that he had ever committed. Thus ended this contest which occupied the Court more than an hour and half. The evidence of this accomplice was then admitted.

Patrick Murphy sworn. [Examined by Mr Hamilton]. Stated the proceedings as on his former evidence, and how he had been employed. Pointed out the prisoner, gave him drink in a jug at Arthurstown Chapel [outside of the chapel]; drank it out of the jug, had no glass remarked the prisoner. [It was a dry might, can't tell whether it was moonlight or not]. Asked Malone (who was executed) who he was. Malone said, it is a wonder you don't know him, and you working in the County Louth; this is *Captain McCulla*. Prisoner was mounted, saw him at Arthurstown first. (Looks at him again) is positive that is the man.

Cross-examined by Mr Murray. Does not remember the night of the week, but remembers it was the week of Hollintide. Never swore that he did. First met at Campbell's the night before the burning. Does not know McElroy, never saw him to his knowledge. Does not know Gubby. Knows Gilogly very well, was very intimate, was with him at Sillery's robbery, never at any other. Remembers the night of the burning, was a dry night. Does not know whether it was moon light or no, can't tell. Got drink at Arthurstown. Saw Gilogly get drink also. Saw him get drink out of a jug. Saw prisoner give it to him. Never saw him before that night. Got some drink from Malone also. Went on to Wildgoose Lodge. Saw prisoner on horseback. Went on to a boggy place where horses were held. Does not know where others went. Saw some horses at a small house near Lynch's. Does not know whose they were. Can't describe the horse. Did not take notice to it particularly because it was night. Was stationed at the back of the house in a garden. Can't describe it. Thinks it was ground. It appeared to him to be ground. Would remember a man sooner than a house. Will not guess how many perches. Got the flax in a garden. Did not go into any house for it. Was taken up and convicted of murder. This was after the burning. Was a Ribbonman. Took an oath when made a Ribbonman, to aid and assist a brother in every cause when called upon, and to obey his committee men. Took another oath after the murder, never to describe it to any person, not to his clergy. Took this oath in an old house which they called America. Malone and Campbell with him. No more in the room. This was the night after the burning. Came last from the Jail of Dundalk. Was out of the Jail last night. Was in the Police Office. Gilogly was with him. Went because he did not wish to be in the Jail when the prisoners came back. It was in the night, was brought back this morning. It was daylight. First gave his information to Mr Pollock. Did not then charge all the persons he knew of. Was too weak. Named 8 or 9 to him. It was the night before or the morning he was to suffer, he does not remember which. Did not confess this to a priest. Did confess other things. Told the priest of other crimes, who said he should tell it to a Magistrate. Did not desire him, only said he should do it. It was Father Lynch. Did not tell him of this murder. Confessed to unload his conscience to a magistrate when going to die. [Three of the Sillerys took him; was not knocked down; took him to Kilmainham, road and fields were full of people; and when they went to Kilmainham the town was full; knew none but Reilly and the Sillerys; did not see McQuillan there; he might be there; the horse might have passed the wet part of the lane; he never saw Gubby to his knowledge; swore against Gaynor yesterday].

Arthur Pollock, Esq., examined by counsellor Staples: [His evidence from *Dundalk Examiner*, 22 October 1881]. Is a magistrate; saw Murphy at the gaol of Trim, who sent a second message for him, on the morning he was to have been executed; held out no hopes of pardon to him; he appeared in a wretched state, had to give him water to support him between seven and eight o'clock; was about an hour and a half with him; what induced him to give information was his father whom he took with him, who fell upon his knees and desired him to confess all the robberies he had been at, which was all the atonement he could now make, having but a short time to live. His father being turned out, he made a full confession of the burning of Wildgoose lodge; he told him he had been induced to go there by a man who had since hanged as he understood.

Peter Gilogley [Gollogly] sworn. [Examined by Counsellor Hall]. Points out prisoner, who gave him drink at Arthurstown. Heard him say there that he had a party that would not fail to do any thing they were desired. Told Campbell that if any of his men would flinch he would be the first man to shoot them. Saw the prisoner when he came back, where he held the horses. Heard him say that they were a fine party of men fit to go to any *engagement*. Is positive of the prisoner.

Cross-examined by Mr Perrin. Lives at Carrickblecke in Co. Meath. Knows McCulla (the prisoner) by eyesight. Does not know where he lives. Does not know he was a yarn bleacher. He (prisoner) was on horseback the night of the burning. [Was on horseback part of the way, three miles; dismounted at the Cross-roads of Churchtown; went the short road across the fields to the chapel, got liquor there from the prisoner; drank out of a jug.]. Got liquor at Kenstown. Prisoner gave it to him in a jug. Drank what he pleased. It had the taste of whiskey. Never was at a murder but Sillery's and Lynch's. Knows Murphy very well. Was with him at Sillery's. Saw him at Wildgoose Lodge. Witness held horses. Lives convenient to Murphy. Went home with him. Took an oath about two years ago, not about Wildgoose Lodge. Was sworn to secrecy. Has not kept it. Does not remember what night of the week the burning was. The night was dark. Did not confess to a priest this long time.[as a Catholic, has given up attending confession since he began such business]. Was at the police office last night. Murphy was with him. Came back to the Jail this morning.

Thomas Gubby sworn. [Examined by Sergeant Joy]. Started their proceeding from Stonetown Chapel. Heard the door broke. Heard that it was to burn a loft upon which a man [Lynch] stood. (Looks round, and points out the prisoner McCulla). Saw him there positively. Heard him say to another man at the burning, 'Did he think that the *Goose* would be well *roasted*' [the man replied that he thought the goose and also the gander would soon be very well done]; upon this they shook hands, and gave a hearty laugh. (Witness looks at the prisoner again). Has not the least doubt of it; sure he is the man.

Cross-examined by Mr McNally. Is a Catholic. Knows the first question in the Catholic catechism – 'Who created and placed you in the world?' Knows the commandments – one of them 'thou shalt not commit murder'. Has not kept it. Was of the party. Heard the cries of those who were *roasted*. Knew they were fellow-mortals. Did not interfere to save them, though he knew his catechism. Had no compunction at that time. Did as he was commanded. Was sworn to do so. Evidenced now to disload his conscience and to atone for his guilt. Does not think that he can ever do penance enough. Never witnessed at Armagh. Had bad notes when taken up. Did not get them honestly. Never told a Priest. Confessed to a Priest after being taken up. Had told a Magistrate before the Priest. Believes he would have refused him the rites of the church if he had told him. The Priest advised him to confess fully to a Magistrate.

P. Halfpenny sworn. [Examined by Counsellor McCartney]. States how the fire was taken from his house in a piece of a pot, and what he saw of the burning. Knows the prisoner these many years. Knows him to always have very good character.

[Cross-examined by Counsellor Murray. One part of the road leading to Lynch's house is not passable for a horse; knew Wildgoose lodge before it was burned; knew the pig-sty before the door; the house behind is four perches back from the house; the pig-sty is two perches distant from the front; thinks a man might know that Lynch's house was on a hill; knows the prisoner McCullough; he lives two miles distant; never knew him to be connected in any thing bad before.]

THE DEFENCE

James McCulla sworn. [Examined by Counsellor Perrin]. Is brother to the prisoner. Lives at Ardee. Has lived there only two months [twelve months]. Lived there before at Rathn[i]estan. Lived there all his life, until he got married, and then went to Ardee. Heard of the burning. Lived at that time at Rathniestan. His brother lived there also. They kept looms weaving [had six or seven looms]. Kept a bleach-green of yarn. Would have some time from one to two hundred pounds worth at once down. Prisoner and witness slept in the green as watch. Slept in a hut or cabin [made of straw and stick]. Had no door. Had two dogs with him. Was on watch every night. Slept some time in the day [till 8 or 10 o'clock], and some time in the night, but always on the watch. Prisoner had an ailment in his knee, a little swelled. Was lame of it the time of the burning. Was with him that night, as usual, on watch. [Had a large quantity of bleach that night]. Not absent that night. [Went to bed at night fall; got their supper in the house at 8 o'clock.]. Generally took supper in the house, and then went to the hut. **Cross-examined by Serjeant Joy.** Is brother to the prisoner. Lived at Rathn[i]estan, one mile from Arthurstown [chapel]. Does not know how long he might ride it – in fifteen minutes. Kept yarn on the bleach. Was there from a fortnight before May until that time – Hollintide. Was always buying and selling yarn [it was his brother's yarn]. Slept there every night from May until that time. Always slept with him in the Bleach-green. Prisoner was there that night. Knew he was there every night. Felt him there every night. [The hut was just a bed, had a four-post bed in it]. [His brother Michael did not go to watch the yarn because he did not learn the trade]. His brother Michael attended at Drogheda market. Heard of the burning at 10 o'clock next day. The bleach is in a lonesome place. Could not see [the chapel nor] Wildgoose Lodge from this house. Prisoner did not hobble out that night. Had no crutches at that time. Could walk with a stick. Swears he was ill. Slept with him from May.

James Carragher [Callaghan, *Belfast News-Letter]* **sworn. [Examined by Counsellor M'Nally].** (Witness for character). Knows Thomas McCulla, the prisoner, 8 or 10 years. Is a very good man. [Was always considered an honest proper man].
[Cross-examined by Counsellor McCartney. Had he heard that there were Riband-men in the country. Answer, he did.]
Henry Blackwell sworn. [Examined by Counsellor Murray]. Knows him [he prisoner] 9 or 10 years. Knew Rooney, Lynch's son-in –law, to be on good terms with the prisoner. Remembers they were school-fellows [heard Rooney say]. Heard that they were relations. [Never heard of him having a bad character until this; witness is a Protestant].
[Cross-examined by Counsellor Hamilton. He knew the prisoner had sore foot for five or six days before the burning].
Rev. James Marron sworn. Is a Catholic Priest. Knows the prisoner.['since he came into the parish', *Belfast News-Letter,* 7 April 1818] Is his parishioner. Knows him to be a peaceable industrious man.
Here **Serjeant Joy** attempting to ask him some questions was interrupted by the Counsel for prisoner. He persisted: he enquired if witness knew where one Shanley was. Witness pretended not to know. At length, as if recollecting himself, said he was not in his parish.
Serjeant Joy, 'I know, Sir, he is not in your parish. Is he not hanged, Sir?'.
Witness, 'O very good, very good'.
Serjeant Joy, 'It may be very good for you, but not so for him. By virtue of your oath, was he not your Clerk?'
Witness said he was.
'And you came forward to give him a character?'
'I did'.
'Well, Sir, now I presume you know where he is'.
The Revd. 'I hope he repented'.
'Indeed and I hope you will repent too, Sir.'

JUDGE'S ADDRESS

His Lordship then addressed the Jury, and commented upon the evidence, which lasted an hour and 25 minutes. He stated that this was a more important case than any of the former. The peculiar situation of this man required their most serious consideration. He proceeded to state, that it was his duty to make any observations that he should see necessary upon the peculiar situation of the persons engaged on that night. It was his duty to make such remarks. It was his duty to see that the proceedings on the trial were legal. It was his duty to explain the case as it stood in law, but it was their province to decide on the guilt or innocence of the prisoner, & for that purpose he begged of them to divest their minds of all prejudice upon the occasion. He said that the prisoner appeared to be a man that could not be induced from low circumstances in life or such causes to enter into this conspiracy. If he did enter into it at all, his motives must be of the most diabolical nature.

What was [t]his most infernal conspiracy, this dreadful nefarious outrage? It was a most malignant conspiracy against all laws. It was a conspiracy of a band of ruffians, a conspiracy formed against all those who would dare to defend their property or appeal to or take refuge under the laws. Yet this is a man who might be expected would have supported the law. It had appeared to them in evidence that he was a man who had a considerable property to defend and consequently it was more natural to expect that he would have supported the laws than enter into this foul conspiracy, to oppose the distribution of justice. If this was an argument in his favour, it was for their most serious consideration. His Lordship stated that such proceedings as the transactions of that horrid night affected all ranks and degrees of men, the lowest peasant as well as the highest gentleman. It was wisely ordained by Providence that ranks and degrees among men should exist, and it was impossible for one to subsist without the other. If such proceedings were suffered, what would be the consequence? It would drive all men of property, all who had any regard for the laws and their personal safety, out of the country; and if they should succeed in making the county Louth a desert, what would it serve? They would next, like voracious wolves cut each other's throats, and quickly put an end to the community. As he before observed, one rank of mankind depended upon the other for subsistence. If the higher and middle order of men were driven out of the country, how were the lower ranks to get employment? If the Gentlemen of property were forced to leave the country, they would drain it of its wealth for their support, and spend it elsewhere. 'I do not address this solely to you. I address it to all who hear me, and I wish it may make that impression upon their minds which it ought. I entreat you not to visit any such remarks upon any individual'.

The Learned Judge proceeded to comment upon the evidence. The witnesses, he said, were men stained with the foulest crimes, and their testimony was to be weighed with caution and jealousy, but the law allowed of their evidence if it appeared to be so connected, so linked as to deface every doubt of its being a fabricated story, so supported by other evidences in some important particular as to satisfy their minds that they were detailing facts which had actually taken place; in such instances the law allowed this testimony to be competent; for, gentlemen, said he, the testimony of one bad man must go for nothing, the testimony of two bad men can be no better than that of one, nor is that of three or four, of any more weight, if not corroborated by some other facts. It was therefore their duty to examine, to scrutinize the testimony, which had been delivered by men who confessed themselves guilty of the most atrocious crimes. If it appeared to them that they had corroborated each other in facts stated by them differently, yet the same; if it appeared to them that their testimony was such as excluded a doubt of its being a fabricated system, why then it was for their consideration. If on the other side, they had not a doubt, a rational, reasonable doubt of the guilt of the prisoner, it was their duty to bring in their verdict accordingly; but if they had a rational doubt, such as men of rational and reasonable minds should have, it was his duty, and the most agreeable part of it to tell them – to conjure them, to let the prisoner have the benefit of that doubt.

The Jury retired for three minutes and returned a verdict of *Guilty*.

The prisoner then proceeded to declare his innocence in that hardened manner practised on former trials of this case. His Lordship addressed him in the most impressive manner, pointed out his aggravation in persisting in thus denying his guilt, which to him appeared in the clearest manner, and, he was certain to all those who had been witness to his long and impartial trial. He had had the benefit of a most impartial investigation of his case, the talents of the most able Counsels in his defence, and nothing that could be done for him had been omitted. His Lordship declaimed against the practise used on these trials by wretches suborned to come forward to prove what was vulgarly called *alibis* – but what appeared to him, and must to every thinking mind, to be the most glaring perjuries. Here this unfortunate man brought forth his more unfortunate brother to perjure himself in the most palpable manner. This he considered a crime almost equal in magnitude to the murder in question. He then pronounced the sentence of the law in the most feeling and awful manner.

Here followed a scene of the greatest confusion imaginable. The prisoner had attempted to interrupt the Judge more than once, while addressing him. He now deliberately laid down his hat, which he had held in his hand, and, putting his hand into his pocket, was pulling something out – the jailor seized his hand and pocket, and the alarm was given that he had a pistol. The Judge left the bench, and went into the Grand Jury-room, and in a moment the dock was surrounded by the police. The prisoner got enraged for being dragged and held. He seemed to be more astonished than any one present, what could be the cause. When his hand was extricated, lo! the pistol which had occasioned all this confusion became a prayer book, that he had concealed in his pocket for the purpose of swearing his innocence.

His Lordship left the Court, and the prisoner was led quite peaceably to the Jail.

Belfast News-Letter **version, 7 April 1818:** After the sentence was pronounced, the prisoner put his hand into his breast, and seemed to search there for some matter concealed under his waistcoat. At this moment some person called out, that the prisoner was armed with a pistol, upon which a very great confusion and disorder arose in the court, and several persons jumped over into the dock and seized and searched the prisoner. However it proved that the unhappy man had not any pistol about his person, but that he had been endeavouring to take out a testament, upon which, he said, he wished to attest his innocence. He was immediately ironed and sent to the jail, and order became again restored in court.

The prisoner McCullough was a man of most interesting appearance. He is six feet in height, well proportioned, and was genteelly dressed. He was a man of wealth, supposed worth 1000*l*. and was a principal leader among the party.

The *Newry Telegraph* (extract in *The Correspondent* 4 April 1818) commented on Thomas McCullogh:

> 'It is astonishing that such a man should have been so weak in intellect – so depraved in morals, as to associate himself with a nefarious gang of assassins, at the hazard of losing the advantages which he possessed in society, and even life itself'. On Judge Fletcher it remarked, 'In the course of his speech, he made honourable mention of the very proper behaviour of the Catholic Clergy, exemplified in their conduct to Murphy and Gubby. He observed that the ribbandmen are bound by oath to preserve the secrets of their associate inviolate. Hence he inferred, that the Roman Catholic Clergy do not possess any information of the schemes and acts of that illegal and desperate banditti'.

On the incident of McCullogh attempting to draw out his prayer book it records:

> When McCullough heard his awful sentence, he suddenly plunged his hand, in a hurried manner, into his coat pocket. And now, the cry of 'A pistol! A pistol!' was uttered by many voices. Judge Fletcher, alarmed by this exclamation, retreated precipitately from the Court. The lawyers fled *pari passu*. The gaoler instantly seized the hand of the convict – the police gathered round him with drawn swords – reiterated cries of 'Seize him! Seize him! A pistol! A pistol! A rescue! A rescue!' resounded from all quarters. McCullough who is a strong man, made some resistance, and his struggle kept up the interest of the scene. At last he was overpowered, and the gaoler drew from his pocket the object of all this bustle and terror – a little Book. *Parturiunt montes nascetur ridiculus mus*. On his book he intended to swear, that he was innocent of the crime for which he had been sentenced to die.

TRIAL OF WILLIAM BUTLER, THOMAS SHEENAN AND JOHN KEEGAN

The trial took place in Dundalk on 2 April 1818. *Drogheda Journal*, 4 April 1818 with extra notes throughout from the *Dundalk Examiner*, 29 October 1881:

> *Thursday, April 2*. William Butler, Thomas Shienan [Sheenan], and John Keighan [Keegan], were put to the bar [for the burning of Wildgoose Lodge].
> [The judge (**Fletcher**) entered the court at the usual hour.]
> **Counsel for the Prisoners**, Messrs McNally & Hamilton.
> **Mr McNally** observed, that the case of Butler would appear to be a different one, respecting the defence, to any heretofore brought

forward upon his occasion. Therefore he would wish him tried alone. The prisoners being willing, however, to join in their challenges, they were all retained at the bar. After a very few challenges, the following Gentlemen were sworn as **Jurors**:
Henry McNeale, Strangfield [Strandfield]; Robert Thompson, Ravensdale; James Johnson, Waterbridge [Falmor]; Robert Getty, Dundalk; Robert Sheridan [Sheedon], Dundalk; Benjamin Atkinson, Mount Bailie [Dundalk]; Alexander Donaldson, Philipstown; Robert Dickie, Clonale[e]nan; John Morgan, Dillen; William Munkittrick, Ardee; John Baillie, Shorstown [Shortstone]; John Coleman, Rathory.

Serjeant Joy opened this trial with a short but comprehensive speech, addressed to the Jury. He stated, that, as no peculiarities appeared upon this case, he would not detain his Lordship or the Court with any remarks, the facts were all known to them already; some of them, if not all, had sat upon former trials. He stated that against two of the prisoners there would appear upon evidence some particulars of a more corroborating nature than had yet appeared, and they would be prepared to give them that weight, which in their better judgement they would seem to deserve.

Alice Rispan [Rispin] sworn. States that the house of Wildgoose Lodge was burned upon the night of the 29th of October, 1816, and that she could identify her son, &c. [Deposed to Mr McCartney as she did before; the eight bodies were found lying in a closet, opposite the door of the back entrance].

Thomas Gubby sworn. Examined by Mr Bell]. Remembers the burning of Wildgoose Lodge, and states the proceeding from Stonetown Chapel. [Heard some of the persons inside say 'for God's sake to save our lives', and the mob answered 'no'. He points out all the three prisoners at the bar, recollects them all being there, particularly recollects Butler, remembers him [Butler] meeting with McCulla (who was convicted yesterday) - McCulla asking him [Butler] in a jesting manner '*did you think would the Goose be well done*,' to which he replied, '*that he thought that both the Goose and the Gander would be well done shortly'*. These remarks were followed by a cordial shake hands and laugh. Witness saw Kieghan carrying straw to the fire, and fell over the stile at the garden, after which he heard him complain of hurting his foot.

Cross-examined by Mr McNally. He acknowledged flying from the county Tyrone [his birth place], for being charged with a robbery, was of the party, was taken in Drogheda [by Mr Armstrong], had forged notes, but never passed any, they were given to him, paid nothing for them, [was acquitted at Armagh upon a charge of taking up arms, because his prosecutor perjured himself, thinks everyman should be acquitted whose prosecutor would perjure himself, would not perjure himself knowingly for the world] was one at Lynch's murder, went for that purpose, wanted to punish Lynch for prosecuting such rogues as him, could not avoid going, was seduced, never saw Lynch in his life, never heard of him before, had no malice, had no revenge to gratify, heard a man from within as if calling for mercy, and heard answers from without, confessed to a magistrate, never called to the bar here, was called to the bar in Tyrone (*a laugh*), would not swear false, would be afraid to perjure himself, lest he should be damn'd, did help to burn eight people.

A Juryman: Did you know Butler before?

No, never saw him since 'till in Jail, never saw any of them since, but described them to Mr Pendleton, in the presence of the Solicitor General, in Kilmainham, before he saw them.

Peter Gilogly sworn. [Examined by Mr Staples]. Points out Butler. Does not know his name, but remembers his person, remembers him very well, saw him first at Arthurstown Chapel, had a pistol, saw him go before him with the rest of the party, saw him return again [where he was holding the horses], had still the pistol, did not see him since, but saw him often before, is certain that he is the man, saw him in the Jail [yard], saw him with others, knows him perfectly, could point him out among them.

Upon being cross-examined [by Mr McNally]: He stated that he had no acquaintance with him, only saw him at a fair, but persists that he is sure of him; witness is a taylor, left off that business to become a robber. [Was not charged with crime until Sillery's robbery, was at it, twelve months last February since; saw Butler often at the fairs of Mullacrew and Ardee, and at many other places; knows the prisoner to be the man he saw there that night].

The *Belfast News-Letter*, 7 April 1818, has some additional reporting:

Alice Rispan [Rispin] called up again [examined by Mr Hall]: She knows the three prisoners. The last time she saw John Keegan was about two months before the burning. He then said to her, she was right in taking her son out of Rooney's house, for Lynch and Rooney were rogues and had turned traitors to their country; he said he would be the first of 12 men who would stand forward to burn Lynch, his house and family, to ashes, and they should not eat their supper on Holy-Eve night. [Her son was a weaver, and had been apprenticed to Lynch]. A few days after a particular day upon which her son had been brought by the constables to Rosy Park, to state to Mr Fortescue and other Magistrates what he knew of the original breaking of Lynch's house, she went into Thomas Sheenan's house, upon which he said, 'Your son is a fool for meddling with Hugh McCabe, [that if he went thirty miles off he would be known by] the colour of his hair and eyes, and other marks and other tokens, will attend him till he shall meet the usage of a *Stag*, meaning an informer'.

Cross-examined: Did not tell Lynch precisely what she had heard from those particular prisoners, or mention their names to him, but she often warned him to be aware, for his life was threatened. It was rumoured by the country that he and his family would be burned. Her son, often after the first attack, went to Lynch's house, against her will and advice to him. He son used to say to her, in reply to her warnings not to go to Lynch's house, that people could not be murdered so easily as she seemed to fear.

[*Here the prosecution ended*]

WILLIAM BUTLER'S DEFENCE

Mary Butler [examined by Mr McNally]: Lives at Aclint, half a mile from Wildgoose Lodge, across the bog. It is a longer distance by the road. [Has five sons.] The prisoner is her son. The prisoner and her other sons are weavers. [Has a shop beside the house where the boys sleep]. Remembers the burning at Lynch's house; from her own house saw the house burning at night. Lynch's house was situate on a rising ground. She had been up late baking bread. She came into the house, awoke her husband, and told him of the burning. He got up immediately, and went to some neighbours to alarm. She called her three sons (the prisoner amongst them). They slept in their weaving shop. She saw them get up, and standing in their shirts on the floor, before they dressed themselves. After supper her sons went out to the shop. She did not see them after till she saw them in bed.

Cross-examined [by Serjeant Joy]: It was between one and two o'clock at night when she saw the house on fire. [She was baking bread at that hour]. She was late in that baking, because it was late when she got the word from her husband to bake. It was supper time when the baking was thought of. [as they were going to dig potatoes next morning]. Supped sometimes late and sometimes early, generally earlier than 10 o'clock, but it was about 10 o'clock that night. [She sometimes goes to bed earlier than ten o'clock.] The night was within one or two of Hollintide, and was not very dark. Her sons were to dig potatoes the next day. The potato field was about two miles from their dwelling-house. [The boys went to bed after supper, between nine and ten o'clock; did not see them again until between one and two o'clock; she knew Lynch's house and saw it burning at two o'clock; it was not blazing hard at two, but it blazed more after she went in; was very fond of Lynch's people; was afraid they would be killed if they went to help Lynch that night; could not tell that her sons were anxious to go to assist; could not tell where they went after supper].

James Butler [Examined by Mr McNally]. Father of the prisoner Butler. Witness has three other sons besides the prisoner. Was well-acquainted with Lynch. His house is not far from witness's house. [half a mile]. Remembers witness's wife (the last witness) raising him out of his sleep [between one and two o'clock; gave order to bake bread at supper; supped between nine and ten o'clock], and telling him that Lynch's house was on fire. He got up immediately, and went out in his shirt, and saw the house burning. He then dressed himself, and went to alarm the neighbours [there were four cabins in his neighbourhood; alarmed them; went to Michael Moghan]. He left the prisoner and his

[two] brothers behind him at his house [in the shop where there were two looms]. Witness had called them up. They came out of the house, in their shirts, to see the fire, and sons afterwards went back to dress themselves, when witness went off to the neighbours. [He was asked again by the counsel how many sons he had in all; he then said five; why then did he say four; because the younger one was only a little boy about ten or twelve years old].

Cross-examined [by Mr McCartney]: Did not go to Lynch's [when he saw the fire], or let his sons go there, because he heard firing of guns, and a great noise of bloody war there. His sons went out to the shop after supper. They used to sleep there. Does not think they could have been at the fire, after they had gone to the shop, and before he saw them in their bed. Lynch was the best neighbour he ever had. He was a good doctor, and used to bleed his family and horses and cows, and give then advice without charging him any thing. Witness and his family, and indeed the whole parish, were very sorry for Lynch's fate. The fire could not be seen from his house, but from a situation about a perch from the house.

John Butler. Brother to the prisoner. Remembers his father alarming him and his two brothers, William and Patrick. [Went to bed after supper]. They were all lying together. Witness lay in the middle and William lay at the far side of the bed near the wall [because he always lay there; they had all shirts upon them]. They got up in their shirts and went out, about a perch from the house and saw the fire [saw the roof of the house fall in, had seen other houses burned and the roof fall in; it was his father who rapped and told them to get up, as Lynch's house was set on fire; saw his father abut half an hour after Michael Moghan came there; did not go over for fear of being killed; it would have been his duty to have gone to help to put the fire out, if it had been accidentally burned; the neighbours were all in a 'perspiration']. They then returned and dressed themselves. From the time they had gone to bed together none of the three brothers ever left the shop where they slept. None of witness's family ventured to go over to Lynch's. They were afraid. The fire might have happened accidentally, but witness heard two shots fired just after his father called him. [Did not see his uncle]. Saw Mohan [Moghan], a neighbour, at witness's father's house that night, and a labourer of his, named Halfpenny. [Were all very sorry for Lynch, has four brothers, the youngest between thirteen and fourteen years of age].

Patrick Butler [Examined by Mr McNally]. Slept in his father's loom-shop, with William and John Butler on the night of Lynch's burning. His father knocked at the door of the shop and bid them get up smart, that [Edward] Lynch's house was on fire. They, in their shirts, and before they had put any thing more on them, ran out and saw the house on fire. It wanted three hours of day. Neither witness or any of his brothers had stirred from the time they had gone to bed to the time their father had called them. Knew Lynch very well. Had not seen him in his house recently before the burning. Used sometimes to call on him to doctor witness's family when any of them were ailing. Saw

Mohan's people, some of the Taaffes, and some other neighbours at his father's that night, after the alarm. None of the entire party gathered at Butler's house went to assist Lynch, though they saw the house on fire. They heard several shots and were afraid.

[**Cross-examined by Mr Staples**]. Knew Lynch very well; he was a great friend to all the family; was shortly in Lynch's house; would go for him when they wanted to bleed any of the family; does not know of arms being in the house; heard there was a guard at it; dare not go to assist him for fear. Saw Taafe and Moghan in the barn; durst not go for fear of the numbers and shooting that were there. John slept in the middle and William next to the wall.]

Thomas Halfpenny. [Examined by Mr McNally]. Knows James Butler, father of the prisoner. Witness saw Lynch's house on fire. James Butler, the prisoner's father, had called him. Witness was asleep at Mohan's house, where he lived. He heard a knocking at the door. Made no answer. Got up and saw that James Butler was the person who had rapped at the door, and then had gone down to Mohan's room window, at which he rapped likewise. Heard but one shot fired after witness got up. Heard the noise of people. Went to Butler's house, because he saw a fire lighting in the house and the door open. Mohan came there too after witness. Saw the prisoner and his brothers in the house when he went there, but none others.

[**Cross-examined by Mr Hall**]. Was asleep when the knock was given at the barn door; heard one shot fired two minutes after he got up; went to Butler's; was afraid to stay at the barn; saw light there; went there before his master, Moghan; was afraid when he heard the shot; heard the voices of many people; was afraid to go to Lynch's to assist in putting out the fire, for fear of offending the neighbours; no person went to Butler's but Moghan and him.

Michael Mohan. [Examined by Mr McNally]. Lives in Aclint. The last witness (*Halfpenny*) is his labourer [servant]. He lay in witness's barn that night. Witness was called by James Butler. He saw the burning after but did not hear any shot fired. He found the prisoner in his father's house, on his going there, which he did soon after he was called up out of bed and had dressed himself. [It was about a mile to go round by Lynch's].

Cross-examined [by Sergeant Joy]. Does not know whether Butler came to him and to the other neighbours to bring them to his house merely that they might see his son in the house, or for what purpose he called them. Went to Butler's of his own accord. Found the prisoner and his brothers Pat and John and their mother, as also Halfpenny, his labourer, there. The deceased Lynch's sister was married to witness's wife's brother.

[Went to Butler's house, because of the alarm that was in it; went to see the boy. Why did old Butler go about at two o'clock to see his son at that hour? Why! Did you all go there for the purpose of seeing his son? Could not tell. A smart young man could return from Lynch's house before two o'clock. Did not prevent any one from coming forward, nor never encouraged any one to prosecute Lynch's murderers; he liked

Lynch, would tell on any one who murdered him. Lynch's sister was married to his brother. All about the street were trembling about the fire; William Butler had his clothes on, and looked as well as ever he had seen him.]

John Coleman. One of the Jury. Has known Butler (*the prisone*r), these five years. He never knew a man in his sphere of life bear a better character.

Michael [Nicholas in *Drogheda Journal* and *Dundalk Examiner*] **Kelly.** Knows Butler for a very long time. His character was unequalled in the county for propriety of conduct.

James Lynch. Is brother to the unfortunate man who was burned. Knows the prisoner Butler all his life [since he was christened]. Never heard a better character than the prisoner enjoyed. There never was any thing between Lynch's (*deceased*) family and Butler's family but friendship and good neighbourhood and he does not believe Butler would have joined in hurting witness's brother more than witness himself would have done.

THOMAS SHEENAN'S DEFENCE

Daniel Murphy. Recollects the night of the fire. Lay in Sheenan's house that night. Saw Sheenan there. Went to bed between eight and nine o'clock. Lay in the same bed with him all night. Did not get up till day-light. Sheenan was in bed with him all night.

Cross-examined [by Counsellor Macartney]. Lay awake all night. A woman took labour that night., which kept him awake. Nelly Reilly was her name. Saw the child next morning. [He slept in the room because the standing bed was there in the kitchen.] She lay in the kitchen. Witness's sister attended her. The groaning of the woman kept him awake all night. [how could he sleep with the grunting she kept? Is a married man; always left the house when his wife was in labour] There was a sheet put against the door-way in the room where he lay. There was no door. Saw the woman on a straw bed in the morning. Is a besom-worker. Can't sleep whenever he hears a noise. The child is a girl.

Catherine Murphy. Is sister to last witness [who is a besom-maker]. Lodged in Sheenan's house the night of the fire. A woman took sick and was bought to bed that night. [The woman that was in the house spinning wool was big with child]. Witness attended her. She was very sick. Did not moan much. Prisoner, and his son, and last witness slept together. The besom-maker slept at the outside and prisoner in the middle. His son refused to sleep next the stranger. [Put up a sheet between the room and the kitchen, as there was no door.] Prisoner did not stir from going to bed till morning. Heard some shots fired.

[Cross-examined by Counsellor Hall. Lynch's house was not far from where she was that night; knows the lane going up to the house; Sheenan's house was on the side of that lane; heard no shots, no horses, nor footmen that night; put the men to the room; does not recollect that there was a standing bed in the kitchen; recollects no bed but the one that was in the room; her labour began about eight or nine; the men never got up; the woman made very quiet moaning; did put up a sheet to prevent the men from seeing what the women were doing.]

Bryan Sheenan. Is son to the prisoner. Witness and his father slept, on the night of the burning, in the bed with Daniel Murphy, on a bed of straw in the little room. [Daniel Murphy lay next the stock, his father in the middle; is sure his father slept in the bed all night.] Witness always slept with his father. Heard no noise that night of firing, or huzzas, or shouts. Heard horses passing. Thought they were going to the bog to draw away turf, which the people were in the habit of stealing that season, firing being scarce.

Elenor Reilly. She knows Sheenan. Recollects the night she was brought to bed in his house. She lay that night in the place in which Sheenan's family spun their wool. There were also in the house two men that were besom or broom-makers. They got lodging in Sheenan's that night, and Sheenan's wife was angry on account of the throng in the house. She lay on the straw. There was a standing bed in the kitchen in which the children lay. [Nobody was in the house but Sheenan, the woman, the besom maker, and the prisoner's son].

JOHN KEEGAN'S CASE

Patrick Halfpenny. Knows Keegan. He lived near witness's house at the time of the burning [near Wildgoose Lodge]. Witness called at prisoner's house about two hours before day-light on the morning after the burning. He and his wife were then up. They were outside at the end of the house. His wife was crying. He went with prisoner to Lynch's house that morning and assisted to put out the remains of the fire, clear out the ashes and rubbish, and find the bodies.

Thomas William Filgate, Esq. Has known Keegan a great number of years past [Knew the prisoner has been out of the country nine years]. He worked for him long ago. His character then was a very good one. **Mr [John] Coleman**, one of the Jury, the same one who had been examined as to the character of the prisoner Butler, says, he has known Keegan 20 years and upwards. Never heard any thing against him or his character. His character was a very good one and as fair as any poor man's like him in the country.

VERDICTS

The **Jury** retired a few minutes before three o'clock, and the Court was then adjourned. At nine the Learned Judge resumed his seat on the bench, and the Jury being called, delivered a verdict of *Guilty* against Sheenan and Keegan, who heard the verdict with the most perfect indifference.

The Jury not having agreed in the case of Butler, they were ordered to return, and remained locked up until half-past eleven o'clock on Thursday. Being again called into Court, and asked, had they agreed?, said they had not. The Judge told them they must be discharged at the verge of the county.

Serjeant Joy observed, that he understood the verge of the county was several miles from Dundalk, and as they had suffered so much from long confinement, he hoped the distance would be shortened, and, if the opposite Counsel had no objection, let them be discharged convenient to town.

This was acceded to by Mr McNally.

The Jury were marched out, attended by the Sheriff and a guard of soldiers. They remained sometime waiting for his Lordship, who arrived, and discharged them. Butler lies in gaol until next assizes, to be again tried.

RELEASE ON BAIL OF OTHERS ACCUSED

The Correspondent of 7 April 1818 contains an extract from the *Newry Telegraph* recounting the release on bail of six men who were regarded as not among the leading suspects. Some extra details are provided from the *Dundalk Examiner* 5 November 1881.

P[at]. Malone, E. McQuillan, J. Lochlan [Lochran], N[M.]. Clark, J. Morris, and H. Turnan, being put to the bar and arraigned, **Mr Serjeant Joy** rose and addressed the Court, saying:

That he congratulated his Lordship, and the county of Louth, that this unpleasant, disagreeable business was for the present postponed. He felt it his duty to state that the Crown wished, in the commencement of the prosecution for the murders at Wildgoose Lodge, to select from amongst the great numbers who were concerned in that nefarious transaction, those who were most active in the horrid deed, and the principal ringleaders in the conspiracy. It is certain that numbers were present on that night, who knew not, when they set out, for what purpose they had been collected together. The Crown wished to select for punishment, those who had planned and conducted the conspiracy. They had, in a great measure, been able to select these leaders. It was his wish, as leading Counsel for the Crown, that those men at the bar should be admitted for the present to bail, and that such bail should be taken for them, as would not preclude the possibility of their enjoying the advantage of this indulgence extended to them by the Crown. It depended on their own good conduct, and the peace of the country, whether they would ever be called on again. He wished to impress it on their minds, and the minds of all in Court, that it was not on account of any failure of evidence on the part of the Crown that this was granted. They had, indeed, sufficient evidence to identify them as being of the party on that night, though not actively or prominently engaged in the conspiracy.

Some of the leaders had already paid the forfeit of their lives. Others were convicted and sentenced to die, but there remained yet unapprehended, some of those ringleaders, whom (if they are apprehended, and apprehended they will be) there is sufficient proof to convict, and they will most assuredly pay the forfeit of their lives to the offended laws of their country.

The trials of Lynch's murderers have closed for the present. The Crown intends to prosecute all the ringleaders of this infernal conspiracy, and to extend mercy to the minor villain. To these a kind of conditional amnesty is extended. They will be admitted to bail; and, if they and their associates in wickedness cease to disturb the peace of the community, they will be suffered to drag out the remnant of their miserable existence, undisturbed by the hangman. They will escape all temporal punishments, except that which may result from the scorn of their fellow-subjects, and the stings of endless remorse. They are held as a kind of hostage for the peace of the country; and the slightest deviation from the rules prescribed to them by the crown, will precipitate them and their coadjutors in crime into eternity.

The *Belfast News-Letter*, 10 April 1818, reflecting back on the trial, reported on the address of Judge Fletcher.

Previous to the Court rising at Dundalk on Friday, the **Hon. Judge Fletcher** addressed himself to the multitude who were present. He bewailed the wretched state of the country, which appeared, by these proceedings to be deluged in perjury! What perjury, and what subordination of perjury, had appeared upon these trials! Even boys had been brought forward, and had been taught to swear what they knew was false! He verily believed that the whole of this wicked transaction may be considered as built upon this horrid foundation – the deluded people thinking that by perjury, and subordination of perjury, they would be able to escape the punishment due to their crimes; that they would succeed in hoodwinking a Jury. And thus they deceived themselves, and led others into wickedness and vice. It had appeared on these trials, that all their proceedings had been regulated by oaths, some were adduced to take them, and thought themselves bound to keep them secret. Thus they had hesitated not to commit the most diabolical crimes; and then, in order to escape the punishment which the law inflicts, they are obliged to suborn their fathers and mothers, brothers and sisters, and even children to perjure themselves, by coming forward, as they did upon these trials, and swearing that at the very time the prisoners were at home, or in such a place as made it impossible for them to commit the crimes they stood charged with.

The venerable Judge, in a feeling and pathetic address, exhorted the lower orders to abandon those illegal societies, which have brought several of their fellow men to an ignominious death, and has entailed disgrace and affliction on their unfortunate families and friends. He trusted this appeal, that proceeded from a love for his country, and the best feelings of his heart, would have its due weight, and that their future good conduct would atone for their past transgression.

As in the case of Thomas McCullagh, Judge Fletcher in similar words again commended the Catholic clergy for their conduct towards Murphy and Gubby:

> In the course of his Lordship's address to the Jury on the trial of Sheinan [Sheenan], Keigghan, and Butler, he made honourable mention of the very proper behaviour of the Catholic Clergy, exemplified in their conduct to Murphy and Gubby. He observed that the ribband men are bound by oath to preserve the secrets of their association inviolate, even from their spiritual Pastors. Hence he inferred, that the Roman Catholic Clergy do not possess any information of the schemes and acts of that illegal and desperate banditti.

EXECUTION OF THOMAS McCULLOGH, PATRICK McQUILLAN, JAMES SMYTH, THOMAS SHEENAN, JOHN KEEGAN

The executions took place at Reaghstown on 7 April 1818. Report in the *Belfast News-Letter*, 10 April 1818 [reprinted in the *Dundalk Examiner*, 5 November 1881]:

> Extract of a letter from Dundalk – April 7.
> This morning, a little before eight o'clock, the five convicts, McCullough, McCullan, Smith, Shienan, and Keighan, were led forth from the gaol, and placed in a jingle, attended by the Rev. Mr Duffy, the chaplain, to be taken to Reaghstown for execution. McCullagh was remarkably clean, and seemed to have a white dress under his great coat. After they were seated, McCullan got up, as if going to speak, but sat down again. In a few minutes he again rose, and exclaimed, 'That my soul may perish if ever I saw Wildgoose Lodge'. The other four made no observations. They appeared, particularly McCullagh, quite composed, and behaved with the greatest propriety.
> The procession moved forward at a quick pace. The prisoners were escorted by a party of the 14th light dragoons, with three or four officers; Samuel Pendleton, Esq. and the horse police of Dundalk; the high and sub-sheriff, gaoler, and executioner.
> At the place of execution they were joined by the staff of the Louth and some detachments of the 46th regiment of foot [45th according to *The Correspondent*, and *Dundalk Examiner* 5 November 1881]].
> Since their conviction, these unhappy men continued to evince the most determined resolution of dying declaring their innocence.
> On their arrival at Reaghstown, they suffered on a temporary gallows erected for the purpose, and continued to deny their guilt to the last moment.
> McCullagh's body was taken to Louth and gibbeted. The other four

were brought back to town, and are to be delivered to the hospital surgeon for dissection.
Nothing remarkable occurred at the place of execution, but that, at the earnest request and persuasion of the Rev. Mr Marron, McCullagh said that he forgave the world.
The Right Hon. John Foster, the Lord Viscount Jocelyn, with many others who composed the Grand Jury, attended this awful ceremony.

In his Journal Henry McClintock described Tuesday 7th April 1818 as a 'showry' day. He does not mention the executions. For Wednesday 15th April he writes, 'I dined in the Barracks at the mess of the 14th Lt. Dns. with Colonel Brotherton'.

DR JAMES MARRON, PARISH PRIEST OF TALLANSTOWN

Rev. Dr James Marron, who testified at the trial of Thomas McCullagh and attended his execution, is commemorated by a lengthy epitaph in Latin on the wall of Tallanstown church.[221] The 'difficult times' mentioned in it would include the atrocity at Wildgoose Lodge and the sequel of trials and executions. In translation it reads:

'Pray for the soul of Rev. James Marron, D.D., rector of the church of Tallanstown for 37 years. He was born at Drogheda in 1764, and died the 14th day of December, 1839. Instructed at Drogheda in the first elements of learning and in the Humanities, he studied philosophy and theology at Paris, and adorned with the laurels of the doctorate he was raised to the order of the priesthood A.D. 1788. Associated with the Most Rev. Richard O Reilly, archbishop of Armagh, in the pastoral charge of Drogheda, he exercised the office of curate for 14 years. Finally, in 1802, he was promoted by the said Most Rev. Archbishop to be parish priest of the church of Tallanstown, which church he ruled until his death. He was a man assuredly distinguished, adorned by common agreement with piety, learning, zeal for souls, skill in the conduct of affairs in difficult times, and all other virtues which become the excellent pastor. In memory of the best of pastors and a much esteemed uncle, Patrick Marron his brother's son reverently raises this stone'.

Dr Marron was born in Drogheda on 30 April 1764 and was baptized on 15 May as appears in the Register of Baptisms of St Peter's Church. His parents were Patrick Marron and Catherine Jennett, and his sponsors were Michael Connor and Mary Cruice.
Dr Marron directed one of his parishioners, Pat Gernon of

Knocklore, probably a schoolmaster judging by his excellent work, to compile a census of the Parish of Tallanstown. The date 'October, 1834' is inscribed on the cover of the register. It lists the heads of households in each townland and denotes their religious denomination. It is an excellent guide to the families who would have inhabited the parish in the period of the Wildgoose Lodge murders. Fr Diarmuid Mac Íomhair published it in the *County Louth Archaeological Journal* (xiv, 1957).

A letter written by Dr Marron on the day of the executions to a friend, Mrs Margaret O'Reilly, Knock Abbey, who was then living in Cheltenham, has survived. Mr George Patterson who wrote the first truly historical article on the burning of Wildgoose Lodge for the *County Louth Archaeological Journal* (xii, 2, 1950) published part of it and gave the background of the letter. He was alerted to its existence by Fr Diarmuid Mac Íomhair, who remembered that many years ago Canon P. Finnegan, parish priest of Donaghmore, County Tyrone, had seen a letter at Knock Abbey containing a reference to Wildgoose Lodge. A copy of the letter was procured from Colonel C. H. O'Reilly then owner of Knock Abbey. Patterson wrote:

> Mrs O' Reilly was the daughter of Myles Dowdall, Esq., of Cairne, County Meath, and married (as his second wife) in 1789, Matthew O'Reilly, esq., of Knock Abbey, by whom she had issue five sons. Two charming miniatures of the lady and her husband are in the possession of Colonel O'Reilly and he has in his service a man who is a definite link with the Wildgoose Lodge episode, his forebears having been compelled to guard Lynch and Rooney following the first attack on the premises, a claim substantiated by a reference in a monograph on Wildgoose Lodge published by John Mathews (editor of the *Dundalk Examiner*) in 1882, wherein such protection is mentioned.

The postmark on the letter is dated 13 April and was directed to Mrs Margaret O'Reilly, care of the Post office, Cheltenham. The full text of the letter reads:

Rathbody

> 7 April 1818
> My Dear Madam,
> I hope this letter will find you out. I could not get a more particular address from your worthy sons William & Walter; I met them in Drogheda about six weeks ago at the Primate's Month's Mind.[222] They returned to Dublin that evening & would not stay to dine with us. We had Doctor Troy and several other Bishops and clergymen from Dublin

& elsewhere; sixty three sat down to dinner, the executors paid for it - £70. He bequeathed £200 to the Ursuline Nunnery of Drogheda & £50 a piece to the charity schools, also something to his servants. The residue to the Doyles. An auction was called for the sale of his effects & his Villa, which was purchased by a Custom House clerk for £180. I do not think, nor can I learn that he died rich; we know not as yet who will be his successor.

By writing to you, dear Madam, I hope to cheer the melancholy state I have been in these latter days, particularly this morning, having attended five criminals from Dundalk who were executed near the chapel of Reastown, within view of Wild Goose Lodge, for the burning of which they were convicted. Four of them my own Parishioners, late Mat McCullow's son Thomas; Smyth the mason's youngest son; his son-in-law Keegan; and a man in years Sheenan; also a Co. Meath man McCullin. I have constantly attended them since Sunday morning and they all to the last moment asserted their innocence of the crime for which they suffered. The Co. Meath man declared he never knew where the lodge was untill he saw it from the scaffold. There were Ten executed about three weeks ago on the same spot; there was but one of my flock amongst them, McCabe the turfman's son, and he with five others asserted their innocence: report says that seven of them attested their innocence. I could not exactly say how many, for though I was at the place of execution, I would not be permitted to go near them – of this they bitterly complained. All this is most melancholy. The late Speaker with whom I had some conversation this day about their last dying declarations, and all our great folks are extremely puzzled. Your old friend Faithful Fortescue, our present High Sheriff, has conducted himself with humanity and applause. Indeed our popular Judge Fletcher and the juries are at a loss how to act. The evidences for the Crown, the most infamous of characters, frequently tell the truth; whilst the *alibis* in defence of the criminals are mostly supported by flagrant perjuries. John Coleman by holding out in opposition for near 24 hours to the entire of the jury in defence of one Butler, a lad of excellent character, well defended by an evidence for an alibi, put an end to the special commission last week. Fletcher on his way to Dublin, brought the jury with him a part of the road, and then scattered them. A ludicrous circumstance occurred on the verdict against McCullow. 'My Lord', said he, putting his right hand under the left side of his coat. 'Secure him', said the judge, thinking he intended to draw out a pistol, and ducking his head he fled to the Grand Jury Room. 'Clear the court', was then the word – some leaped out the windows etc. On examining McCullow it was found he only intended to draw out a prayer-book & attest his innocence. Indeed you are happily away from this – nothing but Gibbets offend the eye. Four in chains at Louth, four more at Corcreah, and three beyond Dundalk. Still the ribbon-men are very numerous, I am told, in the neighbouring counties, but inoffensive. I most sincerely wish myself out of this Co. Louth. I met Matw [Matthew] yesterday in Dundalk and enquired about all his friends. He told me Mrs Dean was well and had lately brought a son to the world; that he lately had a letter from you and a note from Miss Lissey saying you were well and pleasingly situated. Since the anniversary of Mr O'Reilly I have not been within the gates of Thomastown, as neither the heir nor his brother go to any religious worship, which gives great publick scandal. How to reclaim them I know not. I am told Lord Louth proposed to him that he should marry his sister-in-law Rose of Dunsany; he objected to the match saying the lady had not sufficient fortune. In consequence his Lordship has renounced his acquaintance; the coolness has subsisted upwards of six weeks. Peter Coleman's affairs are as yet unsettled, but he and his family are well. At Fane Valley all are well; the same I can say of your former connections here.

Mrs Taaffe will soon return to Smarmor. Sir Edward Bellew and family are in Paris; he writes home that the City is so corrupt he cannot trust his sons to any place of publick education. The poor tenants of Thomastown are all as you left them. I am sorry I have not more pleasing intelligence for you. But I never knew this country so dull. I hope your little family is well and that Richard & Miss Lissey are in good spirits. Tell her I never forget our compact. Indeed you are all daily present to my mind. I never expect to meet again such friends. Should you do me the favour to write to me, I hope to be able to send you occasionally more interesting letters. I have the honor to remain with esteem & gratitude

Your very humble & obt servant

James Marron

Pray remember me to poor Mary Anne. Excuse the inaccuracies of this letter, as I had frequently to suppress a gush of tears whilst I wrote it. I thought I could post this letter in Drogheda, but have to send it from Ardee: here Dr Lee makes many kind enquiries about you. Our winter has been long and very severe – our spring so wet & winter-like that our gardens are uncultivated and our farmers cannot sow their crops. 10th April.

11
Trials and Executions (3)

TRIAL OF WILLIAM BUTLER, OWEN GAYNOR, AND MICHAEL KEARNAN

The trials took place in Dundalk on 3 April 1818 and 3 July 1818. Henry McClintock wrote in his diary:

> Friday 3d July 1818, Dundalk. Showry day – the Assizes began here – I attended at the Custom House – Bessy & I dined at home – we passed the evening with my mother & sister Fortescue – my brother John was there also.

For the trial of these men we have to return to the Spring Assizes, 1818, for the first part of their ordeal. The trial took place in the new Court House, Market Square, which replaced the old Sessions House in Church Street. The *Belfast News-Letter*, 7 April 1818, reported:

> Friday, April 3
> *George McCullan [McQuillan], Owen Gainor [Gaynor],* and *Michael Kiernan [Kearnan]*, were put to the bar, charged with the same offence as the other prisoners and pleaded *not guilty*; but stated they were not ready for their trials, in consequence of their witnesses not attending – this excuse was humanely admitted; and Serjeant Joy said he would not press the trials at present, and that they should remain in gaol until next assizes; they were accordingly remanded. The jailer received orders to mitigate their confinement as far as safety would permit, provided they conducted themselves properly.
> *Patrick Waters* was indicted for a burglary at Lynch's house; he pleaded *not guilty*, and said he was ready for trial. On being asked if he knew on what charge he was going to be tried answered, for the burning of Lynch's house; but when he was informed that was not the crime he stood charged with, but for a burglary in company with Shanley, who had been prosecuted by Lynch and Rooney, said he did not expect such a trial to be brought on, and was unprepared for trial. He was ordered to be remanded until next assizes.
> *Hugh Kiernan [Tiernan], Patrick Malone,* and four others, were indicted for murders at Wildgoose Lodge. Being placed at the bar, Sergeant Joy addressed the Court, and said he was happy to say that the painful duty he had to perform was brought to a conclusion. He had prosecuted to conviction those who took an active part in the transactions of that horrible night. Others had put off their trials for the

present. He hoped to God the people of the country would take warning from the examples that had been made, and come to know the blessings attendant on a life of virtue and industry; that they should avoid all illegal associations and pursue honest employments, for their happiness and comfort. As for the six prisoners at the bar, although there was abundant proof of their guilt; yet as it appeared they had not being acting in the savage manner others had, whom it was necessary to make examples of, he would tell them, that that law, which they had set at defiance, would now humanely suffer them to be discharged, on entering into bail, to appear when called upon, which would entirely depend on the peaceable state of the county. *Gainor* who had been acquitted, is also to give bail. Samuel Pendleton, Esq. the Chief Magistrate, has a discretionary power given him, to take such bail as he approves of.

William Butler, Owen Gaynor and Michael Kearnan duly were brought to court again at the County Louth summer assizes held in Dundalk. The proceedings are taken here from the *Belfast News-Letter*, 7 July 1818 with some added details from *The Correspondent*, 8 July 1818 and the *Dundalk Examiner*, 5 and 12 November 1881:

The assizes for the county commenced at Dundalk on Friday [3 July 1818]. The following are the **Grand Jury**:
[Right Honourable John Foster, Foreman], Lord Jocelyn, T.B. Balfour, Esq., Mathew Fortescue Esq., Chichester Fortescue, Esq., Alexander Filgate, Esq., Nicholas Coddington, Esq., William P. Ruxton, Esq., Thomas Lee Norman, Esq., John McClintock, Esq., John Taafe, Esq., Henry Brabazon Esq., G. Sheils Eccleston, Esq., Mathew O'Reilly, Esq., Thomas W. Filgate, Esq., Philip Pendleton, Esq., Thomas Lloyd, Esq., Thomas Tisdall, Esq., William Filgate, Esq., C. Moore, Esq.
Baron McClelland addressed the Jury in a few words. He congratulated them, that he had the pleasure of addressing them in a place suited to the administration of justice (the new court-house) [thanks for the neatness and comfort of the court-house] that they were at length relieved from the inconvenience of the temporary one which they had so long occupied. He remarked with pleasure, that the calendar contained but very few prisoners in addition of those left over at the last assizes, and even those were for crimes of a trifling nature. He was happy to learn, that those disturbances which had so long disgraced their country had subsided; those deluded people had found that the arm of the law was too powerful for them to contend with, and he hoped that the peace of the county would not be again disturbed. His Lordship remarked that it was not necessary for him to say any thing to excite them to dispatch, as the burden they had to do was very trifling.
William Butler, Owen Gainor, and Michael Kiernan [Hugh Kiern or

Kiernan in the *Belfast News–Letter*], were indicted for the murder of Edward Lynch and family, at Wildgoose Lodge. They severally pleaded not guilty, and stated that they were ready for trial.

William Butler. After the panel was called over, previous to the jury being sworn, Counsellor Scriven addressed the Court on behalf of Butler. He said that Butler had stated in an affidavit (which he produced) that his agent, Mr John Wallace, was absent at the Armagh election; that he had no other person employed or instructed in his case; nor did he know it until it was too late – that he had been produced for trial at the summer assizes of 1817 – also at the spring assizes of 1818 – both times his agent attended, but his trial was put off; that at the Special Commission he was tried, and, the Jury not agreeing, was remanded to prison. He further stated, that as his case was a peculiar one, he hoped that his lordship would take it into consideration and permit his trial to stand over until the next assizes.

Here his Lordship desired the affidavit to be produced, which, when read, he remarked was defective in every particular upon which he could claim a delay of trial – not having stated therein when he was apprised of Mr Wallace not being able to attend, and in other respects so defective, that he could not postpone his trial.

Serjeant Joy rose, and said, that, as his Lordship had remarked, the prisoner at the bar had no legal claim to a delay of trial – yet as the leading Counsel for the Crown, he was invested, in this case, with a power which his Lordship had not – and, as the trial of this man seemed to be of much more importance than any of the preceding, it was his wish that every advantage should be allowed him – that though his document was so defective that he had not, in point of law, shewn just cause of delay [at the same time he must observe that Butler when asked by the clerk of the court if he was ready for his trial, said he was, and in his mind, it was the legal gentlemen who were concerned for him, that felt they had not a good defence, and took advantage of the absence of the agent to put off his trial.] For that very reason, and that it was in the power of the Crown to proceed to trial, he, on the part of the Crown, assented to his trial being postponed until next Assizes. He was then remanded to prison.

The following account is taken from the *Dundalk Examiner*, 12 November 1881:

— **Keiran [Michael Kearnan]** and **Owen Gainor** were indicted for the murder of Edward Lynch and his family by burning them with fire at Wildgoose Lodge on the 29th of Oct. 1816.

Mr Serjeant Joy opened the case in his usual style of impressive eloquence. He said that he could have wished when he last took his leave of the gentlemen of the jury, that it has been a final adieu, but circumstances prevented the fulfilment of that wish. The prisoners at the last commission were not ready for their trial, and on that ground had put it off. They were indicted for the murder of Edward Lynch and his family by fire on the 29th of October 1816. Gentlemen, if you had heard that a whole family had perished by fire, your hearts would have been wrung with sympathy, but if you had heard that it was not by accident, but that a band of ruffians assembled and destroyed them for revenge, you must have been struck with horror. He then proceeded to state the facts as they appeared afterwards in evidence.

Kieran [Kearnan] was the person who gave information to Mr Pendleton, respecting the burning of Wildgoose Lodge, and when brought forward last assizes, foreswore all he had sworn to in his examination.

The same chain of evidence which was brought forward on all the former trials, was followed up on this. **Gollogly** identified the prisoner Gainor.

During the examination of **Mr Pendleton**, he produced two separate informations, which he had taken from the informer, Murphy, in Trim: in the first information he finds the name of Keiran [Kearnan] – Gainor's is in the second.

James Corrigan, a policeman , proved that Kieran [Kearnan] had made an application to him in the month of August last, saying he had sent a message to Mr Pendleton, and had not got an answer, and said he was the boy could give him the information respecting Wildgoose Lodge; he never held out any threats or promises to him; was present when Mr Pendleton took the confession.

This witness was cross-examined by Kieran [Kearnan], with intent to show that he had held out inducements to him to make his confession. **Samuel Pendleton**, Esq., examined a second time. Produced the confession of Kieran [Kearnan], in which he gave information respecting the Wildgoose Lodge burning. In these he swore against Laurence B[o?]nd, Terence Marron, Kelly the Rake, Hugh McCabe, Pat Craven, Edward McQuillan and several others.

THE DEFENCE

Kieran [Kearnan] called **Henry Ogle**, a policeman and **Thomas Woods**, the under gaoler to prove that they had heard different conversations between Corrigan and him, wherein Corrigan held out inducements to him to give information. They swore positively they did not hear any such conversation.

Gainor attempted to prove an alibi but failed.

The learned **judge** in recapitulating the evidence gave a very clear and impartial charge to the jury.

The **jury** retired for a short time, and returned a verdict of guilty.

The prisoners had no counsel. Gainor cross-examined several witnesses with a great degree of shrewdness, and behaved during the trial and receiving sentence in a proper manner – but Kieran's [Kearnan's] behaviour was outrageous.

The miscreant Kieran [Kearnan] left the court bellowing forth the most horrid imprecations against his prosecutors. On his way to the gaol his blasphemies and curses struck the people who heard them with horror. **Owen Gainor**, and **Hugh Kiern**, or **Kiernan** [*recte* **Michael Kiernan**] were then set to the bar. They were found guilty at a late hour, on Friday evening, after a trial which lasted several hours. The prisoner Gainor appeared affected; but Kiernan [Kearnan] was hardened to a degree beyond conception. Whilst every one was melted by his Lordship's pathetic address, the wretch who was the object of their compassion uttered horrid imprecations upon his prosecutors. Of all the miscreants brought to trial for this diabolical crime, Kiernan [Kearnan] seemed to be the most hardened and wicked. He was taken back to the gaol, uttering execrations all the way. Gainer behaved with decency. They are to suffer on Monday.

It is to be remembered that the Chief Magistrate Samuel Pendleton in his chart states that Michael Kernan was arrested in County Monaghan on 12 March 1817 by himself, with his servant and five of the County Meath Constables. He was identified by the approver Patrick Murphy. He adds, 'had been admitted as an approver, when produced as a witness, denied his Confession, at the Gallows admitted his guilt'.[223] Pendleton states that Hugh Tiernan, brother of Michael Tiernan, hanged for the original burglary, was arrested in County Louth by the Louth Police on 22 December 1817, was identified by the approver Patrick Murphy and was admitted to bail on 4 July 1818. The *Belfast News-Letter* is mistaken in referring to Gainor's co-accused as 'Hugh Kiern and Kiernan'. Also admitted to bail on 4 July were George McQuillan, Edward McQuillan, Patrick Malone (2), James Laughran, and James Morris.

The *Dundalk Examiner* of 24 December 1881 reprinted the account of the further trial of William Butler at the Spring Assizes in Dundalk 6 March 1819 before the Rt Hon. Baron McClelland for the murder of Edward Lynch, his family, and others.

> At the opening of the court, Mr A.C. McCartney made a motion on behalf of the Crown to obtain leave to postpone till next assizes the trial of the prisoner William Butler. On a former trial the jury could not agree to a verdict, and Butler was again put forward for trial at the following Summer Assizes; but with the consent of the Crown, Butler was allowed to postpone his trial. Counsel, stated that at that time the Crown were prepared to go on with the trial, but now they were not, and he therefore asked that Butler's trial be postponed till next assizes. The prisoner (Butler) strongly opposed the application. He said he was in Prison for two years, and that was a long time and hoped that the Crown would proceed with his trial, without any further

postponements.
Ultimately it was agreed between Counsel on both sides that he be admitted to bail on his own recognizances in £100.

Butler disappears from the assizes' reports and it is presumed that the case was not pursued.

EXECUTION OF OWEN GAINOR AND MICHAEL KEARNAN

The execution of Owen Gainor and Michael Kearnan on Monday 6 July 1818, is reported in the *Belfast News-Letter*, 10 July 1818 (and in *The Correspondent* 11 July 1818):

> Monday last, about twelve o'clock, a temporary gallows was erected in front of the jail of Dundalk. At one o'clock the unhappy culprits attended by the Rev. Mr Duffy, Catholic Chaplain. Gainer declared he bore no malice to any person, and Kiernan [Kearnan] confessed his guilt, saying bad company brought him to his untimely grave. They were then launched into eternity; and after hanging thirty minutes, their bodies were cut down and sent for dissection to the County Hospital. It may be remembered that Kiernan [Kearnan] offered himself as an approver, and appeared anxious to give evidence; but, when brought forward in March last, he recanted, and showed it was a design to destroy the evidence of the other witnesses.

Henry McClintock wrote in his diary:

> **Monday 6th** Very fine day – after breakfast I walked into Dundalk & attended at the C. House – two men were hanged in this town for the burning of the Wild Goose lodge, eighteen men have now been hanged for that burning – Bessy & I dined at home – Louis and Marianne with us.

MURDER OF TERENCE CASSIDY

On the night of 3 July 1818, the first day of the Summer Assizes, Terence Cassidy was murdered. As is clear from a petition of his widow Mary Cassidy to the Lord Lieutenant, 2 March 1819, seeking assistance, he gave information about the 'Threshers'and on that account was murdered by them.[224] In 1816 Bryan Coleman, John Coleman, and Bryan Durneen, were indicted for administering oaths to Terence Cassidy but the case against them does not seem to have come to court. It is likely that Terence Cassidy gave information to the authorites and named them. Other documentation, as we have seen, more specifically states that he also gave information regarding the burning of Wildgoose Lodge. Although the comment is not made in any document or newspaper it may be that he was related to Ann Cassidy who died in the fire at Wildgoose Lodge. The following report is from the *Belfast News-Letter*, 10 July 1818. A few details are added from the reprinted account in the *Dundalk Examiner*, 5 November 1881:

> Murder – Friday night, a man named Cassidy who was returning from Dundalk to his own house, was most brutally murdered [near his own house]. It appeared on the Coroner's Inquest, from the testimony of John James Biggar [Esq.,], who was the only witness examined, that he was conversing with him about half after two o'clock on Friday evening. It was generally supposed by the lower order of the people in that county, that Cassidy had given private information respecting the burning of Wildgoose Lodge. He is reported to have advised Kieran, who was hung, and had got the mark of gun powder in his face, to give information, for that his face would betray him.

Mr Henry Brabazon, Dundalk, processed Mary Cassidy's petition in a letter, 4 September 1819, to Under-Secretary William Gregory:

> Understanding that government have granted an annuity of £15 per annum to the widow of Cassidy from the date of his murder which happened on the 5 or 6 July [*recte* 3-4] 1818 by which one year was due to her last July & she not having any means of getting it in Dublin & as she lives now near this town, if you would have the goodness to order that sum to be sent to me here, I will give it to her & get what voucher you require from her for it. She is a great object of charity having six [*recte* seven] young children & no means of providing for them. There has been £800 sent to Mr Hamilton to reward the four informers, Murphy, Gilroy, Gologly & Gubby, being a portion of the reward at first offered by this County, which leaves them no excuse for remaining longer in this country.[225]

Mary Cassidy's petition read:
To Charles Lord Chestwynd Earl Talbot Lord Lieutenant of Ireland.

> The humble petition of Mary Cassidy widow of the late Terence Cassidy of Ratheady, County of Louth humbly sheweth. That your poor petitioner's late husband was murdered on the road returning from Dundalk upon the 1st night of the last assizes. It being reported and understood in the country that he had given informations against the Threshers & that he was to give evidence at that assizes, and your petitioner having been on this account left a widow with 7 children, and having only received on this account one pound sterling, Petitioner begs to submit her case to you, and to hope your Excellency will have the enquiry made of the Grand Jury of the County of Louth, for the truth of what she states, which would have been sooner done but for her distress of mind & she and her whole family being in the fever since, for the truth of which she begs to refer your Excellency to Matw Fortescue Esqr of Stephenstown who sent a doctor to attend them – and that your Excellency would order some assistance to give to her and her distressed family for the loss of her husband she will as in duty bound ever pray. Mary x (her mark) Cassidy now resident in Dundalk.[226]

Subsequently a payment was made to Mary Cassidy on 9 September 1819.

In 1963 more of the Filgate papers referring to the burning of Wildgoose Lodge and its consequences came to light when F. C. Freeman of the Mint Stamp Co, of Dublin consulted a postal historian, the Reverend W. Edwin Davey, an English Presbyterian minister, regarding postal history material he had received from W.R. Filgate of Tallanstown, County Louth. Filgate then presented Davey with four boxes tied with red tape in which there was a bundle of newspaper cuttings, handbills, letters and a child's drawing, relating to Wildgoose Lodge, an indication that the Filgate family over some years had kept material on the tragedy. On examination of the documents, Davey became interested in the story of Wildgoose Lodge. The County Library, Dundalk, purchased a quantity of this material in an auction held by Ian Whyte in Dublin on 4 July 1992. The material also included a copy of a lecture that Davey once gave on the Wildgoose Lodge tragedy. Some of the letters in the bundle bear the hand-stamp 'Kilmainham Penny Post' and were written by Thomas Duffy a prisoner in Kilmainham Gaol. He alleges that he was one of the murderers of Terence Cassidy and, obviously in the hope of an early release or reprieve, purports to give details of the murder. His evidence is hardly credible but is an indication as to how far some prisoners would go to obtain release. The letter is marked 'Kilmainham Penny Post, 2 o'clock 8 Au. 1821'.

> Kilmainham 7th August 1821
> Sir,
> I take the liberty sending a short statement of my case to your honour concerning a murder that Was Committed on the Body of Terrance Cassidy of Mullacrew about three years and half last spring about two miles of Dundalk ... the ignominious party who murdered this Man I will tell your honour as soon as you come up or send me an answer ... the number 5 persons and myself ... I was getting no Rest night or Day so I hope it may not be amiss to submit a short statement to you honour in the case.
>
> Sir I am Yours
>
> Thomas Duffy
>
> from Dundalk
> Excuse me only for the man
> you sent letters is here to as you
> Promised to be up its to the
> Speaker Foster I would write

A second letter, signed by James Gilford, with no postal markings, obviously delivered to Filgate's brother by hand, enclosed Duffy's statement. It is dated 18 August 1821,

> My Dr. Sir,
> A man of the name of Duffy who is under sentence of transportation here, has requested that I wd. Forward the Enclosed to your brother Wm. And he wishes much if your Brother is in Town that he wd. take the trouble of calling on him as he has much useful Information to give him.

ENCLOSURE

> The Depisciton and Information of Thomas Duffy that Thomas Rooney, Peter Gilooly, Thomas Conlin, Patrick Magennis, Thomas Callaghan, Robert John Devine and me hid behind a bank until Cassedy came up the road wit a lofe of bread under his aram.
> Thomas Conlin struck him on the back of the head with a large stone. Thomas Rooney struck him with a Blunderbuss, and Thomas Callaghan struck him with a stick ... with Casedy crying murder and for mercy But ther was non for they niver left of Beating him untill that they utterly deprived him of life ... Rooney did not let eany of the party disper untill he swore each to be true and never to devilge the murder
> ...
> Thos. x (his mark) Duffy

In his lecture the Reverend W. Edwin Davey quotes more extensively from Thomas Duffy's deposition, which was among the Filgate papers he had acquired. This particular piece is not among the papers acquired by the County Library, Dundalk. Davey says he has put it into 'more intelligible English'. It is to be noted, of course, that the Thomas Rooney mentioned is not to be confused with the victim of the Wildgoose Loge burning who bore the same name.

> They intended to put an end to Cassidy which was put into execution on the same night in the following manner - that Tomas Rooney, Peter Gilooly, Thomas Conlin and me did all go behind a bank, but I most solemnly declare that I did not know that they ever intended to commit murder or I would not have gone with them. But as soon as this was communicated to me I objected and wished to go back, but Thomas Rooney did instantly present a blunderbuss to me and swear that if I did not go forward and be like the remainder of his comrades he would put or drive the contents of the blunderbuss through my body. I was compelled to go with them and remain behind a bush until joined by Patrick Magennis (who is at present in Dundalk gaol), Thomas Callaghan, and Robert John Devine. The first who came in sight was Patrick Magennis wo gave a signal by whistling and all immediately rushed out as Cassidy came up the road with a loaf of bread under his arm. Thomas Conlin struck him on the back of the head with a large stone and knocked him on his knees and then Thomas Rooney struck him on the head with the blunderbuss, and then Thomas Callaghan struck him several blows with a stick. Cassidy cried out Murder and begged for mercy but there was none, for Thomas Conlin, Thomas Rooney and Thomas Callaghan never left off beating him until they utterly deprived him of life. As soon as the murder was completed they counselled to leave him in the ditch but Rooney said that he must not but to leave him on the road. Rooney went forward to Cassidy, lifted up his head and put the loaf of bread under it. Rooney would not let any of the party disappear until he swore each and every one of them to be true and never divulge the murder, but Robert John Devine was not present at the murder but was left on the road that is nearer to Dundalk as a guard. Rooney and all went on to Knockbridge but I would not go any more with them, and a little way on the road to Dundalk from where the murder was committed the first man I met was Robert Devine who asked me 'was that business done' – that is to say, was Cassidy murdered. I answered that I did not know anything about the murder ...

This 'deposition' had been taken from Duffy by a fellow-prisoner in Kilmainham, as this letter to William Filgate on 12 August 1821 (postal markings: 'Kilmainham Penny Post 2 o'clock afn 14 Au 1821') explains:

Honord Sir,
I beg leave to trubel your honr with this hoping that your honr will pardon me for this. But from the seriousness of the case I consider it my duoety in the sight of both God and Man to aid and asist in being the instrumental means of bringing the prepretirators of shuch a most unhumain murder to Divin Justis as the person can neather read or write that has called on me to take down his de[cl]aration. The person is a Thomas Duffy a convict in Killminham that has called on me to take his depision [deposition] which I have done frome his own mouth word by word and he has signed his mark to the seam which remains in my custody untill your arivel hear - that Thomas Duffy having frome a serious consideration in his own mind that it is but just and right in the sight of God to bring to punishment the persons that was conserned and was auctealy [actually] the murders [murderers] of a Terrince Casidy that was murdered some time back near Knock Bridg on the Louth Road, that he was an eye-witness to all the murder and most solomly declears that he never did lift his hand aganst said Casidy but acconoweledgs [acknowledges] that he was sworn not to devulge [divulge] or make known the seam. But he having weghed the matter in his own mind and having comunicated the seam to me – a Thomas Kidd - in seam prison I at his request have taken down all ther neams and pleace of residence and where each and every one of them can be got at present being six in number and I have alsow taken down the maner how the plot was conspired and transacted and how the murder was completed and I consider that his testimony is right for I know each and every one of them frome others information in this goal of other depridations that some of the seam party has been guilty along with them makes it appear that they are the very murders [murderers] of Terence Casedy and should your honr approve comming to Dublin he will give your honr the information - for he says that he do not wish to give the information to eany other. He has alsow decleared in seame deposion [deposition] that Thomas Roony after Casedy was murdered that there was but one bad member moor [more] in the country and that was a Mr Willam Fillgeat a magestrate and that he would have him put out of the way the very first opportunity that is he would put a perioud to his existence for he was the means of hanngin [hanging] all the men for the Wild Goos bussnes [business]. Hond [Honoured] I have don only what I thought to be my duety before God and if you wish me to send you a copy of the deposion [deposition] or the origineal I will and I will hold the seame in my possion [possession] untill I hear frome you & I have the honr to be Sir your most obed[t]ent with and Respet

Thomas Kidd

Killminham Goal, Agust 12th 1821
N.B. I beg leave to apolege [apologise] that you will be under the necesity [necessity] of freeing eany letters you may send as I am not at present in ability (?).[227]

Two days later Kidd followed with another letter giving information on a threat to William Filgate's life and more information on outrages in County Louth.

Postal markings: 16 Au 1821.

> Honord Sir,
> I beg leav to transmit this Smal Epistal to you honr. It may be that your Honr will Be ofended with me for this trubl – but I hop that you will eagus [excuse] me as I have done the seam with the rest of your honrs trubl hear – for I am thankful your honr could not think ... your Life ... I have to ... a moment if you wear after hearing and heeding the Declartions and testomony of a Patrick Murry and a Thomas Duffy that is in this goal and I have taken down ther Declarítions and they have singed them and thy ar in my posseson and will remain untill I hear From you.
> I sent your hr a letter befor this but I had no answr – Patrick Murry has Declamd all he know abot Henrys robbery and from his testomy I am of opining you will be eabel to trace the murder of Patt Hnery – as alsow the Conspircy againt your selfe ... Duffys testomy as ... with regard to the ... Murry says that he can do more but he will not give any more untill he hears or sees you. Both Duffy and he has sinde ther marke and I hav singed my neam to them. I hav all ther neams and how evry thing was carried on and how both Fergus Hinry and the Consprid againt your life and a parte of Henries Robery and Terrins Casidys murdr. I will hold all untill I hear from your honr. I only considr this my duty in the sight of god and man to do as I am doing.
> I hav the honr to be sir your obeidnt with deffrinc and Respet
> Thomas Kidd
>
> Kilmainham goal
> Agst 14th 1821   N.B. ples to eagus the want of peapr

On 25 September 1821 John Crowe, governor of Dundalk Gaol wrote to William Filgate Esq at Lisrenny, Ardee, dismissing the evidence of Thomas Duffy. It would seem, perhaps through the instigation of William Filgate, that Duffy was transferred to Dundalk Prison to be confronted by Patrick Magennis who was about to be executed. Crowe interviewed 'McGuinness' in the prison and he denied that Duffy was even present at the murder.

> Sir,
> Agreeably to your desire I mentioned the circumstance to Mr Duffy who in my presence after the most serious caution to McGuinness opened the matter respecting the informations given by Duffy against him, and he most solem[n]ly and satisfactorily declared on a Book which he then, (and when we went into the cell) had in his hand, in the presence of that God whom he expected in a few days to meet that he

never seen or knew Duffy until in this prison after he was committed, and that all that he had known concerning the murder of Cassidy, & those concerned in it he mentioned without reserve; there was a man of the name of Lee who was of their party but he did not join them at the time; he feighned sick and remained behind, 'sure' said he 'I would not be such a man as to give the names of those whom I was not certain were concerned as I really would consider it a murder and the Blood of them on my head'; he also said he 'was positive Duffy was not at all at the murder for he was no party man, and a stranger living so far out of the Country, & that should there be any more they were all from the neighbourhood'; he stated that the only party men that went up with that batch of Transports were Drumgoole, Curtis, & young Hoye the latter of whom had declined it for some time back; from the solemn manner in which he gave this declaration to Mr Duffy, I am doubly satisfied that what I set forth to you yesterday was correct, and as McGuinness stated, that his being so positive Duffy was not there, that he was no party man and that none but party men were concerned.
I remain Sir with the most profound respect your ever faithful & obedient servant In Crowe

On 12 July 1821 (Postal Marking: 3 o'clock 18 Jy 1821) Pat Murray, a prisoner in Kilmainham Jail referred to by Thomas Kidd, wrote to William Filgate alleging a threat against Filgate and protesting the innocence of his brother who had been transported:

Kilmainham Gaol.

July the 12th, 1821.
Sir,
I Begg lave to inclose you those few lines Conserning leting your Honour now that the infermation I Gave you when my Brother was in Dundalk preson it being the best infermation ever you got Conserning the Safety of your own life for their is plans laid a gainst you that you are Not a ware of Altho you made little of it at that time and it is on that account that and you being the mains of Sending my Brother a broad that I did Not give you any infermation when I was in Dundalk for I did not blame you for sending my self but was willing to suffer any punishment for the crime I had committed but instead Sir I am not so Dul of understanding but I know that my infermation is of now hurt to any Person while I am here or it is Not on that account I am Going to Give you any infermation but to let your Honour now that you transported my brother innocent and besides to let you Now these people that fixed many a plan to take your life and the same people in the country yet that Committed the Crime that my brother was sent a broad for and not Crime is lone but several others crimes. Sir I wish to let your Honour now that I have a great dale more to tell you when I

have the opportunity of talking to your Honour that I dont wish to minshin any thing about to any person that rites for me for I never rote any my self but sir if you think it worth while to Come here I will give you the hole infermation about all I now and if you wish to find my infermation out in being true rite to George Henry Eqr. in the parrish of Dunmine and he will give you some infermation about Hugh Sherrey Robery and then you can now whether I am rite in that part or not. Sir you need not wonder at me being dark against you for at the time that Robert Nevil went and sarched the house when my Father and Brother was in Dundalk gaol when he cud get nothing anlawful he went and brought some yarn that my poor old mother spoon and when he seen that the Feagans would have Nothing to do with it he went and left it and said you sir would not allow him to give it and sir he sold it since as I am told.
Patt Murry Convict

12
Rewards and Payments

Reference has already been made to the various memorials to the Lord Lieutenant seeking the rewards that had been offered for information leading to the apprehending of people involved in the burning and murders at Wildgoose Lodge. Peel on a number of occasions sought Pendleton's direction in assessing rewards. Pendleton judged in favour of John Armstrong over Constable Wright in the apprehending of Thomas Gubby. In an early letter of 29 July 1817 to Peel he advised no payment for the arrest of Gubby as he then regarded his confession as dangerous and useless.

A list was furnished to Pendleton in September 1817 asking his opinion regarding payments of rewards. The list and Pendleton's reply are as follows:

> **George Payne**. C. Chief Constable 3d Division: prays £200 for apprehending Pat Divan. Certificate of Magistrates of 3d Division.
> **William Leary**: prays £200 for apprehending Pat Divan. Henry Brabazon's letter. Leary's affidavit.
> **John Burke**: apprehending Divan, prays £200. His affidavit.
> **John Shore**, postmaster of Navan: prays £200 for apprehending Bernard McIlroy [Gilroy]. Letter of G.D. Hamilton as to belief.
> **John Shore**, postmaster of Navan: prays £100.
> **George Wright**, Sub-Constable, Co. Tyrone: prays part of reward for apprehending Thomas Gubby. Ld Caledon gives a good character. Pendleton's letter.
> **William Smart**, Gaoler of Trim: prays £20 for useful information, reward offered in the *Hue & Cry*. A. H. Pollok's certificate.
> **John Armstrong**, chief constable, Drogheda: prays £200 apprehending Thomas Gubby. Certificate from John Foster, Pendleton, R. Smith, G. D. Hamilton.
> **Thomas Hunter & others** [police constables at Corcreaghy]: prays benefit of reward in such proportions etc. for apprehending 12 persons.

Letter of Samuel Pendleton to William Gregory, 23 September 1817, assessing payment of rewards.

> Sir
> In obedience to your direction I have given the best consideration I am capable of, to the subject of the several claims made under his Excellency's proclamation of the 18th of Novr and conceive that under

it *three rewards each of £200* have become fairly and justly payable - one for the apprehension of *Devan* who was executed; one for Bernard *Gilroy,* and one for Pat *Clarke,* who being both principals 'concerned in' the same offence, were admitted approvers, and were the essential witnesses, by whose testimony Devan was convicted.

For the first of these George Payne and Wm Leary are claimants. From my own knowledge of the circumstances I am obliged to say, that the facts are not correctly stated in the memorial of the *former.* It was not 'by any diligent search made by him through the City of Dublin' that the place of Devan's employ was discovered. The truth on the contrary is, that (having *previously fully ascertained both where he worked and where he lodged*) I had sent two of my own men who knew his person to Dublin, to have him and another person taken, and came myself the day after principally for the same purpose. I gave my warrant to *Payne,* that his being a known city peace officer might prevent any attempt at rescue, when he should be arrested, and I directed him to be at the Custom House Docks shortly before the labourers there would quit work, where Devan would be surely found, and identified by my men. This was all done with correctness, and precision, but I do not conceive that Payne being the bearer of the warrant, or Leary the person who made the actual capture, (as stated in his memorial, and confirmed by his, and J. Burke's affidavits) should entitle *either* of them *exclusively* to this reward. I would therefore humbly suggest, that as it appears the *James's St. and Louth* police equally participated in the arrest, (and nothing beyond the ordinary exercise of their duty, being done by any, so as to give a *special* claim) that the sum of £100, being the moiety of the reward be given to each, to be distributed in such manner as the respective Magistrates of these establishments shall think best.

I consider that *Mr John Armstrong* for having well concerted and *Mr John Shore* for having effected the *arrest of B. Gilroy,* are *each entitled to a moiety of £200 for his apprehension.*

I am also of the opinion that *Thomas Hunter, Francis Davis, William Leary, John Robinson, Robert Hunter and Joseph Sillery are entitled to equal proportions of the reward of £200 for the apprehension of Patrick Clarke.*

I do not conceive that any reward can yet with propriety be claimed for apprehending Thomas Gubby. - Wright (the Tyrone constable) is misinformed as to having contributed by his testimony to the conviction of any persons. He [Thomas Gubby] has neither been used, nor *yet* admitted as an approver. It has not yet *judiciously appeared* that he was 'concerned' in the crime, neither is it certain that any publick advantage will *ever* be derived from his confession.

As to the claim of Mr Wm Smart to the reward of £20 offered by the Head Police Officer, for having procured the information of Pat. Murphy, which (as he says) led to the conviction of Devan, I consider it to be entirely unfounded. Supposing the certificate of Mr A. Pollock to be correct, which I do not conceive it is, no part of the information so given by Murphy either directly or indirectly contributed to the conviction of Devan. For my accuracy in this, I beg to refer (if necessary) to Mr Baron McClelland, and the Solr General.[228]

In March 1819, in a climate of more tranquil times, moves were made by local gentry to remove the 'Peace establishment', which had been put in place under the Peace Preservation Act and parallel with the Insurrection Act. Obviously the expense of maintaining it was weighing heavily on them. Since peace reigned it was also thought to be an appropriate time to pay out the rewards offered. On 19 March John Foster at Collon wrote to Chichester Fortescue suggesting that a meeting of magistrates should be held to consider 'the state of the country as to any necessity of the police establishment being continued longer in the four proclaimed Baronies' and also to ascertain 'the claims of rewards offered by us in respect to the late horrid murders at Wild Goose Lodge and of immediately collecting the proportion of each subscription necessary for the payment'.[229] There followed an exchange of letters[230] between Fortescue and Foster as to who should call the meeting, Fortescue suggesting the Clerk of the Peace in a letter of 24 March 1819. Foster replied on 26 March: 'I never have been brought to consider the Clerk of the Peace as any other than an officer of the sessions and only to act where they were concerned, nor do I recollect as instance of his being called upon to convene a meeting, except under the Insurrection Act, where the Law made him an instrument by express enactment and that Law is now expired'. Accordingly, having taken for granted that there was a general desire for the meeting he had put an advertisement in the *Drogheda Journal* fixing the 5th April as a date for it. Foster duly made out a list of names of 'Magistrates summoned by post for C. Bellingham on Monday April 5th 1819'. On 2 April, Neale MacNeale at Faughart wrote saying that he could not attend the meeting due to illness but he recommended that the Barony of Lower Dundalk be 'relieved from the enormous expense of a Police establishment'.[231]

The meeting addressed the two matters of the ending of the 'Police establishment' and the rewards. A memorial was drawn up and signed by 19 magistrates.

> *To his Excellency The Lord Lieutenant* –
> The Memorial of the undersigned magistrates of the County of Louth assembled at Castle Bellingham on Monday the 5th of April 1819 –
> Sheweth
> That the four Baronies of this County which have been in a state of

disturbance are to the best of their judgement & observation now restored to peace & good order, and they therefore pray his Excellency to take into his consideration the present state of those Baronies viz. Ardee, Louth, & Upper & Lower Dundalk & to proclaim their restoration to peace & good order, if His Excellency shall in his wisdom think proper so to do, which is submitted with great respect
Louth, Matthew Fortescue, William Filgate, Gervais Tinley, James Forde, George Forster, Thomas Fitzgerald, Faithful Fortescue, T. W. Fortescue, James Wright, John Foster, T. S. Skeffington, Edward Bellew, B. Balfour, Chichester Fortescue, John McClintock, Samuel Little, H. Brabazon, R. Thompson.[232]

At the 5th of April meeting a resolution was agreed and signed by John Foster, chairman, that Samuel Pendleton, George Forster, Revd Gervais Tinley, Henry Brabazon, James Ford, John Stratton and Thomas Filgate 'be appointed a committee to ascertain the amount of the sums subscribed for procuring information etc respecting the late horrid murders at Reaghstown, to examine into the demands upon those subscriptions & to call in such a percentage of them as may be necessary to discharge them & to make their report to the magistrates at the end of Quarter Sessions'.[233] On the same day Foster sent a copy of this resolution to Samuel Pendleton with an instruction.

I am desired to inform you that it is their wish that all money due to Mr Charles Evans for printing, advertizing etc be in the first instance ascertained & reported for payment.
That they have further agreed that the sum of 250£ shall be laid out in the purchase of an annuity for Alice Rispin for her life from some of the Insurance companies to be vested in Trustees for her use & that Gubby, Gilroy, Murphy & Gallogley are each entitled to the Reward of 200£ offered by them in Nov. 1816.[234]

The payment to George Evans was probably for the account from the *Drogheda Journal* for £221 2s. 8d in respect of the publication of requisitions, resolutions *etc* of the magistrates.

Foster must have written to the Under-Secretary William Gregory at Dublin Castle seeking a meeting with the Lord Lieutenant to pursue the matter since Gregory wrote to him on 7 April 1819 informing him that the Lord Lieutenant was unwell but would be pleased to receive Foster when he had recovered. The question of withdrawing the police would be considered, he wrote, when next the Lord Lieutenant was in Council.[235]

On 17 August 1819 the Committee appointed on 5 April 1819 wrote to Viscount Jocelyn suggesting August the 25th as an appropriate date for the meeting to authorise the payment of the reward money.[236] Jocelyn then wrote to Foster suggesting Monday 23rd August as a more convenient date.[237] The magistrates meeting at Castle Bellingham on that day resolved that the rewards of £200 each should be paid to the informers, and that those in arrear with their subscriptions to the reward money should be circularised and asked to pay immediately.[238]

I reproduce here also a copy of a printed page of the proceedings of a committee appointed by Louth magistrates to reward persons giving information respecting the burning of Wildgoose Lodge. It was printed by Parks, Printer, Dundalk. Rewarded were the approvers Gilroy, Gollogly, Gubby and Murphy, the widow Alice Rispin, crown witness and mother of the servant boy who lost his life in the fire and one Halfpenny.

To the Magistrates of the County of Louth

> We the undersigned being the Committee appointed at your Meeting, at Castlebellingham, on the 5th April 1819, for the purpose of collecting a sufficient Sum from the Subscription, entered into, in order to Reward Persons, giving information respecting the Burning of Wildgoose Lodge, think it necessary to report their proceedings
>
> Your Committee have by applications to the several Subscribers, raised the Sum of £1064 18s. 0^1/$_2$d. being Sixty per Cent. on the original Subscription of such Individuals as have contributed to the above Sum. Several of the original Subscribers have not, however, paid their proportions; and your Committee are of opinion, there is little or no hope of being able to raise any more Money. A list of the defaulters shall, nevertheless, be laid before you, at the next Meeting you may choose to appoint for the consideration of the state of the Wildgoose Lodge Funds.
>
> Your Treasurer has, by order, made Payments from this Fund, to the amount of £1064 1s. 4^1/$_2$d, and a Balance of £178 16s. 8d. now remains in his Hands, to be disposed of as you may think most fit. But your Committee deem it right to inform you, that besides the four Prosecutors, viz. GILROY, GOLLOGLY, GUBBY, and MURPHY, to whom a sum of £800, has been paid, three other persons have made applications for remuneration, from this Fund, viz. the Widow of TERENCE CASSIDY, a woman Named ALICE RISPEN, and a Man of the name of HALPENNY

TO THE
MAGISTRATES
OF THE
County of Louth.

WE the undersigned being the Committee appointed at your Meeting, at Castlebellingham, on the 5th April, 1819, for the purpose of collecting a sufficient Sum from the Subscription, entered into, in order to Reward Persons, giving information respecting the Burning of Wildgoose Lodge, think it necessary to report their proceedings.

Your Committee have by applications to the several Subscribers, raised the Sum of £1242 18s. 0½d. being Sixty per Cent. on the original Subscription of such Individuals as have contributed to the above Sum. Several of the original Subscribers have not, however, paid their proportions; and your Committee are of opinion, there is little or no hope of being able to raise any more Money. A list of the defaulters shall, nevertheless, be laid before you, at the next Meeting you may choose to appoint for the consideration of the state of the Wildgoose Lodge Funds.

Your Treasurer has, by order, made Payments, from this Fund, to the amount of £1064 1s. 4½d. and a Balance of £178 16s. 8d. now remains in his Hands, to be disposed of as you may think most fit. But your Committee deem it right to inform you, that besides the four Prosecutors, viz. GILROY, GOLLOGLY, GUBBY, and MURPHY, to whom a Sum of £800, has been paid, three other persons have made applications for remuneration, from this Fund, viz. the Widow of TERENCE CASSIDY, a Woman Named ALICE RISPEN, and a Man of the name of HALFPENNY.

Your Committee beg leave to suggest, that as the 7th February next is appointed for holding a Sessions, for the investigation of Presentments, it probably might prove convenient to enter into the business of the Wildgoose Lodge Fund, on that Day, when your Treasurer will be ready to lay before you a detailed account of his Receipts and Payments.

HENRY BRABAZON.
GEORGE FORSTER.
JAMES FORDE. } Committee.
GERVAIS TINLEY.
JOHN STRATON.

PARKS, PRINTER, DUNDALK.

> Your Committee beg leave to suggest, that as the 7th February next is appointed for holding a Sessions, for the investigation of Presentments, it probably might prove convenient to enter into the business of the Wildgoose Lodge Fund, on that Day, when your Treasurer will be ready to lay before you a detailed account of his Receipts and Payments Henry Brabazon, George Forster, James Forde, Gervais Tinley, John Straton. Committee.[239]

Regarding the fate of the informers, Patrick Murphy, Thomas Gubby and Peter Gollogly, it is likely that they went abroad for safety. This seems to have been the case at least with Patrick Murphy. He wrote to John Foster on 14 August 1819 asking for payment of his reward:

> Sir, I beg your pardon for sending to you but I am detained this week back but Mr Pentland told mee you were to give mee the 100 pound that was sent to mee and Mr Hambleton [Hamilton] told mee to acquaint your honor and you would not delay and I hope your honor will bee so good as to rite to Mr Hambleton [Hamilton] when I can get it for while I stop here I am at great expens. Kind Sir my passage is paid this week past and I don't know the minute the ship will seal. I hope sir you will be so good as to consider us and send to me by return of post. Direct to Mr Hambleton [Hamilton], Sacfell [Sackville] St. I remain with respect your humble servant. Patt Murphy.[240]

Foster wrote from Collon on 23 August to Robert Hamilton enclosing a copy of the order for £800 to Messrs Gordon and Hamilton, Crown Solicitors, made at the Magistrates' meeting, and asking him to pay the informers – 'Two of the men, Gubby & Murphy, desired their money might be paid to you. I am sure you will excuse our troubling you with the money for the other two'.[241] On 28 August Thomas Gubby and Peter Gologly wrote to Foster from Dublin informing him that Stratton had not yet sent the money to Hamilton: 'We most humbly take the liberty of making the present application and most sincerely returning your honour our sincerest thanks for your former trouble in regard of us – we understand that your honour has sent the order to Mr Hamilton to pay us £200 cash, but Mr Stratton has not sent the money as directed in your honour's order – and under said circumstances we are exposed to danger in detaining so long in the City'.[242]

A number of letters extant among the Filgate papers now in

the Public Records Office of Northern Ireland relate some of the further misfortunes of Alice Rispin. On 1 June 1818 she wrote to William Filgate, Lisrenny, informing him of the detention of another son, John Hill, in Monaghan Jail and asking Filgate to 'interfere for him and use your interest' on his behalf.[243] There are two letters from John Hill from the prison to his mother[244]: 2 June 1816 requesting his mother to have him freed by obtaining references from either Justices of the Peace or Gentlemen and sending them to him through his jailer John Short; 10 June 1816 stating that a few lines from Mr Filgate to Mr Dacre Hamilton [?] on his behalf might free him and informing her that threats had been made by the 'Inspector over the Jail' to ask the Judge to deal harshly with him if he was not freed before his trial came up.

Alice Rispin further wrote to Filgate on 15 March 1820 regarding the state of her finances.[245] As late as 12 March 1825 Lord Oriel, Collon, wrote a letter to Filgate enclosing a letter from Alice Rispin concerning her allowance [letter not now attached].[246]

Other letters in the Filgate papers brought to light in 1963 give further details of her living in Dublin and Kildare, her sense of danger and her continual seeking of sustenance funds.[247] A letter, with no postal markings (delivered then by hand) addressed to Alexander Mangin Esqre, Dublin (endorsed 'This order I never received'.), reads:

> My Dr. Sir,
> At the last meeting at the Castle on the business of Mrs. Rispen's demand it was agreed that she should get £15 in advance in addition to the quarterly payment of £3. 15. 0. Perhaps you would be so good as to give her the fifteen pounds and get rid of her Importunities. She calls here daily.
> Yours most faithfully
> Robert Hamilton
> 21st Sept. 1819
> Sackville Street

Apparently Alice Rispin did not receive the fifteen pounds because the following March she pleads again for help:

> Postal marking: 15 Mr 1820.
> Dear Sir,
> On the first Monday in August 1819 a settlement took place between

me and Mr Pentleton [and] Robert Hamilton Esqr. Sackville Street, Dublin. Mr Pentleton [Pendleton] promised me Thirty Pounds p. annum and help from the County of Louth to put me in a way of doing. Mr Cafferry was calld and ordered to provide me in safe and secure lodgeings … accordingly I had lodgeings at Island Bridge County of Dublin but left in care of no Person but the Almighty. I then went to Mr John Taylor in the Castle of Dublin and Recd. Three pounds Fifteen shillings and was told that was Goverment Money and that I was to get it quarterly in future and Fifteen pounds p. annum from the County of Louth … also the state of the times and the distress of my Family obliged me to quit Island Bridge and seek a Retrate in Kildare and I remaind there till the next quarters money came due. I went to make my markets and saw my danger in that Place and came to Dublin. Surcumstanced as I am I throw my Self and my Poor Family afairs intirely upon the worthy Gentlemen of my own County as my whose dependance …

Dear Sir – I expect to receive an answer in a few days and Remain with the most Profound Respect.

     your very humble servant
     Alias Rispin

Address for me at Dublin
Richard Filgate Esqr.
March the 15th 1820

Another letter in 1825 records once again further demands of Alice Rispin per Lord Oriel. There is no cover to the letter. It is endorsed 'Wildgoose Lodge, Lord Oriel, Recd. 12th Novr. 1825'.

Collon

Nov. 12 1825
My Dear Filgate,
I enclose letter about Alice Rispen and will trouble you for information about the statement in the letter, which if I recollect aright, does not state the truth. Tell me what allowance she got from our Subscription. I think she neither did nor could get any from the Gr. Jury as she asserts.

     Ever yours most truly
     Oriel
     Will. Filgate Esqr.

PAYMENT BOOKS

Two payment books (CO-904-4 and CO-904-5) in the Public Record Office, Kew Gardens, London, contain entries relevant to the Wildgoose Lodge story:

1816

Feb 17 Lennox Bigger Esq, Dundalk, for Thos & Pat. Kirk who defended their house £20

May 25 Lennox Bigger Esq, Dundalk, reimbursement of expenses for information, search for offenders etc : £100

July 30 Saml Pendleton Esqr, Co. Magistrate, Co. Louth, subsistence of informer: £19-2-6.

Do for information and guides: £7-10

Oct 22 S. Pendleton Esqr. for Lynch (Co. Louth), half year to 10 October: £7-10

1817

Feb 19 Lennox Bigger Esq, Dundalk, for information: £30

April 24 J. Armstrong, C. Constable, Drogheda, for bringing up Thomas Gubbey: £3-8

April 28 Rev. M. Wainwright, Trim, clothes for Gallagly & Murphy: £4

June 2 Rev. Mr Wainwright, Trim, for Murphy & Galloghly, subsistence to 31 May: £6-14

July 7 Mr Wainwright, Trim, for Murphy & Gallagly. Subsistence to: £4-14

Aug. 21 Rev. Mr Wainwright, Gallagher [sic] & Murphy's subsistence: £5-6

Sept 4 Mr Farrel, police officer, expense of Murphy & Gallagher from Trim: £9-17-2 ?

Oct. 15 Dunn for Murphy's wife: £1

1818

Jan. 16 Mr Pendleton for Rev. Mr Duffy, R C Chaplain, Dundalk Gaol: £50

Feby 20 Mr Dunn of Kilmainham, on acct of conveying Murphy to Dundalk: £15

March 21 Mr Dunn of Kilmainham, Ditto for subsistence of Gallagly's & Murphy's wives to same period (15 March): £5-12

April 2 Mr Farrell, peace officer for subsistence of Murphy (Wild Goose Lodge): £1-4-5

May 1 Mr Dunn for Gallogly's wife, (Ditto) subsistence (from 16 March to 26 April) same period: £4-4-.

May 12 Dunn of Kilmainham for conveying Murphy & Gilloghly, approvers, to Naas Gaol: £5

June 24 Dunn for Murphy & Gillogley's wives (from 27th April to 31 May): £3-10

July 15 G. Dunn Ditto for subsistence of Gilloghly's & Murphy's wives from 25 May to 12 July: £4-18

Aug. 22 Gaoler of Trim for subsistence of Murphy & Gollogly from 13 May to 30th June: £10-14

Sept. 7 G. Dunn for Murphy & Gollogly wives subst (for do) from 13 July to 14 Aug.: £3-10

Sept. 11 G. Dunn for sub. Of Murphy & Gillogly's wives: £2-2
Oct. 8 G. Dunn for s. of M.'s & Gillogley's wives: £2-8
Novr. 12 Ditto for s. o Murphy and Gilloghly's wives from 1 to 31 Octr: £3-2
Dec. 8 G. Dunn for sub. of G. & M. wives, 1st to 30 Nov.: £3

1819

Jan. 2 Geo. Dunn of Kilmainham (for attendant on) for subsistence of Murphy & Gillogly's wives Dr at Is. per day: £3-2
Feby 3 Geo. Dunn for Gillogly's & Murphy's wives Ditto: £3-2
Feby 3 Moorehead, Gaoler, Naas for subsistence of Murphy from 23 Aug. to 7 Feb.: £13-13
March 2 G. Dunne for G's & M's wives. Subsistence in Feb.: £2-16
April 2 G. Dunn Subs for G's & M's wives in March: £3-2
May 10 S. Pendleton Esqre for the Revd Mr Duffy R C Chaplain, Dundalk Gaol: £50
May 31 G. Dunne S. of G & My's wives in May: £3-2
July 10 G. Dunn for G & M's wives in June: £3-11-11
July 19 Keeper of Gaol at Naas for subs of Murphy to 25 July: £13-13
July 20 Moorehead, Gaoler at Naas, expence of conveying Murphy to Kilmainham: £2-14-9
Aug. 16 G. Dunne subs. Gallogly & Murphy's wives to 2 Aug.: £4-5
Aug. 17 Honble Col. Le Poer Trench, expence of sending Judith Lynch home from New Brunswick: £28-7-8.
Aug. 17 Alice Rispin. Witness in the case of the Burning at Wild Goose Lodge 1 Q[uarte]r to 1 Octr.: £3-15
Sept. 9 Widow Cassidy. Witness per Mr Brabazon, an year's advance from 1 July 1819. (Wild Goose Lodge): £15
Novr. 3 Alice Rispin 1 Qr allowance to Ist Jan.: £3 –15

1820

Novr 1 Alice Rispin 1 Quarter to 1st Jan.: £3-15

1821

May 4 Alice Rispin 1 Qr to 1 July: £3-15
Nov. 3 Alice Rispin 1 Qr to 1 Jan. 1822: £3 15.

The Account Book C O 904 5 shows similar but irregular payments quarterly to Alice Rispin up to 1827. That for 3 November 1824 was paid per R. Warburton Esq.

13
The Gibbets

Twelve of those executed for the burning of Wildgoose Lodge were gibbeted. This measure was intended to strike terror into local inhabitants and act as a deterrent. Anton of the 42nd Foot regiment, author of *Retrospect of a Military Life*, who seems to have acted as a guard at the gibbets, comments on them in his narrative:

> The regiment having received the route in June 1818 for Dundalk, the detachments were all ordered in to Armagh whence they proceeded to occupy their new quarters.
> Dundalk is the assize or chief town of the county of Louth and here the trial of a number of criminals concerned in the burning of Wildgoose Lodge took place and for which eleven (recte twelve) unhappy wretches suffered death and were afterwards suspended on gibbets. Detachments were posted at the respective places to prevent any of their criminal associates from consigning the bodies to the grave.
> How far the sentence of the law in thus exposing the carcases of criminals may have the intended effect of deterring others from attempting the like crimes, I shall leave for the consideration of those who are more deeply versed than myself in the workings of the human mind. I am led to think, however, that where the criminals form only the operative part of an extensive body it might be better to let their bones lie hid in the dust with their crimes than to excite public feeling in favour of sorrowing relations and oath-bound associates who register the criminals in the calendar of martyrs and saints. When the condemned has been guilty of some crime the deliberate act of individual malice and wickedness the case differs for most likely no friend will indulge in sympathizing for him and his bones may get leave to bleach in the wind without exciting any other feeling than that of contempt for the criminal and horror at the crime for which he suffered.

The Grand Jury Presentment, General Assizes, 1818, record the cost of erecting the gallows and gibbets and 'an Execution and Fees issued against said Matthew O'Reilly':

> To Alex. Shekleton for erecting gallows, gibbets etc £283 – 11 – 5.
> To Matthew O'Reilly, Esq. and Patrick Halfpenny, inhabitants of the parish of Phillipstown, in the barony of Ardee. ... being the amount of an Execution and Fees issued against said Matthew O'Reilly, Esq. one of the said inhabitants; for damages sustained by said parish, in consequence of the burning of the house of Townley Patten Filgate,

situate at Wild Goose Lodge, in the parish aforesaid, and recovered by Action at suit of Townley Patten Filgate, against the aforesaid Matthew O'Reilly; pursuant to Acts (23 and 24 Geo. 3, Chap 29, Sec. 7, 10 and 12) for the more effectually punishing persons who shall obstruct the freedom of the Corn Trade &c £125-16-8'.[248]

Henry McClintock in his diary mentions a visit to three of the gibbets in October 1818:

> **Sunday 11th** Morng fine – day wet – Bessy, Louis, Marianne, Louisa & I went to church – then Bessy & I rode (she on Ireland & I on a borrowed horse of Mr Brown's) to Hackballs Cross & saw three gibbets there of men executed for the burning of Wild Goose Lodge – we got wet to the skin & rode there & home again in under an hour and a half – Surgeon Noble & his son Wm. dined with us.

The gibbets were taken down in 1819. A few documents record the event.

John Foster to William Gregory. Collon. 5 April 1819:

> I have the honor of enclosing a Memorial from the Magistrates of Louth assembled at Castlebellingham this day which they request you will have the goodness to lay before his Excellency the Lord Lieutenant.
> Allow me also to mention their general wish that before the Police be withdrawn the bodies on the several gibbets may under his Excellency's authority be taken down & buried in the Gaol Yard, & the gibbets removed. It is their earnest hope that they have remained sufficient time to impress on the people the ready & determined resolution of the Magistrates to apply with energy, the powerful arm of the Law - to check and put down any attempt tending to disturb the peace and tranquility of their County and to bring to severe justice the promoters and perpetrators of any more attempts.
>
> To His Excellency the Lord Lieutenant etc, etc.
> The memorial of the undersigned Magistrates of the County of Louth assembled at Castle Bellingham on Monday the 5th of April 1819.
> Sheweth that the four Baronies of this County which have been in a state of disturbance are to the best of their judgment & observation now restored to peace and good order, and they therefore pray His Excellency to take into his consideration the present state of those Baronies viz. Ardee, Louth & Upper & Lower Dundalk, & to proclaim their restoration to peace & good order if his Excellency shall in his wisdom think proper so to do. Which is submitted with great respect. Louth, Mattw. Fortescue, Will. Filgate, Ger. Tinley, James Forde, George Forster, Tho. Fitzgerald, Faith. Fortescue, F. W. Fortescue, Jos. Wright, John Foster, M. [T.H.]. Skeffington, Edw. Bellew, B. Balfour, Chi. Fortescue, John McClintock, Sam. Little, H. Brabazon, R. Thompson.[249]

Joseph Holmes, Under Sheriff of the County Louth. Dundalk. 12 April 1819:

> I have to acknowledge the receipt of the order of the Lord Lieutenant in respect to the taking down of the bodies on the several Gibbets within this County and the removal of the same, and shall have such duly executed in pursuance thereof.[250]

Wildgoose Lodge itself fell into ruin. It is unlikely that it was inhabited again. The unreliable Carleton says in his autobiography that when Fr Edward McArdle, Kilanny, related the story of the Wildgoose Lodge tragedy to him: 'I was so completely absorbed by the interest it excited, that I went to the very low elevation on which the house stood, and observed the scenery about it. The house had been rebuilt and was inhabited by a decent and very civil family, named Cassidy, if my memory does not fail me'.[251] The owner, Townley Patten Filgate, refers to its fate a few times in his farm diary:

> Monday, 1 June 1818. I went to Drogheda and had an inquest before the sheriff to ascertain my loss at Wild Goose Lodge and had a finding for £90. I also took administration to Lynchey.
> Tuesday, 26 January 1819. The old kitchen grate was taken out and given over to farm work. The kitchen grate saved from Wildgoose Lodge put in its place.[252]

14
Conclusion

Inevitably the Reaghstown murders reverberated for generations in the parishes of Tallanstown, Louth and Ardee and indeed in all County Louth. H. G. Tempest says in his *Gossiping Guide to Louth* (1952), 'Continuing on the road towards Knock Abbey we pass a moderate hill on the right, the scene of the burning of the "Wild Goose Lodge" over the heads of its occupants on 30th October, 1816 – a lurid memory of crime in County Louth to this day ... The crime is still remembered with horror, as also is the creaking on windy nights of the gallows at Reaghstown Chapel and elsewhere on which the corpses of the murderers and those of some believed to be innocent were left to decay'.[253] The story inevitably drifted into myth and folklore, much of it centred on the fate of two of the informers. The lore is not to be trusted but it is intriguing. Mathews records a traditional account of the deaths of Patrick Clarke and Bernard McElroy. Mc Elroy, he says, without evidence, came from Forkhill.

> The greatest consternation prevailed througout the country when it was known that Clarke had become an informer, as it was certain he could hang hundreds by his evidence. However, immediately after Devan's execution Clarke became ill of the yellow fever, which then prevailed to a fearful extent, and was sent to the large store opposite the Steampacket Quay (known at that time as Taylor's store), where such patients were treated, and from here he disappeared in the most mysterious manner. Some say he was taken over in a boat to Cooley; be that as it may, to the great joy and satisfaction of many he was never afterwards heard of. He never informed on any man but Devan. ...
> There are various rumours as to the death the notorious McElroy got. But the correct one is, that he was taken out of a wakehouse, mid-way between Ballymahon and the town of Longford, and brought into a field where a number of young horses were grazing. He was tied to two of the horses, which were hunted off in different directions, and thus the unfortunate wretch was torn limb from limb. A number of men were arrested but there being no evidence against them whatever they were discharged. McElroy's identity in the wakehouse was discovered by a carman from Dundalk, who was going with a puncheon of whiskey from the Dundalk Distillery to the town of Boyle, in the County Roscommon, and when about five miles from Longford

the cart got into a rut which was in the road; seeing the light in the house, he went in for help, and there beheld the informer whom he knew well. He called out a few of the men and told them who McElroy really was. "Well", said they, "he'll never hang another man". They took him out to assist the carman, and then gave him the death as they said "that every stag should get" '. [254]

In 1964 and 1965 Michael J. Murphy, collector of folklore for Roinn Bhéaloideas Éireann, University College, Dublin, recorded a number of tales regarding Devan, the origin of the Wildgoose murders, and names and fate of 'stags' or informers.[255] Annie Lynch, his principal informant and native of the district, told him ghostly stories of the suicide of 'Little Father McCann' (and she thinks there were two priests who committed suicide and were connected with the Wildgoose Lodge episode, both perhaps called McCann). There is no evidence whatsoever that Fr McCann committed suicide but perhaps the story indicates that the horror and tragedy affected his health and personality. Another tradition recorded by Michael J. Murphy from a McCoy of Creggan, South Amagh, maintained that the informer McElroy came from Cullyhanna. All these stories are far-fetched and hardly credible but they do indicate the lingering fear and disturbance of mind that remained amongst local people for generations.

In his article 'Poets and Poetry of Kilkerley'in the *County Louth Archaeological Journal*', 1916, Fr L.P. Murray mentions a tradition connected with Wildgoose Lodge: 'In the early years of the nineteenth century the house (Kilkerley House) was in possession of a younger member of the the family of MacKeowns of Belrobin. One member of this family, Kitt (Christopher) MacKeown, is popularly believed to have been one of the leaders in the burning of the Wild Goose lodge. He gave the largest donation to the fund for the building of Kilkerley Chapel in 1820'.[256] One further reference, in the *Dublin Evening Mail*, 24 May 1826, may be of interest: 'The offices of Mr James Mulloy within 2 miles of Kells were maliciously set on fire in consequence of the occupying tenant having been ejected the day before. Mr Mulloy some time back received several letters threatening himself and his family with Wildgoose usage should he persist in ejecting the tenant'.[257]

The Rev. James Leslie in his *History of Kilsaran* (1908) tells a folk story, which he thinks occurred about the year of 1816, the year of the burning of Wildgoose Lodge. The story was told to him by Very Rev. Dr Ovenden, Dean of Clogher, who related to him that his mother's father, Rev. Thomas Parkinson, Rector of Stabannon, stopped a party of 'rebels' who came to burn Stabannon Rectory, halting them in their tracks by reading to them from the Book of Revelation and applying the text of Babylon, the Mother of harlots, to the Church of Rome and the work they were doing in her name.[258]

William Filgate, magistrate, closely associated with Wildgoose Lodge and witness at the trials subsequently came under threat. Families who believed that members were innocent and were unjustly treated by police, magistrates and informers nursed their grievances and Ribbonmen still gathered to plot revenge. Among the Filgate papers recovered in 1992 and in the County Library, Dundalk, is a scrap of paper evidently anonymously sent to William Filgate: 'If you don't leave this pleace you will be Burnt alive in Short time you and family'. Another paper is a letter written on 1 January 1820 from John Crowe, Governor of Dundalk Gaol, to William Filgate sending him information regarding an allegation of a threat to his life.

> Sir,
> Having this morning received Information thro' Mary Lynch or Mathews, that a conspiracy had been formed by some people between Dunleer and Colon to take advantage of you when Hunting in that part of the Country by getting you at any time by yourself and when you would come to a leap surrounding you at the ditch and when you might light off to pretend to take your horse and at the same time seize yourself and break your neck that it might appear from the way they would leave you it was from a fall from your horse. I therefore thought it my duty to loose no time in apprizing you of the matter in order that you might be prepared to repel any attack that they should at any time attempt to make upon you. As far as I can learn this information came from Biddy Campbell whom you committed a few days back for Cow Stealing; and there would something further come out only she was prevented by some of the other women. However I shall use my exertions if possible to find out those concerned in that dreadful scheme and I shall remain Sir your faithful and obedient Servant.
> P.S. I send this letter by Mathew's Husband.[259]

It was probably around the same time that Filgate received a letter from 'G. F.', who may have been a relative:

> What I would with you is that a fellow of the name of Derry (our pig friend) has given me Information concerning the murder of Thornton at Castletown six years back. *He was one of them*. I have all concerned in custody. He also has told me *he was one* of six that were sworn to murder you. Before I spoke more to him on the subject I wished to see you also. Now that you know what I want come at your own time. I wrote to Lord Oriel on the subject to know how I should act. You may see him at Ardee but not me. ...[260]

Three statements, dated 20 January 1823 and witnessed by William Filgate, from Alexander Shiels, Philip Shirley and Peter Halfpenny confirm an incident which had occurred at Shiels' house.[261] It is to be remembered that Bob Shiels was the steward of William Filgate's father and that it was he who on the morning of the fire rode over to Kiltybegs, County Monaghan, to inform William Filgate of the catastrophe.

> County of Louth to wit. **Alexr. Shiels** sworn saith that on Monday the 13th Jany inst. Bryan Brenan, Philip Shirley, & Peter Halfpenny came to his House, and after some conversation with said Brenan in the presence of sd Shirley & Halfpenny sd Brenan said it was Robt Shiels of Lisrenny & his uncle Peter Brenan, that made Thos Rooney hang the then first man for Wild Goose Lodge. On sd Shiels ordering Brenan out of his House he again said it was Robt Shiels and he Alexr Shiels that hung the rest of the men that was charged for W.G.L. On said Shiels shutting his door after puting him out sd Brenan called to Halfpenny & Shirley to come out and not to be drinking in an Orangeman's House. Alexr. Shiels
> **Philip Shirley** sworn saith he heard Alexr Shiels and Bryan Brenan in Argument & understood they were arguing somethings about Wld Goose Lodge. Shiels sd the Country accused his family of it, & the Congregation of Reaghstown wd not clear them of it – when Bryan Brenan said He cleared his Hands out of it – but that it was his (A.S.) father & his own which done it. Alexr Shiels told Shirley the argument was, who urged Tommy Rooney to swear agst the three first men that were Hanged. Saw Shiels put Brenan out of the House & wd not swear that whether Brenan did or did not mention Orange Man. He did not hear Orange Man mentioned. Had heard Alexr Shiels say he did not care if he was called more or Orangeman. He does not recollect Bryan Brenan making use of the expression. Philip Shirley
> **Peter Halfpenny** sworn saith he was in Liquor and does not recollect anything that took place between Shiels & Brenan till he saw Shiels putting Brenan out of the House & does not know of any thing that took place more on the subject whether that was in the House or not, but Brenan and Shirley came away with him. Peter Halfpenny

The catchword 'Wildgoose Lodge' led to a humble explanation from Berkeley Buckingham Stafford, Mayne, Castlebellingham to William Filgate explaining the truth about a rumour he was alleged to have spread at election time. He wrote to Filgate on 29 September 1831:

> Having been yesterday informed in Dundalk that a report is current throughout the county that I indulged in abuse of you in a speech I made on Sunday last, I take the earliest opportunity of rising to you on the subject, to put you in possession of the truth, in case you may have heard the rumour.
> I certainly mentioned your name, but it was coupled with no disparaging or vituperative expressions. I had myself been told that morning that you proposed standing for the county in place of Sir Harry Goodrick who had resigned. I merely observed to the people that 'ignorant as I was of the fact, I could not positively contradict it, but on reflection was inclined to give no credit to the report, conceiving that scarcely any Tory Gentlemen in Louth would consider it advisable to risk his money in the attempt to defeat a Liberal candidate; that therefore the independent freeholders might keep up their spirits etc etc.' I am reported to have mentioned Wildgoose Lodge and to have connected it with your name. I can assure you, on the honour of a gentleman that not only I did not mention the name of Wildgoose but that I did not even hint or glance at it in the most remote degree – nor was the idea present in my mind on that occasion. If I know myself, I consider it would be impossible for me to allow my politics so to make me forget gentlemanly feeling as to indulge in personal abuse of parties different from me in opinion: nor could I conceive my political cause advanced by such a line of conduct. Knowing the evil effects of the mistaken or malicious rumours, when uncontradicted and desirous to retain the favourable opinion, as to private character, I may have hitherto heard in your mind, I hope you will think me justified in addressing you.[262]

M.R. Beames in his article on Ribbonism in *Past & Present* (1982) gives a few references to the continuance of Ribbonism in County Louth in the second quarter of the nineteenth century, mentioning two arrests in Ardee in 1839, one a baker, Owen Kearney and the other a hackler called Reilly. Kearney was described as a man with an 'extensive trade in the baking business ... in the habit of sending bread to a great many gentlemen in the counties of Louth and Meath'. He gives an interesting list of the occupations of Ribbon suspects in County Louth in 1842:

5 labourers (one lately in the army), 4 farmers, 3 publicans, 2 masons, 2 shoemakers, 1 son of an extensive farmer, 1 son of an extensive farmer and miller, 1 wheelwright, 1 butcher, 1 tailor.[263]

One of the main features of the trials of those prosecuted for the Wildgoose Lodge atrocity was the use of informers who were also involved in crime. The acceptability of the evidence of accomplices raised legal questions both in Britain and in Ireland. In 1824 a pamphlet, *Observations on the Corroboration of the Testimony of Accomplices*, apparently written by John Mayne a barrister at law, was published by M.N. Mahon, Grafton Street, Dublin.[264] The writer set out to elucidate the following principle: 'That an accomplice is a competent witness has never been fairly questionable. It is founded on necessity and good sense. His credibility, however, is a different thing, and with regard to it the Judges of England appear to have very early laid down the rule – that the testimony of an accomplice requires corroboration, and that they would always in the exercise of their discretion so direct a jury. I state the rule to be, that corroboration must be in some point affecting the identity or individual guilt of the person on trial: in other words, that *some* evidence must be given against him, independent of the accomplice, and in support of the testimony. This appears to me, upon a review of all the cases, to have been the construction of the rule adopted in England. Corroboration of the testimony of accomplices has, indeed, repeatedly become the topic of animated discussion, but always in the endeavour to give favour of the prisoner. The counsel for the prosecution or the court have never sought to confine it within narrower limits than those I have assigned'. Having further clarified this principle, the author enumerated sample cases from England and concluded his treatise with a commentary on the case of the Wildgoose Lodge. Although the pamphlet was not primarily written on this subject, a new edition, revised and corrected, and printed in 1824 by James Kelly, Catholic Booksellers, Drogheda, made bold to give it a new title, obviously for local interest – *A Full Report of the Important Trial and Execution for the Burning of the Wildgoose Lodge*.[265] It is a very impaired commentary on the trial for the author refers to the trials at the spring assizes of 1818 presided over by Judge Fletcher, while Patrick Devan's trial took place at the summer assizes of 1817 where the judge was Baron McClelland. He has Devan's trial in mind in analysing the strength of the witness of the accomplices. He has no knowledge of the doubts of the authorities as to the trustworthiness of the evidence of Thomas Gubby or that he was the sole witness in the cases of John Keegan and Thomas Sheenan. He does not, as he says, attempt to give a true report of the case but the *nature* of it – witnesses who came from different parts of the country, who were kept in separate places of confinement and yet corroborated the general details of the story of the other. He says, 'The credibility of the testimony arises from the coincidence between the accomplices in particulars which could not have been preconcerted between them; and this is a corroboration to the full as satisfactory as any to be derived from the usual one by witnesses of unimpeached integrity'.

The Wildgoose Lodge atrocity easily provided missiles for insult among families and neighbourhoods. It is ironic that the collective action of the 'lower orders' would within a generation of its occurrence become a factor to be reckoned with and a class to be wooed in the political rivalry of the local gentry. The Ribbon men could empathise with the bold defiant articulation of O'Connell's call for rights for Catholics and the Catholic emancipation campaign gave them a psychological feeling of a risen people. With Catholic Emancipation in 1829 the servile peasantry had moved a long way from the contempt and oppression of the first quarter of the century to dictating on occasions the success of the more liberal line of politics. The anti-tithe agitation became a national political issue. Agrarian violence, protests against tithes, evictions and unfair leases continued to foster the Ribbon society and it became more organised in later generations. John Mathews in his account of 1882 points out that Richard Lawlor Sheil referred to the tragedy of Wildgoose Lodge in a speech in the House of Commons in April 1839.[266]

After the trials, the executions, and the gibbeting some of the major figures in the story moved on to other business. The four informers Gilroy, Gollogly, Gubby, and Murphy were each paid £200 with a view, it would seem, to leaving the country for their safety. A report of a court case in the *Irish News*, 16 November

1912, indicates that 'Gubby' was still used as a term of abuse in Eglish, County Tyrone, Thomas Gubby's home place, a hundred years after the events of Wildgoose Lodge. At Moy Petty Sessions on 15 November, before Mr Henry Tohill, JP and other magistrates, Francis Stafford, Savanaghanroe, summoned Patrick Daly, Crubinagh, for having used threatening language towards him on 2nd October and 1st November. Stafford had lodged a complaint against Daly who had been a rural postman, on account of a letter having been delayed. Daly in consequence had been dismissed and it was alleged that after that he gave Stafford a lot of annoyance – 'On 21st October, when passing defendant's house, the latter came out and called witness an informer, a traitor and a bankrupt, and said he was "as bad as Gubby". Defendant's wife tried to pull witness off the road. Mr Tohill, JP: "To be called 'Gubby' is vey bad. He was a well known informer in the old days" … Defendant was bound over to keep the peace for twelve months'.

There is mention of a Judith Lynch in Payment Books. On 17 August 1819 Honble Col. Le Poer Trench was paid £28-7-8, the expense of sending her home from New Brunswick.[267] She may have been a member of the Lynch family, perhaps a daughter of Edward Lynch. By 1820 Samuel Pendleton was in Castlegar, County Galway, and there are some letters from him to Dublin Castle in the months of March and April of that year reporting from Castlegar on the police establishment there, on prosecutions and executions.[268] Robert Curtis in his *History of the Royal Irish Constabulary* wrote of the limitations of the police in dealing with disturbances in the post 1816 period:

> For three or four years from that period, 'the peelers' were allowed to cope with these 'untoward circumstances,' and, perhaps, they did their best; but chief magistrates, chief and other constables, sheriffs, local magistrates, and special constables to boot, failed to restore peace; and it is not to be wondered at that the force – if such it could be called – appointed under that Act, found no great favour with either the public or with the government. It was not their interest to be altogether successfully efficient, and they never became popular with the people; while they kept the authorities in many instances 'in hot water'. They continued, however, to eke out an unsatisfactory existence for some time after the Act was passed, which created the present constabulary force … [269]

Conclusion

Judge Fletcher died on 20 March 1823. Daniel O Connell in a letter to his wife at Tours, Monday 9 June 1823, wrote, 'Judge Fletcher, my neighbour, is dead. He has left a large fortune to his only child, his son, the barrister who is an odd looking but a worthy creature. He will be succeeded it is said by Sergeant Torrens'.[270] A tablet in St Patrick's Cathedral, Dublin, commemorates him and his family, 'This tablet is erected to the memory of the late Justice Fletcher of the Court of Common Pleas, Ireland, who died the 20th of March 1823 aged 73 years. Also to his widow Sarah Fletcher who died the 14th February 1838 aged 78 years. Also to William Fletcher, Barrister at Law LL.D, who died the 9th of February 1845 aged 49 years. Also to Franciska Fletcher his widow, youngest child of the late Archibald Hamilton Rowan of Killylea Castle, Co. Down, who died on the 28th of August 1861 aged 58 years'.[271] In his will[272] he had left his wife comfortable regarding money, right of entry to residence and a choice of 300 books for her own library from his. He left his house on Merrion Square and demesne and house of Mont Rose to his son William. He had already given him his entire law library.

Peel in 1829 was to change his tune regarding government repression in Ireland when, shortly after Catholic Emancipation, he cast a glance back on the coercion laws in Ireland. He who had been so bitterly anti-Catholic and even racist at times in his outlook towards the Irish, who had strenuously opposed Catholic Emancipation and would not consider remedying the evils and sources of the causes of agrarian disturbance, now for political effect and purposes softened on both of them. As J.A. Partridge remarks in his book *The Making of the Irish Nation* (1886)[273]: 'It was not till O'Connell's election for Clare, in 1828, that Peel and Wellington yielded to the Irish people, as in the following year they also abandoned the penal code. They then excluded O'Connell, who had been elected, and disfranchised the 40s. freeholders who had elected him. But listen (it is worth while) to Peel's indictment of his master's policy':

> I ask you to examine the state of His Majesty's Government for the last thirty-five years ... I begin with 1794. From that period there has been disunion in the Government on account of the Catholic question, and the administration of Irish affairs. The consequences have been most

unfavourable to the administration of this country (England). The cabinets have been in general nearly equally divided. Ireland has been governed, almost inevitably, upon the same principle - at one time a Lord-Lieutenant adverse, and a Secretary favourable. The law offices of Ireland divided; the subordinate members also. What has been the consequence? Jealousies and suspicions between honourable men embarked in the same cause, and subject to the same responsibilities.

Let us now turn to the legislature ... What is the result? Each party can paralyze the other; nothing effectual can be done, either by the means of coercion or relief. But what becomes of Ireland if these party conflicts without a result shall continue? I will not presume to affirm that the dissensions in our councils and the distractions of Ireland stand to each other in the exact relation of cause and effect, but they have been very nearly concurrent.

Let us cast a rapid glance over the recent history of Ireland, trace it from the Union. What is the melancholy fact? That for scarcely one year during that period that has elapsed since the Union has Ireland been governed by the ordinary course of law.

In 1800 we find the Habeas Corpus Act suspended, and the Act for the suppression of rebellion in force. In 1801 they were continued. In 1803 both Acts were renewed. In 1804 they were continued. In 1806 the west and south of Ireland were in a state of insubordination, which was with difficulty repressed by the severest enforcement of the ordinary law. In 1807 the Act called the 'Insurrection Act' was introduced. It gave power to the Lord-Lieutenant to place any district by proclamation out of the pale of the ordinary law; it suspended trial by jury, and made it a transportable offence to be out of doors from sunset to sunrise. In 1807 this Act continued in force, and in 1808-9, and to the close of the session of 1810. In 1814 the Insurrection Act was renewed; it was continued in 1815, '16, and '17. In 1822 it was again revived, and continued during the years 1823, '24, and '25. In 1825 the temporary Act intended for the suppression of dangerous associations was passed. It continued during 1826 and 1827, and expired in 1828. The year 1829 has arrived, and with it the demand for a new Act to suppress the Roman Catholic association.

'Put down', exclaimed Lord Palmerston, 'the Association! They might as well talk of putting down the winds of heaven, or of chaining the ceaseless tides of the ocean ... The Catholic Association was the people of Ireland. Its spirit was caused by the grievance of the nation; and its seat was the bosom of seven milllions of its population. It was therefore idle to talk of putting down the Association except by removing the cause to which the Association owed its existence. (10 February 1829, Hansard)

'They might as well talk of putting down the winds of heaven, or of chaining the tideless tides of heaven'. The two great revolutions, the French revolution and the industrial revolution, could hardly be suppressed. It would be a long time before governments would look favourably on democracy and the social welfare of all the citizens of Ireland. As J. S. Donnelly remarked in his conclusion to his article on the Whiteboys of 1769-76, 'A wiser government would have undertaken social reform and not relied exclusively on the gun and the gibbet'.[274] It took Peel a quarter of a century to face the problem of the Irish land system; he set up the Devon commission in 1843 to examine the question and introduced in 1845 and 1846 some measures of compensation to the Irish tenant farmer for improvements made by them. The commission in general attributed agrarian violence to the great poverty of the peasantry but no measures to revolutionise the land system were effected. The state had largely gained control over the peasantry through its new police, its magistracy and its law courts. The barbarity of transportation and the great numbers sentenced to capital punishment at all assizes throughout the country continued and embittered the poor against the cruelty of inadequate government. The Great Famine reduced the numbers and moral solidarity of the peasantry by starvation and fever. The holdings of the tenantry were deceased in drastic fashion by death, emigration and eviction leaving the landlords a freedom of action in agriculture, which they had long sought. The local agrarian societies, however, would return in a generation and, thinking there was no other way, would once again by outrage and injury seek relief from their social problems of poverty, famine and oppression. Unfortunately there would be other Wildgoose Lodge tragedies within contexts of grievances, violence and state counterviolence.

NOTES AND REFERENCES

1. P. Ó Gallachair, 'Clogher Clergy, 1535-1835', *Clogher Record* (1969) p. 98; J. E. McKenna, *Parishes of Clogher*, Vol. i, pp 418-30.
2. David J. O'Donoghue, *The Life of William Carleton*, p. 129. Benedict Kiely, *Poor Scholar*, pp 38-9.
3. Benedict Kiely, *Poor Scholar*, pp 38-9.
4. Seamus Piondar, 'Terrible Story of the "Wild Goose Lodge"', *Ireland's Own*, 1 Dec. 1951; Michael Ward, 'The Tragedy of the Wild Goose Lodge', *op. cit.*, 10 June 1983; Michael Ward, 'The "Wildgoose Lodge" Murders', *op. cit.*; Sam Hanna Bell, 'The Terrible Affair at Wild Goose Lodge', *Ulster Tatler*, December 1970. Ballads in County Library, Dundalk: 1. Begins 'The Hills gaze down from Reaghstown on the valley there below'. 2. Begins 'Eighteen Sixteen was the date of the year'. For the murder of the Sheas in Co. Tipperary cf. J.F. McCarthy, 'Agrarian Warfare in Co. Tipperary: the Burning of the Sheas', *Clonmel Historical and Archaelogial Society Journal*, 1954-5. No. 3, pp 9-12.
5. p. 318.
6. *Leaders of Public Opinion in Ireland*, vol.ii, p. 53, 'There is no danger in poverty; it is the smug, saucy and venturous youth of the farmer class that plot and perpetuate all the predial mischief'.
7. Donal McCartney, *The Dawning of Democracy: Ireland 1800-1870*, pp 80-1.
8. 'Signor Pastorini', pseudonym of Charles Walmesley (1722-97) author of *The general history of the christian church from her birth to her final triumphant state in Heaven, chiefly deduced from the Apocalypse of St John the Apostle* (1771). Cf. McCartney, *idem*, pp 99-102.
9. P.R.O.N.I, D.O.D.562/3869.
10. Tom Garvin, 'Defenders, Ribbonmen and Others', *Past and Present*, No. 96, (1982), p. 137.
11. *British Journal of Sociology*, Volume 29, Number 1 (March 1978), pp 22- 40.
12. Michael Beames, 'Cottiers and Conacre in Pre-Famine Ireland', *Journal of Peasant Studies*, Vol. v (1975), pp 352-3.
13. p. 43.
14. Lady Gregory, *Mr Gregory's Letter Box*, pp 98-103.
15. pp 110-113.
16. For the pre-Famine era 1815-45 cf. articles by Timothy P. O'Neill listed in the biographical section.
17. pp 2-3.
18. p. 35.
19. *University Review*, Vol.2 (1959), p. 9.
20. T. Desmond Williams ed., *Secret Societies in Ireland*, p. 27.
21. cf. Timothy P. O'Neill, 'Fever and public health in pre-famine Ireland', *R.S.A.I. Jn.*, ciii, 1, pp 1-34; N.A. O.P. 474 'Typhus Fever Epidemic 1817-18'.
22. *Co. Louth Arch. Jn.*, xii, 2 (1950), p. 162.
23. pp 7-8.
24. HO.100: Vol.189-191, Letters and Papers, Ireland. Jan to Dec. 1816.
25. Galen Broeker, *Rural Disorder and Police Reform in Ireland 1812-36*, pp 95-6.
26. Paterson, *op. cit.*, pp 161-3.
27. O'Neill *op. cit.*, pp 2-3.
28. K.H. Connell, *Population of Ireland, 1750-1845* (1945), p. 231.
29. Robert Carl Shipkey, *Robert Peel's Irish Policy*, p. 84. The number of deaths officially attributed to fever was 6,101.

30   Norman Gash, *Mr Secretary Peel*, p. 225.
31   S.J. Connolly, 'Union government, 1812-23', in *A New History of Ireland*, V, p. 62.
32   HO.100: Vol. 192-3, Letters and Papers, Ireland, Jan. to Dec. 1817.
33   HO: 100: Vol. 194-5, Letters and Papers, Ireland, Jan. to Dec. 1918.
34   pp 11-12.
35   Editorial note by Pádraig Ó Néill in *Journal of Henry McClintock*, p, 239, 'A plaque to his memory can be seen in Saint Nicholas' Church of Ireland (Dundalk) – 'Erected by the inhabitants of Dundalk and its vicinity to the memory of George Gillichan, M.D. His unwearied exertions to alleviate the sufferings of the poor, during a contagious fever, with which Providence was pleased to afflict this country, deprived society of his talents and his virtues and consigned him to an early grave, Decr 24, 1817, aged 26. T.Kirk Sculp Dublin'; cf. H.G. Tempest, *Notes on the Parish Church of St Nicholas Dundalk* p. 20, 'A large mural monument in the south transept represents the story of the Good Samaritan. It commemorates Dr George Gillichan ...We read in the records that at the special wish of the committee the sculptor made the Samaritan a portrait of the doctor'.
36   'The State of the Poor in Dundalk, 1800-1850', *Irisleabhar Cuimhneacháin na mBráithre Críostaí, Dún Dealgan, 1869-1969*, p. 31.
37   'Ardee Dispensary Minute Book, 1813-1851', *Co. Louth Arch. & Hist. Jn.*, xvi, 1 (1965), pp 8-9.
38   O'Neill, *op. cit.*, p.10.
39   The editor of *Tempest's Annual* was not able to identify this clergyman.
40   Quoted in Brian Inglis, *The Freedom of the Press in Ireland 1784-1841*, p.134.
41   p. 99.
42   For the activity of priests in Killaloe diocese in attempting to maintain peace cf. Ignatius Murphy, *The Diocese of Killaloe 1800-1850*, pp 31-3; .
43   Tadhg Ó Ceallaigh, 'Peel and Police reform in Ireland', *Studia Hibernica*, No.6 (1966), p. 27.
44   Charles Stuart Parker, *Sir Robert Peel from his Private Correspondence*, Vol. i, p. 141.
45   cf. for the history of Irish police: Robert Curtis, *History of the Royal Irish Constabulary*; Galen Broeker, *Rural Disorder and Police Reform in Ireland 1812-36*; Séamus Breathnach, *The Irish Police: from earliest times to the present day*; T.G. F. Paterson, 'The Royal Irish Constabulary', in *Harvest Home: The Last Sheaf*; R. Barry O'Brien, *Dublin Castle and the Irish People*; Michael Beames, *Peasants and Power: the Whiteboy Movement and their Control in Pre-Famine Ireland*. The County Constables for Ardee and Louth are listed in the *Query Books*, County Archives, Dundalk – 'Ardee: High Constable, Laurence Bellew (*Ardee*), Sub-Constables, James Hurst (*Lowth Hall*), John Geddis (*Drumcar*), Thos Anderson (*Hurlestown*), Alexander Graham (*Collon*), George Henderson (*Churchtown*), James Hardman (*Ardee*), John Collon (*Stabannon*), Thomas Eaton (*Ardee*), John McAllester (*Ardee*). Collector of the Cess – Laurence Bellew (*Ardee*). Louth: High Constable, Arthur Holland (*Killincoole*), Sub-Constables, Alex Pilkington (*Rathbody*), John Hall (*Killincoole*), Robert Govers (*Stonetown*), George Walsh (*Castlebellingham*), Eph. McCullogh (*Channrock*), Bart Eagar (*Whiterath*), Michael McQuee (*Stephenstown*), Joseph Claxton (*Glydefarm*), William Kelly (*Louth*), Thos Thompson (*Lurgangreen*). Collector of the Cess – Arthur Holland (*Killincoole*)'.
46   Daniel Gallogly, *The Diocese of Kilmore:1800-1950*, pp 16-17.
47   pp 55-6.

48 p. 66.
49 T.G.F. Paterson, *Harvest Home: the Last Sheaf*, p. 187.
50 Charles Stuart Parker, *Sir Robert Peel from his private correspondence*, Vol. i, p. 145.
51 W.E.H. Lecky, *Leaders of Public Opinion in Ireland*, Vol. ii, Daniel O'Connell, p. 53.
52 Broeker, *op. cit.*, pp 48-9.
53 Vol.ii, p.338. For other references to Judge Fletcher cf. James Kelly, 'That Damn'd Thing Called Honour': Duelling in Ireland, 1570-1860, 239; Allan Blackstock, *An Ascendancy Army: The Irish Yeomanry 1796-1834*), p. 289; G. Locker Lampson, *A Consideration of the State of Ireland in the Nineteenth Century*, pp 228-9 where the author refers to 'the uncouth and voracious Judge Fletcher' and notes, 'At a certain hour every day he used to become suddenly seized with a ravenous desire for food, as though he had a wolf in his stomach. This sometimes took place in Court, which made it very inconvenient for all parties concerned. He was a rugged, but humane man'.
54 Charles Stuart Parker, *op. cit.*, p. 153.
55 *Ibid.*, pp 153-4.
56 *Ibid.*, p. 154.
57 *Ibid.*, p. 154.
58 Gash, *op. cit.*, pp 132, 182.
59 Lady Gregory, *op. cit.*, pp 85-6.
60 Tadhg Ó Ceallaigh, 'Peel and Police Reform in Ireland', *Studia Hibernica*, No. 6, p. 43.
61 *Agricultural History*, No. 46 (1972), pp 380-1.
62 Gash, *op. cit.*, p. 175.
63 Ó Ceallaigh, *op. cit.*, p. 44.
64 Copy in County Museum, Dundalk.
65 John Mitchel, *History of Ireland*, pp 145, 150-1.
66 Wm Vesey Fitzgerald: Chancellor of Irish exchequer, 1812-16; M.P. Co. Clare, 1818; defeated by O'Connell on seeking re-election; created English peer by Peel, 1835. cf. John S. Crone, *A Concise Dictionary of Irish Biography*, p. 69.
67 *The Burning of Wildgoose Lodge* (pamphlet), pp 2-3.
68 Daniel J. Casey, 'Wildgoose Lodge: The Evidence and the Lore', *Co. Louth Arch. & Hist. Journal*, xviii, 2 (1974), pp 146-7. Transcription, H.P.E. Filgate, 11 March 1867.
69 Noel Ross ed., 'The Diary of Marianne Fortescue, 1816-1818', *Co. Louth Arch. & Hist. Journal*, xxiv, 4, (2000), p. 495.
70 Copy in County Library, Dundalk.
71 'County Louth Grand Jury Indictment Book, Spring Assizes 1805 to Spring Assizes 1889', *Tempest's Annual*, 1938.
72 N.A., S.O.C. 1763/19; summary in Private Official Correspondence. Magistrates. 1815/16.
73 N.A., Private Official Correspondence. 1815/16.
74 *Idem.*
75 *Idem.*
76 *Idem.*
77 *Idem.*
78 *Tempest's Annual*, 1938.
79 Vol. ii, pp 332-3.
80 *The Burning of Wildgoose Lodge* (pamphlet), p. 3.

Notes

81 Gale E. Christianson, 'Secret Societies and Agrarian Violence in Ireland, 1790-1840', *Agricultural History*, No. 46 (1972), p. 378.
82 Charles Stuart Parker, *op. cit.*, p. 207.
83 Grand Jury Presentment Book, County Louth (National Library, Dublin).
84 N.A., SOC/1763/41; *Parliamentary Papers: Papers relating to Disturbances in the County of Louth; Session 28 January 1817 – 12 July 1817 (Vol. viii)*
85 Information through the courtesty of Elizabeth Balcombe and Noel Ross; entries found by Elizabeth Balcombe in N.L.I. Ms. 16.963 Lowther Lodge Farm Diary recorded by Townley Patten Filgate.
86 Noel Ross, *op. cit.*, p. 502.
87 Daniel J. Casey, *op. cit.*, p. 146.
88 N.A., SOC/1763/34.
89 N.A., SOC/1763/33. Published in *Parliamentary Papers: Papers relating to Disturbances in the County of Louth: Session 28 January – 12 July 1817 (Vol. viii).*
90 H.O. 100: Vol. 189-191, Letters and Papers, Ireland, Jan. to Dec. 1816.
91 N.A., SOC/1763/35.
92 P.R.O.N.I., D.O.D.562/3763.
93 P.R.O.N.I., D.O.D.562/3764; the proclamation enforcing the Peace Preservation Act in baronies of Louth is printed in *Parliamentary Papers: Papers relating to Disturbances in the County of Louth; Session 28 January 1817 – 12 July 1817 (Vol. viii)*
94 H.O. 100: Vol. 189-191, Letters & Papers, Ireland, Jan. to Dec. 1816; *Parliamentary Papers: Session 1 February 1816 – 2 July 1816 (Vol. ix).*
95 Gash, *op. cit.*, p. 219.
96 P.R.O.N.I., D.O.D. 562/?
97 N.A., SOC/1763/31A.
98 N.A., SOC/1763/32.
99 P.R.O.N.I., D.O.D. 562/5762.
100 N.A., SOC/1763/36.
101 Noel Ross, *op. cit.*, p. 502.
102 N.A., SOC/1763/36.
103 N.A, SOC/1828/15; *Parliamentary Papers: Papers relating to Disturbances in the County of Louth; Session 28 January – 12 July 1817 (Vol. viii).*
104 N.A., SOC/1763/36.
105 P.R.O.N.I., D.O.D., 562/3766.
106 P.R.O.N.I., D.O.D., 562/3767.
107 N.A., SOC.1763/36; *Parliamentary Papers: Papers relating to Disturbances in the County of Louth; Session 28 January 1817 – 12 July 1817 (Vol. viii).*
108 Idem.
109 N.A., SOC/1763/37.
110 N.A., SOC/1763/36.
111 N.A, SOC/1763/39.
112 N.A., SOC/1763/36.
113 Idem.
114 P.R.O.N.I., D.O.D. 562/3769.
115 N.A., SOC/1763/36.
116 N.A., SOC/1763/38.
117 N.A., SOC/1763/46; *Parliamentary Papers: Papers relating to Disturbances in the County of Louth, Session 28 January – 12 July 1817 (Vol. viii)*
118 N.A., SOC/1776/46 & 60.
119 N.A., SOC/1838/1.
120 N.A., SOC/1838/2.

121	N.A., SOC/1838/13.
122	N.A., SOC/1838/14.
123	N.A., OP/482/8.
124	*Idem.*
125	Charles Stuart Parker, *op. cit.*, p. 236.
126	*Studia Hibernica*, No.6 (1966), p. 45.
127	N.A., OP/1561/15.
128	N.A., OP/1565/23, 24, 27, 28.
129	N.A., OP/1565/50.
130	N.A., OP/1561/17.
131	N.A., OP/1712/60, 61, 64.
132	N.A., OP/1711/24.
133	N.A., OP/1765/15-20.
134	N.A., OP/1776/60.
135	N.A., OP/1763/4, 5.
136	N.A., OP/1765/69, 70.
137	P.R.O.N.I., T2354/2/13, 15; letters also in County Library, Dundalk.
138	N.A., SOC/1813/38.
139	N.A., SOC//1817/3.
140	*Tempest's Annual*, 1938.
141	N.A., SOC/1763/12.
142	H.O. 100: Vol. 189-191, Letters & Papers, Ireland, Jan. to Dec. 1816.
143	N.A., SOC/1763/28.
144	N.A., SOC/1763/40.
145	H.O., 100: Vol. 189-191, Letters & Papers, Ireland, Jan. to Dec. 1816.
146	N.A., SOC/1763/41.
147	N.A., SOC/1763/41.
148	N.A., SOC/1763/36.
149	N.A., SOC/1763/48.
150	N.A., SOC/1763/49; *Parliamentary Papers: Papers Relating to Disturbances in Ireland; Session 28 January – 12 July 1817 (Vol. viii)*
151	H.O., 100: Vol. 189-191, Letters & Papers, Ireland, Jan. to Dec. 1816.
152	N.A., SOC/1828/1.
153	*Tempest's Annual*, 1938.
154	N.A., SOC/1828/6.
155	N.A., SOC/1828/7.
156	N.A., SOC/1828/5.
157	N.A., SOC/1828/8.
158	N.A., SOC/1828/15.
159	N.A., OP/1963/9, 11.
160	N.A., SOC/1954/31.
161	H.O., 100: Vol. 154-5, Letters & Papers, Ireland, Jan. to Dec. 1818.
162	N.A., OP/2075/21.
163	N.A., OP/2075/28.
164	N.A., OP/2075/24.
165	N.A., OP/2075/34.
166	N.A., OP/2075/37.
167	N.A., OP/2075/37.
168	N.A, SOC/1828/16.
169	N.A, SOC/1828/17; N.A..SOC/1828/16.
170	*Tempest's Annual*, 1938.
171	N.A., SOC/1828/17.
172	*Idem.*

173 N.A., SOC/1829/15.
174 N.A., 1828/16,17.
175 N.A., 1828/16.
176 *Idem.*
177 *Idem.*
178 N.A., SOC/1829/19; 'Information of Peter Gollogly', in County Library, Dundalk.
179 N.A., SOC/1829/27.
180 N.A., SOC/1829/55.
181 *Idem.*
182 N.A., SOC/1828/17.
183 N.A, SOC/1828/17.
184 N.A., SOC/1828/17.
185 N.A., SOC/1828/15.
186 N.A., SOC/1828/10.
187 N.A, 1828/17.
188 N.A., SOC/1828/16.
189 N.A., SOC/1828/12.
190 N.A., SOC/1829/27.
191 N.A., SOC/1828/9.
192 N.A., SOC/1828/15.
193 N.A., SOC/1828/15.
194 N.A., SOC/1828/10.
195 N.A., SOC/1828/15.
196 N.A., SOC/1828/11.
197 N.A., SOC/1828/17.
198 *Idem.*
199 *Idem.*
200 N.A., SOC/1828/12.
201 N.A., SOC/1828/13.
202 N.A., SOC/1828/17.
203 *Idem.*
204 *Idem.*
205 N.A., SOC/1828/15.
206 N.A., SOC/1828/17.
207 *Idem.*
208 *Idem.*
209 *Idem.*
210 *Idem.*
211 *Idem.*
212 N.A, SOC/1828/16.
213 N.L.I. Ms. 16.963, Lowther Farm Diary recorded by Townley Patten Filgate.
214 F. Elrington Ball, *Judges in Ireland, 1221-1921*, Vol.ii, pp 335-6.
215 *Ibid.*, p. 342.
216 N.A, SOC/1828/14.
217 Noel Ross, ed. 'The Diary of Marianne Fortescue' *Co. Louth Arch. & Hist. Jn.*, xxv, 2 (2002), p.115.
218 For much of this information I thank Fr Hugh Fenning, O.P., and Pádraig Ó Néill. Rev. Patrick Duffy received £40 0 0 in 1823, presentment, *Query Books*, County Louth Archives.
219 O'Connell, Maurice ed. *The Correspondence of Daniel O'Connell*, Vol. ii, 1815-1823, Letter 601.

220 Copy in Royal Irish Academy, Broadside 4, 3B53-56/492.
221 I am grateful to Noel Ross who provided me with notes on Dr Marron by Fr Thomas Gogarty and a copy of the text of Dr Marron's letter to Mrs Margaret O'Reilly.
222 Primate Richard O'Reilly (+31 Jan. 1818) lived in Drogheda. He was friendly with the O'Reilly family of Thomastown and sometimes visited there as is clear from his letters to his Vicar General Dr Conwell. Cf. the calendar of these letters in the Cardinal Tomás Ó Fiaich Memorial Library & Archive.
223 N.A., SOC/1818/16.
224 N.A., OP/2075/27,2.
225 N.A., SOC/2075/38.
226 N.A, SOC/2075/27.
227 Copy of Thomas Duffy's statement also in P.R.O.N.I., T2354/2/16A & B.
228 N.A., SOC/1828/16.
229 P.R.O.N.I., D.O.D.562/3770.
230 P.R.O.N.I., D.O.D.562/3771, 3772.
231 P.R.O.N.I., D.O.D.562/3373.
232 P.R.O.N.I., D.O.D.562/3775.
233 P.R.O.N.I., D.O.D.562/3776.
234 P.R.O.N.I., D.O.D.562/3778.
235 P.R.O.N.I., D.O.D.562/3779.
236 P.R.O.N.I., D.O.D.562/3781.
237 P.R.O.N.I., D.O.D.562/3782.
238 P.R.O.N.I., D.O.D.562/3783.
239 P.R.O.N.I., T2354/2/11.
240 P.R.O.N.I., D.O.D.562/3787.
241 P.R.O.N.I., D.O.D.562/3788.
242 P.R.O.N.I., D.O.D.562/3789.
243 P.R.O.N.I., T2354/2/8.
244 P.R.O.N.I., T2354/2/9, 10.
245 P.R.O.N.I., T2354/2/14.
246 P.R.O.N.I., T2354/2/22.
247 County Library, Dundalk.
248 National Library Ireland.
249 N.A., SOC/2975/31.
250 N.A., SOC/2075/29.
251 O'Donoghue, *op.cit.*, p. 131.
252 N.L.I. Ms. 16/063.
253 p. 152.
254 *The Burning of Wildgoose Lodge* (Pamphlet), p. 9.
255 Roinn Bhéaloideas Éireann, University College, Dublin. Iml. 1691, lgh 54-79; 1693, lch 62; 1236, lgh 211-3; 976, lgh 92-3.
256 Vol. iv, No. 1, p. 60.
257 Information from Noel Ross.
258 pp. 144-5.
259 P.R.O.N.I., T2354/2/13.
260 P.R.O.N.I., T2354/2/12.
261 P.R.O.N.I., T2354/2/20.
262 P.R.O.N.I., T2354/2/26.
263 No. 97, pp 130-1.
264 Royal Irish Academy, Haliday Pamphlets relating to Ireland, 1320, Trials 1824.

265	*Idem.*
266	*The Burning of Wildgoose Lodge* (Pamphlet), pp1-2.
267	P.R.O., Kew Gardens, London, CI-904-4, CO-904-5. There is a reference to her in the calendar of Official Papers NOT EXTANT, National Archives, Dublin, under Crown Witnesses and relating to Wildgoose Lodge.
268	N.A., SOC/2172/33, 44, 64.
269	pp 8-9.
270	O'Connell, Maurice, *op. cit.*, Letter 1027.
271	*Memorials of the Dead in Ireland* (Journal), Vol. vi, p.531.
272	N.A., T16912.
273	pp 118-9.
274	*Proceedings of the Royal Irish Academy*, Vol. 83, C, No. 12, p. 331.

CONCISE BIOGRAPHIES

ARMSTRONG, JOHN, Chief Constable, Drogheda, and Constable of Ferrard.

BALFOUR, BLA(Y)NEY T., (1799-1882), eldest son of Blayney and Lady Florence Balfour of Townley Hall, Co. Louth.

BALFOUR, BLAYNEY, (1769-1856), residence at Townley Hall, Co. Louth.

BELL, J.

BELLINGHAM, SIR WILLIAM, Castle Bellingham, Co. Louth, d. 26 October 1826.

BELLEW, SIR EDWARD, Barmeath Castle, Co. Louth, d. 15 March 1827.

BIGGER, LENNOX, (1769-1857), magistrate, residence at Richmond, Dundalk.

BLACKWELL, DR HENRY MUNRO, physician and coroner of County Louth and for the victims of Wildgoose Lodge burning. Residence in Collon, Co. Louth.

BOOTH, JOSEPH, (1784-1857), attorney, Sub-Sheriff of County Louth, 1816; residence in Dublin and Darver Castle.

BOURNE, JOHN, d. 21 April 1829 aged 59 years; Clerk of the Peace for County Louth, William St, Dundalk; appointed by John Foster and acted as 'his unpaid election agent' (cf. A.P.W. Malcomson, *John Foster: The politics of the Anglo-Irish Ascendancy* pp 256-7); residence at Priorland, Co. Louth.

BRABAZON, HENRY, residence at Drumcar and later Dromiskin; a magistrate of Co. Louth.

BRABAZON, WALLOP, (1770-1831); residence at Rath House, Termonfeckin, Co. Louth.

BUSHE, CHARLES KENDAL, b. 1767. d. 10 July 1843; renowned legal figure in the nineteenth century and celebrated orator in the Irish House of Commons; opposed the Union; 3rd Serjeant-at-Law July 1805; Solicitor General 1805-22; Chief Justice of the King's/Queen's Bench 20 Feb. 1822-41; residence at Kilmurry, Co. Kilkenny and Dublin.

CASSIDY, TERENCE, Ratheady, Co. Louth, murdered by 'Threshers', 3 July 1818.

CHESTER, HENRY, Carstown b. 1808, son of Henry Chester, Co. Meath; M.P. for Co. Louth 1837-40.

CHETWYND, LORD CHARLES, 2nd Earl Talbot, Lord Lieutenant of Ireland, 1817-21.

Biographies 345

CODDINGTON, HENRY,

CODDINGTON, NICHOLAS, b. 1765, d. 31 August 1837; residence at Oldbridge, Co. Meath.

CROWE, JOHN, governor of Dundalk gaol; died 19 November 1849, aged 81 years. Crowe Street in Dundalk is named after him.

DALY, ST. GEORGE, b. c.1757; called to the Irish bar 1783; prominent in promoting the Union; became prime serjeant and a privy councilor 1799; was appointed a baron of the Exchequer 1801; was transferred to the King's Bench; resigned 1822; resided in Dublin and at Eyrecourt, Co. Galway.

DAWSON, JOHN

DEVAN, PATRICK, weaver, teacher, clerk of Stonetown church; local leader of Ribbonmen; hanged at Wildgoose Lodge, 23 July 1817.

DOYNE, PHILIP, Reverend, curate in Ardee, 1816, followed by his son Reverend John Doyne in same year.

DUFFY, PATRICK, O.P., Father, Catholic chaplain to Dundalk prison.

ECCLESTON, GEORGE SHEIL, Dromiskin, Co. Louth.

FILGATE, ALEXANDER, b. 17 Sept.1771, d. 30 April 1827. 1st son of William Filgate (b. 1740) and brother of William Filgate (d. 1875); Lieutenant-Colonel Louth Militia.

FILGATE, THOMAS WILLIAM, (1818-1868); residence at Arthurstown, Co. Louth.

FILGATE, TOWNLEY, Reverend, b. 16 July 1784, d. 28 Dec. 1822; 4th son of William Filgate of Lisrenny; m. Isabella eldest daughter of William Ruxton of Ardee House; curate and then vicar of Charlestown, Co. Louth.

FILGATE, TOWNLEY PATTEN, Lowther Lodge, Balbriggan, Co. Dublin; owner of Wildgoose Lodge; buried 14 July 1828, aged 74 years.

FILGATE, WILLIAM, b. 1781, d. 23 Nov. 1875; residence at Lisrenny, about four miles from Ardee.

FITZGERALD, THOMAS, rich West Indian merchant who established himself at Fane Valley, Co. Louth (cf. A.P.W. Malcomson, *John Foster: the politics of the Anglo-Irish Ascendancy*, p. 329); MP for County Louth 1832-4; d. 29 October 1834.

FLETCHER, WILLIAM, b. 1750, d. 20 March 1823; elected member for Tralee 1795; associated with the opposition group in the Irish parliament and at the Bar; 2nd Justice of the Common Pleas, 21 Oct. 1806; delivered a famous charge on current political questions in Wexford, 1814; supported Catholic emancipation and parliamentary reform; presided at some of the Wildgoose Lodge trials; resident at Montrose, Co. Dublin.

FORDE, JAMES, Dundalk.

FORSTER, GEORGE, (1796-1876); son of Rev. Sir Thomas Forster, rector of Barronstown; m. 20 May 1817 Anna Maria Fortescue, daughter of Mathew and Marianne Fortescue.

FORTESCUE, CHICHESTER, b. 12 Aug. 1777, d. 25 Nov. 1826; residence at Glyde Farm, Co. Louth; High Sheriff of County Louth 20 Feb. 1800; Lieutenant-Colonel, Louth Yeomanry.

FORTESCUE, FAITHFUL, (1781-1844), Corderry, High Sheriff of County Louth 1818.

FORTESCUE, FAITHFUL WILLIAM, b. 1773, d. 23 Aug. 1823; residence at Milltown Grange, Co. Louth; High Sheriff of County Louth 1821.

FORTESCUE, MARIANNE, daughter of John McClintock of Drumcar, b. 17 May 1767, d. 14 Oct. 1849; m. 1st Jan. 1787 Mathew Fortescue of Stephenstown (d. 10 Nov. 1802); her diary edited by Noel Ross in *Co. Louth Archaeological and Historical Journal*.

FORTESCUE, MATHEW, b. 3 Sept. 1791, d. 21 Jan. 1845, son of Mathew and Marianne Fortescue; residence at Stephenstown House, near Dundalk.

FOSTER, HENRY, b. July 1750, d. 7 Nov. 1838; residence at Daghanstown, Co. Louth.

FOSTER, JOHN, b. Collon, Co. Louth, (28) Sept. 1740, d. 23 Aug. 1828; last Speaker of the Irish House of Commons, 1785-1800; hostile to Union and Catholic claims; MP in English parliament for Louth; created Baron Oriel 17 July 1821; Captain, Collon Infantry 1796.

FOSTER, THOMAS HENRY, see Skeffington.

FOSTER, WILLIAM, Barronstown, Co. Louth.

GOLDING, GEORGE R., Lime Park, barony of Dungannon, magistrate.

GORDON & HAMILTON, Crown Solicitors.

GREGORY, WILLIAM, (1766-1840); Under-Secretary at Dublin Castle 1812-31.

HAMILTON, FRANCIS D., Portreeve (Sovereign) of Navan, 1817; residence at Leighsbrook, Navan.

Biographies

HOLMES, JOHN, Under-Sheriff of Co. Louth, 1819.

JOCELYN, LORD, John, b. 1769, d. 21 Jan. 1828, fourth son of the first earl. M.P. Dundalk 1798-1800, M.P. Co. Louth 1807-10 and 1820-6, m. Margaret, dau. of Rt Hon. Richard Fitzgerald and had an only dau. Anne Charlotte who m. 3 Aug. 1820 Richard Burke (later the fifth Earl of Mayo). Captain, Dundalk Corps, Yeomanry.

JOY, HENRY, (1763-1838); youngest son of Henry Joy, owner of the *Belfast News-Letter*; called to the Irish bar 1788; Second Serjeant 1816, and First Serjeant 1817; resided in Dublin in Temple-street and near Dublin at Woodtown.

LAMBERT, GEORGE, Reverend, vicar of Ardee 1806-20; and held also the vicarage of Clonkeen 1804-19.

LITTLE, SAMUEL, Reverend, b. 1752, d. 4 April 1823; rector of Louth 1789-1823, and Dunleer1789-1809; residence at Grange townland near Stephenstown.

LLOYD, THOMAS, agent to Lord Clermont; residence at Ravensdale; died 9 August 1821.

LOUTH, LORD, Thomas Oliver Plunkett, (1764-1823); 11th Baron of Louth, residence at Louth Hall.

LYNCH, EDWARD, resided at Wildgoose Lodge, burned to death by the Ribbonmen.

MACAN, TURNER, b. in Bengal *c.*1795, d. unmarried in America; residence at Greenmount, Castlebellingham, Co. Louth; High Sheriff of County Louth, 1817.

McCANN, THOMAS, Father, native of Knockbridge; parish priest of Louth 1799-1822.

McCLELLAND, JAMES, b. *c.*1768, d. 1831; m. Charlotte, daughter of Acheson Thompson, Ravensdale, Co. Louth; was appointed solicitor-general 1801; became a baron of the Exchequer 1803; resided in Dublin and at Annaverna, Ravensdale, Co. Louth; judge at trial of Patrick Devan.

McCLINTOCK, HENRY, b. at Drumcar, 28 Sept. 1783, d. 27 Feb. 1843, author of diary (edited by Pádraig Ó Néill); officer, Dundalk Corps, Yeomanry.

McCLINTOCK, JOHN, b. 14 Aug. 1769, d. 5 July 1855, eldest brother of Henry.

McNALLY, LEONARD, b. 1752, d. 1820; counsel for the prisoners at some of the 'Wildgoose Lodge' trials.

MacNEALE, NEALE, residence at the 'Major's Hollow', Faughart.

McNEALE, J.W., residence at Faughart.

MARRON, JAMES, b. in Drogheda 1764, d. 14 Dec. 1839; parish priest of Tallanstown.

MOORE, C.

MOORE, HUGH, residence at Nootka Lodge, Carlingford, Co. Louth; a magistrate; died 5 October 1851.

MURRAY, CAPTAIN WILLIAM, Drumfields, magistrate, Dungannon.

NORMAN, THOMAS LEE, High Sheriff of County Louth in 1820.

O'REILLY, MATHEW, residence at Knock Abbey, Thomastown, Co. Louth.

PAGE, ROBERT, collector of excise, Dundalk

PARKER, JOSEPH, printer in Dundalk.

PARKS, PAUL, postmaster and coroner, Dundalk.

PAYNE, GEORGE, Chief Police Officer, James' St, Dublin, 1817.

PEEL, SIR ROBERT, (1788-1850), tory politician; Chief Secretary for Ireland 1812-18; Home-Secretary 1822-7, 1828-30; Prime Minister 1834-35, 1841-46.

PENDLETON, PHILIP, Mooretown, Co. Meath.

PENDLETON, SAMUEL, residence in Dublin 1798 when he supported Edward Hardman against Ralph Smyth in a by-election in Drogheda; perhaps a brother of Philip Pendleton, Mooretown, Co. Meath, who supported Hardman in the same election; ex-soldier, Chief Magistrate in Co. Louth after the burning of Wildgoose Lodge.

PERRIN, LOUIS, born in Waterford 1782; was called to the Irish bar 1806; assisted in the defence of Robert Emmet 1803. (cf. F. Elrington Ball, *Judges in Ireland 1221-1921*, Vol. ii, p. 349).

POLLOCK, ARTHUR HILL CORNWALLIS, Justice of the Peace; Mountainstown, Co. Meath.

PURCELL, JOE, officer Dundalk Corps, Yeomanry.

PURCELL, WILLY, officer Dundalk Corps, Yeomanry.

REI(A)D, JAMES

RISPIN, ALICE, mother of James Rispin who was burned to death at Wildgoose Lodge; witness at Wildgoose Lodge trials.

RICHARDSON, W. HENRY, d. 1867; resided at Prospect, Co. Louth.

ROGERS, ALEXANDER, solicitor, d. 16 August 1831, aged 77.

ROONEY, THOMAS, married to Biddy, daughter of Edward Lynch; principal witness in conviction of three Ribbonmen for the first attack on Wildgoose Lodge; perished with his wife and child in the revenge burning of the lodge.

RUXTON, JOHN FITZHERBERT, d. 1826, eldest son of William and Anne Ruxton of Ardee and Shercock.

RUXTON, WILLLIAM (P), residence at Red House, Ardee.

SALLERY, WILLIAM OGLE, Chief Constable of the barony of Morgallion, Co. Meath.

SHEILS, BRABAZON DISNEY, High-Sheriff of County Louth, 1816; residence in Newtown-Darver, Co. Louth.

SHORE, JOHN, postmaster of Navan, 1817.

SHEKELTON, ALEXANDER, (1786-1845); founder of Dundalk Iron Works; officer, Dundalk Corps, Yeomanry; residence, Dundalk, Co. Louth.

SHEKELTON, Lieutenant, Collon Corps, Yeomanry.

SIDMOUTH, Henry Addington, (1757-1844); tory politician, Prime Minister 1801-4; created Viscount Sidmouth in 1805; Secretary of State for Home Affairs, 1812-22, responsible for the harsh repression of radicalism in England, especially with the introduction of the Six Acts in 1819 after the Peterloo massacre.

SKEFFINGTON, T.H., (Thomas Henry), (1772-1843), son of John Foster; m. Lady Harriet Skeffington and assumed that name; Colonel of the Louth Militia.

SMART, WILLIAM, gaoler of Trim prison.

SMYTH, RALPH, Deputy Mayor of Drogheda, 1817; magistrate.

STRATON, JOHN, (1763-1821), lived at Lisnawilly, Dundalk; married to Lady Emily Jocelyn, youngest daughter of the Ist Earl of Roden; Collector of Customs for port of Dundalk.

TAAFFE, JOHN, Smarmore Castle, Co. Louth.

THOMPSON, Acheson, residence at Ravensdale, Co. Louth.

THOMPSON, ROBERT, (1766-1835), linen manufacturer, brother of Mrs Baron McClelland, Anaverna; residence at Ravensdale, Co. Louth.

THORNTON, PATRICK, miller, murdered at Castletown 4 March 1816.

TINLEY, GERVAIS, Reverend, master of Dundalk Grammar School, and also curate Dundalk; m. (1) Mary Eastwood, d. 1813, (2) 23 May 1815, Letitia, sister of John Page, Dundalk.

TIPPING, FRANCIS, residence at Bellurgan Park, Co. Louth.

TISDALL, THOMAS,

WAINRIGHT, Rev. M., inspector of the gaol of Trim.

WHITWORTH, CHARLES, Lord Lieutenant of Ireland, 1813-17.

WOOLSEY, JOHN, land agent for Mrs J.W. Foster.

WRIGHT, JAMES,

WRIGHT JOSEPH, Reverend, 'm. Mary, only child of Stephen Filgate of Ardee, by whom he had Rev. Joseph; was curate Ardee 1797 and rector Killincoole from 1815 with which he held Heynestown till his death in 1847' (J.B. Leslie, *Armagh Clergy and Parishes*).

YOUNG, ROBERT, Ardee; captain Ardee Corps, Yeomanry.

(*I am indebted to the notes of Noel Ross in his edition of 'The Diary of Marianne Fortescue' in* Co. Louth Archaeological and Historical Journal, *and to notes received from him and to Pádraig Ó Néill's 'Brief Biographical Details' in his edition of* Journal of Henry McClintock.)

BIBLIOGRAPHY

PARLIAMENTARY RECORDS

Reports: Session, 28 January 1817 – 12 July 1817; *Papers relating to Disturbances in the County of Louth* (Vol. viii)
Reports: Session, 1 February 1816 – 2 July 1816; *Nature and Extent of the Disturbances which have recently prevailed in Ireland, and the Measures which have been adopted by the Government of that Country, in consequence thereof* (Vol. ix)
Reports: Session, 27 January 1818 – 10 June 1818; *Report from the Select Committee on the Contagious Fever in Ireland, with an Appendix; Second Report from the Select Committee on the Contagious Fever in Ireland* (Vol. vii)

MANUSCRIPT & PAMPHLET COLLECTIONS

National Archives, Dublin
    State of the Country Papers
    Official Papers
    Official Papers Not Extant: 1790-1831 has references to Wildgoose Lodge (Macartney. A.C. to Sergt Joy, and Judge Fletcher to W. Gregory on Special Commission to be held at Dundalk to try Wildgoose Lodge prisoners – 11 March 1818, Carton 291, No. 1996/181; Wildgoose Lodge, Mary Farrelly's letters to be intercepted – 18 March 1817; crown witnesses – Wildgoose Lodge. Jan.- Dec. 1818, 2013 and Judith Lynch, Jan.- Dec. 1819, 2129.)

National Library Ireland
    Grand Jury Presentments, County Louth, 1818 General Assizes
    Ms.16.963, Lowther Lodge Farm Diary recorded by Townley Patten Filgate

Royal Irish Academy
    R.I.A., Haliday Pamphlets relating to Ireland, 1320, Trials 1824
    R.I.A., Broadside 4, 3B53-56/492

Public Record Office Northern Ireland
    Foster/Massereene - D.O.D./562/-
    Miscellany of Papers re Wildgoose Lodge (copy with permission of Sion Mills Rectory) – T2354/2/-

Public Record Office, London
    H.O. 100: Vols. 189-191;192-3; 194-5; 196-7 (letters and Papers, Ireland (microfilm in National Library, Dublin)

County Library, Dundalk
    Papers relating to Wildgoose Lodge

County Archives, Dundalk
    Query Books, County Louth
    'County Louth Grand Jury Indictment Book: Spring Assizes 1805 to Spring Assizes 1889', *Tempest's Annual* (1938). Some extracts from the vellum bound original book entitled Co. Louth Grand Jury Indictment Book. Spring 1805 to Spring 1895. List of True Bills found and the Bills ignored by the Grand Jury.

County Museum, Dundalk

Poster relating to proclaimed areas in County Louth, 1816

Irish Folklore Commission, Dublin
    Historic & Local Events: Wildgoose Lodge, Louth, Co. Louth (collection of Michael J. Murphy)

NEWSPAPERS AND PERIODICALS

Annual Register
Belfast News-Letter
The Correspondent
Drogheda Journal
Dundalk Examiner and Louth Advertiser
Dublin Evening Post
Dublin Evening Mail
Enniskillen Chronicle and Erne Packet
Freeman's Journal
Newry Magazine
Newry Telegraph

Ireland's Own
Ulster Tatler

BOOKS AND ARTICLES

Anton, James, *Retrospect of a Military Life*. (W.H. Lizars: Edinburgh, 1841)
Atkinson, A., *Survey of Irish Population*. (Baldwin, Cradock and Joy: London, 1823); Extract, 'Dundalk in 1817', *Tempest's Annual* (1952)
Ball, F. Elrington, *The Judges in Ireland, 1221-1921*. 2 vols. (John Murray: London, 1926)
Barker, F. & Cheyne, J., *An account of the rise, progress and decline of fever lately epidemical in Ireland, together with communications from physicans in the provinces* I (Dublin, 1821)
Bartlett, Thomas, *The Fall and Rise of the Irish Nation: The Catholic Question1690-1830*. (Gill and Macmillan, Dublin, 1992)
Bassett, George Henry, *Louth County Guide and Directory*. (Sealy, Bryers and Walker: Dublin, 1886)
Beames, M.R., 'Peasant Movements: Ireland 1785-1795', *Journal of Peasant Studies*, Vol. 2, (1975), pp 502-506.
Beames, M.R., 'Rural Conflict in Pre-Famine Ireland: 1837-1847', *Past and Present*, No. 81, (1978), pp 75-91
Beames, M.R., 'The Ribbon Societies: Lower-Class Nationalism in Pre-Famine Ireland', *Past and Present*, No. 97, (November 1982)
Beames, Michael, 'Concepts and Terms: Cottiers and Conacre in Pre-Famine Ireland', *Journal of Peasant Studies*, Vol, v, (1975), pp 352-3
Beames, Michael, *Peasants and Power: The Whiteboy Movements and their Control in Pre-Famine Ireland* (The Harvester Press, Sussex & St Martin's Press New York, 1983)
Bell, Sam Hanna, 'The Terrible Affair at Wild Goose Lodge', *Ulster Tatler*, (December 1970)
Blackstock, Allan, *An Ascendancy Army: The Irish Yeomanry 1796-1834* (Four Courts Press, Dublin, 1998)
Boué, André, *William Carleton, romancier irlandais (1794-1869)*. (Publications de la

Sorbonne: Paris, 1978)
Breathnach, Séamus, *The Irish Police: From Earliest Times to the Present Day*. (Anvil Books: Dublin, 1974)
Brett, William, *Reminiscences of Louth*. (Dundalgan Press, 2nd edition, Dundalk:1913)
Broeker, Galen, *Rural Disorder and Police Reform in Ireland, 1812-36*. (Routledge & Kegan Paul: London, 1970)
Brown, Thomas N., 'Nationalism and the Irish Peasant, 1800-1848', *The Review of Politics*, Vol. 5, No. 4, (October 1953), pp 403-445
Burke's Irish Family Records. (Burke's Peerage Limited: London, 1976)
Carleton, William, *Traits and Stories of the Irish Peasantry: With the author's latest corrections*. (Illustrated by Daniel Maclise, R.A. J. & R. Maxwell: London)
Carleton, *The Black Prophet: A tale of Irish Famine*, Irish University Press, 1972
Casey, Daniel J., 'Wilgoose Lodge: The Evidence and the Lore', *County Louth Archaeological and Historical Journal*, Vol. xviii, No. 2, (1974), pp 140-164, Vol. xviii, No. 3, (1975) pp 211-231
Casey, Daniel J., 'Carleton and Devaun', *The Carleton Newsletter*, I, (January 1971), pp 19-22
Casey, Daniel J., Rhodes, Robert E., ed. *Views of the Irish Peasantry*. (Archon Books: Hamden, Connecticut, 1977)
Chesnutt, Margaret, *Studies on the Short Stories of William Carleton*. (Acta Universitatis Gothburgenis: Göteborg, Sweden, 1976)
Christianson, Gale E., 'Secret Societies and Agrarian Violence in Ireland, 1790-1840', *Agricultural History*, No. 46, (1972), pp 360-384
Clark, Samuel, Donnelly, James S., Jr, *Irish Peasants: Violence and Political Unrest 1780-1914*. (Manchester University Press, 1983)
Clark, Samuel, 'The importance of agrarian classes: agrarian class structure and collective action in nineteenth-century Ireland', *British Journal of Sociology*, Vol. 29, No. 1. (March 1978), pp 22- 40
Connell, K.H., *The Population of Ireland, 1750-1845*. (Oxford, 1966).
Connolly, S. J., *Priests and People in Pre-Famine Ireland, 1780-1845*. (Gill and Macmillan, New York: 1982)
Corcoran, Moira, 'Two Drogheda Voters' Lists': 1798 and 1802', *Co. LouthArchaeological and Historical Journal*, Vol. xx, No. 4 (1984).
Corrigan, D.J., *Famine and Fever, as Cause and Effect in Ireland ...* (Dublin, J. Fanning & Co.)
Crotty, Raymond D., *Irish Agricultural Production: Its Volume and Structure*. (Cork University Press: Cork, 1966)
Curtis, Robert, *History of the Royal Irish Constabulary*. (London, 1878)
D'Alton, John, & O'Flanagan, J.R., *The History of Dundalk* (Dublin, 1864)
Donnelly, J.S., 'Irish Agrarian Rebellion: The Whiteboys of 1769-76', *Proceedings of the Royal Irish Academy*, Vol. 83, C, No. 12 (1983), pp 293-331
Donnelly, James S., *Landlord and Tenant in Nineteenth-Century Ireland*. (Gill and Macmillan: London and Dublin, 1973)
Donnelly, James S., 'Hearts of Oak, Hearts of Steel', *Studia Hibernica*, No. 21 (1981, pp 7-73)
"Down the Quay": A History of Dundalk Harbour. (Teamwork Scheme, Dundalk, 1988)
ffolliott, Rosemary, 'Co. Louth Game Licenses in 1813', *The Irish Ancestor*, Vol. xii, Nos 1 & 2.
Fortescue, Thomas (Lord Clermont), *A History of the Family of Fortescue in all its Branches*. (2nd edition, London, 1880)

Freeman, T.W., *Pre-Famine Ireland: a study in historical geography.* (Manchester,1857)
Gallogly, Daniel, *The Diocese of Kilmore.* (Cumann Seanchais Bhréifne, 1999)
Garvin, Tom, 'Defenders; Ribbonmen and Others: Underground Political Networks in Pre-Famine Ireland', *Past and Present*, No. 96 (1982), pp 133-155
Gavin, Joseph, O'Sullivan, Harold, *Dundalk, A Military History.* (Dundalgan Press: Dundalk, 1987)
Gash, Norman, *Mr Secretary Peel: The Life of Sir Robert Peel to 1830.* (Longman: London and New York, edition 1985)
Gregory, Lady, ed. *Mr Gregory's Letter-Box 1813-1815.* (London, 1898)
Harmon, Maurice, 'Aspects of the Peasantry in Anglo-Irish Literature from 1800 to 1916', *Studia Hibernica*, No. 15 (1875), pp 105-127
Hughes, T. Jones, 'Society and Settlement in Nineteenth-Century Ireland', *Irish Geography*, 5, No. 2 (1965), pp 79-96
Inglis, Brian, *The Freedom of the Press in Ireland 1784-1841.* (Faber and Faber: London)
Inglis, Brian, 'O'Connell and the Irish press, 1800-42', *Irish Historical Studies*, Vol. viii, No. 29 (March 1952)
Kelly, James, *'That Damn'd Thing called Honour'; Duelling in Ireland, 1570-1860*, Cork University Press, 1995)
Kiely, Benedict, *Poor Scholar: A Study of William Carleton.* (The Talbot Press: Dublin, 2nd edition, 1972)
Kiely, Benedict, 'Return to Wildgoose Lodge', *Irish Times*, 12, 26 July; 11, 21, 29 August; 8, 21 September 1972
Lampson, G. Locker, *A Consideration of the State of Ireland in the Nineteenth Century.* (Constable: London,1907)
Lavelle, Patrick, *The Irish Landlord since the Revolution.* (Dublin, 1870)
Lecky, W.E.H., *Leaders of Public Opinion in Ireland*, Vol. ii, *Daniel O'Connell.* (Longmans, Green & Co.: London, 1912)
Leslie, James B., *History of Kilsaran.* (Dundalk, 1908, reprint 1986)
Leslie, J.B., *Armagh Clergy and Parishes.* (Tempest, Dundalk, 1911)
Lewis, George Cornewall, *Local Disturbances in Ireland.* (first published London, 1836, Tower Books: Cork, 1977)
Love, H.W., 'Georgian Society in Louth', *Co. Louth Archaeological and Historical Journal*, Vol. xviii, No. 3 (1971).
McCartney, Donal, *The Dawning of Democracy: Ireland 1800-1870.* (Helicon Limited, Dublin)
McCarthy, J.F., 'Agrarian Warfare in Co. Tipperary: the Burning of the Sheas', *Clonmel Historical and Archaeological Society Journal* (1954-5. No. 3, pp. 9-12)
McDowell, R.B., 'The Irish Executive in the nineteenth century', *Irish Historical Studies*, Vol. ix, No. 35 (March 1955)
McDowell, R.B., 'The Irish courts of law, 1801-1914', *Irish Historical Studies*, Vol. x, No. 40 (September 1957)
MacDermot, Brian, ed. *The Catholic Question in Ireland & England 1798-1822: The Papers of Denys Scully.* (Irish Academic Press. Dublin, 1988)
MacIvor, D., 'Census of Tallanstown Parish, 1834', *County Louth Archaeological Journal*, Vol. xiv. No. 1 (1957), pp 14-25
McKenna, J.E., *Parishes of Clogher*, Vols 1,2. (Enniskillen, 1920)
Malcomson, A.P.W., *John Foster: the politics of the Anglo-Irish Ascendancy.* (Oxford University Press, 1978)
Mathews, John, *The Burning of Wildgoose Lodge.* (Reprinted from *The Dundalk Examiner*, 1882)

Mitchel, John, *History of Ireland*. (Cameron & Ferguson, Glasgow, 1849)
Mokyr, Joel, *Why Ireland Starved: A Quantitative and Analytical History of the Irish Economy, 1800-1850*. (George Allen & Unwin, London, 1983)
Mooney, Desmond, 'The Origins of Agrarian Violence in Meath 1790-1828', *Ríocht na Mídhe*, Vol. viii, No. 1, 1987, pp 45-67.
Mooney, Desmond, 'Popular religion and clerical influence in pre-famine Meath', *Religion, Conflict & Coexistence in Ireland*, pp 188-218, ed. R.V. Comerford, Mary Cullen, Jacqueline Hill & Colm Lennon. (Gill and Macmillan: Dublin, 1990)
Murphy, Ignatius, *The Diocese of Killaloe 1800-1850*. (Four Courts Press, Dublin, 1992)
Murray, A.C., 'Agrarian Violence and Nationalism in Nineteenth-Century Ireland', *Irish Economic and Social History*, Vol. xiii (1986)
Murray, L.P., 'Poets and Poetry of Kilkerley', *County Louth Archaeological Journal*, Vol.iv, No.1 (1916), pp 42-60
Murtagh, Michael, *St Patrick's Dundalk: An Anniversary Account*. (Dundalk, 1997)
Nowlan, Kevin B., 'Agrarian Unrest in Ireland, 1800-1845', *University Review*, Vol. 2, (1959), pp 7-16
O'Brien, Eileen, 'An Irishman's Diary', *Irish Times*, 5 December 1983
O'Brien, R. Barry, *Fifty Years of Concessions in Ireland, 1831 –1881*. 2 vols, (London 1909)
Ó Ceallaigh, Tadhg, 'Peel and Police Reform in Ireland, 1814-18', *Studia Hibernica*, No. 6 (1966), pp 25-48
O'Connell, Maurice R., ed. *The Correspondence of Daniel O'Connell*, Vol. ii, 1815-1823. (Irish University Press for the Irish MSS Commission, 1972)
O'Connor Morris, William, *Present Irish Questions*. (London, 1901)
O'Donoghue, David J., *The Life of William Carleton: being his autobiography and letters; and an account of his life and writings, from the point at which the Autobiography breaks off*. 2 vols. (Downey & Co.: London, 1896)
Ó Fiaich, Tomás, 'The 1766 Religious Census for Some County Louth Parishes', *County Louth Archaeological Journal*, Vol. xiv, No. 2 (1958), 113-117
Ó Gallachair, P., 'Clogherici: Clogher Clergy, 1536-1835', *Clogher Record* (1969), pp 89-104
Ó Muireadhaigh, S., 'Na Fir Ribín', *Galvia*, Vol. x, (1964-5), pp 18-33.
Ó Muirí, Réamonn, 'The Burning of Wildgoose Lodge', *County Louth Archaeological and Historical Journal*, Vol. xxi, No. 2 (1986), pp 117-147
Ó Muirí, Réamonn, 'Thomas Gubby alias Hughes: Informant on the Burning of Wildgoose Lodge', *Dúiche Néill*, No. 8 (1993)
Ó Néill, Pádraig, *History of Knockbridge*. (1994)
Ó Néill, Pádraig, transcribed and edited *Journal of Henry McClintock*. (Dundalgan Press: Dundalk, 2001)
O'Neill, Timothy P., 'The Catholic Church and Relief of the Poor, 1815-1845', *Archivium Hibernicum*, Vol. xxxi (1973), pp 132-45
O'Neill, Timothy P., 'Clare and Irish Poverty, 1815-1851', *Studia Hibernica*, No. 14, (1974), pp 1-27
O'Neill, Timothy P., 'Poverty in Ireland, 1815-45', *Folklife*, Vol. xi, (1974), pp 22-3
O'Neill, Timothy P., 'Fever and Public Health in Ireland', *R.S.A.I. Jn.*, Vol. ciii, (1973) pp 1-34
O'Sullivan, Harold, 'The State of the Poor in Dundalk, 1800-1850', *Irisleabhar Cuimhneacháin na mBráithre Críostaí, Dún Dealgan1869-1968*, pp 29-33
O'Sullivan, Harold, 'Dundalk in 1817', *Tempest's Annual*, 1952
O'Sullivan, Harold, 'Ardee Dispensary Minute Book, 1813-1851', *County Louth Archaeological and Historical Journal*, Vol. xvi, No.1, 1965

Ó Tuathaigh, Gearóid, *Ireland before the Famine 1798-1848*, Gill and MacMillan, Dublin & London, 1972
Parker, Charles Stuart, *Sir Robert Peel from his Private Correspondence*, 3 vols, (London, 1891-99)
Partridge, J.A., *The Making of the Irish Nation*. (London, 1886)
Paterson, T.G.F., 'The Burning of Wildgoose Lodge', *County Louth Archaeological Journal*, Vol. xii, No. 2 (1950), pp 159-180
Paterson, T.G.F., 'The Royal Irish Constabulary' in *Harvest Home: The Last Sheaf*, ed. E. Estyn Evans (Dundalgan Press, 1975)
Peel, George, ed., *The Private Letters of Sir Robert Peel*. London, 1920
Piondar, Seamus, 'Terrible Story of the "Wild Goose Lodge", a Grim Tale of Co. Louth', *Ireland's Own* (1 December 1951)
Ross, Noel, 'The Diary of Marianne Fortescue', *County Louth Archaeological and Historical Journal*, Vol. xxiv, No. 2 (1998), Vol. xxiv, No. 3 (1999),Vol. xxiv, No. 4 (2000), vol. xxv, No. 2 (2002)
Shipkey, Robert Carl, *Robert Peel's Irish Policy: 1812-846*. (Garland Publishing, Inc.: New York & London, 1987)
Strutt, Guy, 'The descendants of Robert McCann of Cloghoge, Co. Armagh', *The Irish Ancestor*, Vol. v, No. 1 (1973).
Tempest, H.G., *Gossiping Guide to County Louth*. Vol. iii. (Dundalgan Press: Dundalk, 1952)
Tempest, H.G., *Gossiping Guide to Dundalk*. (Dundalgan Press: Dundalk,1952)
Tempest, H.G., *Notes on the Parish Church of St Nicholas Dundalk*. (Dundalgan Press: Dundalk, 1955)
Tempest's Annual,1938, 'County Louth Grand Jury Indictment Book, Spring Assizes 1805 to Spring Assizes 1889'
Ua Dubhthaigh, Padraic, *The Book of Dundalk*. (1946)
Vaughan, W.E., *Ireland under the Union, 1. 1801-70 – A New History of Ireland*. (Clarendon Press: Oxford, 1989)
Ward, Michael, 'The Tragedy of the Wildgoose Lodge', *Ireland's Own*, 10 June 1983
Ward, Michael, 'The "Wildgoose Lodge" Murders', *Ireland's Own*.
Whitmarsh, Victor, *Memories of Dundalk: A Pictorial Record*. (Dundalk, 1977)
Williams, T. Desmond, *Secret Societies in Ireland*. (Gill and Macmillan: Dublin, 1973)
Winstanley, Michael J., *Ireland and the Land Question 1800-1922*. (Methuen: London and New York, 1984)
Wolff, Robert Lee, *William Carleton Irish Peasant Novelist*. (Garland Publishing, Inc.: New York & London, 1980)

SELECTED PLACE-NAMES

Aclint, co. Louth
Anaverna, at Ravensdale, north co. Louth
Annamuna (Tully), Annaghminnah, co. Louth
Ardee, co. Louth
Armagh city
Arthurstown, Tallanstown parish, co Louth
Aughaloe, Aghaloo, co. Tyrone
Ballylark, Ballyleck (?) barony of Monaghan
Ballymakenny, co. Louth, three miles north of Drogheda
Ballymascanlan, barony of Lower Dundalk, three miles north of Dundalk
Ballynavoreen, co. Meath
Barronstown, near Hackballs Cross, north co. Louth
Belfast
Bellurgan Park, co. Louth
Benburb, co. Tyrone
Cadian, co. Tyrone
Cairne, co. Meath
Caledon, village, co. Tyrone
Camily Ball, Camlyball, townland, South Armagh
Canafanauge, three miles north-west of Dundalk
Carlingford, village beside Carlingford Lough
Carricklane, co. Monaghan
Carrickleck, co. Meath
Carrickblecke, co. Meath
Carrickmacross, co. Monaghan
Castlebellingham, co. Louth, situated in the valley of the Glyde river
Castleblayney, co. Monaghan
Castlegar, co. Galway
Castletown, Dundalk, co. Louth
Cavan, county
Chamberstown, co. Meath
Channel Rock (s), Chanonrock, six miles south-west of Dundalk
Charleville, near Castlebellingham, co. Louth
Churchtown, two miles south-west of Wildgoose Lodge
Collon, barony of Ferrard, six miles north-west of Drogheda.
Cooley, north-east of Dundalk, co. Louth
Corcreagh, Corcreeghagh, in the barony of Ardee, eight miles south-east of Dundalk
Cornavon, co. Meath
Correcklick, Carrickleck, co. Meath
Creggan, South Armagh
Crosakill, Crossakeel, co. Meath
Cullyhanna, village in South Armagh
Darver, mid-county Louth
Deranoon, near Castleblayney
Donaghmore, co. Tyrone
Drogheda, co. Louth
Dromas, Drumass, parish of Inishkeen (Inniskeen), co. Monaghan
Drumban, co. Monaghan
Drumbride, co. Meath
Drumcar, barony of Ardee, between Dundalk and Annagasson, co. Louth.

Drumfields, Dungannon, co. Tyrone
Drumgowna, near Corcreeghagh, co. Louth
Drumleck, co. Meath
Dublin
Dundalk, co. Louth
Dungannon, co. Tyrone
Dunleer, village, in mid-eastern co. Louth
Edmondstown, barony of Ardee, western part of co. Louth, bordering Monaghan
Eirdnagrena, Ednagrena, parish of Inishkeen, co. Monaghan
Enniskeen, Inniskeen, Inishkeen, village in co. Monaghan, on the border of Louth, seven miles west of Dundalk.
Errigle, Errigal, co. Tyrone
Errigle Trua, Errigal Truagh, co. Monaghan
Farnham Lodge
Faughart, north of Dundalk, co. Louth
Feras, Feeras, Feraghs, Louth parish, co. Louth
Fintona, co. Tyrone
Glack, co. Louth
Glasdrommond, Glasdrummond, South Armagh
Glyde Farm, co. Louth
Gort, parish of Clonfeacle
Gortin, Gorteen, near Inishkeen
Grimskeen, co. Louth
Hackball's Cross, four miles west of Dundalk
Irishtown, near Ardee, co. Louth
Jonesborough, village in South Armagh
Kells, co. Meath
Kenstown, co. Meath
Kilkerley, co. Louth
Killanny, parish in Louth and Monagham
Killtibegs, Kiltibegs, Kiltybegs, co. Louth on border of co. Monaghan
Kilmainham, co. Meath
King's Court, Kingscourt, co. Cavan
Knock Abbey, at Thomastown, co. Louth
Knockbridge, village three miles southwest of Dundalk
Knocklore, Tallanstown parish, co. Louth
Leighsbrook, Navan, co. Meath
Lime Park, Dungannon
Lisrenny, near Tallanstown, co. Louth
Louth, county
Louth Hall, parish of Tallanstown, co. Louth
Louth parish
Louth river, the Glyde
Louth village, seven miles southwest of Dundalk
Lordship, co. Louth
Mansfieldstown, a mile east of Castlebellingham, co. Louth
Mayne, Castlebellingham
Meath, county
Meath-hill, Meath Hill, co. Meath
Mill(s) of Louth, parish of Tallanstown, co. Louth
Monaghan county
Monaghan town
Mount Bailie, Dundalk

Morgallion, barony in co. Meath
Mountainstown, co. Meath
Mountrush, co. Louth
Mullacrew, one mile from Louth village, one mile fom Tallanstown
Navan, co. Meath
New Brunswick, Canada
Newtown-Darver, co. Louth
Omagh, co. Tyrone
Paris
Parknamuddagh, near Louth village
Pepperstown, north of Ardee
Philipstown, three miles north-east of Dunleer, co. Louth
Rampactown, Rampark, north co. Louth
Rathbody, parish of Tallanstown, co. Louth
Rathneestan, Rathneestin, townland in Tallanstown parish, co. Louth
Rathory, parish of Tallanstown, co. Louth
Ravensdale, village four and a half miles north-east of Dundalk
Reaghstown, western part of co. Louth
Redbarns, Dundalk
Reskmore, near Dungannon, co. Tyrone
Riverstown, village, eight miles north-east of Dundalk and four from Greenore
Roach, Roche, parish of Roche, north co. Louth
Rosy Park, co. Louth
Scotstown, co. Monaghan
Seatown, Dundalk
Sheelagh, north co. Louth borderng South Armagh
Shortston, Shortstone, north of Hackballs Cross, north-west co. Louth
Smarmore, a medieval parish two and a half miles south of Ardee, co. Louth
Stabannan, village three miles north-west of Dunleer, co. Louth
Stephenstown, near Dundalk
Stonetown, north of Corcreeghagh, Tallanstown parish
Stormanstown, co. Louth
Strandfield, co. Louth
Tallanstown, village beside river Glyde, three miles north of Ardee, co. Louth
Tankardsrock, co. Louth
Tatebawn, Tatebane, near Dundalk
Thomastown, Tallanstown parish
Townley Hall, name from the Townley Balfour residence, four miles north-west of Drogheda
Trim, co. Meath
Truoah, (Mountain Bar), co. Monaghan
Tully, (Annaminnah), co. Louth
Tullykeel, co. Meath
Tydavnet, co. Monaghan
Waterbridge (Falmor), co. Louth
Wexford
Wildgoose Lodge, Reaghstown, co. Louth
Wm Hillard's Cross, Tallanstown, co. Louth